# TITO
## A Biography

# TITO
## A Biography

PHYLLIS AUTY

**McGRAW-HILL BOOK COMPANY**

New York    St. Louis    San Francisco
Dusseldorf    Mexico    Panama

Library of Congress Catalog Card Number: 75-107283
02498

Printed in Great Britain

# CONTENTS

# ILLUSTRATIONS

All photographs, with the exception of nos. 15 and 16, reproduced by courtesy of Foto-Tanjug, Belgrade.

*The maps are drawn by Edward McAndrew Rucell*

### MAPS

# A NOTE ON PRONUNCIATION

Serbo-Croat, the language used by the majority of people in Yugo-slavia, is written in the Latin script in Croatia, but in Serbia, Monte-negro, and for the Macedonian language, the Cyrillic alphabet is used. Diacritic marks have been used to indicate certain consonants which have a separate sign in Cyrillic.

C is pronounced like *ts* as in *fats*; Č like the *ch* in *beach*
Ć a similar sound sometimes represented by *tch*
Š is pronounced like the *sh* in *shock*
Ž like the *s* in *pleasure*
J has the sound of *y* in *yet*
ai is pronounced *i* as in *white*

Pronunciation of some of the proper-names is as follows:

Čopić        — as Chopich
Mihailović — as Mihi (with long *i*) lovitch
Pećanac    — Pechanats
Pašić        — Pashitch
Šubašić     — Shubashitch
Žujović      — Z (pronounced like the *s* in *pleasure*) uyovitch
Jajce        — Yi(long *i* as in wh*i*te)tse

# PREFACE

Attempting to write the biography of a great man is always a formidable assignment, and is especially daunting when the subject is still living, an internationally important figure and head of state. In the case of Josip Broz – Tito, President of Yugoslavia – the difficulties are increased because of his quite exceptionally full and varied career. He was born at the end of the nineteenth century in a world that was on the brink of great change. His whole career has been closely linked with that change and with revolutionary developments in European society as they have evolved during the twentieth century.

Various phases of his long life have been in places and circumstances that make it difficult – sometimes impossible – for the biographer to investigate in detail. He was a soldier in the Austrian army in the first world war, a prisoner in Tsarist Russia, an observer of the Bolshevik revolution. He made long visits to the Soviet Union during the Stalinist period, was employed by the Comintern in Moscow and narrowly escaped being eliminated in Stalin's great purge. During the nineteen-thirties he worked as an illegal communist organizer, hiding from the police, using different aliases and covering his tracks as he travelled about Europe from Yugoslavia to Italy, Austria, France, Switzerland or Czechoslovakia. After a long passage of time it is far from easy to uncover the true facts about this kind of existence. The biographer has to rely on peoples' memories – and memory tends to be selective in what it retains. Tito himself has an excellent pictorial memory, especially vivid for the dramatic incidents of his past; many of these have been retold in anecdotes that have become fixed like a still photograph, so that some early accounts of his life are like a collection of old snapshots in a family album. For the early years of Tito's life – up to the first world war – it is difficult to get away from the stereotype.

When it comes to the second world war Tito's biographer is faced with a different problem. His total involvement with Yugoslavs of all kinds, from all parts of the country in a war that brought indescribable suffering, and eventually – against all odds – triumphant success, made him even before the end of the war into a hero of mythical character. Hero-worship, natural in the circumstances, was also cultivated to help unite people in war effort and for postwar reconstruction under communist government. It is sometimes not easy to distinguish between Tito the real man and Tito the mythical hero. Until recently the various histories of the Partisan war were very much affected by this heroic concept, and there is as yet no critical objective military history of the Partisan war. I have not attempted such a reappraisal, which is outside the scope of this biography. I have omitted much of the detailed military history and have concentrated on an examination of the political results of Tito's career during the war. Military history is at present being written by Yugoslav, British and American historians whose books will be available to later biographers of Tito.

Writing a biography of a living person has posed the problem of respecting the reticences and reserve which I judge to be the right of all living individuals, even though they may be public personalities. Later historians may not have such limitations. I should, however, put on record that on the occasions when I have been given interviews by President Tito, he answered all questions frankly and fully without hesitation or evasion, giving the impression that he was content to let his record stand up to any examination.

The official biography of President Tito is being prepared in Yugoslavia by a special institution with research workers collecting all possible material about his life. Such a total biography cannot be undertaken by one person. My book aims only to be an interim historical biography – between those written in the nineteen-fifties, especially those of V. Dedijer, Sir Fitzroy Maclean and K. Zilliacus – and the many that will come later. When I started work on this book I approached people in Yugoslavia who had access to material about Tito's life. I was told 'We all have to begin with Dedijer's book.' This I have found to be true. Its English edition was called *Tito Speaks* and it was based largely on autobiographical material which Tito told to the author. In this sense the book is an original source for all future work on Tito's life, even though much has since been discovered to correct and complement it. Sir Fitzroy Maclean's book *Disputed Barricade* is also an original source. It was written after Maclean had worked with Tito during the second world war and become his friend. The life of Tito by the late K. Zilliacus also has special value as a source because it was written in the difficult years after Tito's break with Stalin in 1948. Konni Zilliacus, who spoke Russian fluently and understood Serbo-Croat, had the benefit of many long talks with Tito at that time. My book has no claim to such special value, though I have had two interviews with Tito himself and during the years when I have been working on Yugoslav affairs I have also interviewed many of the top leaders – and others – who have been associated with Tito in different phases of his career.

My aim has been to write a biography making use of earlier works, adding new material – of which there is a great deal for some parts of his life – and drawing on my own knowledge of Yugoslav affairs. I have also had the advantage of having been allowed access to archive material in Yugoslavia which has only recently become available to historians, much of which is still unpublished. I have had very generous help from many people, Yugoslavs, British, American and others, and am most grateful to all of them. None has any responsibility for the judgments expressed in this book. It may seem invidious to mention some names and not others, but I should like to express special gratitude to some who have given time to discussing various aspects of the subject with me, and have helped me to find material. I would like to mention S. W. Bailey, S. Clissold, P. Damjanović, W. F. Deakin, Air Chief Marshal Sir William Elliot, Colonel V. Kljaković, J. Marjanović, W. Roberts, D. Russinov, J. Tomasevitch, V. Velebit, V. Vinterhalter and W. Vucinich. I have received invaluable help from the authorities in charge of the archives at the Institut za Radnički Pokret in Belgrade and from General Fabian Trgo and the staff of the Vojna Istoriski Institut. I was greatly helped by the authorities at the Institut za Radnički Pokret in Zagreb and at museums in different parts of Yugoslavia. I have had unfailing help in getting contacts and material from Yugoslav ambassadors and their staff at the Yugoslav embassy in London, and from a number of government departments and institutions in Yugoslavia. I should also like to pay tribute to the late Professor Rudolf Bićanić of Zagreb University who gave his time so unsparingly on innumerable occasions to discuss with me many aspects of the historical and social background to Tito's life. His wide knowledge and penetrating understanding of the Croatian aspects of this period were unique, and his death has left a gap that cannot be filled. I owe a special debt of gratitude to Mrs Sheila Kidd for helping me to prepare the manuscript for the press, and to Mrs Edna Robinson for her cheerful, intelligent and expert secretarial assistance. I should like to express my thanks to Ghita Ionescu of Manchester University for his sustained interest and for many helpful discussions about the communist world. And finally, I have to thank Christopher Hibbert, for without his encouragement this book would never have been begun, let alone completed.

AUSTRIA — HUNGARY

RUSSIA

• VIENNA

• BUDAPEST

Jassy

Ljubljana
(Laibach)

Trieste

Zagreb
(Agram)

CROATIA - SLAVONIA

Galatz

RUMANIA

BUCHAREST

BOSNIA-
HERCEGOVINA

BELGRADE

Sarajevo

SERBIA

Split

Varna

BULGARIA

SOFIA

Dubrovnik

MONTENEGRO

ITALY

ALBANIA

MACEDONIA

OTTOMAN EMPIRE

CONSTANTINOPLE

SOUTH-EASTERN
EUROPE
1892

Salonika

GREECE

POLAND

CZECHOSLOVAKIA

RUSSIA

• VIENNA

AUSTRIA

• BUDAPEST

HUNGARY

Jassy

ITALY • Ljubljana

RUMANIA

• Zagreb

Galatz

BELGRADE

Zara
Zadar
(Italian)

Split

YUGOSLAVIA

• Sarajevo

BUCHAREST

Varna

Lagosta
(Italian)

Dubrovnik

BULGARIA

SOFIA

ITALY

ALBANIA

• Skopje

ISTANBUL

SOUTH-EASTERN
EUROPE
Treaty of Lausanne
1923

Salonika

GREECE

TURKEY

AUSTRIA

Maribor

*Annexed by Hungary*

*Occupied by Hungary*

*Drava*

SLOVENIA **1**

*Governed by Germany*

Celje

Varazdin

HUNGAR

ITALY

*LJUBLJANA*

Sava

ZAGREB

Bjelovar

Drava

SLOVENIA

*Governed by Italy*

Kupa

Karlovac

Sisak

Daruvar

CROATI

Kopa

Rijeka

Vojnić

Senj

Bos Novi

Sava

Vrbas

**3**

B

Brioni

Pula

Cres

Rab

Bihać

Krupa

Banja Luka

Do

Korenica
(Titova)

Gračanica

Losinj

Pag

Udbina

Drinci

Mrkonjic Grad

Banov

Velebit

Drvar

Jajce

BOS

Grahova

Ministra

Fojnica

Dugi
Otok

Zadar

Dinara

Glamoč

SARA,

Prozor

Duvno

HERZEG

Šibenik

Split

Alps

Kal

Makarska

Mostar

**Adriatic Sea**

DALMATIA

Brač

Neveginje

Ga

Bjelas

Vis

Hvar

Korčula

ITALY

Lastovo
(Italian)

Ljub!

B

Dubrovnik

Dalma

**1** *Annexed by Germany — Slovenia*

**1a** *Governed by Germany*

**2** *Serbia occupied by Germany —*
*with a Quisling Serbian Government*
*headed by General Nedić*

**3** *Independent State of Croatia ruled by—*
*POGLAVNIK ANTE PAVELIĆ*

**4** *Territory annexed to Italy (Slovenia & Dalmatia)*

**4a** *Montenegro under Italian occupation and Government*

**4b** *Territory included in Greater Albania under Italian occupation and*

MONTENEG

*under Italian occu*
*and Governme*

# Yugoslavia

### DURING THE SECOND WORLD WAR

Boundaries
1939—1945

Danube

*Occupied*
*by Hungary*

Tisza

Zrenjanin

RUMANIA

ek

Vinkovci

Novi Sad

*Governed*

**1a**

Vršac

Ruma

*by Germany*

**BELGRADE**

Šava

Dvina

Danube

Kladovo

Sopot

*Homoljske Planina*

Zvornik

Valjevo

Struganik

Kragujevac

Zaječar

danj

Ravna
Gora

**2**

V. Morava

orina

Rogatica

Ilijce

Požega

Čačjak

Z. Morava

Kraljevo

Zlatibor Javor

Priboj

**SERBIA**

Gorazde

NA

Nova Vareš

Niš

Pljevlja

Prijepolje

Raška

Pirot

Lim

Tara

Bijelo
Polje

**4a**

Lebane

hljak

Ibar

avnik

Kolašin

Berane

šić

Blaganik

Andrijevica

Prištine

Titograd

Peć

**4b**

Cetinje

Orahovac

J. Morava

Trgovište

BULGARIA

Bar

Skadarsko J.

**GREATER**

Šar Planina

*Area occupied*

**ALBANIA**

**SKOPJE**

*under Italian occupation*
*and Government*

*and annexed*

Veles (Titov)

Vardar

**ALBANIA**

*by Bulgaria*

Ohrid

Bitola

ent.

Ohridsko J.

Prespanko J.

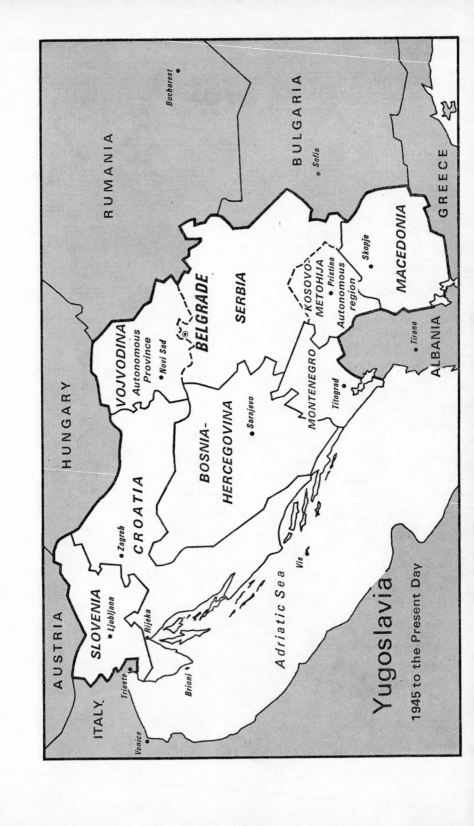

Yugoslavia

1945 to the Present Day

# PART I
# THE MAKING OF A COMMUNIST

# 1 CHILD AND YOUTH

Tito gave his own explanation of why he became a communist to a court packed with sympathetic supporters – long-haired youths and *avant-garde* bobbed-haired girls – on a bleak November day in 1928. Thin, after a recent hunger strike to force a hearing of the case, short and bespectacled, Tito addressed the court and argued with the judge with outspoken and courageous sincerity which a newspaper report the following day described as something more than a display of arrogance. He tried to make a statement about his background and how it had led him to communism, but was cut short by the judge, who said that all that had been gone into already. His explanation of why he became a communist lay in the injustices of society, the poverty and oppression he had seen as a child, which were being continued in the bourgeois-ruled society of the new Kingdom of Yugoslavia. He admitted that he was an active member of the illegal Communist Party, but denied the validity of the law under which he had been indicted because that law, he said, 'was not passed by the people'. In spite of his eloquence he was sentenced to five years' imprisonment and was led away shouting 'Long live the Communist Party of Yugoslavia'. It is almost certain that this prison sentence saved his life.[1]

When he started his sentence on 14 November 1928, he was thirty-six years old, headstrong, defiant, ready to challenge the law and the whole state apparatus. 'I am quite prepared to suffer,' he told the judge who had chided him for pigheadedly sacrificing years of his young life. He repeatedly declared that he was not afraid of the law. When he came out of gaol five years later he was no less fanatical a communist, but less foolhardy, less ready to indulge in open and violent challenge against the all-powerful state. He was far more experienced and far more dangerous. Even when the facts are known about Tito's origins and the historical and social background which he had tried to tell the court had led him to communism, there remains the elusive question of why Josip Broz, seventh child of an ordinary peasant family in Croatia, should have been one of the few to become such a dedicated communist when others of his family and generation did not.

Josip Broz was born in the village of Kumrovec in Croatia on 7 May 1892. His parents were Franjo Broz, a Croat, and Marija (*née* Javeršek), a Slovene from a village only ten miles from Kumrovec, but outside the frontiers of Croatia. Josip was the seventh child born in the first ten years of his parents' marriage; only three others, two boys and a girl, had survived. For the Broz family to rear seven of the fifteen children born to his mother before she died at the age of fifty-one in 1918, was something better than the average for Croatian peasants at that time; in those days a high proportion of children – Tito himself said about 80 per cent – died before the age of fifteen.[2]

The Broz family was by no means the poorest in the village. They owned a farm of about ten acres and were what later were called 'middle' peasants – between the few rich and the many poor who were landless or had very small farms. Franjo Broz also had horses and a cart which he used for a carrier's business, bringing in a little money with which to supplement the food obtained from the land. This implied more substance and use of money than was customary in most peasant families. Franjo had inherited from his father one of the best houses in Kumrovec, a substantial small farmhouse solidly rebuilt and improved less than fifty years earlier. His wife's family too owned land.

It was sometimes said that Marija Javeršek had married beneath her, but her husband was intelligent and occasionally hardworking, though at times too, and increasingly as he got older, shiftless and drunken, as were many of the peasants in those days. He at least accepted the fact – unwillingly at first – that his children must leave the village if they wanted a better life. He was the first father in Kumrovec to allow his sons to become apprentices. His wife Marija had the reputation of being the stronger character and was the careful manager in a family that had too many mouths to feed, which always had difficulty in making both ends meet, which sometimes suffered real hardship and hunger, and was almost always in debt. 'When the debts became intolerable, the soft and good natured Franjo gave up and took to drinking, and the whole family burden fell upon my mother' Tito remembered later.[3] Even so, the family was at the top of the social and economic scale in Kumrovec at the turn of the century. This does not say much, for the small village of about two hundred families had no resident aristocracy, no middle class and no rich peasant families.

Kumrovec lies north of Zagreb, main town of Croatia, in the beautiful but infertile district of Zagorje, a lovely countryside of many small, steep hills with orchards and vineyards on their sharply rising slopes. In the valley is the river Sutla and its tributary streams, with water meadows and marshy fields used for grazing. There is little arable land; the region has neither the rich soil of the valleys of the Sava and Drava further east, nor the stony aridity of the Lika, the part of western Croatia that lies between Zagreb and the Adriatic coast. Tito's generation was the first to leave the villages in great numbers, for the land could no longer support the rapidly increasing population. Thousands emigrated, others like Tito sought work in the towns, most being absorbed into the urban proletariat. Nearly all retained links with their families left behind in the villages where many aspects of life remained unchanged, old customs and ways dying hard. Many features of Zagorje life and characteristics of its people have continued down to our times. Even today the men of Zagorje are renowned for their stubbornness, tough endurance, hard drinking, virility and longevity. Tito retained many of the characteristics of a true son of Zagorje.[4]

Croatia in Tito's childhood was in the Hungarian part of the Austro-Hungarian empire, a multiracial dual monarchy ruled by the Habsburg dynasty. From 1848 the ruling Emperor was Franz Josef who in 1900 was seventy years old, steeped in conservatism and unable to understand or control the many problems that nationalism and economic change had brought to his empire in the second half of the nineteenth century. Prominent among these problems were the relations between the two ruling peoples – Germans in Austria and Magyars in Hungary, and their relations with minority races, especially the Slavs who included Czechs, Poles and Slovenes in Austria, Croats, Serbs and Slovaks in Hungary.

In 1867 Hungary became autonomous except in matters of foreign affairs and defence. Her capital of Budapest was as magnificent, and except that it was not the seat of the imperial chancery, almost as important, as Vienna. The Emperor had to be separately crowned – with an ancient and symbolic iron crown – as King of Hungary. The Magyars jealously guarded their hard-won autonomy and tried to increase and extend their privileges and powers within the empire. But the autonomy they had exacted for themselves as a national right was not extended to the Croats. They treated the minority races within Hungary with harsh disdain, the more so since they feared that any concessions to the rapidly increasing nationalism among Croats and Serbs in Hungary would weaken their own position in relation to the Germans of Austria.

Croatia had a special position within Hungary for it had its own parliament or *Sabor*, meeting in the ancient capital of Zagreb, its own President or *Ban* (though he was appointed by Budapest and represented Magyar rather than Croat interests), and some measure of self-rule in matters of local government. This independence amounted to very little in the period of Tito's childhood. Though peasants in Croatia had been freed from serfdom in 1848 they remained miserably poor and without political influence. There were still in Croatia many large estates owned by landed aristocracy who were mostly Magyars. Representation in the *Sabor* was controlled by the high land and tax qualification required for franchise, and by outright intimidation and bribery of the electorate. The people were eighty per cent peasants and nearly all were disenfranchised. Out of a population of about two million, only 30,000 had the vote. Kumrovec in Tito's childhood had three voters among two hundred families. It was generally reckoned that a good goulasch and a litre of wine on the morning of an election, or one new boot before voting and one after, could procure the peasants' votes.[5]

The Croatian *Ban* from 1883 to 1903 was Count Kuehn Héderváry, who was hated by the Croats for his policy of ruthless Magyarization. He used every method to weaken Croat nationalism and was expert in encouraging antagonism between the Catholic Croats and the Orthodox Serbs who also lived in that part of Croatia which had formerly been a military frontier against the Turks. He was afraid that the Serbs and Croats might make common cause against Magyar rule.

Croats also complained at this time of Hungarian economic discrimination against their territory. In an age of extensive railway development Croatia did not get enough railway lines to allow major industrial development and consequent prosperity. Rivers were the main highways for trade, and these were neglected. After 1873 the port of Fiume on the Adriatic, which Croats considered theirs by historical right and commercial need, was taken over by Hungary. The crude policy of the Hungarian government was that Croats should be kept poor and Magyarized, and industrial development in Croatia was purposely limited to this end.

The battles on most of these issues were fought by Croat middle-class intellectuals in Zagreb or Budapest, far away from the villages.

Newspapers, which became plentiful in Zagreb and the towns towards the end of the nineteenth century, were not commonplace in the villages.[6] Nearly all the older generation of Croatian country people were illiterate, though there was a higher degree of literacy among peasants in nearby Slovenia; the peasants in any case could not afford the money to buy papers and were predominantly interested in their own local affairs. Yet they were well aware of Magyar domination. The Magyars were the foreign rulers, the extorters of taxes, the military officers, the source of irritating or harsh regulations, the people to blame for daily troubles, to be held responsible for poverty and misfortune in the villages.

A vivid memory of Tito's childhood was of a revolt in the Zagorje villages in 1903 when he was eleven years old, against increased taxes. Peasants near Kumrovec showed their feeling by pulling down the Hungarian flag from a local railway station. Magyar police opened fire on demonstrators, killing one man and wounding ten others. This inflamed the situation and there were many arrests. As a punishment to the district, Hungarian troops were quartered on the Croat peasant families. Tito's parents had to support four of them for a month – a heavy extra burden on the family's meagre supplies of food.[7] Magyar rule made many Croats into strong, sometimes fanatical Croat nationalists. Tito may have had some element of this during his village boyhood, but it was not a feature of his mature manhood.

* * *

There were other radical influences on Tito's childhood. Stories of folk history told of the terrible experiences of Zagorje peasants under centuries of feudal oppression when the majority of Croats had been serfs without legal rights under Hungarian law. In Tito's childhood the villagers of Zagorje travelled little, and only had the entertainments they could make for themselves. The dramatic stories of their own past were told and retold. The heroes of these stories – in which good was identified with their own people, the poor and oppressed, and evil with the ruling class – were those who showed independence, defied authority and usually died horribly. The drama was heightened by the fact that the stories were based on historical events and local associations.

An incident which had a deep and lasting influence, although it happened over three hundred years before Tito was born, was the peasant revolt in 1573 in Croatia and Slovenia, led by Matija Gubec.[8] Peasant revolt was endemic in Hungary and Croatia in the late Middle Ages. There had been a very serious one in Hungary in 1514 which had been savagely suppressed. Yet, fifty-nine years later, Gubec and three other leaders were able to plan a rebellion which gained the support of tens of thousands of peasants in Croatia and Slovenia. General causes of the rebellion lay in the rapid deterioration in conditions of life in this region in the sixteenth century, after the Turkish defeat of Hungary at the Battle of Mohacs in 1526. Immediate causes contributing to the Gubec rising were the atrocities indulged in by local lords. Part of the testimony of a rebel leader, Ilija Gregorić, captured and taken to Vienna for interrogation by torture told of the behaviour of a local lord, Franjo Tahi, and of his extortions from the peasants. He said that 'they would have suffered all this misuse had Tahi not pestered and raped their daughters and virgins in a most unchristian and tyrannical way. . . . After the death of his wife, Tahi would ride on horseback into the fields to look at the women working there. Those that pleased his eye were dragged to his castle by his servants and undressed stark naked. If he then took a fancy to any, he would have her bathed and rape her. . . . On one occasion the serfs showed the commissioners fourteen virgins beaten and raped by Tahi. The daughter of a peasant was imprisoned in Tahi's castle of Susjedgrad. When her father protested, Tahi's son cut him about the face with his sword and gouged out his eyes.'[9] These were only some of the misdeeds that aroused the peasant anger.

Gubec's followers put cock's feathers in their hats as a symbol of revolt – a detail that Tito always mentioned when he told the story, saying they had done this too in the games of his childhood. Led by Gregorić the rebels set out on the morning of 29 January 1573 to capture the castle of Cesargrad, whose ruins in Tito's childhood still stood on the top of the steep hill above Kumrovec dominating the valley of the river Sutla and the route into Slovenia. They stormed and set fire to the castle, beheaded the hated bailiff and seized muskets and arms from the arsenal. It was the signal for general revolt throughout the surrounding districts and far into Slovenia and Carinthia to the north. The lords, at first taken by surprise, called up their feudal levy in areas unaffected by the revolt, and promised huge payments to professional soldiers and to any peasants who would support them. Finally the governor of Croatia, Bishop Juraj Drašković, with a comparatively well equipped army of cavalry and infantry, met the rebels at Donja Stubica in the valley not far from Kumrovec. The rebels' resistance was broken. They fled into the surrounding countryside from which they were rounded up for summary execution or torture during succeeding weeks. It was said that in Zagorje alone between four and six thousand serfs were killed, and that hundreds were strung up on trees in all the villages of the district.

A terrible fate was reserved for Gubec because he had set himself up as leader of the peasants. Bishop Drašković had written to the Habsburg Emperor Maximilian: 'We shall crown him as an example, if your Majesty allows, with an iron crown – a red hot one too.' A contemporary historian describes the execution which took place in Zagreb in the old town not far from St Mark's church: 'He was first tortured with red-hot tongs, while his deputy Andrija Pasanec was killed before his eyes. After that he was crowned with a red-hot iron crown and finally quartered like a criminal.' A Croat historian wrote that before being done to death he was led in a carnival procession while the mob jeered at him shouting '*Ave rex rusticorum*' ('Hail king of the peasants').[10]

Tito believed that his ancestors, who were said to have moved to the Zagorje from Dalmatia in the middle of the sixteenth century, took part in this revolt. Throughout his childhood the story with all its local associations and details was the basis of games and plays. He remembered that when any of the children woke up at night, his mother frightened them into silence by saying that if they did not go back to sleep the Black Queen of Cesargrad – Baroness Barbara Erdödy, notorious for her savage punishments after the rebellion – would come and take them away. The traumatic story remained a living memory of cruelty and injustice.[11]

Tito was also brought up on other, more recent, stories of the injustices of serfdom, which had been abolished in Croatia only in 1848. Conditions of serfdom varied. Before the abolition serfs and their families lived on a farm from generation to generation, but the land belonged to the lord. The serf had to give the lord a proportion – in Croatia a ninth – of all crops, wine and livestock, pay a special house tax and do labour service for so many days a year, providing his own tools and cart. The serf was not a slave, but he was subject to the jurisdiction of the lord, who could inflict corporal punishment – and frequently did on both males and females – for the flimsiest reasons. If the lord had the *ius gladii* (right of the sword) he could, in the presence of judges, condemn a serf to death.[12] Not all lords abused

9

their serfs but many did, and misuse of powers was so well known that the Habsburg rulers from the eighteenth century made various attempts to impose legal limitations on the lords. These things were still talked about in Tito's childhood.

When the manifesto abolishing serfdom was made public on 25 April 1848, Tito's paternal grandparents were living in Kumrovec where the Broz family had settled as serfs of the Erdödys in 1684. Like the rest of the serfs they were freed and allowed to buy their house and land from the lord. Peasants who did not have the money were able to borrow the rather large sum required and repay it over a period of twenty years. 'The rate of interest was nominally eight per cent,' said Tito in later life, 'but commission and extras raised it to twenty-four per cent.'[13] The abolition of serfdom initiated revolutionary social and economic changes in peasant life. The sale and purchase of land-holdings became big business. Many lords sold their interests to speculators. The Erdödy family sold out and left the district for good after living there for over five hundred years. Their estate was bought by an Austrian banking house which then loaned the purchase money to peasants who wished to buy the land.

Up to this time the Broz family, like most other peasants in the district – and indeed like most of the South Slav peoples – had been living in an extended family group called a *zadruga*.[14] This was a very ancient institution dating back to the beginnings of the South Slav settlement in the Balkans, originating in the need for people to band together for defence against enemies. In a *zadruga* all related members of a family lived together in one house or group of buildings under the authority of its head, usually the oldest male – just occasionally the oldest female – called the *Gospodar* (master) or *Starešina* (the old one). *Zadrugas* varied in size from two or three married couples with their children to as many as a hundred families living together. The principle was that sons stayed in the *zadruga*, bringing home their brides and building on extra sleeping huts till the whole *zadruga* looked like a beehive. Daughters joined their husband's *zadruga* as they married. Under the *Gospodar* every member had a place in a social hierarchy in which age had priority, but any males were superior to females. The *Gospodar* had patriarchal authority over all members, and his wife ordered the life and work of the women, who prepared communal meals which were eaten together. Major decisions about communal property, work on the land and other matters were taken after consultation between the males.

The *zadruga* tended to produce a static, conservative society. It had been well suited to feudal conditions in an almost self-sufficient economy in which little money was needed. It had been encouraged by the government as it made tax-gathering easier and meant that when men were called for military service agricultural work suffered less since a *zadruga* would spread the work load. It was not suited to the free society and changing economy that succeeded the abolition of serfdom. Many *zadrugas* could not provide a living for all members of the family after arrangements had been made to pay for the land and they began to disintegrate. But it was some years before legal permission was given for them to disband.

When a law of 1853 allowed *zadrugas* to be divided, some families, including that of Tito's grandfather Martin Broz, acted on it and divided up the land and possessions. By the first world war there were few left, but there are people alive today – Tito among them – who can remember *zadrugas* still in existence in Croatia in the period between the two world wars, and traces of them still exist in parts of Yugoslavia today.

Although Tito never lived in one himself he was brought up in a society that was still greatly influenced by the patriarchal customs and close family ties of *zadruga* life. Though his father, Franjo Broz, was 'weak and good-natured', he had authority as head of the family. He made the final decision on what his sons should do in life, and they accepted it. As a boy Josip seems to have been both conformist and obedient. At every stage in his life before he was launched on his own in the world, help was arranged through some member of the family clan – the grandparents, the mother's brother, father's cousin, and sometimes mutual help between Josip and his brothers. These traditional close family ties gave Josip a strong sense of paternal authority and family responsibility which became part of his essential character. When he became a wage-earner he sent money to his family; when his father was an old man, he paid his sister to look after him until he died in 1936; when he became head of state after 1945, he unobtrusively looked after members of his family who were in need.

* &ast; &ast; &ast;

The years after the abolition of serfdom were a difficult time of social and economic readjustment for the peasants of Croatia. The pattern of life which had lasted for centuries had been disrupted. It was also a period of political change. The power of the Habsburg monarchy was declining, its imperial possessions shrinking under pressure from external enemies and the rising tide of nationalism among the many different peoples of the empire. The Emperor Napoleon III of France helped Garibaldi and Cavour to victories which deprived Austria of her Italian provinces which were joined to the new state of united Italy. Austria's centuries old influence over German states was undermined by the emergence of a strong Prussia under Bismarck. In 1866 Austrian armies were decisively beaten by the modern professional Prussian army in a startlingly short war. After that Austria's international influence was permanently eclipsed by the new state of united Germany.

Following the loss of prestige, provinces and revenue, the Emperor Franz Josef and his advisers tried to strengthen their hold over the remaining non-Austrian provinces. But from all the non-German peoples they encountered increasing opposition which they were unable to cow or appease. In 1867 by an *Ausgleich* with Hungary they divided the Habsburg empire into a dual monarchy, giving Hungary a large measure of autonomy and allowing her virtual control over Croatia – a control that only sharpened antagonism between Croats and Magyars and led to more insistent demands for freedom for the South Slavs in the empire, not only for the Croats, but for Slovenes and Serbs who also lived in the Habsburg empire. These demands were encouraged by political activists in the neighbouring state of Serbia which had obtained its autonomy from Turkey in 1829 and became an independent kingdom in 1878. Its political leaders had expansionist visions of a state that would one day embrace all the South Slavs including not only Croats, Serbs and Slovenes from the Austro-Hungarian empire but also other South Slavs still under Turkish rule, as well as those from the small but independent state of Montenegro.

A major factor in international politics in Europe in the second half of the nineteenth century was that as Turkey became politically weak and economically bankrupt both Austria and Russia hoped to inherit the influence and territories she still held in the Balkans. Russia pressed her claims against Turkey by going to war in 1877–78, but it was Austria that was granted the right to administer the former Turkish province of Bosnia-Herzegovina by the Treaty of Berlin which ended the war. This was a purely Slavonic province inhabited by Croats, Serbs and Muslims of Slavonic race. Its annexation by Austria in 1908 poisoned relations with Serbia who claimed it by ethnic and historical right. It antagonized Russia for it thwarted her ambitions to use the Balkans as strategic background for her attempts to control Constantinople, which guarded the entrance from the Black Sea into the Mediterranean. From Bosnia-Herzegovina the Austrians were in a position to push through weakly held Turkish territory in Macedonia down to the port of Salonika on the Aegean Sea. These issues led directly to the confrontation of Austria and Russia on opposite sides when war broke out in 1914. They seemed very far away from the peasants of Croatia but they had a vital influence on the lives of those Croats who, like Josip Broz, were born at the end of the nineteenth century and came to manhood just before the first world war.

Echoes of international events must have reached the villages of the Zagorje. Tito's father Franjo was born in the year of the Peace of Paris that ended the Crimean War; he was ten years old when war came nearer and the Austrians were defeated by the Prussians at Sadowa, fourteen when Bismarck conquered France, almost twenty-two and still unmarried when the Russian armies fought Turkey in the Balkans and got within sight of Constantinople in 1878. It was an age of great insecurity. Increased taxes to pay for Austria-Hungary's wars affected the peasants at a time when prices were rising and most families were still paying off the loans and interest for the purchase of their holdings. Between 1870 and 1890 there was a disastrous series of bad harvests in Croatia, in common with most of Europe. Grain from America, where farming was booming, was imported for the home market in Austria-Hungary. But when local harvests were plentiful again the peasants found that prices for their produce were forced down because cheaper foreign grain was still being imported. In good years peasants failed to sell their crops successfully, in bad years they had little food left after January and had to borrow money to tide them over the spring sowing to the summer harvest.

Grandfather Martin Broz had married a peasant woman, Ana Blažičko, who was proud of coming from a family of peasants who had been free men for two hundred years. He eked out his living from the property he had received in the share out of the *zadruga* by a carrying trade which he plied with horse and cart between the towns within reasonable distance from Kumrovec – such as Zagreb, Sisak and Karlovac. His main concern was to make enough to feed his wife and seven children, to avoid having to sell land to pay his debts, and to tide the family over times of trouble – bad harvests, sickness, childbirth, and the deaths and burials that all families had to face. The Austrian law of 1853 forbade the eldest son to be sole heir to property and required equal shares to be assigned to all children. This was an extra burden to peasants for it caused fragmentation of holdings into farms too small to support a family.

The Broz family was seriously affected by this law. In the winter of 1878 Grandfather Martin was injured and died when his cart carrying a heavy load of salt lost a wheel and overturned. His only son, Franjo, inherited his father's property but had to buy out six sisters. He borrowed money to do this, but eventually was obliged to sell land to pay it back. When he married he had fifteen acres left; by the time of Josip's childhood this had been reduced to ten acres.[15]

\* \* \*

Franjo Brox married in January 1881 when he was twenty-four years old. His bride was sixteen-year-old Marija Javeršek, eldest of the fourteen children of a family Franjo had met when he crossed the river Sutla to go up into the woods of Slovenia to cut firewood. Wood was an important item in peasant life for it was needed as fuel for bread-ovens, cooking fires or stoves, and to heat the flat-topped, tiled corner stoves that warmed the family living rooms in winter. Cutting wood in the lords' forests or on common land had been one of the few privileges of peasants during their centuries of serfdom before 1848. When they received their freedom, forest and common land was retained by the lords as their private property; the privilege of free fuel was lost. Peasants in Kumrovec were left with little woodland and often had to buy their fuel. Franjo made part of his living by collecting wood in Slovenia and selling it in the village. He probably had some arrangement with the Javeršek family, who owned sixty-five acres of farm and woodland in the high hills above the village of Posreda about ten miles from Kumrovec.[16]

On a snowy January day the Javeršek family gave a big wedding party for the marriage of their eldest daughter. Five sleighs brought the groom and his party from Kumrovec. The wedding took place in the village church and the celebration in the family home in the Slovene village lasted several days with dancing and feasting. The bridal couple made a good-looking pair – Franjo of medium height, wiry, with an aquiline nose and curly black hair, a 'real Dinaric type' as Tito later described him – Marija a fairly tall, blonde, attractive-looking girl, dressed in traditional Slovene peasant costume. When the time came for them to make the journey back to Franjo's house in Kumrovec, Marija took with her the usual peasant dowry of clothes, bed linen, rugs and household effects. Among these were the religious pictures – St George and the Dragon, Adam and Eve, Mary and the Child Jesus which can be seen in the Kumrovec house today. The picture of Mary was a special treasure for it is a musical box which plays a hymn tune. Marija maintained close relations with her family which was only half a day's journey away, and when she had children they enjoyed visiting their Javeršek grandparents. Josip, who was his grandfather's favourite, remembered his long visits to them as the happiest days of his childhood.

The house in Kumrovec where Franjo and Marija Broz lived all their married life, and where their children were born – including their seventh child Josip – was built in the traditional style of the Croatian Zagorje peasant dwelling. It had been sturdily rebuilt in 1860, shortly after the dissolution of the Broz *zadruga*, which shows that the family was still prosperous at that time. A tiled roof and well-plastered walls replaced the thatch and rough lath and plaster of the earlier dwelling, and it was built to provide separate living for two families. It had strong wooden floors instead of the bare earth of the poorer houses. In Josip's childhood it was one of the most substantial dwellings of the village. The house today is a museum and has the smartened, depersonalised appearance and atmosphere of such national monuments, virtually unrecognizable from the home that Josip lived in.

But the layout inside the house is only a little changed. From old photographs and some original, some reproduction, contents in the house today, it is possible to reconstruct something of the background to Tito's own accounts of his childhood there. There is an entrance hall used as a store place for outdoor boots and all the paraphernalia of a large family working on the land and living much of its life out-doors. On either side of the hall are two living rooms, the one on the right that of Josip's family, that on the left occupied by their cousins. These combined living and sleeping rooms – about eighteen feet by twelve – called *Hiša* were the centre of family life. Each has a flat-topped stove in one corner, the one in Tito's home patterned in relief with a holy motif of the cross. A large – but single – bed is along one wall. Double beds were unknown among the peasants though a bench alongside – called a *Stiblica* – was sometimes used for extra width.

There was little privacy here, little room for a large family. Babies could be put to sleep on top of the stove when they had outgrown the wooden cradle which can still be seen in the house. The older children slept on the floor in a loft under the roof. Off the main room there was a smaller one – twelve feet by nine – called the little chamber or *komarica*. This had a single bed and could be used for the guest chamber, or for occasional privacy.

A further exit from the entrance hall leads to a sizeable communal kitchen shared by the two families, each using one side. Here a solid beamed roof is equipped with hooks to hang the meat for curing in the smoke of the two woodburning fires, and there are hooks for cooking pots. Behind the fires are huge bread ovens – one for each family – perhaps the most important equipment for any peasant house. Bread was the staple food, eaten for every meal, its quality varying from white flour bread to sour black rye and maize bread, depending on the prosperity of the times. Meat was not eaten every day, fat was a delicacy, sugar a luxury; vegetables and fruit were eaten according to season. Peasants had no equipment for processing food, no money to buy sugar for preserves, so that a glut of fruit and vegetables often went to waste, to be succeeded by periods of want.

Scarcity of food is a recurrent theme in Tito's memories of his childhood in Kumrovec – the locked larder, how the children would ask for bread in front of relatives knowing their proud mother would not refuse though she might beat them later; a teacher who often gave young Josip a slice of bread; the time he stole his grandfather's special sugar, and dropped it in the river; the occasion when his parents were out and Josip led on his brothers and sisters to cook a pig's head which his mother was saving for New Year, and they made themselves sick overeating. It is noteworthy that in his memoirs Tito often described the times of scarcity in his childhood and only once mentioned the feasts that took place in times of plenty, at harvest time, weddings and on traditional feast-days, though he must have attended plenty of these.

Food production was the basic employment of all members of the family, and the children were put to some kind of useful work from earliest years. Young children could watch over the hobbled cattle in the fields, the geese feeding in the valley. They fetched water from the well and had to work the heavy grindstone which ground the corn into flour. This implement with its long pole fixed into a hole near the circumference of a large stone, which Tito remembered pushing round for long hours, is still on view in the kitchen. His mother's distaff is there too; it was used for spinning the flax and wool for homemade clothes for the large family. Weaving was done by hand-loom in a shed outside, which with the cowsheds and other outhouses has now been demolished.

In fact a great part of Josip's earliest years was not spent at the family home at Kumrovec, but with his maternal grandparents at Posreda in Slovenia. Josip, who was a favourite of his grandfather Martin, was sent to live with him to ease the family budget. This long stay in Slovenia gave him a loving, secure, relaxed and happy environment for his early years. His grandfather was a small, stocky man whom Tito may resemble. He called the young boy 'Josek' – little Joey – and Tito remembers him as a gay, witty, friendly man, given to practical jokes, a taste which Tito said he inherited from him.[17]

Here Josip enjoyed the outdoor life, with enough to eat and plenty to occupy him about the farm, fetching water, minding the cattle, learning to ride the horses and going up into the woods with his grandfather, who was a charcoal burner. Here he learnt country lore that was to be invaluable to him in later life when he led a guerrilla army through forest and mountains in the second world war, and it gave him a love of hunting, fishing and country occupations that he kept for the rest of his life.

It was during these formative years with his grandfather that he learned to speak Slovene, a language different from his native Croatian. Though Slavonic it had a different language structure, different stresses from the Croatian language of Zagorje. Josip spoke with a Slovene accent when he returned home. To this day experts can detect traces of Slovene influence on Tito's Croatian, and his speech is atypical. It has often been said by people who note something unusual in his manner of speech that Tito speaks with a Russian accent, and though this may have been true in the early 'twenties when he returned from Russia, Slovene has had a more lasting influence on his speech.

These years, and perhaps an element of Slovene inheritance in his temperament, gave him an understanding of Slovene people and their orientation towards the west. In the 'thirties when he came out of prison and was a prominent communist living an illegal, hunted life, crossing the frontiers from Yugoslavia to Italy and Austria, it was to the villages of Slovenia that he had known as a child that he went for safe hiding, not to his family village in Croatia.

In 1900, at the age of nearly eight, Josip went back to live at home, and in retrospect it always seemed to him that the happiest years of his childhood ended with the nineteenth century. At eight he was considered, like other peasant boys, old enough to be a useful worker and was sent out into the fields to hoe between the rows of corn, weed the vegetables and look after the animals. The stories that Tito told later about his boyhood are the common currency of a normal peasant childhood in Zagorje in these years – the games with the lads of the village, fights with Slovene boys across the border in which Josip had to deny his Slovene affiliation and protest his support for Croatian Kumrovec; stealing apples and walnuts from neighbouring trees, fishing in the brook, hiding his sister's wedding wreath as a joke. But he is reticent about the more intimate family life – his mother's annual pregnancies, his relations during these years with his brothers and sisters and with his father, are rarely mentioned. He says little, too, about the religious side of his upbringing.

Croatian peasants were all Catholic and the church played an important part in their lives. Tito's mother was pious and Josip, with the other children, attended church, was instructed in the catechism and basic Catholic teaching, and made his first communion. The memories he cherished later were all against the church; how the friars from Klanjac collected forced contributions of grain in January when the peasants could least afford it; how he stopped being an acolyte (not why he was chosen) after a priest had slapped him when he was slow and clumsy in removing the priestly robes after mass; how his mother gave him money as a present for the priest who had prepared him for communion and he stole some of it, although his friends told him that he would be struck down by God for his sins. The church did little to alleviate poverty in the village, was extortionate and taught acceptance of existing conditions as God's law. Its higher officials were associated with the ruling class and it had large estates and temporal possessions. These are the things that memory selected after Tito had become a communist and had rejected the Catholic Church as a capitalist institution associated with oppression and exploitation.[18]

In 1899 a village school was opened for the first time in Kumrovec, in a small hall, replaced by a new building in 1902, opposite the Broz house. Schooling in Croatia had been compulsory since 1890, but it was not popular with the peasants, who considered that it took their children away from useful work. 'My people were peasants and took the typical peasant view that education was rather putting on airs and the work of the farm was more important,' Tito recalled in later life. 'I used to be told to do jobs at home which would have meant missing school. So I sometimes played truant from home in order to do my schooling.'[19] But the records for the years 1902 to 1904 still show that Josip Broz was frequently absent. This was not only due to family work, for when he was ten he was ill with diphtheria, which was endemic in the villages and often caused death. There was no doctor for the villages round Kumrovec, but there were many homely remedies and, as still today, many local practitioners of 'folk' medicine. Stamina was the real healer, and Josip, in spite of a later reference to himself as having been 'a frail boy', was basically strong and healthy.

Kumrovec village had about 200 families, but the school also served outlying hamlets and Tito recalls that there were 350 children in attendance when he was there, and only one schoolmaster. Juraj Marković the first schoolmaster, became a lodger in the Broz house, living upstairs in the loft. He was tuberculous. He used to spit blood into his one handkerchief which young Josip would take to wash in the brook and bring back to dry over the schoolroom fire. This may well have given him immunity from the disease which claimed so many Croatian peasants. When Marković's mother fetched him away to die the children wept as he waved goodbye with the handkerchief. For a brief time they were taught by a woman, remembered for her strictness. When she married there came a mild man, Stjepan Vimpulšek, 'always considerate to his pupils, although he had a large family and many domestic worries'. A letter from him about the Broz family says 'Josip's father was the cleverest of his brothers and wanted to make a better living for his children. He asked me what kind of worker Josip should become. I saw he had practical ability and advised he should become a mechanic.'[20]

Josip does not seem to have caused any trouble when he did attend school, and it does not appear that he received any influence from his teachers likely to lead him to be a political revolutionary, except the skill of literacy, a thirst for reading and the advice to go out into the world. Tito said himself that he had difficulty in learning and this is not surprising considering the circumstances of his schooling. Yet his school report for 1904, the year he left school, was uniformly good. Behaviour – excellent; reading – both understanding and elocution – very good; catechism, religious instruction, mathematics and practical work also very good; church and lay singing and gymnastics were marked as good. As he had no opportunity to go on to secondary school he was immediately set to work to keep himself and help support the family, so that at first he had little opportunity to use his learning.

For some months he worked for his uncle Martin Javeršek, his mother's brother, earning his keep and with the promise of a new pair of boots at the end of the year. Josip felt he was cheated on this arrangement for the pair he got in the end were inferior to his own old ones. After words with his uncle he returned home and soon came under the influence of a visiting relative on leave from the Austro-Hungarian army, staff-sergeant Jurica Broz. He told Josip old soldiers' tales about life in the big world and how to get on by leaving the village. Jurica had connections in a nearby garrison town where he was stationed. He said he could get his relative a job there, but first Josip had to be persuaded that it was an opening not to be missed. Jurica advised him to become a waiter as a means of having plenty to eat, being always well-dressed and meeting nice people, without too much hard work.

His father was less keen on the idea. Josip was a useful labourer on the farm, a potential source of income. He would have liked to send him to the United States. Many peasant families in Croatia were helping their sons to emigrate in those years. It was a fruitful form of family investment if they could raise the fare of 200 forints at a time when wages were little over a forint a day. The Broz family could not raise this money.[21]

Franjo Broz was bowing to the inevitable when he at last agreed to Josip following in the steps of his older brother Martin – who had left home some ten years previously – to leave the village and find work in the town. The drift to the town of the younger generation of peasants was part of the process of disintegration of feudal patriarchal society which had coincided with his father's generation. By the end of Josip's schooldays economic difficulties in the village were forcing the pace of change. There had been a great increase in Croatia's population in the later years of the nineteenth century – fifteen per cent natural increase in the years 1881 to 1890 alone – bringing more mouths to feed, and pressure on the peasants to produce more food. In Zagorje round Kumrovec the land was poor and could not be made to produce more without investment of skills and capital which the peasants did not possess.

A new radical political influence appeared in the Croatian villages at this time. It was a peasant movement started by the brothers Antun and Stjepan Radić who founded in 1905 a Croat Peasant Party, the first political party with the aim of mobilizing the passive but discontented peasantry as a force in political life. It had elements of the populist movement that had been active in Russia in the nineteenth century. Its object was to make them conscious of their needs and rights. Stjepan Radić, a peasant by origin, travelled round the villages wearing peasant clothes, speaking to the people in the language and simple terms they understood, very different from the sophisticated town ways of the usual political leaders. They had many meetings in Zagorje and the peasants of Kumrovec must have heard of them, but there is no evidence that they had any direct influence on the Broz family. Their slowly growing influence was a sign of the times, of the changes ineluctably evolving in village life.

In 1907, when he was fifteen years old, Josip Broz left Kumrovec with his cousin, staff-sergeant Jurica, to go to find work in the garrison town of Sisak some fifty miles south-east of Zagreb. This was the end of Josip's life as a peasant, though he returned home on a number of occasions – especially in times of difficulty – for his family ties were still very strong. There is no evidence to suggest that Josip was a budding young revolutionary when he left home. Stories that as a boy he had burnt the midnight oil reading Marx and Engels secretly in the loft can be discounted. He left home in search of his fortune, probably with no greater ambition than to be able to earn enough to eat well, dress smartly, with new town clothes not cast-off peasant outfits, and show his family and the village that he had been a success in the town.

The formative years of his childhood had provided him with a heritage of which he was at that time quite unconscious. He had been born near the bottom of the scale in a stratified society, at a time of increasing social and political tension. The folk history of the Croatian and Slovene people had given him radical feelings about social injustice – rich soil for the political seed he was to encounter later. He had some experience of poverty, though little of the real harshness of life, for his childhood had been emotionally, if not economically, secure. He had learnt to expect and accept help from a closely-knit family which embraced a wide kinship group. He had made warm personal relationships, and these influences remained with him for life. He may well have been deeply affected by the fact that he had an inadequate father and a strong, loving mother. But in general he was

21

a healthy, well-adjusted peasant boy, mature in knowledge of the natural world, very immature in the sophisticated sense. He had never been in a town, never travelled on a train. He was excited, curious, eager to learn, anxious for independence. But with it he had a native shrewdness and caution characteristic of peasant people. He started on a new life which was soon to offer multiple opportunities. At this stage there was no certainty of which way he would develop.

## 2 BOY INTO MAN

Compared with the village Josip had left, the small town of Sisak was a metropolis. It had a military garrison, some shops, an old medieval and Turkish fortress used as a prison, a few restaurants and small industries. The town stood at the confluence of three rivers – the Odra, the Kupa and the great Sava. These were still used by boats and barges for commercial traffic; with the recently built rail link to the main Zagreb–Belgrade railway line they brought people and business to the small market town. Yet it was big enough to open up a new world to young Josip who was found a job in a restaurant kept by a friend of his cousin. The restaurant had a gipsy band, a garden and bowling alley under the chestnut trees, and was patronized by officers and NCOs of the garrison regiment. The job of potboy, assistant waiter and general factotum turned out to be an arduous one, for he had to be at work at the sink or the tables or the skittle alley until all clients had left; tips, the first money of his own that Josip ever had, soon seemed small when he had learnt enough to assess their value. But he accepted the situation philosophically; in a way characteristic of his reaction to opportunity throughout his life, he made the best of what he had until he saw the occasion to move to something better.

It was not long in coming. He soon made contact with youths of his own age who were training as apprentices to a locksmith. He listened to their boastful talk. A trained locksmith was a general mechanic, a mechanic was an engineer, engineers built ships, railways and bridges. They were men of power in the new industrial world. These ideas echoed the words of his schoolmaster, that the future lay with mechanics. Josip plucked up courage and one day, still only fifteen years old, went to see Master Karas the apprentices' employer, a Czech who was a prosperous man of influence in the town. It was the first important decision he had made for himself. It set him on a career that was to expose him to political influences that he might well have escaped, or even rejected, had he become the waiter or tailor that up to that time had seemed possible steps to worldly success.

23

His interview with Karas remained vividly in Tito's memory in later life and he retold it frequently. 'Well young fellow what do you want?' he was asked when, small and rather scruffy in his poor clothes, he was led into the presence of the master. 'I want to be taken on as an apprentice. I want to be a smith. In our family there is always someone who is a smith . . .' The wording of the conversation varies a little as Tito repeats the anecdote, but the gist is always the same. He explained that he did not like the life of a waiter, wanted to train to be a smith, and felt his family tradition gave him some kind of justification. Karas agreed to take him on if his father would sign the legal apprenticeship agreement. The same night he wrote to his father who came and signed, first for Josip and later, with the same master, for his brother Stjepan a year younger than Josip, so that the two boys spent most of their apprenticeship together. According to the apprenticeship indenture, Karas provided training and keep for the apprentice for three years and the father had to provide clothes. Since his father had no money to buy the boiler suit which was the apprentice's uniform, Josip used his small savings from tips and bought his own.[1]

For the next three years, from the age of fifteen to eighteen, Josip lived and worked in Karas's workshop in Sisak. Work was from 6 a.m. to 6 p.m. and apprentices had to attend classes at the technical school in the town twice a week from 5 p.m. to 7 p.m. The community in Karas's workshop consisted of four or five apprentices, and three or four trained workmen-journeymen as they were still called, because they stayed with an employer for only a short time, moving on to gain experience in other places. In some ways it was a patriarchal, almost medieval community, with Karas in authority and each person assigned his place in the hierarchy. The apprentices lived and worked on the job – that meant in the cellars of the house, sleeping on the table near the smithy fire in winter, on hay in the loft in the yard in the summer. Food, plentiful at last if not luxurious, was provided from the family kitchen; and entertainment was what the boys could make for themselves. They kept pets which they traded in a Sunday exchange and mart where they met apprentices from other trades and workshops. They gossiped and sang, were cuffed by the journeymen, fought among themselves, read thrillers to each other during hours of daylight – there was no gas or electricity and candles were rationed – in a close-knit masculine community.

It provided a secure, happy and fairly hardworking life for the years of Josip's adolescence. Whatever awakening of interest in girls and sex that he may have experienced in these years, he never mentions. Going out to dances is only referred to at a later date. Josip seems to have got on well with his colleagues of all ages, to have been good at his work, if undistinguished, and to have taken everything happily in his stride with the exception of one incident shortly before he took his qualifying examinations. One day when he was nearly eighteen, while Karas was out of the way, he was reading a translation of *The Adventures of Sherlock Holmes* to the other apprentices, at a time when he was supposed to be looking after a new drill. Karas returned unseen and caught him in the act, just as the drill broke, at which he lost his temper and slapped Josip on the face. Josip, furious, guilty and ashamed, ran away and hid in a nearby brick works, and Karas informed the police. The fugitive was easily arrested and taken to the fortress prison where he had his first experience of gaol. Had Karas chosen to prosecute, Josip would have lost the whole of his apprentice's training. But the old man had a kindly nature, sent food to his apprentice in prison, and arranged for him to be released without being charged so that he could finish his training, which he did in September 1910.

*     *     *

The years 1907 to 1910 when Josip was in Sisak were ones of dramatic tension in the history of the South Slavs. They were years of mounting nationalism among the Slavonic peoples of the Austro-Hungarian empire, of escalating rivalry between Austria and Hungary and between Austria and Russia in the Balkans. For the Croats they were years of increasing discontent with their position as second-class citizens in Hungary, and of discussion as to what methods could be used to force the Magyars to changes that would ameliorate this situation. Many politically conscious Croats were beginning to think that their only hope of winning self-rule lay in some kind of Yugoslav (South Slav) alliance – joint pressure from Croats, Slovenes and Serbs – within the Austro-Hungarian empire. A few Croats – especially members of a party called the Frankovci – became extreme nationalists rejecting ideas of improved constitutional rights for Croatia in Hungary. Others thought of a so-called 'trialist' solution for relations between the three major races, the Germans, Magyars and Slavs in the Austro-Hungarian empire. Josip must have heard echoes of these political discussions during his youth, but none of them fired his imagination or gained his commitment. Even before he had finished his training he had identified himself with the industrial workers, which led him away from political nationalism towards the international brotherhood of socialism.

At this impressionable age he was exposed to the influence of the Austrian Social Democratic movement, which by the early years of the twentieth century was strongly Marxist, and committed to ideas of international working-class solidarity. This was to be the outstanding influence on his early political development. It led him to communism, and this prevented him becoming any kind of narrow Croat nationalist.

Sisak, unlike Zagreb and Osijek, was not a strong centre for political action among workers. It did not have any trade unions – although these had been legalized in Croatia in 1907, several years after unions were legal in the rest of the monarchy. Only one or two of the journeymen employed by Karas were political activists. One of these organized the apprentices to decorate the workshop with green boughs and flowers for May Day in 1909 and another who attended workers' meetings in a local beerhouse, persuaded Josip to sell and read the socialist newspaper *Slobodna Reč* (Free Word). By the time he had finished his apprenticeship, Josip had gained some idea of the importance of workers' organization, of the need to belong to a trade union if he wanted to get on. As soon as he finished his apprenticeship – having made some iron railings for the District Court in Sisak as his 'set-piece' – he went to Zagreb, and got a job through one of the journeymen who had been with Karas. In October 1910, now aged eighteen, he joined the Metal Workers' Union, which would automatically make him a member of the Social Democratic Party of Croatia at the age of twenty.

He described the receipt of his trade union card and badge as one of the proudest moments of his life. He said later that it made him feel more secure. He recalled that he had taken part in his first workers' demonstration during the two months when he was on his first job in Zagreb.[2] But political activity did not yet play a very important part in his life. His main objective was to go back home to Kumrovec to see his family, and show the village that he had made a big success in the wide world. In this he was to be disappointed. With his first earnings he bought himself a new suit which was stolen from his lodgings within a few hours of its purchase. He had to buy a cheap secondhand one to go home in and was unable to cut a very grand figure. He spent December to January 1911 with his family, and then, his savings spent, and for the first time with no friend or family connection to help him, he went out to make his own way in the world.

His first experiences were sadly disillusioning, his dreams of success as a skilled mechanic shattered by the reality of the labour situation in Austria-Hungary at that time. As a citizen of the Habsburg empire he could travel anywhere in the monarchy in search of work – Hungary, Slovenia, the Czech lands, Trieste, Vienna and the whole of Austria, but in 1910 unemployment was high over the whole area. The lingua franca of the whole central Europe area, especially the western part which was nearest to him, was German, and of this as yet, he had only a smattering.

At the end of January 1911 he left home, was given a lift in his father's cart to the nearest railway station and took a train to Ljubljana, main town of Slovenia. He had little money, no connections and although by now he was prepared to do almost anything to earn money to buy food, he still did not find a job. He decided to try Trieste, a busy port with shipbuilding yards. A measure of his desperate determination was the fact that he walked the sixty miles across the mountains in snow conditions, sleeping rough, and it took him three days to reach the coast. Here too he was unsuccessful. 'In Trieste I was overwhelmed by the harbour and its immense transatlantic liners,' he said later; but at least he was able to go to the branch office of his trade union and collect unemployment relief which the union paid its members. This saved him from starvation and confirmed his belief in the importance of trade union membership. He decided to go home, hitching a ride on a peasant's cart, and walking the rest of the way. By the end of February he was back in Kumrovec again.

'I could not and would not stay long with the family,' he told his biographer Vladimir Dedijer later. 'I spent only a few days resting; as the house was poor, I thought it best to leave as soon as possible.' At the beginning of March he went to Zagreb, where he took a job for four months in a small workshop repairing bicycles, cars and other machines. It was little better than the workshop where he had trained, but at least it gave him a regular wage of two crowns, sixty hellers a day. He was careful to pay up his union dues for the time when he had been unemployed. Short of money though he was, he soon bought himself a new suit.[3] This was the way a peasant showed that he had made a success in the world, and after his earlier failure, the theft of his first new suit and the loss of face during the early months of the year when he had been unemployed, he was determined to retrieve his reputation. He was still in many ways the typical village boy making his way in town.

He soon left Zagreb to try his fortune in Vienna – he wanted to see the world, to learn German and to get away from his father's importunate demands for more and more of his earnings. He accepted his obligation to his family and sent money home occasionally – but to his mother, to prevent his father spending it on drink. Further away from the family he would be freer and have more money for himself. This time he prepared his sally into the world with more caution. Although he bought a railway ticket to Vienna, he was so afraid that the Trieste experience might be repeated that he got out of the train in Ljubljana where he would still be on familiar ground. In the event he was saved a plunge into the unknown by himself, for he obtained work in a fairly large (150 workers) metal goods factory at Kamnik, where he stayed for nearly a year, until May 1912. His own brief account of life in Kamnik shows him still a very ordinary youth, not very politically minded, less interested in the anti-Habsburg propaganda of the gymnastic organization which he joined than in the uniform and feather-trimmed cap – bought from his small wages on hire-purchase – and in marching behind the band and doing gymnastics three times a week. His chance to leave Slovenia came when the factory went bankrupt and its redundant workers were offered a month's wages in advance to go to a larger works in Bohemia where labour was needed.[4] So the unfamiliar journey via Vienna was made with money in his pocket and in the cheerful company of about fifty other workers.

On arrival in Bohemia it turned out that the Slovene and Croat workers had been recruited as strike breakers, and they were prevented from starting work by the Czech labourers who were on strike at the factory. When the management capitulated and granted a rise in wages, the new men also started work at a higher wage. Josip was at last launched as a worker in one of the more rapidly expanding industrial areas of central Europe. He had now gained sufficient self-confidence to branch out on his own, and after two months set off again to take a look at some of the biggest industrial works in central Europe. He had his union card, which insured him against destitution if he failed to find work in Austria-Hungary. He had learnt some

German and increased his experience of various processes of metal working; he had already lost some of the gaucherie and need to show off as a peasant boy in town; he had not contacted his family to tell them where he was and so was free from his father's demand for money.

He travelled during the rest of 1912 from one industrial centre to another, picking up jobs for a short time and moving on. He saw the Škoda arms factories in Pilsen, stayed for a short time in Munich, visited Mannheim and the Ruhr, finally ending up in Vienna in October 1912. When he at last wrote to his mother he received a reply giving him the address of his brother Martin, his elder by eight years, who had left home when Josip was still at school and was now working as a railwayman at the Wiener Neustadt station just outside Vienna.[5] Staying with his brother who had a wife and small baby, Josip was secure in a comfortable family atmosphere. He was also able to get a job in the Daimler works near by. Here at last he got a whiff of the glamour that he had dreamed his training would bring him. He was fascinated by the 'big powerful cars with their heavy brasswork, rubber-bulb horns and outside handbrakes' and 'even became a test driver'. It seems probable, however, that this was not an official position, for in the same account he recollects that he did not have enough money to afford to go into the big coffee houses in Vienna. But he got to know the city which he was to visit many times later in very different circumstances. He also joined another gymnastic association where he trained several times a week. He took up fencing and went to dancing classes to learn the fashionable ballroom dances – high-class social accomplishments that would distinguish him from the kolo-dancing peasants back home. Little by little he was moving up in the social scale. He was still a conformist, trying to better himself in society as he found it. In 1913 when he reached the age of twenty-one he had to go back home to do two years' military service.[6]

\*　　\*　　\*

Service with the Austro-Hungarian army was to bring experiences that changed Josip Broz from a conformist into a potential rebel and social outcast. The change seems in many ways out of character with all the traits that he had showed up to this time, but the events he lived through in the next four years were more than dramatic. Broz saw a social order overthrown during the Russian revolution, and people at the bottom of the ladder, like himself, suddenly elevated to power. It was a heady experience. His own change into a political rebel was not a sudden conversion, but the change when complete was a permanent one, deeply rooted in his personality and linked with his childhood experiences. It had complex causes in which ambition, personal disappointment, idealism and human commitment all played their part.

He had just over a year in the army before the outbreak of the first world war. Unmoved by the irksome discipline, hard conditions and eccentric behaviour of a despotic corporal in his unit, he got on very well in the army, was successful and happy. He had learnt to look after himself and avoid trouble. He was more intelligent, more sophisticated than most of the other recruits, peasant boys, many illiterate, who had come straight from the village. He was in good physical condition thanks to his work and gymnastic clubs, and in the winter of 1913/14 he was trained as a skier. The fencing he had learnt in Vienna stood him in good stead, and he became regimental fencing champion. He was obvious material for promotion and was sent on a non-commissioned officers' training course in Budapest, where he came second in the all-army fencing championship. When he was promoted at the age of twenty-one he was the youngest non-commissioned officer in the 25th Domobran regiment. He already had the makings of a successful soldier.

On 28 June 1914 a young Bosnian nationalist, using arms supplied by members of a Serbian secret nationalist society, the 'Black Hand', assassinated the Austrian Archduke Franz Ferdinand in Sarajevo, capital of Bosnia, the province annexed by Austria in 1908. This caused a chain reaction of events that led to the outbreak of the first world war. Austrian military and political leaders decided that Serbian complicity in the murder plot offered an irresistible opportunity to teach the aggressively nationalist Slav state of Serbia a lesson – a lesson that would be a warning to Slavs within the empire to curb their nationalist demands.

Austria's Chief of Staff, Conrad von Hötzendorf, had had his military plan 'Mobilization B(alkan)' for attack against Serbia ready for some time. It was meant to result in a short localized war. A harsh ultimatum was sent to Serbia, and though it was in the main accepted, Austria declared war on Serbia on 28 July, when her own mobilization was still only half completed. Russia, Serbia's ally, afraid of being involved in war before her preparation could be got under way, also ordered partial mobilization on 30 July. Germany was involved by alliance with Austria. She had to make crucial decisions about which military plan to follow for invasion of France if the war became general. She declared war on Russia on 1 August, and on France two days later, invading Belgium on the same day. Great Britain declared war on Germany on 4 August, and a general war had begun.

Austria was now confronted with a situation far different from the one she had intended. While her troops were invading Serbia she had to face attack by Russian armies on her eastern front in the Carpathians. Conrad had intended to wipe out Serbia with his fifth and sixth armies, keeping the other armies in reserve. The second army, to which Josip Broz's regiment belonged, had been moved into position north of Belgrade as part of the reserve. It had to be withdrawn for use on the Russian front. In September 1914, while the Austrian *blitzkreig* against Serbia was being so unexpectedly thrown back, the 25th Domobran regiment was on its way to Galicia to meet the Russian invasion.

The Croat soldiers had no enthusiasm for the war. 'We all hoped for another heavy [Austrian] defeat like the one the empire suffered at Königgratz, and prayed the hated state would dissolve,' Tito recalled later. 'I hated the war from the beginning,' he said on another occasion. Comment along these subversive lines was general in the regiment, but Broz was reported by one of his loyal *kaisertreu* colleagues. He was accused of having spoken against the war and imprisoned in the Petrovaradin fortress. Since his case was not one for a military court he was released and sent to the front in Galicia.[7]

Once the regiment was in position on the Carpathian front, the situation was very different. The job of soldiering had to be done as efficiently as possible for survival depended on it. As autumn turned into harsh winter, trench warfare reached stalemate. The Croat troops were badly equipped and poorly clothed; their enemies, the Russians were even worse off. 'There were more who succumbed to frostbite in the legs than were killed by bullets,' Tito said later. He strained all his resources to look after his men. His anecdotes told in later life about this period show that he still had the capacity to make the best of things, of the frightful conditions of that winter, even getting some satisfaction out of his job of leading reconnoitering parties behind the enemy lines.[8] He was discovering he had a natural gift for leadership.

The end of this phase of his soldier's career came suddenly on 25

March, Easter Sunday 1915. At 4 a.m. the Russian General Brusilov launched an attack near Okno. 'We found ourselves in a very stupid position which a good strategist would never have allowed to happen,' Tito recalled, 'our troops were pushed into a corner, and the enemy was looking down on us, attacking from high above. They attacked us with artillery, smashed our left flank, encircled us . . . at the beginning, we defended ourselves as best we could.' When a gap had been forced in the Austrian lines, Circassian cavalry charged in, and leaping from their horses began hand-to-hand fighting in the trenches. Josip had a two-yard long lance thrust into his side under his left arm. It penetrated deep and narrowly missed his heart. He fainted and only escaped death from a Circassian sword by the arrival of the less barbaric Russian infantry.[9]

Taken prisoner of war, he was transported to a hospital in an old monastery deep in the Russian interior at Sviashsk on the river Volga near Kazan. He remained there for thirteen months, at first desperately ill. The wound was slow in healing and he had complications including pneumonia and recurrent attacks of typhus, caught from the lice that infested the filthy, overcrowded building where sick men lay on the straw-covered floor. At his worst, he was given up as lost, marked with a red tag and removed to the ward for the dying. But his strong constitution prevailed. He was fortunate to have some care and nursing, and eventually by the summer of 1916 he was well enough to be sent to a small prisoner of war camp near Ardatov in the nearby province known today as Kuibishev. Food was bad, conditions rough, and when some peasants came to look for a mechanic for their flourmill, Broz volunteered to work outside the camp. 'I did not have much work at the mill and had plenty of time for reading . . . I also became acquainted with some anti-Tsarist Russians.' But this comfortable life – which included sauna baths, and the offer of one of the peasant's daughters in marriage – lasted only a few months. Before the end of 1916 he was sent to another prisoner of war camp further east, at Kungur near the town of Perm in the foothills of the Ural mountains. Here, as a non-commissioned officer and still convalescent, he did not have to work. He was put in charge of prisoners who came from various parts of the Austro-Hungarian empire – mainly Rumanians, Czechs and Hungarians, for he had become separated from most of the Croats and other South Slavs.

During the winter of 1916–17 the prisoners were working on repairing the St Petersburg–Siberian railway line. Food, paid for out of their small wages, was scarce, conditions of life severe. As an NCO, Broz was in charge of working arrangements. Surprisingly, the prisoners received Red Cross parcels and were even visited by a Swedish official of the Red Cross Organization to whom Josip Broz later sent a letter complaining that a Russian railway official had been stealing from prisoners' parcels. The Russian soon found an opportunity for revenge. Broz had altered work records to help the prisoners. He was imprisoned in a cellar, and three Cossacks were sent in after him to beat him up. 'They drew their knouts and began to lash me across the back. I received thirty blows I shall remember all my life,' Tito recalled in later life. But that same night another Russian came to his aid with tea and a blanket. Shortly after, at the beginning of March 1917, came the news of the Tsar's abdication. To shouts of 'Down with the Tsar' prisoners were released from gaol and in the ensuing confusion Tito was able to spend some time with a Polish railway engineer who lived nearby. This man was Tito's first close contact with a Bolshevik.

The situation in the small prisoner's camp at Kungur in the early months of 1917 was a reflection of the chaos in Russia. In St Petersburg the Provisional Government was wrestling with problems of the collapse of central authority on the home front and in the army. Soviets were being set up as 'peoples' parliaments' in towns and villages all over the country. It was difficult to know where authority lay and whether the country was still at war or not. The Bolsheviks were not yet in power and were deeply divided on the question of support from the Provisional Government. Lenin, in exile in Switzerland, returned to St Petersburg – in the famous sealed train across Germany – on 3 April. It was after his April Theses, expounding the doctrine of revolution and dictatorship of the proletariat, and as a reaction to continued confusion in St Petersburg, that a revolutionary movement encouraged by the Bolsheviks began to gain support in the Russian capital. In the many prison camps throughout Russia, prisoners of war knew little of what was going on in the capital; they were dependent on who held power in their locality, and even uncertain whether they were still captive or free.

'I had already talked with prisoners of war and we expected there was going to be trouble. The engineer also told me there was going to be a revolution. But someone reported my activities and I was imprisoned, held for three days, and then returned to the same place.' Before long Broz was arrested again and spent fourteen days of April in gaol until his friend the Polish Bolshevik managed to get him released and transferred to work on the railway line at Perm. But life was very insecure with workers being arrested or disappearing. Towards the end of April Broz decided to try to escape. His friend provided him with the address of his son, also a supporter of the Bolsheviks, who was a worker at a factory in St Petersburg. He sold his good military uniform in the market-place and bought a worn-out suit. The jacket was too big for him and he altered it himself; then, aided by the railway engineer he escaped to Petrograd. A little way down the line from Perm, Broz jumped a goods train and, hidden between sacks of wheat, made the journey to the Russian capital, where he arrived in the last days of June. He managed to contact the young Pole and was taken to his flat.[10]

By this time the Bolsheviks had control of the working-class districts of St Petersburg and were gaining increasing support from soldiers and workers in the capital. There were more and more street demonstrations against the government, with Bolshevik slogans – 'All power to the Soviets' – appearing, although Lenin himself was still convinced that it was too soon for a revolutionary bid for power. Tension was heightened when counterrevolutionary forces – monarchists, army officers, ex-servicemen and supporters of the Cadets – began to arm and organize themselves.[11] On 3 July things came to a head with demonstrations of workers and soldiers parading through the streets singing the Marseillaise, demanding the end of the Provisional Government and power to the Soviets. Without organization or leaders the demonstration went on for several days. The Peter-Paul fortress, symbol of the savage despotism of Tsardom, was occupied by the Kronstad sailors who had started the revolt. But the government was able to muster enough support and troops to oppose the demonstrators. Josip Broz was out on the streets in these days. It was his only close contact with the central events of the Russian revolution. Dodging machine-gun bullets fired from the roof of the railway buildings, he was lucky not to be killed. When the government got the upper hand and began to seek out the agitators and Bolsheviks, his friend the Polish factory-worker was arrested. After a few days on the run, hiding by the bridges over the Neva, Broz decided to escape to Finland. Unknown to him, Lenin had also taken this step a little earlier.

Broz, however, on his own and without contacts, had less success. He hoped that his 'white card', a certificate that he was medically unfit on account of his wound, would allow him to get into Finland, which was then part of Russia. He was arrested at Ulenburg on suspicion of being a Bolshevik, sent back to St Petersburg, and by August was incarcerated in a rat-infested dungeon in the Peter-Paul fortress – by this time surrendered by the Bolsheviks – on its island in the Neva river.

'I spent some time in the fortress,' he remembered. 'I was asked several times what I had been doing, what function in the Bolshevik party I had. I answered that I had been doing nothing there, that I was no Bolshevik. I kept saying that I was a white card holder from Viatska Guberniya and that I came to find a job in Petrograd. It was convincing, since I spoke pure Viatska dialect. So I spent three weeks in that prison. Then I got fed up with it. As you know, the Neva flows past the fortress, right below the barred windows. It was misty, damp and frightfully cold. I believed I would leave my bones there.'

'One day they came to ask me questions again. At the beginning I had been afraid to say that I was a prisoner of war. I believed it would be worse for me, especially as I had escaped. When I was taken to the interrogation I said I was a prisoner of war. "Where did you run away from?" they asked. "From Ergach, Permska Guberniya," I replied. "Fool," they answered, "why didn't you say so earlier. You have spent three weeks in here, when you could already have been outside."'

He was ordered back to his own prisoner of war camp, and travelled under guard on the Maxim Gorki train which stopped at every station. At one of these stops, on the excuse of fetching water to make tea, he slipped his guard and escaped. Then he made his way slowly on foot, and by train, first to Yekaterinburg – where he was recognized by a guard from the camp and had to disappear quickly – then to Omsk. On the evening of 8 November, a day after the Bolsheviks took power in St Petersburg – the famous October revolution – he was stopped by a patrol as he arrived in Omsk. 'Who goes there?' they challenged. 'A prisoner,' replied Broz. 'No, comrade, you are free. This is a revolution.' They told him to go to the local fairground where a detachment of Red Guards was being set up. 'Without hesitating much, I went.' With other prisoners of war at the camp he joined a unit of the International Red Guard. He spent the winter months of 1917 to 1918 doing guard and sentry duty for the Bolsheviks on the railway line near Omsk.[12]

These were crucial months for the Bolshevik revolution. On 3 March 1918, Trotsky signed the Treaty of Brest-Litovsk with Germany, and Russia withdrew from the war. Large areas of Russia's western territories were ceded to Germany. This resulted in a very confused situation for Austrian prisoners of war in Russia. Many of the Slavs had been unwilling participants in the fighting against Russia – thousands had given themselves up – and a lot of them, especially Serbs and Czechs, were now eager to get to the west and fight against Germany and her Allies. This feeling was not shared by Croat and Slovene prisoners who were more interested in the situation in their own homelands, and had no army of their own to join. They were unwilling to be incorporated into the Serbian army, and the Serbian government, for political reasons, and with an eye on any future South Slav state would not agree to them forming Yugoslav units.

To add to the confusion, relationships between the Bolsheviks and western Allies had deteriorated, and Allied forces began operating against the Bolsheviks. British troops occupied Archangel in the north of Russia (3 August 1918) and Baku in the south. American forces had landed in Siberia. Earlier in the summer, the Bolsheviks had agreed to allow Czech troops to be evacuated – armed and in military units – across Siberia, and the operation had already begun. But as Allied intervention mounted the Bolsheviks feared that the Czech troops would be used by the Allies against them and began to try to disarm the Czechs. In the resulting fighting Czech troops rose in revolt (May 1918) and began to fight with anti-Bolshevik forces to wrest control of the Siberian railway line from the Bolsheviks. Czech–White Russian forces captured Omsk from the Bolsheviks on 7 June 1918. For a time Omsk was the centre of a Socialist (anti-Bolshevik) Siberian government. In November this was taken over by White troops under Admiral Kolchak who mounted an offensive against the Bolsheviks in the spring of 1919. This failed and Omsk was recaptured by the Bolsheviks between 11 and 14 November of that year.[13]

Tito's accounts of his own movements during these months are imprecise, and it may well be that in recalling them thirty or more years later, he was unable to remember exactly where he was on certain dates. He had to flee from the Omsk region as Czech soldiers were routing out prisoners who had joined the Red Guard; he was hidden for a time by a Russian girl Pelagea Belousova – later to become his wife – but then went further away from the railway line into the steppe country. A mystery about dating in this period was that his Communist Party membership is given as registered with the Omsk party on 19 January 1919. But this was a time when Omsk was in the hands of Kolchak.

At one stage he spent some months – and he mentions incidents in both summer and winter – in hiding with the Khirgiz nomads in steppe country about forty miles outside Omsk. It seems probable that this bizarre and exotic experience lasted the greater part of 1919. He returned to the Omsk region after it had been recaptured by the Bolsheviks in November of that year.

The Khirgiz chief who gave him protection and hid him when bands of White troops rode through the steppe country looking for Bolsheviks, was Hadji Isaj Djaksembayev. His tribe of nomad horsemen – who counted their wealth in horses, the chief himself owning between two and three thousand – roamed the vast steppe country, camping for a while in tents in the summer, in dug-outs in the winter. Broz was able to win favour with Isaj because he knew how to mend a machine-driven flour mill which the tribe used, and because of his prowess with horses. With his adaptability, his humour and toughness, he became accepted by the nomads, and a favoured member of Isaj's entourage, riding across the steppes, breaking in horses, taking part in hunting timber wolves, and at night hearing or telling tales, the involved leg-pulling stories that the nomads delighted in. He dressed like the Khirgiz and learned something of their language, but never became so assimilated that he could stomach all their customs.

On one occasion when Isaj, a Muslim, spoke of the dirty Christian habit of eating pig's flesh, Broz retaliated by denouncing the revolting habit of the chief's women who would serve their men, and then while squatting on their haunches waiting for further commands, would pick huge lice from inside their clothes and crack them between their teeth until their lips were stained with blood. 'It used to make me sick – I could not eat my food,' he said. When Isaj offered him one of his daughters and the opportunity to stay with the tribe, Broz refused. But he did help one of the tribesmen to run away with a woman from a neighbouring tribe.[14]

Towards the end of 1919, when he knew that the region was cleared of Whites and the Bolsheviks were back in power, Broz returned to Omsk to renew contacts with Bolsheviks and prisoners who remained. It was some time before he found the Russian girl Pelagea again, for she too had fled. He met her quite by accident one day when he was walking down a village street. They were married in January 1920 in the Orthodox church of Bogoljuboisko near Omsk.[15]

We do not know if Broz was canvassed by any of the South Slav political groups active in Russia, but if he was it was likely to have been at this time. A conference of ex-prisoners of war had been held in Moscow in April 1918, and Yugoslavs who attended had joined a federation attached to the Russian Communist Party (Bolshevik). Yugoslavs of communist sympathies had also held another meeting in Moscow on 12 November and most had returned home at the end of that month.[16] Some remained for political work among the other returning soldiers. Broz had been too far away from Moscow to have been involved in these activities, but it is virtually certain that he met some Yugoslav communists in Russia before he left. There is no evidence that he was a deeply committed communist at this time, though his sympathies were obviously with the Bolshevik cause, and his name as a former Red Guard must have been listed as a potential supporter once a communist party was organized in Yugoslavia.

Shortly after their marriage, Broz and his wife left for St Petersburg. Broz had decided to go home and not to stay in Russia. He was put in charge of a group of ex-prisoners returning to Croatia. They travelled to Narva, thence by boat to Stettin. In March they started the long, slow journey back by train across Europe. They reached Vienna, capital of a now truncated Austria on 20 September 1920. By this time a Magyar called Bela Kun, who had also returned from Russia but as an active communist, had unsuccessfully attempted to stage a revolt in Hungary which was now an independent state. A new South Slav state had also been established in 1918. It included Broz's homeland of Croatia and other territories of the old Austro-Hungarian Empire which were inhabited predominantly by South Slavs. It came to be called Yugoslavia.[17] Its government was already taking precautions against the influence of any prisoners returning from Russia who might have subversive Bolshevik ideas. Broz took the red star – sign of having been a Red Guard – off his fur cap, although his friends remarked that there was a tell-tale mark where it had been. 'I did not want to make an exhibition of myself [neću da budem karneval]' he said, but in fact it was a prudent action.

He went with his wife straight to his home village, reaching Kumrovec at the beginning of October, only to find that his mother had died in 1918, and his father had moved to a nearby village. He was twenty-eight and had been away for six years. He had had experiences that had made him, if not a changed character, at least a man whose development put him apart from those who had stayed behind.

# 3 EVOLUTION OF A REVOLUTIONARY

Revolutionary changes had taken place in his homeland while Broz had been abroad. Croatia had broken away from the Austro-Hungarian empire, which had ceased to exist, and had joined the new Yugoslav state. When Tito left with the Austrian army to fight against Imperial Russia in 1914 a number of Croats and Slovenes, as well as some Serbs, had even at that time been in favour of Yugoslav union, but few foresaw that the Habsburg empire would not survive the war, and there was no thought then of a new South Slav state. The idea gained ground during the war after the founding in Rome in May 1915 of a Yugoslav committee representing South Slavs in the Austro-Hungarian Empire, and the Pact of Corfu with the Serbs.

How the South Slavs should break away from the monarchy became the burning question, especially after negotiations began in 1917 with Nikola Pašić, the foreign minister of the Serbian government in exile. Croats and Slovenes thought in terms of some kind of South Slav Union in which they would be equal partners with the Serbs. Pašić and many other Serbian leaders thought of an enlarged Serbian state which would include other South Slav lands. He was against the Yugoslav idea, refused to recognize the Yugoslav committee, and refused to allow South Slav prisoners in Russia to form a Yugoslav legion. 'It has always been the ideal of Serbia to free them (the Yugoslavs) from the Austrian yoke,' he said, and claimed that only he (Pašić) had the right to determine what was the correct policy. Serbian officials must obey his orders or go. Wickham Steed, editor of the London *Times* to whom he expressed these views replied: 'Your Excellency speaks like a Sultan, and I must warn you that Allied peoples are not fond of Sultans.'[1] But Pašić was to get his way. On 30 May 1917 the Slovene leader, Father Korošec, read out a declaration in the Austrian parliament demanding that all South Slav lands in the empire be united. By September 1918 Croat and Slovene leaders had decided that the Austro-Hungarian government had no right to speak on their behalf, and the Emperor's proclamation of 19

October promising recognition of national rights, came too late. On 29 October 1918 a Croatian parliament meeting in Zagreb with representatives from all the different regions of Croatia, declared the union with Hungary dissolved and deposed the Habsburg dynasty.

The decision to unite with Serbia came a month later. It was reached in haste without proper agreement of terms, and under pressure of Italian claims for large areas of Croatia and Slovenia. These had been promised to Italy by the secret clauses of the Treaty of London in 1915, which the western Allies had used as a bribe to buy Italian alliance. They too had not foreseen the collapse of the Austrian empire and the creation of a South Slav kingdom which would not willingly agree to Slovene and Croatian lands being given to Italy. Fearful that Italy's bargaining position would be strengthened if the South Slavs delayed the creation of their state by continued disputes over its form, the Croats capitulated to Pašić's demands. They accepted the Serbian Karadjordjević dynasty and agreed to the formation of a centralized government for a united South Slav state.

The new state included Serbia, all the South Slav lands from the Monarchy, Bosnia-Herzegovina, Croatia, Dalmatia and Slovenia, and the prewar kingdom of Montenegro, as well as areas of Macedonia that had remained in Turkish hands to 1914. Its boundaries were to be decided by negotiation at the peace conference. On 1 December 1918 the Regent for the new state, the Serb Alexander Karadjordjević, who was to become its king, received the Croat delegates one at a time, as subjects not as equals. The status of Croatia in the new kingdom had not yet been defined but Serbian intentions were already evident.

By the autumn of 1920 the Yugoslav representatives at the Peace Conference were politically isolated. They were still bitterly disputing among themselves about priorities in frontier claims and far from united. Britain and France were urging the Yugoslavs to give in to Italian demands, and Woodrow Wilson, who had been shocked by the 1915 Treaty of London and had been backing an ethnic solution favourable to the Slavs, had been defeated in the United States and was no longer able to support them. On 10 November 1920 the Yugoslav delegation capitulated to Italian demands. The Treaty of Rapallo with Italy was signed two days later. The Yugoslavs had to abandon their claims to Trieste and Istria and lost Zadar on the Dalmatian coast, some Adriatic islands, and the 'free state' of Fiume, which in effect also became Italian. The treaties of St Germain and Trianon signed in 1919 and Neuilly, in 1920 had agreed frontiers with Yugoslavia's other neighbours. None had given the Yugoslavs their full claims, and her irredentist neighbours remained dissatisfied. When all was concluded, 720,000 Yugoslavs were left living outside the new national frontiers, 480,000, or more than half of them, in Italy.[2]

By the time Broz returned to Croatia in 1920, the rift between Croats and the Serbian-dominated government had already widened. Croats felt bitter that their hopes of self-rule had been dashed. Serbian leaders had become mistrustful of Croats, afraid of their dissatisfaction, and inclined to keep them as far as possible out of positions of authority. The new state had turned sour even before its peoples had elected their first parliament and agreed a constitution.

In the villages of Croatia the peasants may not have known the details of high political negotiations but they were well aware of the political defeat their peoples had experienced. More important to most of the ordinary people was the opportunity for social and economic change which the end of the war had brought. In Croatia during the war, scarcity of food had allowed peasants to profit from a seller's market. Increased prices, and the weakening of authority as the war became progressively more disastrous for Austria, made them bolder. Thousands of soldiers deserted from their units in the countryside. The military tribunal in Zagreb in 1918 had to deal with 100,000 cases of desertion. Peasant outlaws numbering 40–50,000 called 'green corps' took to the maquis to avoid conscription and requisitioning. Peasants began to refuse to pay rents to their landlords. They invaded the large landed estates (four-fifths of which belonged to foreigners, mainly Magyar or German), grabbing lands or possessions in an orgiastic expression of centuries of land-hunger and hatred of the rule of a foreign landed aristocracy. Banja castle in the Zagorje, former property of the Erdödy family, was attacked by a mob of miners and peasants, plundered and dynamited. In 1918 the provisional government in Zagreb, trying to maintain authority while negotiations with the Serbs proceeded, issued on 14 November a proclamation to the peasants promising land reform and the break up of big estates. This was also an urgent problem in many other parts of the new state and one of the first actions of the new government was to issue an Interim Decree for Agrarian Reform on 25 February 1919. Thus before Broz returned home, feudal conditions in Croatia had come to an end, and many peasants had gained land; this did not automatically bring prosperity and conditions in the countryside remained very disturbed.

Croatia had not been the only area to experience disturbances. There were strikes in Slovenia and serious trouble in Montenegro where many of the highland clans, Serb by race, but fiercely Montenegrin by allegiance, were bitterly opposed to the disappearance of their independent patriarchal government, and the loss of autonomy and identity that followed their incorporation into the new state. The situation was even worse in Macedonia where Bulgarian agents of the International Macedonian Revolutionary Organization (IMRO) engaged in terrorist operations to prevent the area being incorporated into Yugoslavia.[3] Opposition throughout the country was put down by Serbian army units which had been part of the Allied army on the Salonika front and which were still at this time headed by the French General Franchet d'Esperey, who did not relinquish his command till after the signature of the peace treaties.

The most serious threat to government authority had been a general strike in July 1919 which had coincided with mutinies in army units led by ex-prisoners of war from Russia who were in contact with communist rebels in Hungary. The Yugoslav government was determined that no such communist or revolutionary movement should gain power in their state. Any excuse for foreign intervention in Yugoslavia must be avoided at all costs, for Austria, Hungary, Italy and Bulgaria were all pressing territorial claims against the Yugoslav frontiers.

The new state had few resources for dealing with the enormous tasks of reorganization necessary to feed, provide shelter and work for all its peoples, and to make the country a viable economic whole. Croatia and Slovenia, poor and backward as they had been under Austria-Hungary, had still been industrially better developed than the rest of the South Slav lands. But their resources and trade, as well as all their major communications, had been with the Habsburg Monarchy. Ownership of banks and factories had been mainly in German or Magyar hands, and their aid was no longer available. During the period of changeover conditions were chaotic and there were tremendous numbers of unemployed. 'Almost nine-tenths of the workers were in the street, unemployed, penniless,' said Tito when describing this period in a speech in 1948. He went on to describe how wages for those who did get work were at starvation rates – two and a half to three dinars a day for unskilled workers, five to six for skilled, at a time when bread, the staple food, cost one and a half dinars for a two and a half pound loaf.[4] There was no large-scale foreign relief. It took the government a long time to negotiate foreign loans, most of which were in any case to be taken up for defence. Inflation and the postwar influenza epidemic afflicted the country simultaneously.

\* \* \*

These were the conditions that Josip Broz and his wife came back to. It was imperative for him to find work, for pride would not let him become again a beggar among his relations, to endure the jibes and snide remarks that went with family charity. There is little material about his life at this time. In talking about it in later years he spoke of the hard conditions of the time, of taking part in a successful waiters' strike – which seems to suggest that he took a job as a waiter for a time – and of making a speech in the Zagreb Trade Union Hall on the anniversary of the October revolution. He said that he ended the speech with the statement, 'The workers can conquer only with the help of arms'; this was the view of the extremists among Yugoslav communists at that time. But we do not know if it was a call to arms or a statement of plain fact.[5]

Some people have concluded that he came back to Yugoslavia as a Soviet agent. There is no evidence to support this. Had he been an active communist agent it seems probable that he would have said so later and claimed credit for it. He would also have been receiving financial assistance, since Soviet agents were paid a small monthly wage, and it is known that some Yugoslav communists were at this time already receiving money from Russia, via Vienna or Budapest. Only a very few returning prisoners were playing any significant part in organizing a Yugoslav Communist Party at this time. Josip Broz was not one of them. Such evidence as there is suggests that he was poor and looking for work. He was politically committed only as a Bolshevik sympathizer and his private life still competed for precedence with his public one. He still thought of himself as a skilled mechanic whose political work would be in the trade unions and in the normal activities of an active social democrat improving conditions of labour. He was not yet totally committed to the new Communist Party, not yet a professional revolutionary.

Before Broz returned to Yugoslavia two important developments had taken place which were to have a determining influence on his life, though he personally at that time had no connection with them. These were the foundation in Moscow of an international communist organization, the Third International, and in the new kingdom of Serbs, Croats and Slovenes, the establishment of a Yugoslav Communist Party. The Third International, later to be known as the Comintern, provided an organization immediately able to aid foreign communists with advice and money, but it had not yet developed the centralized control and total authority over foreign communist parties that it had when Josip Broz first came to be connected with it fourteen years later.

The decision to found a United Workers' Party from the different Social Democrat and left-wing groups in the various regions of the Kingdom of Yugoslavia, was first reached at a unification conference held at Belgrade from 20 to 23 April 1919. The new party was called the Socialist Workers' Party of Yugoslavia (Communist); after a further conference at Vukovar in June 1920, it came to be called the Yugoslav Communist Party.[6]

Opinion among politically active people in left-wing movements in the different regions in Yugoslavia was far from united in support of the new Communist Party. There was sharp controversy about whether support should be given to the revolutionary ideas and tactics of the Bolsheviks, or whether to follow more legal methods of trying to improve social conditions. Even within the Communist Party itself there were widely differing views, with specially bitter controversy on the issue that faced the whole country – should the new state be centralized under Serbian leadership, or should it have some form of federal organization? Alternatives of revolutionary or Fabian tactics also divided the party. Those who supported the more moderate line were gradually superseded by the revolutionary left wing.

Economic conditions also strengthened revolutionary movements in all parts of the country. This was specially true in Croatia, in Bosnia-Herzegovina, and in the Vojvodina, which was only a few miles away from Hungary, where at this time it looked as if Bela Kun's communist revolt might be successful. Radical left-wing policies also had strong support in Montenegro and Macedonia. Italy had agents at work in Dalmatia trying to foment discontent and disrupt the new Yugoslav state. In Serbia, the decisive influence in the move to bring the Communist Party out in support of Bolshevik policies and the Third International, was played by Živko Topalović, later to leave the Communist Party and become an opponent of Josip Broz in the second world war, and Sima Marković, a teacher of mathematics who was eventually to lose his life in Russia, an outcast from his own party because of his independent ideas of communism.[7]

The influence of prisoners of war returning from Russia was very important. They told their stories about how Tsarist power had been overthrown. Dramatic and often romanticized, these helped to swing the masses towards support for the Communist Party. All these influences had their effect on the municipal and general elections of 1920.

In the municipal elections held in March and August, the communists gained victories in many parts of the country. In Zagreb they polled 39 per cent of votes, in Belgrade 34 per cent, thus gaining control of the only two sizeable towns in the country. In the general election held on 28 November 1920, all parties except the Communist were based on regional support. The communists, in spite of divisions among themselves, had followers in all regions of the country. They published thirteen newspapers and hundreds of leaflets which were distributed all over Yugoslavia. They polled the fourth largest percentage of votes (12·4) following the Democrats (19·9), Radicals (17·7), and the Croat Peasant Party (14·3). In the apportionment of seats they became the third largest party in the Constituent Assembly which met in December 1920. One surprising thing about this success was that communist support had been strongest, not in the more industrialized and advanced provinces of Slovenia and Croatia, but in the backward peasant provinces of Montenegro and Macedonia where party organization was at its weakest. Peasant feeling everywhere was strongly radical and revolutionary.[8]

If Russian money was received by some of the party leaders for the expenses of election propaganda it can have had only marginal effect. Communist success at the election of 1920 reflected the revolutionary, radical, frustrated feelings of the times among peasants, workers and regional nationalists in all parts of the country. It could not be ascribed to Bolshevik influence or Russian gold.

Within less than a month of their triumphal entry into the new parliament, the communists received a stunning blow which deprived them of all means of organizing political support and gaining power in the new state. On the night of 29/30 December 1920, the Democrat–Radical coalition government issued a decree – usually referred to as the *Obznana* – ordering, until the passing of the constitution, the dissolution of all communist organizations, including trade unions, and banning all propaganda advocating dictatorship, revolution or any

(*above*): **1. Kumrovec village: Tito's birthplace.**
(*below*): **2. Kamnik, 1912. Josip Broz** (*centre back row*); **his brother, Stefan** (*on his left*).

(*top, left*): **3. Tito in prison, May 1928.**

(*top, right*): **4. Tito in 1928 (not a police photograph).**

(*centre*): **5. Mosa Pijade and Josip Broz in Lepoglava Prison, circa 1931–2.**

(*right*): **6. Tito in Maribor Prison, 1932.**

kind of violence. To the communists, in the euphoria of success, this was totally unexpected. They had not prepared for the realities of the struggle for power. They were not to recover their legal status before the second world war.

There were many reasons why the government had decided to take this authoritarian and, as even non-communist members of parliament maintained, illegal step. The main one seems to have been that the Serbian politicians were prepared to go to any lengths to get their centralist constitution adopted in parliament. To mount a communist scare at this time would underline the need for strong central government and isolate the communist deputies if they remained in parliament. Communist success at the municipal and general elections had also frightened the Serbs who saw the possibility of the Communist Party exploiting regional feelings and widespread economic discontent throughout the country. The party's links with communist revolutionaries in Hungary and with Bolsheviks in Russia were also alarming.

The language and declared policy of the Communist Party had done nothing to allay these fears. 'Long live the Soviet Republic' had greeted cries of 'Long live the King' at the opening session of parliament. Even the milder communist election leaflets had advocated a very different kind of state from that which the Regent Pašić, and other members of the government were determined to create. Communist leaflets had told the electors that they had a choice between 'a state for the rich or a state for the workers and peasants. On one side are monarchists and republican capitalists, on the other is the Communist Party of the working peoples of town and country. A vote for the parties of the rich is a vote for capitalists, bankers, war-profiteers and for their state and dictatorship, a vote for the regime we have today. A vote for the Communist Party is a vote for the end of capitalism, of landowners, merchants and the ruling rich, a vote to abolish the slavery of workers and peasants, a vote for their liberation.'[9] Members of the government had no difficulty in seeing themselves in the description of ruling, rich bourgeoisie; that was in fact what they were.

There had been disorder in all parts of Yugoslavia throughout 1920, and even before the *Obznana* the government had stepped up police measures with increased violence against demonstrators. Violence on one side had bred violence on the other, until it was impossible to distinguish cause and effect. After the municipal elections in Zagreb in March, police had prevented the communist mayor-elect Delić from taking the platform by carrying him bodily from the hall.[10] The general strike in July 1919 caused serious alarm. Serbian troops were used to put down strikes in non-Serbian provinces, and even to prevent what many beside communists believed were lawful meetings. In December 1920 the communists had threatened a further general strike. This seemed like the way revolution had started in Russia.

In retrospect it is difficult to assess the real situation in Yugoslavia at the time of the *Obznana*. In the argument that has gone on about it ever since, truth has been clouded by the fact that supporters of the *Obznana* have exaggerated communist activities to justify the decree, while communists have also exaggerated disorders and their part in them, to show how strong and active the Communist Party was at that time.

Many non-communists in Yugoslavia were against the *Obznana* because it had destroyed political freedom in the new state, and because it was a dangerous precedent which could be turned – as it was later – against other political groups who opposed centralist government. Parliament endorsed the decree and all powers of the state were used to enforce it, introducing an element of bitter violence into political life which was worse than any present before.

Communist deputies deprived of their party, remained in parliament till 11 June 1921, when they withdrew in protest against the arrest and maltreatment of communists all over the country. They were absent on 28 June when a centralist constitution usually called the Vidovdan constitution was passed which denied regional autonomy or any form of regional self-government and gave Serbs the leading position their most fanatical supporters had demanded. It was passed by 223 votes to thirty-five with 165 abstentions. It has since been argued that if there had been no *Obznana*, and if all opponents had stayed to vote, the Vidovdan constitution could not have been passed. In the event the *Obznana* and the Vidovdan constitution defeated their own ends. Violent opposition to the new government was not confined to communists. The situation created by the Vidovdan constitution made stable government impossible throughout the whole interwar period.

The Communist Party had been in existence less than a year when it was banned. It had neither the organization nor the united and effective leadership to control reactions of outraged members in the months that followed. Members reacted violently and were answered by more police violence. A bomb was thrown at the Prince Regent as he was leaving parliament on 29 June. He escaped, but the former Minister of the Interior, Milorad Drašković, who had issued the *Obznana*, was murdered by a communist on 21 July 1921. The assassin was later condemned and executed. The murder led to further draconic legislation. On 30 July 1921 a Law for the Protection of the State annulled the mandates of communist deputies in parliament and local government. It imposed severe penalties – including death – for spreading communist doctrine. The communist movement in Yugoslavia was broken; many of its members were arrested, and its leaders had to go into exile or underground. They became the *ilegalci*, many of whom suffered imprisonment, torture and death in succeeding years in their attempts to keep the movement going.

By 1921 the worst period of postwar economic and political confusion was ended. Conditions in the country were stabilizing and there were some improvements in economic life. In later years many communists, including Josip Broz, who had witnessed the disorders and disastrous conditions of the 1918–20 period, believed that an opportunity for communist revolution had been missed at that time, lost because the working-class leaders did not take advantage of the situation created by the Russian revolution, the Hungarian communist revolt, the disintegration of the Austro-Hungarian empire and return of the South Slav prisoners from Russia, the peasant rebellions in Croatia and nationalist disturbances in other parts of the new kingdom, and the fact that the new Communist Party had 60,000 members and the trade unions 300,000 who could then have been mobilized. 'These were the conditions which made the situation in our country revolutionary at that time,' said Tito in 1948, 'but there was no leadership to take advantage of them.'[11]

Yet this assessment did not list forces which showed that the time was not ripe for revolution. In spite of the numbers enrolled in the trade unions and the Communist Party, there were few industrial workers in the new kingdom, and many of these, like Josip Broz himself, had virtually no experience of organized political life, nor of the techniques necessary for successful revolt. Very few people were dedicated to the idea of working-class power, most wanted better food and working conditions within existing society, and were unsure of what kind of state, what kind of society they wanted. Peasants wanted land – but were less radical once they had got it. In Croatia they gave more support to the Croat Republican Peasant Party of Stjepan Radić than to the communists. All over the country, though peasants were anti-government, anti-townspeople and radical in their attitude to land, prices and taxation, they remained extremely conservative, resistant to social change, and between 1921 and 1942, largely resistant to communist propaganda.

The forces against revolt at this time were also much stronger than the demonstrations and strikes seemed to show. The government had strong leadership intent on centralist power under Serbian control, and had a large and seasoned Serbian army which, when used against Croats, Slovenes, Montenegrins and Macedonians, showed no disposition to side with the demonstrators. If there had been a communist revolution, the Yugoslav government could almost certainly have counted on the same kind of counterrevolutionary intervention that had occurred in Russia. The failure of communism to gain power in the postwar state lay in the unequal forces; but the myth of a glorious opportunity lost continued to influence communist thinking throughout the nineteen-twenties and was partly responsible for continued calls to revolt from some of the leaders which became increasingly unrealistic and wasteful of communist resources.

Josip Broz had been in Yugoslavia only a few weeks when the election took place and the Communist Party was banned. He rejoined the Zagreb branch of the Social Democrat Party in October 1920, a few months after it had been incorporated into the Communist Party of Yugoslavia, thus becoming automatically a party member. He took no leading part in its activities though he was present at meetings and demonstrations in the general election campaign. 'I took part in the campaign in Zagreb,' he said. When the police started to round up communist leaders after the *Obznana* there was nothing to make him a marked man and he was in no personal danger. The police file compiled about him at a much later date shows that beyond the bare fact of his having been a prisoner returned from Russia – suspicious in itself but not incriminating – little was known of him in 1920 and he had no record.[12]

He began to pick up the threads of private life and for a few years in the nineteen-twenties he lived the only period of normal existence as an ordinary family man that he was ever to experience. He showed no haste to take up illegal political work, and for some time had no further connection with the Party, which at that time was in virtual abeyance following the new law. After a short time working as a locksmith in Zagreb, where prices were high and wages poor, he was dismissed. 'There was little to be gained by staying in Zagreb where trade unions were disbanded and mass arrests of workers continued,' he said. He answered an advertisement and took a job – his third of this kind, and perhaps one that he felt was useful to have in times of trouble – looking after a flour mill owned by 'a good-hearted Jew with a large family' in Veliko Trojstvo, a largish (330 houses) village near the small town of Bjelovar, about sixty miles east of Zagreb. His job, which was not arduous, was to look after the engine and as during his similar jobs in Russia, he was his own master as far as work went. His peasant origins helped him to fit into local society and he was accepted by the peasants who brought their corn to be ground at the mill; as a mechanic, an educated and experienced soldier returned from stirring times in Russia with strange stories to tell, he could assure for himself a special place in the community. By his own accounts he was popular with his employer and with the people in the district, who gave him a party when he eventually had to leave.[13]

In three years his wife Polka had three children – additional to one that had died at birth shortly after their return. A boy died of dysentery at the age of eight days, a girl Zlatica only lived a few days and another girl, Hlinka, died of diphtheria aged two; but a son called Žarko born in 1924, survived. This was the normal pattern of life among Croatian peasants at that time. It did not make the loss of these children easier to bear. They were given the usual Christian burial, and Broz himself carved a headstone for the grave of the two girls. He lived with his wife in one room and was little better off than his parents had been before him. Yet the difference between the generations was great, for Josip had far greater hopes and aspirations than his father had ever had. He had seen a social revolution and he never gave up hope that it could be repeated. He spent four and a half years (1921–25) in the quiet backwater of Veliko Trojstvo.

\*     \*     \*

The event that was to change his life came in 1923, when another ex-prisoner of war, a communist Stevo Šabić, contacted Broz at the mill. It is probable that Šabić was already a paid organizer for the Comintern and that his meeting with Broz was part of a deliberate policy to contact former Bolshevik sympathizers and dispersed party members. He and Broz had much in common; both had fought on the

Carpathian front, both had been taken prisoner in 1915, and had sympathized with the Bolshevik revolution. Šabić was an impressive character. He came from a middle-class family, had been an officer in the Austro-Hungarian army, had served as an officer in the Red Army, and had strong communist convictions. He was later an official of a Comintern organization 'Red Help' and was Broz's main connection outside when he later served a long prison sentence. 'At first we had no contact with the underground cells of the Communist Party of Yugoslavia which were formed in the nearby towns of Bjelovar and Križevci,' said Tito later when describing this period. But after the 1923 elections Šabić and Broz met communists who had been arrested in Bjelovar for trying to put up candidates for the elections and with them began Party organization.[14] Broz was given communist leaflets to distribute and his work as a party activist had begun.

This was the classical form of recruitment for a communist and Broz went through the usual phases of 'probationary' service. His political activity was for some time as a worker for the Independent Trade Unions, which was a legal organization allowed by the state. They were used as a front by the Communist Party. Political work by the unions was banned – though this could not be strictly enforced – but activities dealing with conditions of work, pay, and social conditions were allowed. Broz combined the two, legal and illegal, and soon became prominent in all the small groups he worked with. At the beginning of 1924 he was elected to the local Communist Party committee for Križevci. Ambition and idealism made him a tireless hard worker; experience and character made him more daring than many other workers who had never been outside their own locality. He was also more intelligent and more educated than the average worker. As in the army, he had both talent and a taste for leadership.

Soon he was elected a member of a local trade union committee, and as such made a speech at the Catholic funeral of one of its members. In deference to the parents of the dead man, political comrades had not made the customary funeral speech in the house of mourning, but Broz made a short – and cautious – speech at the cemetery. 'Comrade,' he said, standing by the coffin, 'we swear to fight to the end of our lives for the ideas to which you were so devoted.' The Red Flag was unfurled over the comrade's grave to the scandal of the priest and many onlookers.

For this public declaration of communist sympathy he and some other workers were arrested. They were sent to Bjelovar and held in prison eight days, but were acquitted when the case came up. This experience marked off another phase in Josip Broz's career. When the work of the Independent Trade Union was banned in 1924 he was drawn more and more into illegal Party work, visiting Zagreb often to contact members of the Provincial Committee of the Trade Union and the Communist Party. Political extremists in Croatia were still considering the possibility of an armed uprising, and there were contacts between communists and members of Radić's Croat Republican Peasant Party which had not yet accepted the authority of the central government. Arms were collected and stored away in a secret dump. Broz frightened the more cautious secretary of the Communist Party committee for Croatia by suggesting that they could be used.[15] By 1925, when the owner of the flour mill died and was succeeded by his nephew, Broz was already being watched by the police. He said later that they visited his room every Saturday and searched his things.

For the next two years his jobs were decided, not on private or economic grounds, but on the opportunity they offered for political activity among industrial workers. On 21 September 1925 he went to work in a shipyard at Kraljevica on the Adriatic coast where he spent a year repairing torpedo boats which had been sabotaged before being handed over by the Austrian navy to the Yugoslav government, and building a luxury yacht for the politician Stojadinović. Here he was joined by his wife Polka and the baby boy Žarko, who lived with him in one room. He was a member of a party cell of about twelve members which organized secret political meetings in private houses. His work, now directed by the party, was to organize strikes among the workers.

According to his own account, one useful practical approach to this difficult job – there had been no organized union activity there for some years – was to help with the sports and musical activities. He went to Zagreb to buy guitars, and encouraged workers to visit his room to borrow books – works by Jack London, as well as *Mother* by Gogol and works on socialism. Another communist who met Broz at this time, a medical doctor, Pavle Gregorić, who had also been in Russia, described him as a young man with regular features, fair hair and blue eyes, rather serious and austere, with a laconic way of asking factual questions. Elected shop steward, he had no difficulty in rousing the workers because the management were seven weeks in arrears with wages. He backed up the workers' case by letters to the Metal

Workers' Union and the Navy Department in Belgrade. When the strike had lasted for ten days the management capitulated. Shortly after, on 2 October 1926, Broz was declared redundant.[16]

His next assignment from the party was outside his native Croatia at a rolling-stock foundry employing 700 workers at Smederevska Palanka near Belgrade. Here conditions were much harder, the management tougher and more effective. This time he was less successful. Again he was a member of a small cell trying to establish a union branch which could be used as recruiting ground for the party, a weapon for industrial disturbance, and a lever for better working conditions. Broz was in contact with the head office of the Independent Trade Union in Belgrade and frequented its workers' library. There for the first time he met communists working with the Central Committee of the party, among them Juraj Salaj, and Djuro Djaković, who had been trained in Russia and was soon to be proposed by the Comintern as party secretary. But Broz was still a very insignificant party member and there is no evidence that he made any big impression in Belgrade.

Unable to make headway in union activity in the works, he wrote his first newspaper article for a local trade union paper, *The Organized Worker* of 27 March 1927. In this he denounced the management for holding a labour force large enough to allow them to sack undesirables, he attacked it also for paying low wages and exacting a sixteen-hour day, for imposing arbitrary fines, and for intimidation of workers so that only ninety-four out of 300 had dared to vote for a shop steward. 'In such a situation, comrades,' he wrote, 'there is nothing to do but rely on our own forces. Nobody takes care of us, all social institutions are mere words and paper. Comrades, we must all join our militant trade union organization and then carry out an active struggle against the cruel exploitation of the insatiable bourgeoisie.' Ten days after the article appeared he was sacked again.[17]

He had one more job briefly in Zagreb, and then became Secretary of the Metal Workers' Union of Zagreb and a member of the Zagreb Party committee. He never had a job as a mechanic again, and was to remain a political official in many different capacities for the rest of his career. Broz regarded this as the decisive point in his life. Though the first step had been taken two years earlier, it may be that for him this was the point of no return. Shortly after he was arrested again. 'Broz,' said the policeman on being asked what the charge was, 'you have been involved in so much trouble that we could arrest you at any time and choose from a dozen charges.' The police had decided to move against him as a known communist and had acted on information received about his dissemination of communist literature at the shipyard in Kraljevica a year earlier. He was arrested in Zagreb and was taken to Bakar near Kraljevica, where he joined six other arrested workers from the shipyards, and from there, after being detained nine days, the prisoners were moved to the county gaol which was in the ancient fortress in Ogulin. They were marched in chains through Bakar to the railway station with a lame comrade bringing up the rear. When he stumbled the others were pulled down with him. 'It was a humiliating scene and we were relieved to be put on the train for Ogulin,' Tito remembered. Meantime the police in Zagreb had searched Broz's room and found a number of books such as *Trade Unionism in Theory and Practice, Unemployment, Moral and the Class Norms* – all of which could be bought openly in bookshops, but were regarded by the police as suspicious literature for a worker.

Broz had been picked up by the police in June; he was registered as a prisoner in Ogulin on 14 August. By the middle of October there were no signs of the case being heard and he went on hunger strike. 'I wanted to protest against the system prevailing in the gaol,' he said, 'I had been thrown from one prison to another under most difficult conditions. Instead of food, I was given just ordinary slops, and on top of everything else, the court would not question me. . . . I wanted to show through my strike, what we communists are, what kind of fight we were wageing.'

He refused to eat for five days, getting slowly weaker, but carefully maintaining his strength by keeping quite still. 'It is on the second day that the crisis comes in a hunger strike,' he said later. 'You feel overwhelming hunger, but if you can get through this crucial period, your mind falls into a state of light unconsciousness and you cease to feel the hunger so much.' He was still able to speak when a local judge came to see him on the fifth day. This was a liberal Croat, Stjepan Bakarić, whose son was later to become a communist and lifelong friend of the prisoner. He promised that the case would be heard, sent soup from his own kitchen to the weakened prisoner and, impressed by his intelligence and purpose, had him into his house after the hearing and showed him his own collection of Marxist literature in an unsuccessful effort to persuade Broz to keep to legal activities.

When the case was heard on 28 October 1927 Broz was sentenced to seven months' imprisonment and allowed to go free pending appeal to the high court in Zagreb. The sentence was later reduced to five months, but by that time the prisoner could not be found. Broz had left Ogulin a more embittered but more self-confident communist than before. He had come off easily in his first confrontation with the law, and this gave him an uncharacteristic recklessness and contempt for, and underestimation of, the authority he was challenging. He returned to his job as trade union organizer with a new zest, an increased determination to play a leading part in the workers' movement.[18]

# 4 POLITICAL PRISONER

The year 1928 was a critical one in the history of the Yugoslav state, of the Yugoslav Communist Party, and in the personal life of Josip Broz. In 1928 King Alexander's efforts to make his centralist constitution work at last broke down; the event which caused its final collapse being the murder – by another deputy during a debate in the Yugoslav parliament – of Stjepan Radić.

After forcing through the Vidovdan constitution in 1921 King Alexander had spent the succeeding years in trying vainly to achieve stable government by manoeuvring changing and unstable coalitions between the country's diverse political parties and politicians. He was helped by a slow improvement in Yugoslavia's international relations. The Little Entente, a protective alliance with Czechoslovakia and Romania against Hungarian irredentism, was formed in 1921. Italy, the most dangerous enemy and neighbour, became isolated in the 'twenties, and France reluctantly showed itself willing to come forward as Yugoslavia's protector and concluded a pact of friendship with her in 1927. Economic conditions also improved slowly as the government managed to get trade and industry working, especially in the northern ex-Austro-Hungarian areas.

Yet for poorer people throughout the country conditions of life remained very difficult. Unemployment was high, wages low, and harsh working conditions were made worse by the Law for the Protection of the State which limited trade union and all political activity. There was plenty of scope for industrial agitation, but police vigilance made it dangerous work.

The communists were the only political party banned at this time, but they were not the only ones in political opposition to the pro-Serbian king and his centralist government. The King's relations with opposition parties and national groups showed no improvement. The Croat Republican Peasant Party (HRSS), under its popular leader Stjepan Radić, had remained deeply opposed to the regime but was uncertain how best to make opposition effective. Radić changed his tactics continually in unsuccessful efforts to weaken the centralist state.[1] Up to 1924 the HRSS boycotted parliament and refused co-operation with the government. It made unofficial and ineffective contacts with extremist opposition groups, including the banned Communist Party, members of the violent International Macedonian Revolutionary Organization (IMRO), extremist Croatian nationalists called the Frankovci, as well as with more moderate opponents of the King's regime.[2]

In 1924 Radić went to Moscow at the time of the Fifth Congress of the Comintern and signed an agreement joining the communist Peasant International, in the hope of finding international support for the Croat Peasant Party's autonomist aims. Though he said publicly 'We will march with Russia', he privately expressed disappointment. 'The Communists do not want allies only servants,' he told his friend Maček.[3]

By the time of his murder on 20 June 1928, Radić's pro-Bolshevik policy had waned. It had not been popular in Croatia, and Russian help was not forthcoming. He had ceased to boycott the government, was engaged in opposition tactics in parliament and had allied with Serbs from former Austro-Hungarian territories. His murder sparked off violent reactions among people in opposition in all parts of the country, especially in Croatia. On 8 August his party's members seceded from parliament and under their new leader, Vladimir Maček, did not take a cooperative part in government until the very eve of the second world war. The murder was followed by demonstrations all over Croatia and many ended in violence. The government was blamed, if not for the murder, at least for failing to take action against the murderer. He was not arrested until he gave himself up later the same day, and was not tried for over a year. He was sentenced to twenty years' imprisonment. The general situation was aggravated by rapidly deteriorating economic conditions which were part of the general European crisis resulting from the world slump. The Yugoslav government was totally unwilling, even in these grave conditions, to make any political concessions to Croats or democratic opposition, and it was unable to dispel or completely control the widespread discontent.

This was the situation when Josip Broz began to play an active port in communist work in Croatia. By 1928 the illegal Communist Party, from which he took his orders had established a rudimentary underground organization with groups of members organized in cells in different parts of the country. It was dangerous to be a party member, and this was reflected in the enormous decline in their numbers – from 65,000 in 1920 to about 1,000 in 1924. These rose again to 2,300 in 1925.[4] They were by no means all activists and were mainly among the few industrial workers in the country, in areas around Belgrade, Zagreb and in parts of Slovenia and Dalmatia where the country's limited industrial development was located.

The Communist Party used two front organizations as cover for its activities – the Independent Workers' Party, which only had a brief existence in 1923–24, when it was disbanded because it was taking away membership from the communists, and the Independent Trade Union which the government allowed to exist. This union also had to compete with other trade unions, mainly socialist, which had different policies from the communists, and which were stronger because they had inherited the funds of the pre-*Obznana* trade union movement. Josip Broz's trade union positions were with the communist run Independent Trade Union.

Finance for the illegal Communist Party was at this time supplied by the Comintern, and existence on foreign subsidy was the cause of difficulties and dissension as Broz was to discover later.[5] In addition to salaries for officials – both those living abroad who had 'quite good salaries', and those on full-time work in the country – money was provided for publication of leaflets and newspapers, many of which in times of most severe police persecution had to be published abroad, usually in Vienna. These were considered a most important part of political work, and under conditions of illegality were an easier way of conveying party news to secret members than by meetings. Broz was very active in distributing party material – rumour said that he even visited Kumrovec on one occasion and scattered leaflets from a car. Later under a variety of different pseudonyms he was to become one of the most assiduous contributors to party papers.

One of the most famous illegal newspapers, *Komunist*, was founded in January 1925, and had produced three numbers before its editor, a brilliant Belgrade journalist, Moša Pijade, was arrested and savagely sentenced to twenty years' imprisonment – of which he served fourteen – in an attempt to frighten others from similar work. But the deterrent was ineffective. *Hammer and Sickle* was printed in Vienna, *Young Communist* was founded in 1929, and a host of others with national or local appeal appeared at different times. Of these the *Workers' Struggle*, later shortened to *Struggle* (from *Radnička Borba* to *Borba*) was the most famous, and like *Komunist* continues to be published today.[6]

It proved very difficult to organize underground work among the inexperienced, diverse and uncompromising members of the Yugoslav Communist Party. The police were watchful and active, so that communication links throughout the country were always being discovered and broken up by arrests. Reliable couriers were difficult to find, and there were perpetual problems connected with the uncertainties over verbal messages and the dangers of written ones. The weakness of the party made it increasingly dependent on the Comintern, which in any case at this period was bent on centralizing its control and gaining complete authority over communist parties outside Russia. The Yugoslav party proved one of the most difficult to control, not least because of the irrepressible independence of its leaders, who did not at that time include Josip Broz. It thus became most unpopular with the Russian officials of the Comintern.

The major problem was its lack of unity – yet what communist party at this time was united? In Yugoslavia lack of unanimity was not surprising considering the party's origins – many kinds of socialists from the different territories combined in Yugoslavia – the short period it had been in existence before the *Obznana*, and the difficulties of illegal existence. 'It is a thousand times easier for differences to arise in illegal parties,' said the Russian communist Radek about the Yugoslav party, 'and a thousand times more difficult to solve them than in the case of parties that are able to work legally.'[7] Its leaders proved quite unable to agree on basic principles of party policy and work. They argued bitterly over who had been responsible for the collapse of the party after the *Obznana*, on how the party should react to it, and especially over the fundamental and uniquely Yugoslav problem of what should be the party line on the national question, the problem of the regions and national groups that made up Yugoslavia – the Serbs, Croats, Slovenes, Macedonians and others. In all the disputes there were two major opposing groups, and a pattern emerges throughout the whole interwar period, of a communist party divided into two sections.

It is almost impossible to give a satisfactory, simplified explanation of the complex and confused disputes of this period. Most accounts, nearly all from communist or ex-communist sources and almost all with some kind of axe to grind, of necessity describe the disputing leaders as divided into factions of 'right' or 'left'. The rightists in the early period were led by a Belgrade Serb, Sima Marković. They supported the idea of a Yugoslav state under a central government, believing that problems of nationalities existed mainly because of capitalist misgovernment; they would disappear when 'socialist' government was achieved, or could be dealt with by a satisfactory constitution which would allow some form of autonomy. The rightists were also more cautious in their attitude to underground work, sceptical about the results of armed violence and anxious to carry on in a way that would lead to the legal ban on party work being lifted.

The leftists were more extreme. They accepted ideas of separatism for different regions and the need for violence in illegal work. The two sides had their supporters in all regions. Quarrels took the form of personal vendettas which were pursued into party meetings and all activities. They complained about each other to the Comintern and, when the Comintern intervened, refused to accept its ruling. It was Josip Broz's good fortune not to be in any way connected with the earlier phases of these disputes. Very few of those involved at that time survived or were members of the party leadership in later years. Most of them were destroyed because of the Russian-inspired communist law that the party must be monolithic, unanimous; that disagreement on any major issue was treason not only to the local party, but to the workers' movement as a whole and to Russia, its leader. These assumptions were never queried and dominated communist thinking until after the second world war.

At party conferences, congresses and executive committee meetings, the issues continued to be debated – often with heat and venom. Three major Yugoslav Communist Party conferences were held before 1928; the first from 3 to 17 July 1922 in Vienna (twenty-two delegates, but significantly none from Macedonia, Montenegro, Dalmatia and the Vojvodina), the second, also in Vienna from 9 to 12 May 1923 (thirty-four delegates including those from the areas previously unrepresented), and the third in January 1924 in Belgrade (thirty-five delegates from all parts of the country).[8] Comintern officials attended all three and observed the struggle for power between the two opposing groups. Sima Marković dominated the first conference and managed to get his 'rightist' views accepted. The left walked out and two disputing delegations turned up at the fourth Congress of the Comintern in Moscow in November of the same year. Here the right wing threatened to walk out, its leader protesting against the left being allowed observer status. 'This declaration shows that our comrade is far from being in real contact with the spiritual methods of work of the Communist International,' commented the Comintern representative, disregarding precedents from Bolshevik history. 'It is the first time that I hear a delegate declare that if the congress decided against him he will withdraw.'

In the second and third conferences power gradually moved over to the left wing in the Yugoslav party. One of its leaders, Krsta Kaclerović, a Croat, was co-opted to the Executive committee on orders from the Comintern in 1922, and became its secretary in 1923. From this time Marković was losing ground. He did not give in easily and was far from silenced; he had considerable support in Belgrade and among officials of the Independent Trade Union. During a short gaol sentence for being a communist he wrote a book called *The National Question in the Light of Marxism*, in which he quoted Stalin on general theory and expounded his own ideas on Yugoslav nationalities. Stalin had not yet achieved the sinister power in Russia that he was to exercise later, but Sima Marković still showed great courage when he spoke against him in open debate on 30 March 1925, before a Commission appointed by the Comintern to investigate divisions in the Yugoslav Party.

Stalin was already an important Russian leader and Marković was only a candidate member of the Executive Committee of the Comintern. Needless to say, Stalin's view was accepted. It was that the nationalities must be allowed the right to secede or be able to opt for autonomy within Yugoslavia – a Yugoslavia that Stalin assumed would have passed through a 'Soviet' revolution and which would then face the problem of the majority of its population being peasants. 'Marković's ideas,' said Stalin prophetically, 'imply an underestimation of the potential might latent, for instance, in the movement of the Croats for national emancipation.'[9]

In the Party in Yugoslavia, the quarrel was not so easily resolved. Marković was never convinced he was wrong and would not abandon his position. He was eventually expelled from the Party, returning to teaching mathematics and lived for some time in Russia, even becoming a member of the Soviet Academy of Sciences, but disappeared during Stalin's purges. He was one of the Yugoslavs posthumously rehabilitated in Russia after Stalin's death.

With the capture of the Yugoslav party machinery by predominantly left-wing supporters, many of them Croats, and the defeat of the Serb Marković, the main party activity moved to Zagreb, chief

(*above*): 7. Communist group meeting in prison. Mosa Pijade at right.

(*below*): 8. Maribor Prison, 1931–4.

9. Photographs of Tito in forged passports dated 1940:

(top): (a) in the name of Engineer Kostanjšek;

(centre): (b) in a forged Canadian passport In the name of Spiridon Mekas;

(left): (c) in the name of Slavko Babić.

town of Croatia. It was further away from the centre of government in Belgrade and easier for organizing illegal activities. It was also nearer the industrial regions of the country which were still thought to be the best recruiting ground for communists. This brought Josip Broz closer to the centre of party work and inevitably he became involved in the disagreements, especially in relation to the policy of the party and of communist trade unionists towards strikes.

As a result of the recession, workers were being made redundant, prices were rising, and wages were held stable or reduced, resulting in a number of spontaneous and organized strikes in many industries, including the metal and leather workers' industries of whose trade union Broz was organizer. He believed that this was an opportunity for the communists to lead the 'militant enthusiasm' of the workers. This was the Comintern view, but there were people in the party who opposed it as being likely to weaken the party at a time when the police were so powerful. Broz believed that the two sides were wasting their time and energies in fighting each other when they could have been working together to organize strikes and take advantage of 'the most favourable conditions for work and for the strengthening of the Communist Party of Yugoslavia and the trade unions'.[10]

The matter came to a head at a Zagreb party conference held during the night, from 9 p.m. to 5 a.m. of 25/26 February 1928, in a small private house in the suburbs of Zagreb. Thirty-two people and a delegate from the Comintern attended the meeting. Broz, who had been very active in contacting people before the meeting, was a delegate for the Metal and Leather Workers' Union. When the secretary of the party gave a bland report glossing over the failures and differences in the party, Broz – known at this time as Georgijević – became spokesman for a group pressing for rejection of the report. 'It does not represent the real state of affairs,' he said, and went on to criticize the 'factionalism, inactivity, jockeying for position and impeding the work of other people in the party'. He demanded that the Zagreb party should 'take a determined stand', and that a letter should be sent to the Comintern, opposing both left and right factions.[11] It would be interesting to know what were his motives for appealing to the Comintern at this stage: was he entirely disinterested or did he hope to draw attention to himself in Moscow? Had he already conceived an idea that he would like to go there for training as had happened to so many other Yugoslav communists? This was for ambitious people the direct and only way to the top at this time.

His speech and contact work among the delegates had their effect. The secretary's report was rejected, a letter which he helped to draft was sent to the Comintern requesting its intervention, and Josip Broz was elected secretary of the Zagreb Communist Party. He was now an important local Communist Party official, and his name as an activist, if nothing else, was already registered in Moscow. The Comintern replied in April with a stern 'Open Letter' to be discussed by all branches, upbraiding the Yugoslav party for 'fractionalism' and praising the action of Broz's group of militants. It also dismissed the Central Committee of the Party and suggested for appointment a new inner group to be headed by a Bosnian Croat, Djuro Djaković, then being trained at the Leninist School in Moscow.

Broz's group was in line with a new Comintern policy which was being given out to all communist parties. This advocated radical action because it was thought that a new stage of capitalism was now in being which would lead to the disintegration of the whole capitalist system. Renewed attacks by hostile states against the Soviet Union were expected at any time, and local parties were urged to do everything possible to weaken their governments.

Leaflets issued in Croatia at this time reflect the new instructions to the party to go over to 'open war' against the Serbian bourgeoisie and dictatorship. They called for the creation of a 'worker–peasant Soviet state', for a struggle against 'a regime which is killing all progressive and revolutionary people'. They tried to enlist peasant support, reminding the discontented but non-communist peasants of Croatia of their thousand years of sufferings under foreign rule, of the fate of Matija Gubec, of the chance for freedom they had lost in 1920, and the fate they were now experiencing at the hands of the 'great Serb bourgeoisie', the 'bloody, criminal and inhuman regime',[12]

As secretary of the local branch, Broz had to find new and reliable people to help in the intensified work. 'Our committee did a lot to raise new cadres,' he said, 'which is a slow and painful process. One had to be very patient, to go deep into a man's being, to help him, to look at the good in him instead of the bad, to encourage his positive characteristics, to help him get rid of his shortcomings, to make allowances for his background, his educational handicaps, his personal life. Only in this way could cadres be built.'[13]

Broz organized demonstrations for May Day, the traditional

workers' holiday. They were meant to show the strength of the
workers' movement. He himself attended a meeting in the Apollo
Cinema which ended in a free fight with the police. According to a
police report it was a Social Democrats' meeting which Broz had
interrupted by repeated shouts leading to a fight between Social
Democrats and Communists. An account by a communist present at
the meeting says that Broz was arrested when trying to help a
comrade get away from the police.[14] Broz was sentenced to a fortnight's imprisonment. The police dossier made at this time describes
him as dark blond, without moustache, blue eyes, straight eyebrows,
an oval and thin face with darkish complexion; hands long and
narrow, with a wound on the middle finger of the left hand; nose
thick, average, straight; mouth average with some teeth missing;
chest measurement eighty-four centimetres – this was not very broad
for a man of his age and confirms the impression that at this stage in
his career he was overworked and underfed. The dossier lists his
languages as Croatian, German, Russian, and gives an example of
handwriting: 'I have been arrested by the police in the cinema
Apollo.' He was lucky to be released after a fortnight, for he had not
yet served his Ogulin sentence. After this he had to take measures to
avoid being arrested again. He wore dark glasses, a moustache,
different clothes and never slept more than a few nights in one place.
'I always carried a revolver with me,' he said later. It was the end of his
domestic life.

The atmosphere in Zagreb that summer was tense for others
besides Josip Broz. It was electric with frustrated discontent – political
and economic, and many besides the communists seemed to be on the
brink of violence. The charge that exploded this situation came with
the news of the murder of Radić on 28 June, and riots started in
Zagreb.

The police began an intensive search for communists and known
agitators. Twice Broz was nearly caught. Once when he was at trade
union headquarters, a policeman entered and asked 'Is Josip Broz
here?' 'Can't you see he isn't?' replied Broz, and the policeman
saluted and departed. Another time he escaped through the office
window to the roof and jumped on to a table in the yard below where
the ground-floor restaurant proprietor was chopping up meat. The
meat went flying, but Broz escaped. The third time he was not so
lucky. Just before midnight on 4 August 1928, a police informer who
knew him accosted him in the street and said some comrades wished

to see him at a room he occasionally used as a lodging. The police were waiting and this time made sure of his arrest.

Broz managed to get a note out of gaol telling the party what had happened to him. It said: 'Saturday at 12 midnight the 4 August as I was going to bed I was arrested. Police brandishing revolvers grabbed me from behind so that I could not move. Saturday midday they had arrested a man in the house and found 26 books – *Karl Marx, Kommunist Manifesto, Bulletin of the Zagreb Kommunist Party,* 9 copies of *Leninism* – 4 handgrenades, 1 revolver and ammunition of army issue. They said it was all mine. I was tortured in prison and they would not allow me a doctor. Been on hunger strike since 4. VIII and am very weak. Others also fearfully beaten up. No one dare bring us food from outside. Searching me they found some notes. Threatened me with death and that I should be sent to Belgrade Glavnjaca [penal gaol of frightful repute, *ed.*] I would rather die before I. . . . Try all other methods. M. said he will do what he can. Good-bye comrades. I shall soon not be able to stand any longer as I am very weak . . .'[15] This document eventually reached the Comintern in Moscow, where it was seen and endorsed by a Yugoslav official Milan Gorkić. A slightly different version of it was printed by the International Press-Korespondenz under the headline *A Cry from the Hell of Yugoslavia's Prisons.*

Years later, Broz said he had not suffered severe torture in the Zagreb prison, but he had been kept under a glaring light and prevented from sleeping to try to make him talk. He refused to speak, and from time to time was hit on the head, chest and arms. 'I spat blood for a long time after that,' he said in one account, adding in another 'but there was nothing to it really – not what you could call torture.'

As secretary of the Zagreb Communist Party, Broz had been acting in the spirit of the Comintern instructions which urged communists to go over to armed action against the authorities in their countries. Though he denied at the time that the grenades found in his room were his – and technically, no doubt, they belonged to the party – he admitted in later life, 'They were mine all right.'[16]

The police prepared their case carefully, as they believed they were dealing with a dangerous communist. Their records are still extant: the list of what was found in Broz's flat shows that, in addition to books, there were trade union stamps and notes of disbursements, and receipts of small sums of money taken in payment for books supplied and expenses given to various people for travel, money for a woman whose husband had been arrested (200 dinars). A note in code Broz refused to elucidate. An exercise book contained Broz's own notes for a political speech; under numbered headings they indicated the somewhat comprehensive subjects he expected to cover, including both home and foreign affairs.[17]

The trial of Josip Broz, following his arrest, is something of a heroic set-piece in all official accounts of Tito's life. It was not a *cause célèbre*, did not reach the international press, but in its small way it was sufficiently dramatic to be fully reported in the local press. It made an impression among communists, and brought Josip Broz to the notice of higher authorities in the Comintern, as no doubt he intended it should.

Six prisoners were indicted on charges under the Law for the Protection of the State. They came before five judges in the county court in Zagreb on 6 November 1928. Josip Broz's case opened at 11 a.m. on the second day of the trial. A report in a local paper *Novosti* described the court as packed. 'Younger workers and students have taken an extraordinary interest in this trial, squeezing themselves into the courtroom until it is impossible to move', it said. 'They are young men with long curly hair, or young girls with bobbed hair, perhaps the followers of the new gospel, perhaps acquaintances of the defendants. . . . All this strange audience listens attentively, stands patiently, drinking in every word, bursting out laughing at every joke made by the defendants . . .'

'The defendant Josip Broz is undoubtedly the most interesting person in the trial; his face makes you think of steel', wrote the *Novosti* journalist, and a sketch made of the prisoner in court illustrated this. 'His light-grey eyes behind his spectacles are cold, but alert and calm. In his case his attitude in court is perhaps more than a pose, for he has been prosecuted before and has served several sentences for his political beliefs. Many of those present were doubtless aware of the stubbornness with which he maintains his views, and his cross-examination was listened to attentively and in complete silence.'[18]

A Comintern Executive Committee resolution two years previously had reproved Yugoslav communists for not taking advantage of the opportunity that trials gave to publicize the party's ideas. Josip Broz appeared to have taken this lesson to heart, and made full propaganda use of his public hearing. It was his first big public platform, and he rose to the occasion, demonstrating compelling oratorical gifts which were to play an important part in his later career. He answered all questions with a political statement. When asked to plead guilty or not guilty he replied: 'Although I admit the charges of the state prosecutor's indictment, I do not consider myself guilty because I do not accept the jurisdiction of this bourgeois court. I consider myself responsible only to my own Party. I admit that I am a member of the illegal Communist Party of Yugoslavia. I admit that I have spread communist ideas and propagated communism, that I have expounded the injustices suffered by the proletariat, in public meetings and in private talks with individuals. I cannot say where these meetings took place. I have done this ever since the party was banned and became illegal in 1921.'

He went on to attack the police for brutality to himself and the others accused whom he did his best to exculpate. He said he was not interested in the notorious Law for the Protection of the State, though he was aware that his activities had contravened it. 'It is only a temporary law,' he said firmly, 'a law brought in by one class against another, a law that will be swept away.' The State Prosecutor accused him of telling stories against the police in order to martyr himself 'and to get money from Moscow'; to which Broz replied that he personally was not frightened to speak out because he knew that in any case he was going to get a long sentence – that the others accused had not dared to speak the truth as they hoped thereby to be treated leniently.

When it came to the final speech for the defence on 9 November, Broz dispensed with the services of his defending counsel, and spoke for himself. He began to explain from his own life history what it was that had made him become a communist. The judge refused to allow him to continue; the speech was not made, and has never been recorded, though the gist of it may be assumed to be contained in the accounts of his early life that he gave to Vladimir Dedijer and others· When his speech was cut short by the judge, Broz turned to the court room and shouted: 'This shows conclusively that this is a Police State. Long Live the Communist Party of Yugoslavia, Long Live the Communist International, Long Live the Soviet Revolution.' The defendants came up for sentence on 14 November. Two were acquitted, two received two years', and one three years' imprisonment. Josip Broz was sentenced to five years. He was still shouting communist slogans as, manacled, he was taken away.

His behaviour in court had obviously increased his sentence, and it is of interest to ask why he was so foolhardy and defiant. The answers are complex, compounded of conscious and subconscious motives, and instinctive reactions. It is not possible to say how much he was motivated by ambition. He had only just attained a key post in the party, and it was by no means certain that he would return to an influential position after a long absence in gaol. He was still at this time politically naïve, inexperienced in the operations of state power, perhaps self-dramatizing and romantic, accepting the division of the world into white and black, good and bad, that he had absorbed from communist propaganda. 'I am prepared to suffer,' he had told the judge in court, just as he had said to Judge Bakarić two years earlier, 'some people have to be prepared to die'. It is probable that he did not himself understand all his motives; his rather heroic explanation of later years only told part – yet probably a genuine part – of the story. 'Our party needed to be shown that it was a proud and glorious thing to be a communist, that the party is worth all the loyalty and devotion of its members, and worth going to prison for too, without cringing to the bourgeoisie or trying to get off lightly by pretending respect for the police and courts.' Equally genuine appears to be another personal comment made in later life about his own attitude at this time – a comment that confirms that he was already motivated by powerful ambition. 'I regarded the whole question from a purely realistic and practical point of view. I was trying to overthrow their government. It was only natural that when they caught me they should shut me up. I should have done the same in their place. Indeed I had every intention of doing so when I was in their place.'[19]

Broz could not have known what the result of a long sentence would be, but in fact it almost certainly saved his life. It saved him from being involved in the savage and in some cases fatal measures against communists in Yugoslavia between 1929 and 1932, and in the even more deadly extermination carried out by Stalin against Yugoslav and other communists in Russia in the 'thirties.

He spent his five years' imprisonment in two prisons – Lepoglava on the borders of his native Zagorje, where he was from early January 1929 to June 1931. Then, until November 1933, he was in the Maribor prison in Slovenia. It was a long hard period of education in every sense of the word. 'The penitentiary was really a university for many of our people. . . . I put my time in prison to maximum use . . . that is where I learned most.'[20] 'It was just like being at university,' he said later, referring to communist education courses he took part in at both gaols, and perhaps with a suggestion of wishful thinking. It was certainly the longest period of his life when he had plenty of leisure to read, and he was able, in spite of restrictions, to get many of the books he wanted.

His fellow prisoners were a very mixed lot, as a photograph of them taken at Lepoglava shows; but as he was a political prisoner, separated most of the time from criminal prisoners, he was able in both gaols to find some people of political interests and education with whom he could expand his hitherto somewhat starved intellectual life. But he was mixing with men of all types, and the brutalized – sometimes more, sometimes less as conditions changed – prison life sharpened the interplay of the most varied human characters and emotions. In this respect it was an education more valuable for his later life than any academic university. It was also a political education since feuds were continued between members in prison, though these were not often mentioned in the romantic accounts of gaol life told in later years. He had two periods of harsh conditions, the first few weeks at both Lepoglava and Maribor. In both periods he was on a low diet of revolting food, poor quality bread, thin sour soup made of turnip and mangelwurzel, or beans 'with hardly a bean in it' and a small piece of beef twice a week, with little exercise, and cooped up in a cell twenty-three out of the twenty-four hours. His first tedious forced labour at Lepoglava was cleaning goose feathers; in Maribor, in his first weeks of solitary confinement he did not even have this distraction. These were periods of terrible self-discipline to avoid mental and spiritual demoralization. Broz was tough enough to stand up to it very well. In both prisons he was able to escape from this purgatory because of his skill as a mechanic, and was put in charge of the prison's electricity system.

The party's outstanding intellectual, Moša Pijade, was transferred to Lepoglava a year after Broz. He had been in the Mitrovica political prison near Belgrade since 1926 and had served five of his twenty years' sentence. He and Broz took to each other from the start and became firm friends for life. Different in very many ways, they shared a fanatical devotion to communism; their differences complemented each other and enriched a deep relationship. Pijade, a Sephardic Jew from a middle-class family, had been educated in Paris and Vienna. He had the wide culture that Broz came to admire and felt unjustly cut off from by his lowly origins in a socially stratified society. Broz had what was for Pijade the unattainable distinction of coming from a working-class and peasant background. In the Party, intellectuals were in disfavour, though they still provided many of the men who reached the top. The working class were the theoretical élite, but there were few of them to draw on in Yugoslavia. At the fourth Yugoslav Party Congress in Dresden in November 1928 the Comintern representative Togliatti – called Ercoli at that time – had warned that 'intellectuals easily fall under the influence of bourgeois and petty-bourgeois circles from which they originate. That is why they are hesitant at decisive moments. They must learn their role. They must adapt themselves to the working class; they must submit to it. They must not lead it and introduce into its ranks the influence of other classes.' Pijade had learnt his role and he became a very unobtrusive *éminence grise*. 'I was excited to meet a worker-revolutionary of the best type that I could hope to meet in years,' he said later, referring to his first meeting with Broz, who, he added, 'was glad to have someone he could exchange ideas with.'[21]

Pijade was a gifted artist, and a better philosopher and dialectician than Broz would ever be. Both men shared a keen sense of humour – at times of broad humour – and Pijade was also sharply witty, with a caustic tongue. He envied Broz his practical ability, his common touch that was an essential ingredient in the gift for leadership necessary in both prison and in the party. Two years older than Broz, Pijade stood five feet to his friend's five feet eight inches. They made an incongruous pair. It is probable that Moša Pijade was the strongest personal influence on Josip Broz's political career, although in later years he never suggested that he had played such a part in the formation of the character of the Yugoslav leader. Broz himself, with the reticence that characterizes his attitude to all intimate personal matters, never admitted more than that it was a deep and warm relationship.

Broz chose Pijade to be his assistant in the job of running the prison's power station. By hunger strikes and threats the political prisoners had already won considerable concessions. Within the old part of the prison, which had originally been built as a Pauline monastery, they had relative freedom. They were housed in a large dormitory and had their own committee to deal with all their affairs, of which Broz and Pijade were active members. In charge of the electricity supply, Broz moved all over the prison, and even on occasion outside it. He said later that he could have escaped had he

71

wanted to. He was wise not to – perhaps consciously so – since for most communists during these years conditions were far worse outside gaol than in.

In time the committee established educational courses of different kinds for the many young communists and communist sympathizers in the prison. They were in reading and writing, as well as about the theory, practice and history of communism. These classes took place in the afternoons and evenings when prisoners were free. Those who joined the circle were supposed to accept the discipline; they had a weekly task of teaching, learning or observing other prisoners and reports were made to the committee. Contact was established with the party and friends outside, so that books and other necessities could be received. Broz had fixed things so that he could meet contacts in the upper room of a restaurant just outside the prison. Dr Pavle Gregorić, the medical doctor Broz had met earlier, was one of these contacts. He recalled later how after he had gone to visit Broz, he had waited in the upstairs room for an hour. Then, through the window, he saw Broz coming across the road accompanied by four guards who waited downstairs while Broz transacted his business behind a locked door.[22] Broz met others, including a young schoolmistress courier, in this way.

These comfortable arrangements ended abruptly when a prisoner escaped and on recapture informed against the communists. Broz and four other prisoners were despatched in June 1931 to the much harsher prison of Maribor; later Pijade was returned to Sremska Mitrovica where he continued his political organization until his release in 1939.

In Maribor prison Broz met another communist of bourgeois origins, Rodoljub Čolaković, who was serving a sentence for having belonged to the terrorist organization whose members had murdered the ex-Minister of the Interior, Drašković, in 1921. After the first few weeks of hardship they were able to get the political prisoners organized here too, though conditions of life – poor food, no heat, no light and indomitable bed-bugs – remained very difficult. Čolaković describes Broz at this time as thin, pale and ascetic-looking in his prison uniform. He rarely laughed, he said, but when he did he laughed heartily.[23] An informal prison photograph taken at Maribor of Broz wearing pince-nez glasses, instead of the battered steel spectacles of earlier photographs, confirms that he looked ascetic and withdrawn. He was still, it seems, playing to perfection the part for which within his chosen field, fate cast him. But he must have unbent at times, for Čolaković describes the convivial evenings round an old iron stove they managed to get hold of, and called 'La Bourgeoise', when they shared one cigarette between four men; or the Sundays when Broz gave his accounts of the Bolshevik revolution – the prisoners' favourite talk – or the nights when they organized concerts and sang first the International, then revolutionary songs and finally ballads, beginning softly and ending up in a full-throated chorus until the guard came to silence them.

The political courses continued here, too. Prisoners had to work on making paper bags. They worked together streamlining the processes so that they saved time and materials – paper and glue, etc. – and were able to back, disguise and bind copies of the works of communist authors who had an almost symbolical importance for them – Marx, Hilferding, Engels, Rosa Luxembourg and others. In addition, Broz had his own personal reading list, including works of philosophy, psychology and history, to continue his self-education.

When his sentence ended in November 1933 he was told he had to serve the remaining part of the sentence passed on him in 1927. Outside contacts – his old friend Stevo Šabić from Veliko Trojstvo who now worked for a communist prisoners' aid organization called Red Help – had provided him with money. Before he left Maribor he had a suit tailored, and bought good boots. He was taken to Ogulin to serve the last three and a half months.

# PART II
# COMMUNIST AT LARGE

# 5 ILLEGAL COMMUNIST AT LARGE

Josip Broz came out of gaol on 12 March 1934, shortly before his forty-second birthday. He was more mature and experienced, more committed than ever to the communist cause. His conviction, he said later, was overpowering, stronger even than himself. He was far less reckless than in 1928 and had more understanding of the powers of the state he was challenging. He no longer believed that revolution was just round the corner, and was yet prepared to devote a lifetime and risk his life to achieve it.

When he walked away from the grim, round-turreted fortress prison of Ogulin, he was still not a free man. He was accompanied by a guard to see that he reported to the local police station, where he was told that he was not allowed to live in Zagreb or any other town but must go back to his native village and report to the police each day. He had already made arrangements about what he should do after his release. He had been in touch – by notes in cipher – with communist sympathizers among the other prisoners in Ogulin goal, and had given one of them, Nikola Cikara, the address of his aunt in Zagreb where he could be contacted.[1] He had no close ties, for his wife and son had been sent by the party to Russia in 1929. But he looked forward to seeing his own family and set out for Kumrovec.

The new clothes he had obtained in Lepoglava – suit, shoes, matching tie and handkerchief – enabled him to make a good show in the village. His homecoming was not so gay, for his brother Dragutin had recently died and his sister-in-law was in mourning. Friends in the village, though glad to see him and rather admiring his defiance of authority, did not want to get involved with a political rebel. He reported to the chairman of the local council who was an old school friend, and easier to deal with than the police officials in the nearby township. Tito's account in later life, and that of the chairman, Josip Jurak, do not exactly tally, but both are agreed that behind closed doors Jurak congratulated him on the fine show he had put up at his trial, and made it clear – 'by a wink' said Tito later – that he did not need to report each day.[2]

77

He stayed only a few days in Kumrovec – long enough to get used to freedom, fresh air, normal food and normal social contacts; long enough also to be denounced by the village priest as 'anti-Christ'. He visited his relatives across the Sutla in Slovenia, where he had been so happy as a child. Sometime before the end of March he took a trunkful of reading matter that he had kept illegally in prison to his aunt's house in Zagreb, and hid it under the roof. In it were copies of *Kultura* for 1933, of *Literatura* for 1932, the periodicals *Signal* and *Kniževnik*, and some Marxist economic textbooks. The police found it the following year after receiving information from an ex-prisoner who had been re-arrested. In April he visited his sister in Samobor and then went to Zagreb.[3]

Missing from his village, a warrant was soon out for his arrest, but by this time Josip Broz had disappeared. He had decided to go 'illegal', had changed his appearance by growing a moustache, dyeing his hair and wearing gold-rimmed glasses. Spectacles as a disguise were not a new idea. With the exception of one police photograph taken in 1928, all existing snaps of the prisoner Josip Broz at the time of his trial – including the sketch made in court during the hearing – and several snaps taken in prisons when he was serving his sentence, show him wearing a variety of crude spectacles. One shows him wearing pince-nez, usually only worn by middle-class men, which completely transformed his appearance. Did the wearing of spectacles have some psychological significance for this man on the run? He had excellent eyesight and his appearance without them was also a good disguise as some of the photographs on his forged passports show. But they were a practical aid, if not to sight, for they helped him to avoid looking people directly in the eyes – one of the most dangerous things to do when wanting to escape recognition. A more effective change in his general appearance was brought about by a good shave, smarter clothes and changed colour of hair, and by a better diet that slowly removed his cadaverous appearance.

If Tito was a changed man when he renewed his contacts with the Zagreb party in 1934, the world around him, including the Communist Party, was also very different. On 6 January 1929 King Alexander had imposed a personal dictatorship on the country, banning all political parties, the Independent Trade Unions, many periodicals and societies, as well as organized opposition in all parts of the country. Through the Law for the Protection of the State the police were given wide legal powers to arrest political suspects, and were allowed latitude in the methods they used to exterminate those suspected of opposing the King's policies. Maček, leader of the Croat Peasant Party after Radić's death, and many of his supporters spent periods in gaol, as did Dragoljub Jovanović, leader of the Serbian Peasant Party. Svetozar Pribičević, a distinguished Serbian politician in opposition to the King, and other democrats had to go into exile.[4]

Police measures were especially ferocious against the Communist Party. It did not have the mass support of a populist movement as did the Croat Peasant Party, but it was still, as in the nineteen-twenties, the only party with support that cut across regional divisions in the country, and had members in Serbia as well as in Croatia, Slovenia, Bosnia-Herzegovina, Montenegro and Macedonia.

The period of Alexander's personal rule coincided with the worldwide depression which had had catastrophic effects on Yugoslavia, already nearly the most backward country in Europe.[5] While Broz was in goal, at least sure of minimal free daily food, the Yugoslav people had experienced the severest economic conditions. Prices had risen by seventeen per cent and wages dropped. Between thirty-three per cent and forty per cent of all workers were unemployed, only about half of these being able to claim insurance benefit. The huge army of unemployed and the interpretation of strikes as political subversion, allowed conditions of employment in industry to deteriorate still further. In the villages peasants could only obtain lowest prices for the food they sold on the home market and they were unable to sell their crops for export abroad. They had to pay impossibly high prices for any industrial goods – tools, fertilizers, household goods, salt and fuel oil – that they needed. Credit was difficult to obtain and loan interests excessive. In the worst years, in harsh infertile regions like the bare karstlands of the Lika in Croatia and the barren mountains of Montenegro, it was said that interest owed by the peasants was four times as great as their annual income. The situation was intolerable, and yet had to be born; the towns were full of beggars, the villages and hamlets inhabited by gaunt, diseased, half-starved men, women and children. The political and economic situation was so bad that from 1929 to 1932 people were too depressed to be politically active.[6]

In these years Yugoslavia's international position also changed for the worse. In addition to the difficulties at home, King Alexander had

**79**

to face unrelenting enmity from hostile neighbours. The countries which had been forced to cede land for the creation of the new state were still hoping for revenge and restitution. The expansionist policies of Mussolini, by this time well established in Italy and accepted in Europe, and the revisionist aims of Hitler and the Nazis when they came to power in Germany, made Yugoslavia's position more insecure than it had been in the 'twenties. If Italy were to gain her claims in Dalmatia, Austria in Carinthia and Slovenia, Hungary in Croatia, Albania in Kosovo-Metohija, and Bulgaria in Macedonia, the Yugoslav state would cease to exist.

Alexander was trying to work out a policy that would give him powerful friends and allies and prevent his enemies uniting. By 1930 such allies were difficult to find among the Great Powers. The economic crisis had forced Great Britain as well as the United States back on to a policy of non-involvement in Europe. Russia, the traditional supporter of the South Slavs, was now the Soviet Union, a country opposed to Alexander's rule and not in any case recognized by him as he was still a passionate Tsarist. The League of Nations had not developed into an international institution strong enough to protect small nations. France, the chosen ally of the 'twenties, was the only strong power likely to be useful. From 1930 to 1934 King Alexander tried to obtain a military alliance with France. This was difficult to achieve since France needed an ally against Germany and was courting Italy for this purpose; Yugoslavia's need was for an ally in the first place against Italy. The two positions were incompatible and by 1934 King Alexander had only achieved a pact of friendship and understanding – not a military alliance – with France, and the Little Entente (1933) with Czechoslovakia and Romania, countries also threatened by revisionist Hungary.

Between 1929 and 1934 the Yugoslav Communist Party had gone through the worst period of its history. The policy of armed revolt urged by the Comintern before Broz had gone to prison – which had been part of the reason for the conduct which got him there – was continued for some time. It caused the Party to lose members in unequal battles with the police, and discouraged new recruits at a time when general conditions might have led people to look to communism.

In early November 1928 the Fourth Congress of the Yugoslav Communist Party had been held in Dresden, attended by thirty-two

Yugoslav communists and a strong delegation from the Comintern intent on putting an end – as so often before – to disagreements within the party. Again Sima Marković – 'Comrade No. 1' as he was called at first, 'Comrade No. 10' as he became later – was tenaciously defending his own ideas. But the big battalions of the Comintern were now against him. He was denounced by most delegates and especially in a long speech by Togliatti, the Italian communist on the Comintern delegation. Marković made token submission but did not change his views and he was excluded from the party the following year. A new General Secretary was elected after some heavy pressure by Comintern officials. He was Djuro Djaković, who had recently been on a training course in Moscow.

Only a few months later, in April 1929, as police activity began to increase, Djaković was arrested in Croatia together with an official of the Comintern Red Help (N. Hecimović). Both were killed by the police, allegedly when trying to escape.[7] Other arrests followed. According to Tito 'over a thousand party members were arrested and tens of them were killed by the police'. Important communists fled the country and joined the Central Committee in exile in Vienna and elsewhere. The party was shattered. Only a few groups and individuals managed to maintain contact with each other. Some leaflets continued to be circulated, and most of these, in good type and on superior paper, were clearly printed outside the country. Yet their message was unrealistic as before, still urging armed uprising and extreme policies, still anti-Yugoslav and calling for the break up of the state. One such said:

Do Not Pay Taxes, Do Not Pay Back Loans; Long Live the Autonomy and Independence of Workers' and Peasants' Republics in Croatia, Serbia, Slovenia, Macedonia and Montenegro; Long Live the Balkan Federation of Workers' and Peasants' Republics; Long Live the Soviet Balkans; Down with the War-Fascist Dictatorship; Down with the Bloody Monarchy; Long Live the General Staff of World Revolution, the Comintern.

Many years later Tito denounced the leaders, who at this time 'by their stupid and irresponsible decisions caused the decimation of the small number of party members and youth who went heroically to their death and to prison, spilling their blood for the honour of being called a member of the party and a member of communist youth, that is for submitting to party discipline'.[8]

By 1932 the police terror had abated sufficiently for efforts to be made to start up communist activity again, though the leaders did not dare to return from exile. A new Secretary General of the Yugoslav party was appointed in 1932 on orders from the Comintern. He was Milan Gorkić, who was later to become Tito's political chief. His real name was Josip Čižinski and he came from a Ukrainian family from the Polish part of the old Austrian Empire. He had been brought up in Bosnia where his father had been an Austrian government official before the first world war. As a schoolboy he had been active in Mlada Bosna, the radical political organization. After the war he had become a communist and in 1923 had attended a youth congress in Vienna, where his talents had been noted by Comintern officials. He had been invited to Moscow where he worked in the Communist Youth International organization. He spoke Serbian and German, later adding Russian, French and English to his accomplishments. He married a Russian who was known by the name of Beti Glan and was director of the park of Rest and Culture in Moscow.

He rose rapidly in the Comintern and came to be regarded as an expert on Yugoslav affairs. One job he was given sometime between 1924 and 1926 was that of Instructor to the British Communist Party. Travelling on a false passport and wearing expensive clothes as a disguise, he was sent to South Wales to organize communist activities among the unemployed. He was billeted with a miner's family and found them so poor that he never dared to unpack his silk pyjamas. By 1927 he was back in Moscow and was appointed a member of the Central Committee of the Yugoslav Communist Party. He joined its inner circle, the Politburo, the following year. When he became General Secretary four years later he was still only about twenty-eight years old. He was well thought of by the Russians in the Comintern, two of whom, Manuilsky and Bukharin were his friends. But the Yugoslav communists never liked him, partly because he was not a real Yugoslav, and partly because he went so little to Yugoslavia that he gave the impression of being totally out of touch with the situation there. One Yugoslav communist who knew him in Vienna described him as a large man, already becoming rather corpulent, with fine sandy hair, yellowish eyes and a freckled face. He wore tweed suits and brown boots and looked like a prosperous business man or the central European idea of 'a typical English gentleman'. He was in many ways a pleasant and reasonable man to work with, but so many things went wrong with the party during his term of office, that his colleagues eventually came to mistrust him. He was considered to be superficially clever, not a very convinced theoretical Marxist, but he had an aptitude for the manoeuvring and intrigue necessary to success in the Comintern bureaucracy.[9]

In 1932, however, he was hoping for success. He was given ample funds and Comintern directives for a new vigorous policy to put the Yugoslav party on its feet again. It was known that isolated communist groups were already beginning to resume political activities in parts of Yugoslavia. Gorkić had to try to contact these and organize them into a party. He was told to set up local committees and hold local conferences. Though the policy for armed uprising had not yet been rescinded – it still appeared in some leaflets until 1934 – the new plan was to work through legal organizations such as the Democratic Trade Unions, not banned as the Independent Trade Unions had been, and through groups that were now legally allowed, such as sports, dramatic and music clubs. This was the beginning of the policy that evolved into the Popular Front.

Numbers of communists in the country were still small – four hundred in Croatia, three hundred in Slovenia, one hundred and eighty-five in Montenegro. Numbers in Serbia were not known because Sima Marković still had his supporters there working against the new set-up. In 1933 these numbers were reduced again when the Yugoslav police managed to get enough information to make many arrests, especially in Bosnia and Dalmatia. But things improved when a number of the more outstanding communists who had been arrested earlier finished their sentences and resumed work on their release from gaol.[10]

This was the situation when Josip Broz came out of prison early in 1934, and through a bookseller in a very small way, Stevan Galogaža, who helped communists with illegal publications, he managed to re-establish contact with party officials. Accounts vary but are not in basic disagreement about his immediate political position. 'When I arrived in Zagreb and set to work, my comrades elected me to membership of the Provincial Committee, the party leadership for Croatia', Tito told Dedijer. Other accounts say that this was a reappointment to the position to which he had been elected at the time of his arrest in 1928. In discussing his activities when he first came out of gaol with his early biographers, Tito was very reticent. But an idea of actual conditions and the way that Broz set to work can be gained from a long statement made to the police by a communist whom they arrested in 1935. His name was Franjo Kralj and he described how he had first been contacted by Broz in July 1934 and asked to undertake paid work for the party. Although he was unemployed and his family starving, he had refused because of the danger involved. Eight days later Broz met him again and offered him a stipend of 600 dinars a month. Kralj accepted and began to work with Broz and another communist called Brezović. Each one had a different job, Brezović was the contact with local committees, while Kralj worked with trade union groups, and Broz was secretary and contact with what was known as the 'teknik', which was the name for the party organization link which provided money, passports and the official papers for illegal work. Kralj said that he met Broz on a number of occasions between July and October 1934, and after that was given another contact, a woman whose name he did not know 'about twenty-eight years old, medium height and size, blonde and quite pretty'. She continued to pay him, giving him an extra 400 dinars in November for technical expenses, until she too disappeared in February 1935, after introducing Kralj to his next anonymous contact, a man who was 'rather tall, with a long pale face and the appearance of an intellectual'. This man gave him an address in cipher where he could be contacted in Karlovac, but Kralj said he lost the key to the cipher. He was arrested in December of that year, but the three-man cell organization that Broz had been working meant that Kralj had only limited information to give to the police.[11]

This story confirms information now available from other sources showing that Broz was an active communist organizer within a very short time of coming out of gaol, and was provided with funds for his work. All accounts agree that the Zagreb party organization was in a poor way in 1934, and that it was having difficulty in maintaining contact with the Central Committee in Vienna because 'the police caught everybody the Central Committee sent. . . . There were even some who suggested cutting off connections with it.' Broz, confident and eager for work, must have been a godsend. The Zagreb party decided to send him to Vienna, 'to see what the situation was and decide whether it was possible to work with the Central Committee or not'. Before he went he completed an article on Fascism for a communist group at Zagreb university, and spent a short time in

Slovenia. Early in June he stayed in Ljubljana at the flat of a young communist, Boris Ziherlj, and is referred to at this time as a party 'instructor'. He was known as 'Comrade Rudi'. He behaved with great caution but had occasional meetings with local communists including one with a man later to become important in the Yugoslav communist movement, Sergei Krajger. Broz turned up at this meeting well dressed and wearing gold-rimmed spectacles. He was making new contacts while waiting for instructions from Vienna which he had received in cipher and had to decode with the aid of certain copies of the communist paper *Proleter*.[12]

He decided to cross the Yugoslav–Austrian border disguised as a member of a Slovene mountaineering society whose members were allowed to go on climbing expeditions in the Alps and cross for short distances into Austria. As he spoke Slovene it seemed a safer method than relying on forged papers which were so often spotted by the police. Though physically active, Broz was not familiar with the mountain paths entering Austria at places where guards could be evaded, and he had to use the services of a local guide who made a living by smuggling people and goods across the frontier. The journey, which took the whole of one night, proved difficult and hazardous, for the guide was drunk and unreliable. In addition to extorting twice the agreed price of 300 dinars – already a considerable sum – he abandoned Broz before they had reached the frontier. He was left to find his way alone, tearing his trousers as he stumbled down the last rocky descent to arrive, fortunately, in a hamlet inhabited by Slovenes on the Austrian side of the border.

Even so, on 25 July 1934, his arrival was not without incident; after sleeping hidden in a hayloft, he tried to make his way to the village to catch a train for Vienna, but was stopped by armed youths of the Austrian pro-Nazi Heimwehr, wearing swastika badges. Dollfuss had been murdered that day in Vienna. But Broz's disguise as a holiday tourist – complete with climbing boots and rucksack – held good, and he was able to get away and take a train from Klagenfurt to Vienna.[13]

His party contact in Vienna was a ballet student, daughter of a Zagreb doctor, who found him a room and put him in touch with the Central Committee. Its members were delighted to see him as they were avid for information about the situation in Yugoslavia, which they needed for their reports to Moscow. They fell on Broz, as he said in an oft-quoted phrase 'like bees on honey'. Articulate, well-informed, hardworking, resourceful, obedient, courageous and prison-trained, of working-class peasant origins, he seemed the ideal man to work for the Central Committee. Notes of the committee meetings in Vienna at this time record that he attended sessions on 10, 11, 13, 16 and 18 August and is inscribed in the minutes under the pseudonym of Tito. He had many other names and aliases including Rudi, Spiridon Mekas, John Alexander Carlson, Oto, Viktor, Timo, Georgević, Jiriček, Slavko Babić, Tomanek and Ivan Kostajnšek; when he went to Moscow he was known as Valter, and this is the name he used in all his communications with the Comintern, and the name by which Stalin always knew him. Tito was the name he used in Yugoslavia and which eventually became world famous. He said himself that the name Tito had no significance beyond being a name with literary connections in his native Zagorje.[14]

At the offices of the Central Committee he met Milan Gorkić and a number of leading Yugoslav communists who, like himself, had served prison sentences in Yugoslavia and then gone to Vienna. He was set to work writing reports about the situation of the Communist Party in Yugoslavia. These were the basis for Gorkić's reports to the Comintern. A decision had been taken to hold a party conference in Slovenia and Tito was given the job of supervising the preparations for it. He sent a letter to his own committee in Zagreb telling its members what he had found in Vienna and informing them that he had been co-opted on to the Central Committee which automatically gave him a position of authority in the party in Croatia. He signed the letter with his new name.

Sometime in the last ten days of August, Tito returned to Yugoslavia by the same method as he had left it. He was in Zagreb on 30 August when he wrote a report to the Central Committee. He spent most of the first half of September in Slovenia making arrangements about the conference. On 13 September he reported again to the Central Committee saying that he had been unable to attend a conference in Zagreb as conditions there were too dangerous and he had not dared to stay more than three days. He said he had appointed new members to the Slovene leadership, three workers and two intellectuals. In the middle of September he was back in Zagreb again and reported that out of about fifty people he had seen, only one might be considered suitable for membership to the local committee. Gorkić and his colleagues obviously thought this was being over-particular. 'Do not be afraid about the complete integrity of the workers and whether they are very honest and experienced', he was told. 'With the present membership situation, the organization is in no position to exact great qualifications from those who support it.'[15] Police records of statements by communists show that Tito was right to be careful about whom he enlisted, for it was only the fanatical few who refused to give information when arrested.

In addition to this practical consideration Tito accepted the orthodox ideological concept that a 'worker' was superior communist material to an 'intellectual', that the party must therefore build its leadership on workers. This, as he discovered, was an extremely difficult proposition in Yugoslavia where industry was little developed and the proportion of workers to other social groups was small. He himself was later to select quite a high proportion of leaders from those who were only saved from being categorized as 'intellectuals' by devious expedients. Peasants, the largest social group, did not provide many leaders, nor many party members until the second world war.

The Slovene provincial party conference which Tito had been preparing, was held from 15 to 17 September. It was attended by about thirty delegates and was the first, and organizationally the most splendid and daring, of a series of local conferences designed to show that the party was active again. The meeting had the distinction of being held in a large country house about seven miles west of Ljubljana, which belonged to the Catholic Bishop Rozman; this was made possible through the communist half-brother of the Bishop. The brothers had quarrelled and Rozman had banished him to the country. 'About thirty delegates, including myself, attended the conference which lasted two days and nights,' said Tito. 'All the delegates slept and ate in the mansion. The Bishop's brother had the meals served in style in the big dining hall. The tablecloths were white, the glasses were crystal, the plates bore the Bishop's coat of arms. He personally waited at table constantly cursing his brother the Bishop.'[16]

The aim of the conference was to reactivate the party in Slovenia, and speeches by Edward Kardelj, Boris Kidrić and a young communist Jozip Brilej, who was later to become Yugoslavia's ambassador in Great Britain, dealt with various aspects of party work, examining past mistakes and future organization. Tito himself gave a general ideological talk in which he propounded the theory – later to be strengthened by the Popular Front policy – that a proletarian revolution could not succeed by itself, it must be accompanied by a 'bourgeois-democratic' revolution. When the committee for Slovenia was chosen, both Kardelj and Kidrić's names were omitted because they were too well known to the police. They had in fact already been ordered to go to Moscow for training.

It was at this conference that Tito first got to know Edward Kardelj, to whom he had briefly been introduced by Krajger a few days previously.[17] Kardelj was nearly twenty years younger than Tito, but the two men took to each other and were to be associated for the next thirty years in many different kinds of communist party activities – in Yugoslavia, in Moscow during the second world war, and in home and foreign affairs after the war. Tito was looking for people he could trust and work with. Small, dark, studious and quiet, Kardelj was judged by him after these first meetings as a man who was 'an honest revolutionary', and 'not corrupted by factionalism' – that meant a man who would take his orders from the Central Committee. Kardelj, like Tito had been in gaol and had taken part in prison courses on Marxism. He was a schoolmaster *manqué* who had been arrested as a communist while training to be a teacher. Much later in life he was to fulfil his pedagogic and philosophic bent by becoming an exponent of the special Yugoslav interpretation of Marxism. More important in 1934 than his education, was the fact that although he was known to have been very roughly treated when arrested he had not given information to the police.

Shortly after the end of the conference Tito returned to Vienna, and was present at Central Committee meetings there on 23 and 25 September, and 1 and 4 October, after which he returned to Yugoslavia. In the short time that he was in Vienna on this visit he produced reports on the duties of communists when serving prison sentences and on the kind of material that should be printed in party newspapers. He drafted with Gorkić a letter to the Slovene committee about strike action at the coal-mine at Trbovlje; he was asked to write about antimilitaristic work among communists, and about work among trade unions.[18] In addition to his capacity for writing reports, Tito had become an expert in *konspiracija*, the art of working and moving about illegally. He seems to have been stimulated by the challenge and dangers of this kind of life. Responsibility and authority came naturally to him, and he appears to have enjoyed acting out his youthful dreams in the different aliases of successful engineer and businessman that he used as a cover for his illegal political work.

His new life gave him considerable personal freedom, and obedience to a higher authority was a small price to pay for it. He had mastered the communist rules, as can be seen by his written works at this time. He had learnt the formalized language necessary for all party writings and communications. These had to be expressed in certain phrases and words taken from current Soviet practice, many of which have remained in use among presentday communists. Constant repetition made them into clichés almost meaningless to the outsider, but the communist insider knew exactly what they meant. They had the force and message of a ritual. It made writing much easier. Society was divided into 'bourgeois oppressors' and 'working masses'. The Yugoslav government was a 'war-fascist dictatorship'.[19] The Soviet Union was 'the protector of world peace, of small nations' sometimes referred to as *mirnovog mjesta* the place of peace. Obedient and active party members were 'the best party cadres', supporters outside the party 'the progressive elements'. Work within the party consisted of 'correct' and 'incorrect' lines. There were many phrases to describe the behaviour of those who followed 'incorrect' lines, that is the independent, argumentative and disobedient people in the party, of whom there were many in Yugoslavia; these were 'fractionalists', 'adventurists', 'deviationists', 'opportunists', 'reformists', 'obstructionists against the leading party cadres'. Yet the language, stilted as it was, conveyed real meaning, for it applied to real situations, the government was by any standards oppressive, antidemocratic and corrupt, and party members knew in general what they were fighting for, knew that they would not attain it without outside aid which could only come, it seemed, from the Soviet Union to whose help they owed their very existence.

\* \* \*

Tito left Vienna for Yugoslavia immediately after the Central Committee meeting on 4 October 1934. He spent a short time in Zagreb and was back in Ljubljana by 9 October. That evening he was drafting a report to the Central Committee about the successful results of the recent conference, especially on the situation among the miners at Trbovlje. He also wrote about contacts for, and methods of, illegal crossing of the Slovene–Austrian frontier, of which he now had considerable personal experience. Before the draft was finished – it was despatched dated 11 October – he was brought news that King Alexander had been murdered that day, 9 October 1934, at Marseilles.[20] The Yugoslav police introduced special security measures on all frontiers. They began an intensive search for political suspects – including communists – although it was soon established that the murder had been committed by a professional Macedonian assassin, an ex-member of IMRO, hired by the Croat extremist organization called the Ustaši, which was allowed by Mussolini and the Hungarian government to maintain terrorist training camps in their respective countries.

The Central Committee realized that it was too dangerous for Tito to remain in Yugoslavia. He was ordered back to Vienna, which he reached by the end of October. This time he travelled with a forged passport and forged visa made out in the name of a Czech engineer. He looked the part, prosperous and well-dressed, but his documents had been hastily prepared and he was afraid they would not stand up to careful examination. On this occasion luck and his instinct for self-preservation saved him. At the critical time of passport examination on the frontier, he took the baby of a woman travelling in the same compartment on to his knee. The baby chose that moment to relieve itself, wetting Tito's new trousers, and in the ensuing laughter at his apparent discomfiture, the official was distracted and stamped his passport without close examination.[21] He reached Vienna safely and worked with the Central Committee there until the middle of February 1935, attending a meeting on 19 November 1934 held in Brno, Czechoslovakia, because of increased police action against communists in Vienna. For that journey to Czechoslavakia Tito used a forged Austrian passport in the name of Jiriček, a barber.

Prince Paul had taken over power as Regent for the young King Peter II who was still a minor, and the stringent dictatorship regime was at first continued. This did not prevent communists holding small, secret conferences in Serbia, Montenegro and Dalmatia. Tito also set about holding a general conference for delegates from all over the country. It was decided that conditions were too dangerous in Zagreb and arrangements were made to hold it in Ljubljana in December 1934.

For some time past Tito had known that he was to be sent to Moscow for further communist training, as had happened to most of the Yugoslav communists he was working with in Vienna. This was both a reward for past work and a hopeful sign for future promotion.

It had first been suggested that he should be assigned to the international communist trade union organization in Moscow (PROFINTERN). This would have limited his career to work among trade unions and was not what he or Gorkić envisaged for his future. The proposal was changed by agreement with the Russians and confirmed by a Central Committee meeting decision on 18 January 1935 that he should go to the Balkan Department of the Comintern. While waiting to be summoned to Moscow Tito continued preparations for the Ljubljana conference. This took place on 24 and 25 December 1934, in the flat belonging to Ziherlj's mother, where Tito had been hidden earlier. Because of the danger of being caught by the police, only eleven delegates attended, among them Kamilo Horvatin (Hagen), Blagoje Parović (Šmit), Karlo Hudomal (Oskar), Adolf Muk (Zehner) and Boris Kidrić (at this time called Kos, at other times Dobrić and Romić); Kardelj was not present as he had already gone to Moscow. Tito and Gorkić attended only the second day of the conference.[22]

Speed as well as secrecy was a key-note of the meeting. Delegates had been handpicked rather than freely elected. There was no time or opportunity for general debate, and resolutions were passed unanimously. The last six years had been the worst in the history of the party, which for two years, 1930–32, had been all but extinguished. This could be blamed on the severity of King Alexander's oppressive dictatorship, but it was not communist practice to omit a litany of self-criticism. Referring to this, fourteen years later, Tito said: 'The leadership had to admit a whole range of mistakes and shortcomings, for example, its incorrect stand on elections for workers' unions, its incorrect and irresolute stand on the question of local elections – that is, their boycott of elections, also the weakness of its work in the villages and in the army, its neglect of work for the creation of an anti-fascist and anti-war front.'[23]

Delegates also heard speeches about the importance of work among youth and a general foreign policy report dwelling on the dangers of a possible imperialistic war by bourgeois powers against the Soviet Union. As regards the party's policy inside Yugoslavia, instructions were to continue by all means to subvert the 'great-Serb' dictatorship. The conference ended with a rousing collection of slogans – which could not be shouted for fear of the police – 'For bread and work, land and freedom; against great Serb imperialism, for freedom of oppressed peoples; against fascism and imperialistic war; for unconditional amnesty for all political and military prisoners; for unconditional establishment of relations with USSR, for alliance with USSR; against the monarchy, for a workers-peasants soviet state in all lands of Yugoslavia; long live the Communist Party; down with the war-fascist dictatorship, down with the monarchy. Long live workers and peasants' states in Croatia and Dalmatia, Slovenia, Serbia, Montenegro, Bosnia and Vojvodina.' The delegates dispersed into the snowy streets outside to try to evade capture on their several ways home.

Tito attended meetings of the Central Committee in Vienna on 29 December and on 10 January 1935. He and Kidrić were given the job of working on organization of the party among young people, which up to this time had been rather weak. Before he left Vienna he had a disconcerting experience when his landlady's daughter – who had been caught stealing money from her employer – had tried to gas herself. As the police arrived Tito explained that he was only the lodger, but he collected his documents and possessions and fled. A few days later, in mid-February 1935, full of hope for the future and not dissatisfied with his achievements in the eleven months since he left gaol, he set out for Moscow.[24]

# 6 COMINTERN TRAINEE IN MOSCOW

Transfer to a job in the Comintern in Moscow was a big step forward in Tito's career and, like his earlier visit to Russia, it had an important influence on his character and political development. As with so many political émigrés before him, it brought the seeds of disillusionment, not with communism as such, but with many of the methods and policies of Soviet leadership.

Tito's arrival in Moscow coincided with the beginning of Stalin's great purge designed to eradicate first his political opponents and potential opponents among Soviet communists, later extended to remove all foreign communists who had been in any way connected with them. It was fortunate for Tito that he had not been associated with Soviet or Comintern politics before this time. The purge started with the murder on 1 December 1934 of Sergei Kirov – as we now know, though it was not known at the time except to those involved – on the orders of Stalin himself. By the time Tito arrived in Russia early in 1935, many important Soviet communists were already under arrest; but the implication of these events was still obscure, and there was no indication that it would affect the Comintern.[1]

It was fifteen years since he had left Russia, then still in the exciting and uncertain period of the founding of the revolutionary state. His arrival at the Soviet border in February 1935 was a moment of deep emotion, nostalgia for the past and excitement at being in the only existing communist state, the centre from which all communist hope for the future radiated. His attitude to the Soviet Union, the Russian Communist Party and Stalin was as yet one of trusting idealism.

He had travelled by train across Poland, and arrived after a long delay at the frontier at the Russian station of Njegoreloje where red lettering on wooden arches on the grim snow-covered station proclaimed to the few travellers entering from the outside world 'Workers of the World Unite'. He had a feeling of freedom and belonging, and felt uplifted at the sight of the huge portraits of

Marx, Lenin and Stalin, cheered by the optimistic posters of the great industrial development in the Urals and of the romanticized collective farms in the Ukraine.[2] This was what he was working for, what he hoped to see one day in his own country.

Moscow was quite new to him. His earlier travels had taken him to many other parts of the country, never before to its new capital. He was given a small room on the fourth floor of the Hotel Lux in Gorki Street. This was where foreign communists and some Comintern officials were housed. If Tito had looked forward to reunion with his beautiful wife Polka, he was to be disappointed. Though some foreign communists were in Moscow with their wives, family life was not a characteristic feature of society among the crowd of non-Russian Comintern students and workers. Tito found that after Polka had returned to her native land in 1929 she had made other associations in the new Soviet ruling class. She no longer considered herself as Tito's wife, and had let their son run wild, to be brought up by another woman; but their marriage was not dissolved until just before the war. However, documents of this period speak of Tito having a wife. Although Tito continued to see his son occasionally, he remained for some years free of family ties, and this gave him more time for dedicated party work.[3]

He reported for work to the offices of the Comintern in Mahovaya Street, near the Kremlin and Red Square, where he was given an office and secretary, and set to work in the department known as the Secretariat for Balkan Lands. Its head was the German communist Wilhelm Pieck, successor to the Hungarian communist Bela Kun, who had been in Moscow since the failure of the 1919 revolt in Hungary.[4]

Tito spent such spare time as he had visiting the sights of Moscow – Lenin's tomb, the Kremlin, the many museums glorifying communist achievement, the Park of Rest and Culture, and later the factories, schools and collective farms. During his long stay in Moscow he only twice went to the ballet – this was not the entertainment for a serious working communist. He said later that in Moscow he spent a long time reading in his room and in libraries, that his long periods of solitary life in prison had made him used to his own company.[5] But when he wanted it there was plenty of social life available among the residents in the Hôtel Lux, and with his compatriots in Moscow. There were usually about thirty Yugoslavs connected with Comintern work, but others were resident students at the Leninist School and the Communist University for National Minorities of the West (KUNMZ), making about seventy or more, and people were arriving and departing all the time. There were also a number of Yugoslav political émigrés in Moscow, and the total Yugoslav colony amounted to several hundred people. They had their own club and their own Communist Party organization, with frequent meetings. Tito gave an address about conditions in Yugoslavia to a gathering shortly after he arrived. He was introduced simply as 'the comrade from the country'.[6]

There were at this time in Moscow many Yugoslavs who were later to become well known in the Yugoslav party. Besides Tito, these included Edward Kardelj, Rodoljub Čolaković, Djuro Salaj, Vlajko Begović (working in the Communist Youth International) and Ivan Gošnjak, later to become Tito's Chief of Staff. Kardelj was doing a six months' course of study and giving lectures on Comintern history at the Marxist Leninist School for foreign students (known by its initials as MLS) situated at 25 Vorovskoga Street, which was also attended by Čolaković, Gošnjak and a number of others. Students at this school – there were about 700 of many different nationalities – received a stipend of between eighty and 110 roubles from which they had to pay their residential expenses at the school. Conditions there were of the same Spartan standards normal for Russian students, food was coarse and of poor quality – a cause for complaint from the English students at the school as well as from some of the Yugoslavs.

Others doing some kind of political work connected with the Comintern were Vladimir Čopić, Stefan and Djuka Cvijić, Filip Filipović, Ivan Regent, Grgur and Rado Vujović, Božidar Maslarić, Kosta Novaković, Blagoje Parović, Sima Marković, and from time to time the mysterious Comintern agent Mustafa Golubić, who was later to be employed by the Russians on secret service work in Belgrade where he was arrested by the Gestapo shortly after the Nazi invasion and tortured to death because of his refusal to disclose information. Among the Yugoslav communist women in Moscow were Anka Butorac, Cana Babović, Anka Grzetić, Jovanka Horvatin and Zdenka Kidrić. All the foreign communists who were to be engaged in international work for the Comintern were known only by pseudonyms once they arrived in Moscow. Tito was always called Valter. It was thought that this gave them training in *konspiracija* and helped to break any strong national ties they had retained, but there is no evidence that it had much effect in this respect on the Yugoslavs.

H                    95

Pseudonyms were also used by a number of well-known international communists whom Tito met in the office of the Comintern or in the Hôtel Lux. Foremost among these was Georgi Dimitrov – known as *Deda*, meaning grandfather – the Bulgarian who had become world famous the previous year when he had been framed by the Nazis in the notorious Reichstag Fire Trial and had defended himself with such courage that he had been acquitted. Besides Tito's head of department Wilhelm Pieck, there were the Germans, Klement Gottwald and Walter Ulbricht, Otto Kuusinen of Finland, Bela Kun, Maurice Thorez of France, the Italian Palmiro Togliatti, the Spaniard Jose Diaz, the Greek Zahariades, Bulgarians Traiko Kostov and Vasil Kolarov, and for a time, English comrades Harry Pollitt and Palme-Dutt, and Americans Earl Browder and Darcy. Important Russians, officials of the Comintern, held key positions but were too distant to be intimate with junior staff from relatively unimportant countries. The Russian who was closest to the Yugoslavs in the Comintern was a Ukrainian, Dmitri Manuilsky, who has been accused of acting as Stalin's agent throughout, but who liked the Yugoslavs – perhaps better than some of the other nationalities in the Comintern; he did, on occasion, manage to protect some of them. Two other important Russians in the Comintern in 1935, both members of the Soviet Communist Party's Central Committee, were G. Knorin and Ossip Piatnitsky. The latter was in charge of the key Organization Department which handled the finance and administration of foreign agents and communist parties.[7]

After the Yugoslav Central Committee in Vienna had decided to send Tito to work in the Balkan Secretariat, Gorkić had written a letter to Čopić, a senior member among the Yugoslavs working in the Comintern. It said:

We too agree that Tito can take over this work. We leave the final decision with you. If Tito becomes referent, then see to it that people treat him in a friendly way. Tell Valija [Filip Filipović, the Yugoslav member on the Comintern Executive Committee, *ed.*], that he is a worker who has served six years in goal, that perhaps at first he will not be quite so expert [in the routine, *ed.*] as some of those experienced intellectuals. But he knows the Party, he represents the best part of our active workers and after some time – six to eight months – we shall recall him for leadership work in the Central Committee. Therefore no one should treat him as a petty official but rather as a Party member who in the near future will be one of the actual, and we hope, good leaders of the Party.[8]

The fact that such a warning was necessary gives some idea of the relations between members in the Yugoslav community in the Comintern. In Yugoslavia Tito had already started to become a big fish in a small pond. Moscow proved to be not so much a big pond as a political jungle, where careers and even lives were at stake. But he was well able to look after himself. It took a little time to size up the situation and make the adjustment from romantic expectation to stark reality. In the meantime, having sloughed off his illegal *persona* of 'rich bourgeois intellectual', he had no difficulty in taking on the personality and appearance of a quiet industrious party worker, and from his own accounts it is clear that he approached his new life with great caution. In both identities he had the ability to merge unobtrusively into his surroundings – as important in the Soviet Union at this time as it had been under the dictatorship in Yugoslavia.

The Hôtel Lux was a five-hundred-room, five-storey building, with basic but limited facilities for its inhabitants. Entry was by special pass, and no one, however well known to the doorman or however much in urgent need, was allowed in without it. Each floor, reached by an old lift, had a long corridor with rooms running off both sides; many rooms were intercommunicating so that important residents such as Manuilsky, could have several rooms assigned to them as a kind of flat. Ordinary inhabitants like Tito had one long narrow room. It was just wide enough to have an all-purpose cupboard and a washbowl with a cold tap, both near the entrance. Beyond this the rest of the room contained a bed, chair and table.

Other washing and toilet facilities were somewhat inadequate for the large number of residents. Hot water in the shower rooms – separate for male and female – was infrequently available and at limited times, so that to get a good wash several people would share one shower in close and intimate proximity. It was under the shower that Tito met Earl Browder, the American communist. There was a restaurant on the ground floor, but residents could provide their own food, and each floor had a large kitchen with about twenty cookers. Here, while meals were being prepared, gossip could be exchanged between the multilingual international group of European communist élite.

Conditions were not luxurious, but they compared well with the prisons Tito had been in, and it was better accommodation than many Russians were able to have in Moscow in the 'thirties. The worst feature was that even the walls had ears, and the hotel staff, including its manager Gurevich, were agents of the Soviet secret police, the dreaded NKVD. It was necessary – and became more vital as time went on – to keep a very guarded tongue. Unlike some Yugoslavs and other communists, Tito's instinct for self-preservation made him very careful of what he said.

Life in Russia had its own dangers as Stalin's purge gathered momentum and struck at random against foreign communists in Moscow. Fortunately for Tito this first visit coincided with a lull in the purge which lasted from July 1935 to August 1936. So that for a time he was able to enjoy the change from years of prison and months of illegal existence, always on the move between Yugoslavia and Vienna. It allowed the opportunity for relaxation necessary even for the most steely-nerved agent – as Tito certainly was; and in the first six months of his stay he was buoyed up by the conviction – mistaken as it turned out – that in the Soviet Union loyalty and hard work were a sure protection against any convinced communist being unjustly arrested or condemned.

\* \* \*

The Third International – or Comintern as it was called – which played such an important part in Tito's career in the next seven years, had its origins in the prewar international socialist movement. The First International had been founded as far back as 28 September 1864 at a meeting held in St Martin's Hall in Westminster. The purpose of the meeting, which was attended by Karl Marx and a number of British and European socialists, had been to found a Workingmen's International Association, 'to afford', as Karl Marx said in his opening speech, 'a central medium of communication and cooperation for the protection, advancement and complete emancipation of the working classes'. It was replaced by the Second International founded on 14 July (Bastille Day) 1889, which established an International Socialist Bureau to give advice and help to socialist movements throughout the world. The Second International had support from people of very diverse and only broadly socialist views, including a right wing, whose main exponent was Edward Bernstein, a centre, the famous spokesman Karl Kautsky, and the left, which came to be dominated by Lenin and Trotsky. The first world war, forcing members to declare themselves for or against hostilities, precipitated irreconcilable divisions which had always been latent. The Bolshevik revolution in Russia in 1917 gave the left wing the opportunity to create a movement of its own.

Struggling to control internal developments in Russia, Lenin was not able to call an international conference till January 1919. The importance that he attached to it can be judged by the fact that it was convened at such a dangerous and chaotic stage in the revolutionary situation in Russia. It was held in Petrograd, attended by delegations from America, Britain, the Balkans (including prisoners of war), Poland and Sweden, and was dominated by the presence of Lenin and other Bolshevik leaders among the Russians. The result was the foundation of a federation of foreign groups attached to the Central Committee of the Bolshevik Party. At a third session the conference voted – in spite of opposition from the German delegate Eberlein – to found a Communist International. This was the Third – and first purely communist – International which came to be known as the Comintern.[9]

It became an arm of Soviet foreign policy and existed until the end of 1943, when it was officially abolished by Stalin. It built up an enormous administrative machinery in Moscow and exercised great authority over communist parties and individuals from countries outside Russia. This machinery remained in being, without its important foreign officials, even after the formal abolition of the Comintern in 1943. It changed its offices in 1937 and again in 1941, and lost a great part of its foreign personnel as a result of Stalin's purge, but it retained the same administration and some of the same officials to the end. Although abolished as the Comintern, the same administration was in existence in Mahovaya Street again after the end of the second world war, being in effect part of the Soviet department of foreign affairs. This was probably the basis for the administration that prepared the communist takeover in eastern European countries after the war, that founded and ran the Cominform.

Tito became a paid official of the Comintern in 1934. Though he ceased to receive a salary in 1937, he remained an obedient – though towards the end, increasingly independent – worker for the Comintern until 1942. He was not to be completely free from its influence until he broke with Stalin in 1948. Tito's independent development after being one of the apparently most conformist and successful Comintern trainees, is the outstanding and most astonishing feature of his political career.

What kind of an organization was the Comintern which moulded and dominated so many European communists? Much work was done in the 'twenties – especially by Bukharin – on defining its aims. These were finally written into a constitution and programme which was accepted by the four hundred delegates who attended the Sixth Comintern Congress held in Moscow in 1928. The programme listed work under six headings: the world system of capitalism; its development and inevitable downfall; the general crisis of capitalism and the first phase of world revolution; the ultimate goal of the Communist International or world communism. Then followed three sections dealing with the theory of the transition from capitalism to socialism and the dictatorship of the proletariat which would come after revolution had been achieved. According to this programme all capitalist countries were one hostile group threatening Soviet Russia and opposed to world revolution. The Comintern was thus part of Russia's defence system against permanent danger, and its means of organizing help for communist revolution in any other countries where the basic requirements of revolution existed. These 'objective conditions' had been judged to be present in Yugoslavia in 1926, and this had been the reason for the calls to armed revolt that Tito and some Yugoslav communists had tried to act on.

By the time Tito reached Russia in 1935 a radically new world situation had evolved. The success of Mussolini and Fascism in Italy and, even more directly menacing, the recent triumph of the Nazis and destruction of the communists in Germany, caused the Russian leaders to re-evaluate their methods of using foreign communist parties. This was the subject of discussion in the early months of 1935 and was to result in the adoption of the idea of the Popular Front policy as a new tactic of Soviet foreign relations. Once a line of action had been agreed on by the Soviet leaders it was accepted by the Comintern and put into effect by its numerous employees and institutions.

The basic structure of the Comintern was simple, though the ramifications of its many departments were extremely complex. According to the 1928 constitution, its ultimate authority resided in a World Congress supposed to meet every two years. In fact, after its Sixth Congress in 1928 it met only once more, in 1935. In between congresses, supreme authority lay with its elected Executive Committee which met twice a year. Decision making was in the hands of a Presidium – nineteen members and twelve candidate members in 1935 – which met every fortnight, and an even more powerful Political Secretariat composed at this time of seven members and three candidates. In fact real authority resided with the Soviet leadership and was exercised through Russian members on all these committees.

Directly responsible to the Political Secretariat were seven lesser secretariats – called Länder Secretariats – which divided the world according to geographical region. Each of these was headed by a member of the Presidium. Tito's work was with the second of these, the Balkan Secretariat which dealt with Yugoslavia, Bulgaria, Greece and Romania. Before 1928 foreign communist parties and members had used the facilities and money supplied by the appropriate department of the Comintern, but retained some residual autonomy in running their own affairs, some independence in expressing opinions on policy. After 1928 this completely disappeared and the Comintern became totally centralized, increasingly dominated by Stalin's arbitrary and fearful authority.

As an employee of the Comintern, and as a member of the Yugoslav Communist Party, Tito was pledged to complete acceptance of this system, as was stipulated in one of the twenty-one terms of membership which every party had to accept on joining the Comintern. These were very precise in laying down the obligation of all member parties to accept its basic ideas and be obedient to its directives. One clause was that the programme of any member communist party might be drawn up in the light of local conditions but must be in accordance with resolutions of the Comintern; it also had to be approved by that body, which in effect meant by the people who composed its Central Committee, of which Stalin was a member throughout the period of Tito's association with the Comintern. Finally, communist parties were required to expel any party members who disobeyed the Comintern and flouted these conditions.

By 1935 the Yugoslav Communist Party was already notorious for a tendency among its members to disregard these obligations, to remain independent and argumentative in the face of Comintern directives and 'Open Letters'. The Comintern had already disciplined two of its members, Martinović and Marić the two party secretaries before Gorkić, and one of their predecessors Sima Marković, by expulsion from the party for a time. The use of this sanction, and the fact that the party was financed by the Comintern, as well as the comparatively high salaries received by senior party officials, all added fuel to the intrigues and personal rivalry between Yugoslavs connected with the Comintern, and these intrigues as well as rivalry between different nationalities, were used by the Russians as instruments in their own policy. When things went wrong in the Yugoslav party it was not possible to blame the Comintern – which by definition was always right – so a scapegoat had to be found. In 1935 just after Tito arrived in Moscow, a new wave of arrests of communists took place in Yugoslavia, and Gorkić, as General Secretary was being criticized and held responsible. He had strong Russian support, and a new phase of the party power struggle had already begun. Tito needed all his wits about him to master these complicated intrigues, which had their centre in Moscow but also had ramifications in the party in Yugoslavia, as well as in Vienna or wherever the Central Committee of the Yugoslav party happened to be.

Tito was already sufficiently experienced to know that lives were at stake in these political intrigues, and he became increasingly wary. He lived the part that was expected of him as a very junior and new member of the Yugoslav community in Moscow. He was enthusiastic for the cause, quiet and hardworking. He gave lectures on work in the trade unions and on the importance of cadres in party work both at KUNMZ and at the Leninist School. He received twenty roubles per lecture – a fairly high rate of pay at that time. He was advised to use some of his spare time in taking a course of study but decided instead to follow a personal programme of reading saying he could do more work on his own. It was a wise decision not be to associated more than was necessary with Comintern institutions. He says he read books on economics, philosophy and military works, especially Russian and German sources, including Frunze and Clausewitz. Unlike some new recruits in Moscow he had no language difficulties. Togliatti, for instance, had to take long courses in Russian from a lady teacher provided by the Comintern. Tito already knew Russian and quickly became proficient in it again. He spoke German easily and in general was well equipped to deal with the mixed European society and multi-language literature he found in the Comintern.[10]

\* \* \*

During Tito's first few months in Moscow, much of the activity in the Comintern was concentrated on preparing for its Seventh – and as it turned out, last – World Congress which was held in Moscow from 25 July to 20 August 1935 and was attended by sixty-five delegations from all over the world. It was an important occasion in the history of the Comintern, and no efforts of organization were spared to impress this on the delegates. The Comintern leaders used this meeting to proclaim a new policy for world communism, the policy of the Popular Front. Reversing previous practice, communists were told to work with social democrat, liberal or other similar bourgeois parties or groups, in order to create a broad united front to fight fascism. In all previous tactics communists had been instructed to keep themselves uncontaminated by alliance with other parties of the left, which had all been considered as equally dangerous enemies of communism. Communists were now allowed to make agreements with bourgeois party leaders in order to create strong opposition to fascist and reactionary governments. The distant aim of seizure of power was not abandoned, but it was conceded that communists needed allies in the interim period of struggle before fascist governments could be overthrown. It was also conceded, along with the Popular Front policy, that some capitalist states such as Great Britain, France and the United States were non-aggressive. 'Not every capitalist state has an equal desire for war at all times', said Litvinov in 1934 when the policy was beginning to evolve, and they should be distinguished from the aggressive fascist states, Germany, Italy and Japan, who were a danger to world peace and to the security of the Soviet Union.

This change in policy was closely connected with the Russian leaders' reassessment of the current international situation and its dangers for the Soviet Union. The main threat to Russia was seen as coming from Nazi Germany, and in 1934 Russian foreign policy was changed in the hope of diverting German aggression from the Soviet Union. The Popular Front policy was to be concurrent with Soviet moves towards some form of collective security and a system of bilateral alliances to balance German power. Russia signed pacts of military alliance with France and Czechoslovakia in May 1934, and joined the League of Nations in September that year. The change of policy was almost certainly a reflection of Stalin's assessment of Russian weakness in comparison with Germany, and of his need to postpone any military clash with the Nazis until Russia was stronger. For though tremendous strides in industrial development had been made since the revolution, production in the 'thirties remained relatively slow, and results of the savage collectivization of agriculture had been disastrous.

The seventh World Congress of the Comintern was held in Moscow in the great colonnaded hall of the Palace of the Trade Unions, once a club for Tsarist nobles. Tito was among the four hundred or so delegates who filled the hall, which had been decorated with gigantic portraits of Marx, Engels and Lenin, with banners and slogans appropriate to the occasion and to the new Popular Front policy. Stalin's portrait was also there, a sign of his increased personal power. He had not had such a position at the last Comintern Congress in 1928. His appearance for the singing of the International and Wilhelm Pieck's opening speech of the first session was greeted by tumultuous applause. On the platform with important international communists (including Pollitt and La Pasionara) he sat silent and impassive beside his hatchet man of the moment, the man who was to become his most hated instrument in the great purge, the 'bloodthirsty dwarf' Yezhov. Stalin, who was always rather contemptuous of the Comintern, referring to it as 'the grocer's shop', made no speech, and departed as soon as the conference was safely under way. The official record of the conference says that every mention of his name was greeted with 'stormy and prolonged applause, ovation and shouts of hurrah' – a mark of the organized appreciation reserved only for him.[11] This was the first and only time that Tito saw Stalin during his stay in Moscow. He first met him personally when he went to Moscow in his capacity of Commander-in-Chief of a triumphant Yugoslav Partisan army just before the Red Army entered Yugoslavia in 1944.

The Comintern Congress was also the first opportunity Tito had had of attending an international communist conference, and for him the occasion was very impressive. It is perhaps not fanciful to suggest that he was at this time at his most impressionable – aged forty-six, and still a junior delegate – that the policy of Popular Front which he heard proclaimed in the speeches of Dimitrov and Togliatti made a profound impression on him and had a lasting influence on his direction of the communist movement in Yugoslavia before and during the second world war.

If Stalin received the greatest applause and adulation – 'every pronouncement Stalin makes', Manuilsky told the delegates, 'is a landmark in the enrichment and deepening of Marxist–Leninist theory' – Dimitrov was the hero of the conference. It was only a year since the Reichstag trial in which he had proclaimed to the court, and to the world, 'for me, as a communist, the highest law is the programme of the Comintern'. And in reply to a German newspaper comment, 'Dimitrov is the Programme of the Communist International made flesh', he had said 'I cannot think of a better description of myself.'[12] It was, therefore, both fitting and a sign of his acceptability to Stalin, that a special position was created for him by the Seventh Congress – that of Secretary-General of the Communist International. He retained this position until the formal ending of the Comintern in 1943, and continued with similar work until he was sent from Russia to Bulgaria in 1947, to take over the Soviet-protected communist government there.

The Yugoslav delegation to the conference was fairly large. It included in one capacity or another most of the Yugoslav communists in Moscow who held, or had held, official position in the party. Names were put forward under their accepted pseudonyms – delegates from the Central Committee, Gorkić (Somer) and Parović (Šmit) – reported to the conference about the situation in Yugoslavia since the last conference. Delegates elected by the party in Yugoslavia were the Dalmatian Ivo Marić (who later was to fight Tito on the leadership issue) and Drago Petrović (Milinković) a printer from Zagreb. The Slovenes were represented by Lovro Kuhar (Valić), the Serbs by a metal worker, Milan Radovanović (Simonović). *Ex officio* members were Vladimir Čopić (Šenko) and Josip Broz (Valter). In addition Filip Filipović (Bošković) was a special delegate. He was an old member of the Executive Committee of the Comintern and had attended its congresses in 1924 and 1928. Stjepan Cvijić (Andrej) and his brother Djuka, were delegates, and Kardelj (Birc), Rade Vujović (Liht) and Božidar Maslarić (Andrejev) were also present in some capacity; Rodoljub Čolaković (Rozenko) and Rudolf Hercigonja (Mironov) organized the delegation's secretariat with the help of August Cesarec (Man) and Ivan Regent (Mateo).[13] With the exception of Tito, Regent, Čolaković, Petrović and Kardelj who managed to leave Moscow, and Parović who was killed in Spain, most of these men were to be put to death by Stalin in the next two or three years.

At its first meeting the Yugoslav delegation chose Gorkić as its leader, and Tito with his fluent Russian as its secretary. In this capacity Tito was able to attend all sessions and many committee meetings, and become familiar with the delegates and the work of the conference. He appears to have done his work well, since when it came to a question of choosing a Yugoslav member for the Executive Committee of the Comintern his name was at one stage suggested instead of Gorkić. Meetings for this nomination were held on 13 and 14 August 1935. The Yugoslav delegation seems to have been unable to chose between three equally backed candidates – Gorkić the Comintern nominee, Kamilo Horvatin and Vladimir Čopić. Tito's name was accepted as a compromise solution. Čopić had the unwelcome task of intervening with his own delegation when Valter's name was rejected by the Comintern leaders. Manuilsky, Gorkić's friend and protector told Tito: 'Since you did not elect Gorkić in whom alone the Comintern has confidence – and it does not have it in you – we will not give you a full member of the ECCI, but merely a candidate member, and he will be Gorkić. This is your punishment.'[14] As candidate member – and this was confirmed by the congress – Gorkić could participate in Executive Committee meetings, but did not have full voting rights. All this was another black mark for the Yugoslav party.

When the conference finished, the members of the Yugoslav Politburo took the opportunity to have a meeting in Moscow before its members dispersed. At a meeting on 21 August – Tito again being co-opted to the committee – it was decided that the gifted Serbian member Parović should go back to Yugoslavia to continue his work inside the country. Tito was ordered to accompany members of the Yugoslav delegation who were joining a group of other delegates from the conference on a three weeks' tour of the Soviet Union.

The tourists, including besides Tito only three Yugoslavs, Petrović, Radovanović and Cesarec, left Moscow in the last week of August and returned in mid-September. They visited the trans-Volga region and western Siberia, parts of the country which Tito knew from his prisoner of war days. They saw heavy industry factories at Sverdlovsk, coal- and gold-mines, and machine factories at Kuibishev. They visited tractor stations and went to some of the new collective farms. The purpose of the tour was to impress the foreign communists. Tito did his work well, interpreting and making speeches to various audiences telling them about the conference that had taken place. He could speak to Russian workers and peasants in language they understood. If he had any reservations about what he saw – it was not long after the bloodily enforced collectivization and fear and resentment were certainly still present – he kept his thoughts to himself. Much later he said: 'I talked with collective farm members, and noticed them nudging each other when they wanted to say something.'

Tito was back in Moscow at final meetings of the Yugoslav delegates on 15 and 17 September and for a meeting of the party's Central Committee, before they dispersed. It had been decided that he should join the Central Committee in Vienna at the end of the year. But before December disquieting news had been received from Yugoslavia, both about continued disagreement over how the new policy should be put into practice, and about wholesale police arrests among party members. Tito was instructed to stay on in Moscow for a time and this is why his sojourn there was twice as long as had originally been intended.[15]

\* \* \*

In Yugoslavia a general election had been held in May 1935 after Prince Paul had become regent following the murder of King Alexander. Parties opposed to the regent's continuation of personal rule formed a united opposition which received a majority of votes, but gained no change in the character of the government. The Communist Party, still illegal, was unable to play an open part in the election campaign, and had been bitterly divided on what tactics to use. Gorkić had first issued instructions that it should put up its own candidates through its legal front organization, the Working Peoples' Party. Shortly before the election, and perhaps on instructions from the Comintern which had already accepted the Popular Front policy that was soon to be promulgated at its Congress, he withdrew this order and told Yugoslav communists to work with, and vote for, the united opposition candidates. In the event, the opposition parties led by Maček refused to accept the cooperation of the communists, who made impossible demands. Many communist supporters voted for the united opposition, and the communists reaped neither benefit nor credit from the result. The united opposition itself gained no benefit from their success either, for Prince Paul appointed as his new premier the right-wing pro-Nazi politician Milan Stojadinović. But many Yugoslav communists felt that in some way an opportunity had been lost and it was necessary to hold a post mortem on the reason why, with the accusing finger pointed at Gorkić. He was also blamed for the fact that after the election the party was again nearly exterminated by the royalist police.

Arrests had begun after a meeting of workers at Sisak had got out of control and communists had demonstrated for the Soviet Union, demanding – quite contrary to the new Comintern policy – the creation of a Soviet Croatia. Shortly after this, a communist courier carrying party documents, Djako Mitrović, had been arrested. Soon the police had lists of active communists all over the country and eventually were able to arrest nine hundred and fifty out of a total of about three thousand members of the party in different regions of Yugoslavia. From interrogations they obtained a lot of information about different party leaders, including fresh information about Tito. The illegal party was once again almost broken, leaving only a few people to carry on the party work. Among these were students in Belgrade including one young communist Milovan Djilas, recently out of gaol.[16]

News of the situation slowly filtered onto the Yugoslav desk in the Balkan secretariat in Moscow, for communications by courier were dangerous and spasmodic. Criticism of the Gorkić set-up in Vienna was now widespread in Yugoslavia, in Moscow, and in the Central Committee itself. In April 1936 when Gorkić was away in Moscow, Čopić organized a meeting of some members of the Central Committee in Prague and Vienna, without consulting either Gorkić or the Comintern. It was, of course, discovered, and the Comintern decided that once again it had to take drastic action over the lack of discipline and unity in the Yugoslav Party.[17]

It acted with its usual authoritarian decisiveness. The whole Yugoslav Central Committee was dismissed, and on 9 September 1936, a new committee chosen by the Comintern was 'elected'. The inner group of this committee then proceeded – no doubt on instructions also – to elect Gorkić again as Secretary-General, and Tito as Organizing Secretary. According to his later accounts it is clear that Tito himself was at least privately against Gorkić by this time, and was publicly advocating the need for the party to have its secretary working in the country, not from Vienna. He says he went to Dimitrov himself with this proposal. 'A heated discussion developed over my proposal,' he said, 'Gorkić in particular opposing it. Finally, it was decided that the Central Committee should split. One part, headed by me, would go home to work, while Gorkić as Political Secretary, would stay abroad. He was given the right to veto all political resolutions and decisions adopted in Yugoslavia. . . . I consented to this decision,' he went on. 'Besides, I wanted to establish a principle concerning subsidies from the Comintern, which in my opinion greatly hampered the party.' 'It was a weak decision,' he commented on another occasion, 'but even so, it helped me to work independently in the country'.[18]

In all this manoeuvring for power inside the Yugoslav party, Tito, now playing an active part, seems to have had Dimitrov firmly on his side. 'My personal relations with Dimitrov were very good indeed. There was very much trust and mutual confidence between us,' Tito remembered later. On another occasion he commented: 'He was completely friendly and understood in detail the difficulties of illegal party work in existing circumstances.' Manuilsky, the chief Soviet representative in the Comintern, was a friend and supporter of Gorkić, so that it was necessary for Tito to proceed with care. 'As to Manuilsky,' said Tito later, 'sometimes he was on our side, sometimes on the other. He first supported the other side, but in the end came to the conclusion that we should have his support.' The reorganization of the Yugoslav Communist Party at this time was being carried on against a background of mounting terror in Moscow, for the lull in Stalin's purge came to an end as soon as the Comintern Congress was over. Those who now lost the struggle for leadership were among the first Yugoslavs to be arrested and in most cases executed, by the NKVD, the Soviet secret police. But for the time being Gorkić himself remained free. He had bested his critics and his main opponents on the Central Committee were excluded, including Čopić, Hudomal, Horvatin and Stjepan Cvijić, who within a short time all disappeared.[19]

In the middle of October 1936, Tito at last left Moscow and joined the Central Committee in Vienna. He had been given his orders to assist Gorkić in reorganizing the Communist Party, and was to be allowed to work in Yugoslavia. He was to enforce discipline and acceptance of the Comintern policy, and to rid the party of members who would not come into line. This was a tall order in itself, for no one had as yet succeeded in regimenting the Yugoslav party. In addition he had been given the job of recruiting volunteers to fight for the Republican Army in the Spanish Civil War, and arranging for their safe despatch from Yugoslavia to Spain.[20] Both tasks were extremely difficult and dangerous. It is probable that no one in the Comintern, and least of all Gorkić, who must certainly by this time have regarded Tito as a rival, thought that he would succeed, let alone survive.

# 7 INTERNATIONAL EXPERIENCE

The terror created by Stalin's great purge had already begun to affect the Comintern before Tito left Moscow in the summer of 1936. Zinoviev, Kamenev and others to be condemned in the Trial of the Sixteen that summer, had been in gaol since December 1934, and many other Russians had been arrested.[1] Foreign communists who had been associated with them, or with any kind of liberal ideas were already under suspicion. It was a good time to be leaving Moscow.

Gorkić, once more in authority over the Yugoslav Party, summoned Tito to Vienna, providing him with forged papers for the journey which was to be routed through Yugoslavia. But Tito already knew that factions in the Comintern and the Yugoslav Party had used badly forged documents, or tip-offs to the frontier police, as a means of liquidating their opponents. He suspected that a number of Yugoslav communist officials had lost their lives in this way. He did not trust the Latvian woman doctor who was to travel with him. 'I obtained another passport and went quite a different way,' he said later, 'because other comrades who got passports through Gorkić were arrested at the Yugoslav frontier.' He travelled from Moscow to Prague and arrived in Vienna in the middle of October 1936.[2]

His special job was to organize the recruitment and despatch to Spain of volunteers for the Spanish Republican army fighting to suppress the revolt of General Franco. On arrival in Vienna, Tito discovered that the situation of the Central Committee had changed because the Austrian police, under new orders from the pro-Nazi Chancellor Schuschnigg, had tightened their security precautions against communists. Boris Kidrić and other Yugoslavs had been arrested in Vienna in June 1936, and the Austrian police had succeeded in getting hold of a lot of the Yugoslav Party archives.[3] The Central Committee had to disperse into hiding, and moved its headquarters to Paris during the last months of 1936. The situation there was much easier for communists because Leo Blum's Popular Front government had been in power since 1935. Although officially following a non-intervention policy in the Spanish Civil War, it was permissive to all

(*above*): **10. Tito in Bosnia, 1942.**

(*left*): **11. Draža Mihajlović, 1942.**

12. Tito, aged fifty-one, at Jajce, November 1943. (A previously unpublished photograph).

kinds of international committees for aid to Spain, since it was already aware that the German and Italian governments were sending military assistance to Franco.[4]

So it was from a Paris office that Tito began to establish secret communications with party members still active in Yugoslavia, and to set up the 'railway' network that took volunteers from Yugoslavia through Austria and Switzerland to France, and then on to Spain. In fact work proved to be far less dangerous than it would have been in Vienna but it required frequent visits to Yugoslavia to set up an organization. It was the first really big job on an international scale that Tito had had to tackle, and it gave him full scope for his *konspiracija* and talent for organization.

In Yugoslavia there was no shortage of volunteers to fight for the Spanish Republican army. They came from all classes, all parts of the country; from communists, left-wing sympathizers, idealists, from people disgusted with the lack of freedom in Yugoslavia, or with the continued lack of employment in the chronically backward parts of the country – and also from people who saw the Spanish Civil War as the last bastion in the fight against Nazism and Fascism in Europe.

First, Tito had to establish his communications with recruiting agents in the country; he had also to make arrangements for safe places where people could hide before being passed on to different stages of their journey. A chain of contacts had to be found in Yugoslavia, Austria and Switzerland and plans made for the journey through France and illegal crossing of the Pyrenees. It was an expensive operation, but money was provided by the Comintern, and by many voluntary contributions to Republican Spain from all over the world. Couriers travelled all the time – men and women, many of them young students – carrying messages, verbal or written, some in primitive code, others written in invisible ink on apparently innocent letters. Careful precautions were needed not only on account of the communists being sought by the police, but because the Yugoslav Ministry of the Interior had banned help to Republican Spain and considered all volunteers as communists.

Living in a small hotel – the Hôtel des Bernardins, rue des Bernardins – on the left bank in Paris, moving between contacts in the working-class suburbs and among students in the Latin Quarter, Tito gained many left-wing international contacts and became familiar with western life. He had to learn French, which he did by ploughing through the French communist paper *Humanité* every day. His headquarters were in a small bookshop called 'Horizonti' in the rue Echaudée near St Germain des Près, but he met many of his contacts in the streets and in cafés.[5] For a time such work in Paris was easy, though it became more difficult towards the end of the Spanish Civil War when right-wing politicians had come to power in France after the collapse of the Popular Front. As the international situation deteriorated, and Laval negotiated with Hitler and Mussolini, Yugoslav communists became convinced that the French Deuxième Bureau was working closely with the Yugoslav police against them.

For volunteers to Spain, the Yugoslav stages of the journeys were the most dangerous. One Yugoslav communist was arrested at his home the morning following his return from two years in Spain. The police had watched the house after reading all his letters to his wife. On interrogation by the police he told a typical story. Dressed as a tourist, he had first set out by train from Osijek to Zagreb. He had taken another train to Samobor and then walked into Slovenia, staying for a few days at a holiday house in Ptuj. From there he had gone hiking in the Alps and illegally crossed the Austrian border, making his way to Klagenfurt. Shortly after, having obtained false papers from a local contact, he had taken a train to Basle in Switzerland continuing a few days later by rail to Paris. There he had stayed at the Hôtel Moderne in the XXth arrondissement, while arrangements were made for his despatch to Spain. He had then travelled to Carcassone, and from there had taken a bus to the Spanish border where guides were waiting to take volunteers across the Pyrenees. The whole journey took about three weeks. He had been lucky on the way out in having an uneventful journey; others who attempted it were arrested, especially on the Yugoslav–Austrian border. But many illegal travellers got through both singly and in groups; some went in parties of three or four, and referred to themselves as 'Singeraši' since they posed as sellers of Singer sewing machines, whose commercial travellers were a common sight in the Balkans and other parts of Europe at this time.[6]

There were, of course, numbers of other volunteers who were not known to the police as wanted communists. They left Yugoslavia legally, travelling on their own passports; people like Koča Popović, who came from rich upper-class families, could travel to France without arousing suspicion. In 1937 Vladimir Dedijer went to Spain as a journalist. The fact that a world fair was held in Paris in 1938 was also a help, since parties could be arranged to visit it as normal excursions.[7]

The most ambitious scheme misfired. It was a bold and simple plan to move about five hundred volunteers by sea direct from Yugoslavia to Spain. At the beginning of March 1937, a French ship *La Corse* was hired for 700,000 French francs, and sent from Marseilles to pick up passengers near Budva on the Adriatic coast of Montenegro. According to Tito, Gorkić took charge of this operation and put arrangements in the hands of Adolf Muk, a former plumber and member of the Central Committee. The plan was grossly mismanaged. It was in any case on a scale difficult to conceal from the Yugoslav police, since hundreds of men converged from all over Montenegro and Dalmatia to a place not far from the Regent's summer residence at Miločer. Many small boats were assembled to row them out to the French ship after light signals had been exchanged with a lookout post in the mountainous hinterland. As darkness fell, and a brisk seasonal wind whipped up the waves, the ship tried to approach the coast. But boarding was impossible on 2 March. By the next night the police, who were already well aware of what was going on, had brought up reinforcements and cordoned off the area. Nearly everyone involved was arrested including Adolf Muk who, dressed as a French sailor, was on the ship when it was boarded by a Yugoslav patrol. A Comintern 'instructor' jumped overboard and escaped. Under interrogation by the police, Muk gave information about the whole communist organization and arrests escalated throughout the country.[8]

This disastrous episode caused trouble for the committee in Paris which was called to account by the Comintern. Although Tito had been involved – he had among other things gone to Brest to make arrangements about hiring a ship – he was able to exculpate himself by proving that the operation had been in the hands of Gorkić. He had been in Yugoslavia at the time and had himself reported the 'sensational news' in a letter the night after it had happened. Gorkić also wrote about it to the Comintern some ten days later, when he still did not know about Muk's arrest. He said that the only reason for the fiasco was the high wind, the *bura*, and asked the Comintern if the same scheme could be tried again a month later. Tito also wrote to Dr Pavle Gregorić to ask if a second attempt to send volunteers by sea was feasible. Gregorić replied that it was impossible as the

113

authorities all along the coast were alerted. So the overland route, getting more dangerous all the time, had to be continued.[9]

About 1,300 Yugoslav volunteers – some 560 being Communist Party members – reached Spain and joined the Republican Army, fighting mainly with the 129th International Brigade in some of its appropriately named battalions – such as Djuro Djaković, Dimitrov and Masaryk. More than half of these (about 700) were killed, or died in prison camp shortly after the war, and over 300 were wounded. A high proportion of the Yugoslavs became officers in the Republican Army – 274 in all including two lieutenant colonels, eight majors, thirty-five captains, 105 lieutenants and eighty-five non-commissioned officers. There were also thirty-nine political commissars, seven at battalion level. One, the former Comintern trainee and Central Committee member who had fallen into disgrace in Moscow, Blagoje Parović, was commissar at brigade level and was killed in the fighting.[10] For the Yugoslav communists this was to have more importance than a mere role of honour, for of the three hundred to get back to Yugoslavia, nearly all joined Tito's Partisans during the war. Their battle experience, their political indoctrination in the International Brigades, their experience of guerrilla warfare, were all invaluable to Tito in building up his army to fight the Germans and Italians. Four of these 'Spaniards' as they came to be called, were in charge of Tito's four main army groups that pursued the retreating Germans in major military operations at the end of the war. Tito himself said he would have liked to be a volunteer, but the Comintern never permitted him to visit Spain. It was fortunate that he did not, since many of those who went to Spain were later to be killed in Stalin's purge.

The other part of Tito's work at this time was to start on his job of resuscitating the Communist Party in Yugoslavia and purging its leadership at home and abroad of people who were factious and disobedient. It was a daunting task. The syndrome of the past few years had been recurring phases of reorganization followed by wholesale arrests; this had been repeated time and again until all but the most daring or foolhardy were frightened to be active in any way. With the spate of arrests following the capture of party documents in Vienna, the Yugoslav police became very well informed. It had always been their policy to infiltrate communist organizations, and with increased information they were able to do this most successfully, and sometimes at the highest level, and possibly among Yugoslavs in the Comintern. Argumentative and undisciplined at the best of times as past years had shown, Yugoslav communists became openly dissatisfied with the way the party was run, and uncooperative with the Central Committee, whose leaders gave orders but ran few risks. Mutual mistrust led to quarrels, and members suspected each other of being police informers.

It was Tito's problem to stop this rot, and even allowing for the hero-worship that was later to glorify all accounts of his work at this time, he seems to have set about it in a most vigorous and methodical way. He spent the greater part of the first seven months of 1937 in Yugoslavia, making brief visits to Paris to deal with volunteers for Spain and to attend Central Committee meetings. He also had to arrange about money – which at this time was supplied from Moscow – and the printing of leaflets and supply of propaganda material. From Tito's reports and from Gorkić's letters to the Comintern, it is possible to follow a good deal of Tito's work in these months. He travelled to most parts of Yugoslavia making contact either with known communists, or meeting personally people who had been recommended as possible communist sympathizers. A number of his assignations were connected with the Comintern's Popular Front policy and he contacted members of other political parties, including the Croat Peasant Party, and representatives of the legal, and mainly socialist trade unions.[11]

It was very dangerous work, and specially dangerous when he travelled across the frontiers to Paris. He had various aliases and changed his appearance and style of clothing, but in general his cover story was that of an affluent and successful engineer whose business interest required a lot of travelling. He lived the part to perfection, but he never became so addicted to it that he was unable to resume equally convincingly the role that he felt was his real self, that of the skilled working man. During the early part of 1937 he was in Split, Zagreb, Slovenia and Montenegro. From contacts that he is known to have made it is clear that he was trying to build-up an entirely new Party organization, with fresh and mainly young personnel who could be used in legal work and would not need to live an underground existence. Most communists with police records were useless for the time being, though he made a few individual exceptions; many of the old Party members were extremely independent and had strong local connections, and many groups were suspected of having been infiltrated by police. Among the people in

115

Slovenia whom Tito retained were Boris Ziherlj and Sergei Krajger. A separate party organization for Slovenia was founded on 17 April 1937 and further developments were left in the hands of the committee and of Edward Kardelj, who had also recently returned from his work in Moscow. In Croatia he contacted Leo Mates and Vladimir Bakarić, son of the judge who some years previously had been kind to Tito in Ogulin.

Work in Serbia was difficult because of strict police surveillance and he decided to begin through university students. The contact who was sent to Croatia to meet Tito to discuss political agitation among students at Belgrade University was Milovan Djilas, who travelled to Zagreb by train 'on the look out in case I was followed by a police agent', as he recalled later. At this meeting Tito told Djilas that the Central Committee of the party was going to stop being situated abroad and be located again in Yugoslavia. He also told him that an organization for Young Communists was to be founded and asked for suggestions for people to help run it. Djilas returned to Belgrade and consulted there with a member of his party cell, Alexander Ranković. Between them they decided to suggest the name of Ivo Lola Ribar to Tito.[12] By 1938 this small group, Kardelj, Ranković, Djilas and Lola Ribar, had become Tito's main lieutenants in party work and stayed with him for many years. With them were associated other members of the Politburo, Miko Marinko, Franc Leskošek and Ivan Milutinović. They were the inner, decision-making core of the Yugoslav Communist Party, and were so well chosen and soon became so well trained, that for the next four years, that is until Yugoslavia became involved in the second world war, they were able to run the party during Tito's sometimes long absences abroad, and during the war they became the nucleus of a military High Command.

Croatia presented a different problem, but it was one with which Tito, being a Croat and member of the Zagreb party, was familiar. The major problem among Croats was still Croatian nationalism, and the problem of whether to support the idea of Croatian autonomy, which the Comintern had previously insisted on, or the Yugoslav idea which had become communist policy with the change-over to Popular Front tactics. Not all Croatian communists had accepted the Yugoslav idea, and the issue remained unsolved until the outbreak of war. This meant that for some time Tito did not have sufficient authority in Croatia to force obedience from independent groups, and from party members who thought of themselves as senior to him. In their eyes he was a representative of the Comintern which itself was heartily disliked by many local communists. Tito tried to satisfy this independence by founding a separate party organization for Croatia which had been decided on by the Comintern as far back as 1934. The inauguration took place at a meeting of nineteen delegates held in the woods outside Samobor (Zagreb was considered too dangerous) in the middle of the night of 1/2 August 1937. Twelve people were elected to form a Croatian Central Committee.[13] This did not, however, put an end to Tito's difficulties in Croatia and for some time he had to proceed cautiously relying on the few people he could be sure of.

One of these friends was the writer Miroslav Krleža. He was also among the few people with whom Tito could relax and be himself, without the need to play a part or be withdrawn. They had known each other for a very long time and shared much common experience. Both had been at the same barracks during the first world war, though Krleža's war service had not taken him to Russia like Tito. They had met at political meetings when Tito had returned to Croatia after the war and discussed 'well-worn political themes' of 'what to do and how to do it'. In the early nineteen-twenties, Krleža had already found that Tito 'always showed complete conviction and certitude, but he was strangely obstinate – one could say he showed constant obstinacy'. In those early days, before Tito's outgoing character had hardened and closed under the protective covering necessary for survival during his years in gaol, his life in underground work and his apprenticeship in the Comintern, Tito had allowed the perceptive Krleža to see something of his innermost character. This remained a bond between them for life, although in later years Krliža often stuck firmly to views that were not popular with the party leaders.

In one of his visits to Zagreb in early 1937 Tito visited Krleža unannounced after a nine years' gap in their relationship. Krleža first thought it was a stranger at the door, but when he heard the 'clear, warm, friendly voice and hearty laugh', he knew who it was. 'At first sight I thought there was little change in him', said Krleža, 'but he had changed a lot, more than that, he had entirely changed. He was calm, sure and simple – like a man who has liquidated in himself all his doubts, and was conscious of his own vocation.' They spent the whole night talking. Krleža had just come back from Italy and told Tito about what he had seen of fascism there. Tito told Krleža how

117

one night when he arrived in Croatia he had been forced by some irresistible homing nostalgia to go back to the village of Kumrovec where he had been brought up, even though his family was no longer there, and even though it was extremely dangerous for him to be seen in the district. He had stood in the dark under the chestnut trees near his old home, had heard the dogs barking and the trickle of the stream, smelt the familiar smells of the village, including the next-door neighbour's dunghill and stables. He felt that nothing had changed – even to the dead cat in the stream and the creak of a broken gate.[14] Romantic nostalgia had evidently vied with the socialist realism and need for revolutionary change he felt he ought to be thinking about. Relaxation of this kind with a friend of his own age, of outstanding character and no less intelligent, was already rare in Tito's life, and was to become even rarer in the future, for he was now on the threshold of another change that was to separate him further from his contemporaries.

Tito was at this time only Organizing Secretary inside Yugoslavia. He was still responsible to Gorkić who was General Secretary with the Central Committee in Paris and had ultimate responsibility to the Comintern. He made two journeys to France in the first seven months of 1937 to report on his work. He attended a Central Committee meeting in Paris on 25 March, and was there again for a short time in mid-May. By midsummer, however, news began to reach Paris that Stalin's purge was beginning to be directed in earnest against foreign members of the Comintern. Gorkić was summoned to Moscow at the beginning of July and nothing further was heard from him. This was ominous; in addition, the Comintern cut off its payments to the Yugoslavs. Two committee members, Rodoljub Čolaković and Sretan Žujović, who had been appointed at the same time as Tito, but to work in Paris, wrote that he had better come to Paris as soon as possible. He arrived there on 17 August.[15] He was told that Gorkić had left for Moscow without too much alarm, saying that he thought he had been summoned for a dressing down – 'headwashing' as it was called in Russian.[16]

Gorkić's letters to the Comintern in the previous months confirm the impression that he had no presentiment of disaster. They had been almost naïvely outspoken and critical of the Russian leadership of the Comintern. They had shown no apparent awareness that the increasing administrative difficulties which he complained of might indicate a change in policy which held dangers for himself and his colleagues. His letters to 'Fleischer' (Ivan Grzetić) who was his contact in the Yugoslav section of the Comintern, had been full of optimistic accounts of his own work and of the reorganization of the party in Yugoslavia. He had complained repeatedly about how he was being hampered by lack of cooperation from the Comintern, with the hardly concealed implication that this was due to inefficiency or hostile intrigues. He said that his letters had not been answered; he had asked for ten sets of illegal identity papers and only received six; he was tired of being asked to send detailed financial reports and estimates: 'Five or six times I have written to tell you what our financial position is, now you are again asking for it . . . you say we shall only get what is necessary for May, yet today is the 22nd May and we still have no payment.' He complained that other communists, Poles, Austrians and Germans, got better treatment, that his own workers did not get consideration for the needs of their own personal lives; he had had no reaction to his request that Kardelj's wife be allowed to join him, that Tito's wife should be sent immediately. Tito, he wrote, had already made two trips down there – to Yugoslavia – and been in Paris twice waiting for his wife, without any result, and had had to go on his travels again. 'When you read this, don't curse us or put it down against the personal account of our people', Gorkić had written. 'If circumstances are such that you have to live like a monk, do not force others to put on a monk's habit and make them face the same temptations that you have had to suffer.' Yet elsewhere in his letters he indicated that he knew that all was not well in Moscow. 'Debelk's wife thinks that there is still "something against us" up there, because she is not allowed to go back home', he had written, apparently unconscious of the fact that wives were retained in Moscow as hostages for the good behaviour of their husbands. At the same time, he was receiving material from Moscow about the trials of Russians caught up in the purge. He had leaflets about this printed, but drew no warning from them for himself.[17] In spite of his experience in Comintern bureacracy and intrigues, Gorkić was clearly too self-confident, and perhaps too soft a man to foresee or cope with the situation that had developed in Moscow by the summer of 1937. He went to Moscow optimistically and without suspicion of the death that awaited him there. His disappearance was Tito's opportunity.

Tito himself believed both then and later that Gorkić had been responsible intentionally, or through culpable inefficiency, for the deaths and imprisonment of many Yugoslavs; that he had purposely excluded from responsible positions many gifted Party members who might have competed with him for the leadership. As late as 1948 Tito's comments on Gorkić were very bitter. But twenty years later he gave a more considered judgment. 'He was a very gifted bureaucrat and spent his whole life as a Comintern employee and for this reason was not popular with our people. But he did not organize well. Yet he was not a fool, and not a spy. He did a great deal of harm to our party, but this was no reason to liquidate him. He was something of a small dictator. I could not say that the things that went wrong in our party were deliberate on his part. Sometimes I had the impression it was intentional, sometimes not. But really he did not have the necessary knowledge of the situation inside our country to protect our cadres.'[18]

*　　*　　*

The news that Gorkić and other Yugoslavs in the Comintern had been arrested started a power struggle between a number of different groups in the Yugoslav party. As Organizing Secretary appointed by the Comintern, Tito had a claim to carry on the functions of Party Secretary until someone was appointed to replace Gorkić. But there were others also who had some kind of special mandate from the Comintern; one of these was Vladimir Čopić, and another was Janko Jovanović a teacher from Šabac who had worked for a long time for the Comintern both in Moscow and in Spain. 'When Gorkić was imprisoned,' said Tito later, 'the fractionalist struggle became more widespread because the question was posed – "Who would now become head of the party?" Those who were leading that fight hoped that I would not be given the mandate. They made various alliances against me and caused me a lot of difficulty.'[19]

Two members of the Central Committee in Paris whom Tito named as his bitterest enemies were Labud Kusovac and Ivo Marić. Kusovac had worked on arrangements for the volunteers for Spain, and it was among them as well as among students in Paris that he tried to get support. Tito had to work against them through his own friends. 'In Paris I was greatly helped by Boris Kidrić, and among fighters in Spain by Maslarić,' he said later. Kidrić was working as a journalist in Paris at that time. He was to remain a loyal supporter and intimate colleague of Tito until his death in 1953. Kusovac and

Marić while attending committee meetings called by Tito in Paris, were secretly in touch with Tito's most dangerous opponent – dangerous because he had a following in Yugoslavia and support in the Comintern – a young Montenegrin called Petko Miletić, who was at that time a political prisoner in Sremska Mitrovica gaol in Yugoslavia.[20]

Tito now made a determined bid to become Gorkić's successor. He saw clearly that if the Yugoslav Communist Party had any future at all, it was inside Yugoslavia, not in Paris, and certainly not in Moscow. He knew also that he must get backing from senior officials in the Comintern. He wrote to the head of the Balkan Section, Wilhelm Pieck on 28 August shortly after his arrival in Paris, giving a businesslike and detailed account of the work he had done in Yugoslavia since he had left Moscow. He stressed that he had followed Comintern orders and had begun to found a new party leadership from 'legal people'. To this letter and a number of others, as well as telegrams sent to Pieck over the next few months, he received no reply; but news filtered through to Paris of the terror in Moscow where Stalin's purge had at last struck in earnest against the foreign members of the Comintern. The Hôtel Lux had become 'something like a frontier village raided nightly by bandits as the NKVD came to take away their victims'.[21] In the middle of October 1937 Tito himself received a summons to Moscow to be interrogated about the situation in the Yugoslav party. He did not go; this was one of the vital decisions of his life. The order was eventually countermanded, by whose authority we do not know, but two Comintern officials whom Tito was later to say had helped him greatly were Wilhelm Pieck – who was probably concerned in this case – and Dimitrov.[22]

Tito's methods of gaining power and besting his opponents during the next few months were very similar to those he used at the beginning of the war. He threw himself with demonic energy into organizing political activity. He held Central Committee meetings in Paris, sent orders to all the people he had working for him in different parts of Yugoslavia requesting them to hold meetings, collect money, collaborate with the legal trade unions, work with the socialist group led by Živko Topalović. He sent Sreten Žujović and Rodoljub Čolaković to work in Serbia on these Popular Front activities, and thereby saved them also from making the fatal trip to Moscow whither they had already been summoned. He wrote many articles in party newspapers to explain his Popular Front policy for he knew that the Comintern always set great store on the printed word. He wrote letters in great numbers, including one to two party members, Nikola Kovačević and Srdjan Prica; the former had been sent to Canada and the United States to try to raise funds which Moscow had ceased to supply. He approached people in Yugoslavia for the same purpose. With the exception of twelve days visiting Vienna and Prague at the beginning of January 1938 to contact the Comintern 'teknik' there he spent the whole winter in Paris waiting for word from the Comintern.[23]

The most obdurate and personally dangerous opposition to Tito during the winter of 1937–38 came as a result of Petko Miletić's activities in Yugoslavia. He was a Montenegrin, younger than Tito and had already spent several years working in the Comintern where he had made friends with some of the Bulgarians. He made a strong bid to get accepted as Party leader, first among the prisoners, then by other communist groups in Yugoslavia, and finally through contacts in Moscow to get Comintern support. In the gaol Tito's old prison friend Moša Pijade was leader of the Tito supporters. Miletić used the weapon often employed by the NKVD against their victims and most difficult to counter, accusing Pijade of being a 'Trotskyist', and tried to have him thrown out of the party organization in the prison. But Miletić had taken on two redoubtable opponents. Pijade sent out coded messages which reached Tito in Paris. 'It was a struggle which lasted without interruption for two and a half months. It was possible to isolate Miletić and a small group of his supporters from the party organization only when Comrade Moša (Pijade) was given the mandate by the CC[ Central Committee, ed.] ... Moša carried the main burden on his shoulders. He did not undress for months. Discussion and disputes by day, while at night he wrote ciphered reports to the CC.'[24] Even when Tito and Pijade had won the encounter in Mitrovica, Miletić was not finished. He was determined to get the position of Secretary General for himself, and when he came out of gaol continued his intrigues against Tito in Moscow.

On 11 March 1938 Hitler's troops marched into Austria which was annexed to the Reich two days later. It was an ominous event for all Europe, and especially for Yugoslavia for it brought the Nazis to the Yugoslav frontier, and was clearly only a stage in further German expansion. Tito immediately wrote a declaration denouncing the *Anschluss* and had leaflets printed to be circulated secretly in Yugoslavia. He now decided that he could not stay any longer in

Paris waiting for orders from the Comintern. He must go to Yugoslavia and stay to clear up the situation there, establish his own authority and leave people in charge of communist organizations in different parts of the country who could carry on if he was summoned to Moscow, and who could be trusted to report back to take their orders from him. He knew he already had a nucleus of such people.

On 12 March 1938 the Zagreb police received a tip-off from an informer that Josip Broz, a member of the Central Committee of the Yugoslav Communist Party would shortly be coming back to Zagreb with the task of reorganizing the Communist Party in Croatia. He would be travelling on a forged Czech passport in the name of Engineer Josef Tomanek, born 15 March 1893 in Klatovy. The source of information was not disclosed but it seems more than likely that this was a case of his enemies giving the police information so that he could be arrested. Yugoslav frontier police were alerted at all possible places of entry along the Austrian and Italian borders with Croatia, and at the ports of Split and Dubrovnik.[25] Before the end of the month Tito under another name and with his hair very inexpertly dyed red – 'Comrade, your hair is not dyed well. A smart policeman would spot you at once,' said an acquaintance – was already in Belgrade.[26] He had used another passport and travelled by a different route. He spent two nights at a hotel, was followed by a plain clothes policeman, but managed to put him off the scent by posing as a visitor. Relaxed and self-assured, he went into a shop and bought a Turkish coffee set – an obvious tourist gift from a prosperous businessman to his wife. But he thought it better to change his lodging. Vladimir Dedijer who, although a sympathizer, was not at that time a party member, was persuaded by his communist friends Djilas and Lola Ribar to give Tito a bed in the attic of the family house in the middle of Belgrade. Tito stayed two nights at the Dedijer house, appearing only in the evening when he was tired and went straight to bed. But as Dedijer's mother pointed out, he was a dangerous guest; his toothpaste was French and his soap was bought in Czechoslovakia.

Two days after he left Belgrade, when the police were still on the lookout for him on the Austro–Italian frontier, Tito arrived in Zagreb by plane – with a ticket obtained by Lola Ribar from a relative working in the air company – 'wearing an elegant suit, looking more like a businessman than an *ilegalac*'.[27] Tito spent three months, from the middle of March to mid-June 1938, in Yugoslavia. He was still only acting General Secretary of the Yugoslav Communist Party, but he felt he had some Comintern support, as on 26 February he had at last received a reply to his many letters and telegrams to Wilhelm Pieck. He returned to Paris on receiving a message from Dimitrov that he was to get ready to go to Moscow. In the middle of July he wrote to Dimitrov: 'I have now been over a month in Paris where I came because you asked me to travel to see you. Although immediately after my arrival all necessary information was sent "above" [to the Comintern in Moscow, ed.], so that everything needed for my journey could be supplied, I am still waiting for my entry visa. The situation in our family [the Yugoslav Communist Party, ed.] makes it imperative that our problem be settled as soon as possible. That is why I beg you to do everything in your power to get my entry visa issued.

'My presence down there in the field is at present necessary for the family, since a whole series of highly important measures must be carried out, not only in connection with the general political situation in the country, but also in connection with the current situation in our family. For two and a half months I have been doing field work in all the more important spheres of activity, but I had to leave suddenly at your request, so that I could not completely achieve the most vital objectives.' He then went on to list the work he had done, including founding 'a provisional leadership to deal with immediate work'. Tito's letter continued 'Comrade Dimitrov, to this day we have succeeded in protecting the party not only against more serious upheavals, but we have also achieved good results. We have proved successful . . . because in the field we have a healthy element devoted to the party and the Comintern. But it is dangerous to prolong the present situation.' He then went on to denounce the intrigues of Marić and Kusovac and said that he had excluded them from party office. Marić, he continued, had been boasting in Yugoslavia that he had the confidence of the Comintern, and Tito suspected that he had been put up to this by some Comintern officials who had had a meeting with Marić without telling Tito. 'Why did he not invite me to their discussion since I was still here at the time?' Tito asked angrily. 'If nothing can be done to help, then at least chaos should not be created. . . . Comrade Dimitrov, would you please try personally to see to an early settlement of our problem? If there is no need for me to travel to meet you at your place, would you please allow me to go back to the country so that I can help as much as possible? If no confidence is placed in me, then it is essential to appoint someone else and to give him moral support. But not anyone from those rotten émigré circles. I feel a great responsibility to the party in the country and I cannot sit here like this any longer. In that connection I insist that we must rely on cadres in the country and that the leadership down there in the country must be under the control of the party. With comradely greetings from Valter.'[28]

Near the end of August 1938 Tito at last left Paris for Moscow. He travelled by plane via Stockholm and arrived in Moscow on the 24th. He found the atmosphere there tense with fear; those who had escaped in the terror of the preceding months were in a state of shock. Many had a fatalistic belief that it would be their turn soon and went to bed at night with a bundle of clothes beside them ready for the NKVD 3 a.m. knock on the door. The population of the Hôtel Lux had been more than decimated. The Comintern had been denounced as 'a nest of spies' and only one person had been left in both Polish and Hungarian sections; all the others had been arrested. KUNMZ had been dissolved, the Leninist School partly closed down and the Comintern offices had been moved in November 1937 from Makhovaya Street to a building in the Lenin Hills suburb.[29] Tito was instructed to go to work in the Foreign Languages Publishing House to help two other Yugoslavs, Čopić and Jovanović (Janković) who had started the job of translating Stalin's *History of the Bolshevik Party* into Serbo-Croat. Since administrative rules still applied in spite of the purge, he was paid quite generously for his work, and he saved the money against future need.

Tito must have been apprehensive, but he had come to Moscow to fight for his position, and his life. He did not intend to give up easily. He felt self-righteous about his own loyalty and had a burning sense of mission about his work. His whole life was committed, and if the worst came to the worst, it would have to be sacrificed. His attitude was a compound of idealism, courage and shrewd common sense. He lived quietly and unobtrusively, worked 'day and night' on the translation and was ready to make out a strong case for himself. He too, was summoned and interrogated about Yugoslavs who had been arrested, and told to write what he knew about them. According to his own account he said he could not do this as he knew very little about any of the Comintern people except Horvatin. He said he wrote objectively about him, saying Horvatin was well trained in theory, clever, of intellectual and not working-class background, that he had some petty-bourgeois characteristics, but was very popular. The next day he was asked if Horvatin was a Trotskyist to which he replied that he did not know. After that, he said, he was always careful to say that he knew nothing about the other Yugoslavs as he had never worked with them. We do not know if he was asked about Gorkić, who in any case had almost certainly been executed before this time.[30]

Over a hundred Yugoslavs were arrested in Stalin's great purge, many of them in November 1938. Some were imprisoned for long terms, but sixty or more, many of them dedicated communists, were killed. They included besides Kamilo Horvatin and Gorkić, Filip Filipović, Crgur, Voja and Radomir Vujović, Kosta Novaković, Vilem Horvat, Akif Seremet, Stjepan and Djuka Cvijić and Karlo Hudomal. Vladimir Čopić, Anton Mavrak and Mladen Čonić were also liquidated. Almost all these were communists who had worked in the Comintern for years. They included hardly any like Tito who were recent recruits to the Comintern. The full story of the Yugoslav part of this terrible episode will probably never be told since most of the witnesses are dead, and those who could talk now know only small parts of the picture. It is known that in addition to those arrested in 1937–38, there were others who met the same fate when they returned to Russia after the end of the Spanish Civil War. A few were released during the second world war to fight in the Red Army, some like Gorkić's wife, Beti Glan, who is still alive, survived long periods in gaol and eventually were released to retire to civilian life in obscurity. Djilas, who did not have personal experience of the purge, wrote that the Bulgarians were lucky because they had Dimitrov to protect them. It is known, however, that Dimitrov intervened on a number of occasions to help Yugoslavs, and Tito himself many times expressed gratitude for the help he received from him at this dangerous period.[31]

Tito was one of the few Yugoslavs in Moscow at this time who escaped with his life. Why and how he managed to escape is a subject for endless speculation. It has been suggested by his enemies that he saved himself by betraying his friends and colleagues, that he was an NKVD agent. There is no evidence to support either of these suggestions, and they are contrary to all we know of Tito's character, nor would such things have saved him had the Russians been bent on his elimination. Comintern procedure had always been to ask members to report on each other, and it is also certain that many reports had

(*right*): **13. Tito and Dr Ivan Ribar after being wounded in the Fifth Offensive, June 1943**

(*below*): **14. Slovenian delegation to the AVNOJ, November 1943, Jajce. Boris Kidrić** (*left*) **and Herta Has** (*second from left*).

(*above*): **15. Tito in Mlinište, Autumn 1942.**

(*below*): **16. Djilas, Kardelj and Ranković. Jajce, November 1943.**

been made on Tito. The character of the purge was such that it was the people with long periods of service whom Stalin wished to exterminate. Other Yugoslavs who, like Tito, arrived in Moscow just as the purge began, and those whose work was in Yugoslavia, were not so much affected. There were also certain elements of luck and random chance in Tito's escape. He was lucky to have been a fairly new recruit to Comintern work, lucky that Gorkić had wanted to use him for dangerous field work in Yugoslavia; lucky too that the Yugoslav party had reached crisis point before he became associated with the leadership so that he could not be blamed for things that went wrong before 1935. He was fortunate in knowing Russian and German well so that he could make himself clearly understood. Perhaps most fortunate of all, he came to the fore at a time when the international scene was changing so rapidly that it favoured the growth of communist support in Yugoslavia and helped him to make a success of party organization.

At the same time Tito's own character and behaviour were also important aids to his escape. He had strong nerves; he had been careful to be obedient and hardworking when in Moscow. He had not associated with any particular clique, nor made friends among the Russians, though he had done his best to win the approval of key people such as Dimitrov and Wilhelm Pieck. He knew how to control his tongue and never to speak about politics in places that were 'bugged'. On one occasion when his son Žarko came rushing into his room in the Hôtel Lux with stories of the latest arrests, Tito had had to lead him out into the park and instruct him on the importance of keeping quiet.

Tito himself believed that his own efforts were more important than elements of luck in saving him from the purge, and it is true that it was his own decision not to go to Moscow in 1937, when even his skill and Dimitrov's and Pieck's protection might not have been able to save him. 'It was my own doing', he said much later when looking back on these events. 'I saw what it was all about and was careful to concern myself only with Yugoslav affairs, and that was why they had no holds to drag me in by. It was certainly not chance.'[32]

# 8 GENERAL SECRETARY OF THE PARTY

Tito was not officially appointed General Secretary of the Yugoslav Communist Party until early 1939; this was more than a year later than has usually been supposed.[1] Even after he had arrived in Moscow in the summer of 1938 it was still not clear whether the Russians who controlled the Comintern would confirm Tito's leadership, or whether they intended to dissolve the party altogether. As Dimitrov had summoned Tito to Moscow it may be assumed that he wished him to have the job of General Secretary, but he had to persuade Manuilsky and the other Russians that this would be in their interests; it was a slow process. Even after Tito's appointment, Manuilsky still spoke of the Yugoslav party as broken up by provocateurs and spies. 'You know when the question arose of appointing a secretary of the Yugoslav Party, there was some wavering,' said Dimitrov to Milovan Djilas in 1945, 'but I was for Valter. He was a worker, and he seemed solid and serious to me. I am glad that I was not mistaken.'[2] 'As to Manuilsky,' Tito remembered later, 'sometimes he was on our side, sometimes on the other. At first he supported the other side but in the end came to the conclusion that we should have his support.'[3]

Tito also remembered how other foreign communists were frightened to associate with Yugoslavs at this time when the purge had not yet run its course. One day when he was eating in the restaurant of the Hôtel Lux with Veljko Vlahović, recently returned from Spain and appointed secretary of the International Division of Communist Youth, Vlahović pointed out that no one would sit at their table. 'It is of no importance,' said Tito confidently, 'one day they will be falling over each other's chairs to sit with us.'[4] These were brave words indeed, for Yugoslavs were still being arrested in Moscow at this time; even Tito's two colleagues working on the translation of Stalin's *History* soon disappeared, though they were men who might have been thought to be immune from arrest. Čopić had been a member of the Comintern's Central Committee.[5]

The real issue facing the Russians was whether they wished to keep the Yugoslav party in being or not. If they wanted to reactivate the party, there was no suitable and experienced Yugoslav left except Tito. He had proved himself to be loyal, tough, hardworking, and above all willing to take orders and accept the current party line. He was also a worker and not a despised intellectual. He had kept the party in being during the past twelve months even though it had been almost totally neglected by the Comintern. All this, however, could have been set aside had the Russians felt it would have served their interests to dissolve the Yugoslav party. But by the end of 1938 they must have known that war in Europe was inevitable, and an active party in Yugoslavia under an obedient leader could be seen as likely to be more useful than no party at all.

Nearly two months after his arrival in Moscow Tito still had not been received by Dimitrov although Yugoslav communists and Tito had had an interview with Manuilsky. On 17 October 1938 he again wrote an urgent letter asking for a decision about 'our question'. He sought permission to go back to Yugoslavia to take charge of communist party work for a general election there scheduled for early December. He asked if he could see Dimitrov and wrote: 'I have long been convinced that my meeting with you will have historical significance, not only for me personally, but for the development of our Party.'[6] Three days later Dimitrov received Tito. At an earlier meeting Dimitrov had said to him: 'Tell me Valter, do you have a party organization in Yugoslavia?' On this occasion, after all his own work in Yugoslavia in 1937 and 1938, Tito was able to give a detailed and optimistic report about the organization that he personally had set up with Yugoslav resources and without assistance from the Comintern. There is no full record of this conversation, though Tito later recounted the gist of it on several occasions. Dimitrov evidently gave Tito a typical Comintern dressing down about the past misdeeds of the Yugoslav party, threatening that it might be dissolved – as had already happened to the Polish party – unless Tito produced the required results. But in the end he confirmed that Russian authorities had agreed to offer Tito the job of General Secretary. 'I accepted Dimitrov's offer and said "We will wash away the stain",'[7] Tito recalled, adding on another occasion 'I had no ambition to take over leadership of the party, nor ever had. But I wanted the leadership to be strong, firm and revolutionary. I had never thought of becoming the head, but I did want the head to be a man who could work. What was important to me was that the collective should be strong, that the leadership should be strong; not one man, but a whole collective.'[8] This was perhaps an understatement, for Tito had certainly made a strong bid for the leadership.

Although Tito had got the mandate for his position of Party leader, it still had to be ratified by the Comintern before he could leave Moscow. Formal confirmation was probably given at a Comintern Secretariat meeting on 5 January 1939. Before this happened Tito had had to deal with a final attempt to undermine his position from Petko Miletić, the man who had fought him for the position of party leader after the disappearance of Gorkić in 1937. Towards the end of 1938 Miletić finished his gaol sentence in Yugoslavia and after a short visit to his native region of Kosmet, he disappeared. He had friends among the Bulgarian personnel of the Comintern, including Karl Lukanov, Stella Blagoieva and Damianov, the powerful secretary of the Balkan Sekretariat Personnel Division. Unknown to Tito, Miletić succeeded in travelling to Moscow via Bulgaria and Istanbul, and was given a job in the Comintern. Travelling on a Moscow bus one day, Tito saw someone whose face he recognized, and eventually realized it was Miletić. Disturbed and annoyed that he had not been told anything about Miletić's arrival, he went to see Damianov who declared he knew nothing about it. Tito, however, realized that Miletić was making a determined effort to ruin him. He learned that Miletić had submitted a report accusing him of Trotskyism, the charge which had sent so many other Yugoslavs to their deaths.

Tito was summoned before the Comintern investigation commission which was the instrument for purging foreign communists. He had to face what he called 'absurd' charges of having put Trotskyist ideas in his translation of the *History*; it was also alleged that he was a member of the German minority in Yugoslavia and had been associated with German Trotskyists. He has never given a detailed account of his investigation, but has said that he managed to prove the accusations were false, and was helped in this by Florin, the German communist who was President of the Comintern Control Commission. It is often said that Dimitrov hid Tito in his apartment on one occasion when the NKVD were looking for him, and it is most likely that it was at this time. Once he had been cleared it was obvious that Tito had won the struggle against Miletić, who left Moscow. His friends had helped him to flee to a holiday home in the Crimea, and he thereafter disappeared. It was assumed that he, too, had been imprisoned or killed. His ultimate fate is not known, though there were rumours that he was seen again in Moscow in 1945 and that he was later associated with the savage Cominform campaign to overthrow Tito in 1948. The fight with Miletić had been a vicious struggle for power in which Tito's life had been in danger, and thirty years later his references to it still show the bitterness he felt about it.[9]

Tito left Moscow at last at the beginning of March 1939. He travelled on a Swedish passport in the name of John Alexander Karlson, born in Stockholm on 23 December 1897. He travelled by sea from Leningrad to Le Havre, then took a train via Switzerland to Yugoslavia. He slipped off the train at Venice and took a boat to the small port of Sušak near Rijeka, where he believed police control was less strict than on the Italo–Yugoslav frontier.[10] It was now the end of March 1939, and the situation in Europe was moving inexorably towards war. On 15 March the Nazis marched into Prague; Czechoslovakia was broken up, Slovakia given independence. On 28 March the Spanish Civil War virtually came to an end with Franco's capture of Madrid. On 7 April Mussolini's troops invaded Albania. The ring was closing round Yugoslavia and Tito knew now that he had very little time left to set up an effective party organization before war broke out. He also knew that he was likely to be recalled to Moscow both to report on his work and because he had not yet finished the tedious job of getting through the press his Yugoslav translation of the *History* – on which the Russians set such symbolically high store.

\*     \*     \*

During the period of Tito's position as temporary acting General Secretary of the Yugoslav Communist Party its members had doubled from 1,500 in the autumn of 1937, to 3,000 in May 1939. They rose steeply again in the next three years; by 1940 they totalled 6,455, and when the Germans finally invaded Yugoslavia in the spring of 1941 they had reached 12,000. Membership figures for the Communist Youth Organization (SKOJ) showed a similar increase – from 2,000–3,000 in 1935 they rose to 9,000 in 1938, and to 17,800 (including active supporters) by September 1939.[11] These obviously rounded figures were based on area reports submitted by local secretaries. It is possible that they were optimistic, but there is no reason to doubt the trend of increased membership that they show. Nor is there reason to doubt that they reflected Tito's energetic and efficient leadership. They also reflected the big impetus to recruitment given by the Popular Front policy which was being carried out against a background of deteriorating political conditions and in an atmosphere tense with expectation of war. Though the blueprint for communist organization was the one that was provided by the Comintern for all communist parties, the method and team spirit in which it was executed in Yugoslavia was determined by Tito himself. Policy was received, doctrine communicated from Russia, its interpretation and methods of execution were decided by the Party's Politburo, whose members were all Yugoslavs. Whether he was in Yugoslavia or Moscow, Tito was the final arbiter. Of necessity he had to delegate much of the work, but he managed to be informed about all that went on and keep control in the hands of the team he had chosen.

There can be no doubt that Tito's position as leader was strengthened by the fact that the Moscow purge had eliminated or discredited almost all the Yugoslav communists who had been important in the leadership in earlier generations. Tito's new leaders were young and very few – other than Kardelj and Tito himself – had been to Moscow for training. A number of Moscow trained Yugoslavs, among them Čolaković and Žujović, were given posts of relative obscurity at this time, and only returned to prominence after the outbreak of war. It was a deliberate policy of concentrating on youth – youth that had no connection with the feuds of the past, that had not suffered the shock of losing colleagues and friends in the purge, that was dynamic and involved with contemporary political issues. This policy had far reaching results.

The young people whom he gathered round him by personal selection between 1937 and 1941 were to become the officer class for his army during the war and, in spite of heavy losses, they later supplied the top people in communist government. Most of them were selected or vetted by Tito, and were known to him personally. Some of them became his friends. And for almost all there was a mystique in their attachment to him which lasted for many years. This owed something to the tense conditions of the times and the heightened emotional relationships of a secret society, for the Communist Party was still illegal. It also owed much to Tito's charismatic personality, his gift for leadership, his capacity to win loyalty and affection especially from men younger than himself.

There was in this relationship a strong element of the masculine comradeship which is roused when men share danger and face death together. There were also elements of the patriarchal society in which men had a special position, a special authority. This was the kind of society in which Tito had been brought up; in varying degrees it was the background of all the other South Slavs, the Serbs, Croats, Slovenes, Montenegrins, Bosnians, who all provided the new leaders. Their folk-inheritance translated easily into the authoritarian, yet in some respects democratic system that Tito had evolved for his own Party. The idea of a heroic leader was traditional among the South Slav peoples. It helps to explain why Tito was so much of a father-figure to his followers. Was it also entirely coincidence that many of his close associates were the young men who had been made fatherless by the great losses in the first world war? Known already to his intimate followers as 'Stari' – the old man – he was a combination of father-figure, village elder, protector and legendary hero, and he knew to perfection how to maintain the right mixture of intimacy, aloofness and authority for this role.

Associates from these days stress that though Tito was very authoritarian, he always discussed problems with them, listened to what they had to say, and tried to make joint decisions with them. Young people were carefully recruited but were not at first pressurized into joining the party. Membership was made to seem difficult, a reward given to those who had proved themselves. An example of this can be seen in the case of Vladimir Dedijer, who worked for the party for over a year before it was suggested that he should become a member. He acted as courier, bringing documents concealed in music sheets back from Paris and fetching Comintern papers from Sofia. He frequently put up visiting communists in his home in Belgrade. On the first occasion when Tito had stayed with him, sleeping in a bed in the same room, they had two general conversations about the ideas of communism. One had been in the watches of the night, while Tito lay awake chain-smoking. The other was at a specially arranged meeting in the Topčider Park. But Tito made no suggestion that he should become a communist. Dedijer was at this time as useful outside the party as in it. He was asked to join the party after the outbreak of war in 1939, and after he had spent a day in goal but had been released because his father-in-law was an ex-royal minister. 'We have tested you. You deserve the honour,' Djilas had said on inviting him to become a member.[12] In the party

Dedijer was first assigned to a cell of shoemakers, to give him at least a suggestion of working-class experience; a month later he was moved to a cell of lawyers.

Another young man with whom Tito worked very closely in these years, whom he loved dearly and treated almost as his deputy in party work, was the gifted and dynamic Ivo Lola Ribar. Since 1937 he had been working as Organizing Secretary for the Communist Youth. Small, dark and highly intelligent, Lola Ribar came from a wealthy Zagreb family. His father, Dr Ribar, had been President of the National Assembly of the new Yugoslav state when the Vidovdan constitution was passed in 1921. Devoted to his two sons, both communists and both to be killed during the war, Dr Ribar became during the 'thirties more and more in sympathy with their political ideas, and helped in many ways with their communist activities. Finally, during the war, he joined the communists himself and became the President of Tito's first wartime parliament.

In prewar Yugoslavia, in which to be upper class (there was no aristocracy) meant to have influential connections in business, government, judicial and senior police circles, Lola Ribar had powerful protection for himself, and sometimes for his associates. On one occasion when he was arrested, his father was able to complain to his friend the prime minister Cvetković, who ordered his immediate release.[13] It was said that Lola Ribar himself had been known to arrive at a communist organized street demonstration in the family Cadillac, driven by a uniformed chauffeur. His resources – which included his own bachelor flat – were put at Tito's disposal and used for disguise, hiding, travel and all the other complicated arrangements of the life of an *ilegalac*. He also helped in finding houses that were above police suspicion for the secret party meetings.

The Ribars had personal connections with students from families of their own class and helped to recruit many useful educated members into SKOJ. These young people accepted without question the derogatory party line about their bourgeois origins and the disapproval of intellectuals. 'Your duty is to prove your allegiance to the working class every day every moment,' a Central Committee man told Vladimir Dedijer.[14] The guilt of belonging to a small privileged class spurred them on to greater efforts. But Lola Ribar, like Tito, had the capacity to mix with young people of all classes and students from other countries, including England, where he had close friends. He was also a brilliant orator, able to whip up support at student meetings for demonstrations of all kinds – against government policy, or for better conditions and more scholarships for students.

SKOJ, which Lola Ribar organized so well, was a semi-autonomous organization, in the Stalinist sense of autonomy. This meant that it accepted the policy and directives of the Moscow-controlled Communist Youth International, and of the Politburo of the Communist Party, but had its own machinery of officers and committees, congresses and conferences for endorsing those decisions, and dealing with the tactics for their execution. Unlike the Communist Party, which Tito had made largely self-supporting after 1937, SKOJ was dependent for some – but by no means all – of its financing on funds supplied from the International Youth Organization in Moscow, with which it had its own means of direct communication. But with Lola Ribar in charge, the position of SKOJ as a subsidiary arm of the Yugoslav Communist Party was never in doubt.

In May 1937 Tito himself had outlined a new policy for SKOJ in an article he wrote in the official party newspaper *Proleter*. The article expounded ideas that had been promulgated in the Comintern and the Youth International in Moscow – especially the Popular Front theme of trying to recruit support among young people of all kinds – peasants and intellectuals, as well as workers. SKOJ's new task, wrote Tito, was to fight against fascism and 'for bread, peace and freedom, for a safer and more cheerful life'. This was not quite such a hackneyed suggestion as might appear nowadays. Many of the peasant and working-class students at Yugoslavia's universities and technical schools were too poor even to stay in residence and attend lectures; having enrolled they returned home with a few books and reappeared at university only to take their examinations, or if communists, to take part in demonstrations. The promise of more bread had a real meaning for them. Peace, freedom and greater security also had desperate importance as the Nazis extended their conquest in central Europe. Tito said that SKOJ must include all youth – peasants, students, young workers and townspeople. It must get down to grass roots, to the real needs and ways of life of young people, and it must make more provision for cultural activities, education, entertainments and sport, the sort of things that Tito himself had found most useful when he had been a youth straight out of the village.[15]

The new SKOJ membership provided plenty of volunteers for the

135

many auxiliary jobs in party organization. Members demonstrated in the streets and universities. One of the biggest successes for the Popular Front policy was the way in which SKOJ managed to gain cooperation from many of the students' organizations and clubs at Belgrade university. Here political activities were relatively easy to organize because of the autonomous status of the university which allowed meetings to be held and leaflets to be printed and cyclostyled without police interference. 'We could carry on revolutionary activities almost undisturbed within the university walls,' said Vukmanović-Tempo, one of the communist leaders who helped to organize communist youth in Serbia. Communists and their sympathizers, students and others, could demonstrate with comparative freedom. If the police chased students into the university precincts, they were infringing university freedom. Some university professors supported the students against the police.[16] SKOJ members also acted as couriers, international as well as within Yugoslavia; they distributed newspapers and leaflets. Numbers of them were arrested, many were beaten up by the police, some even died. Women students were particularly useful in many of these jobs; they were not subject to military call-up, were easier to disguise, and more difficult to apprehend.

There was a higher proportion of women members in SKOJ than in the party. In a society in which the idea of male superiority had deep roots, among women as well as men, the Communist Party made continued efforts to bring women into their activities. They had a variety of periodicals – *Women's World, Today, Woman* – in which efforts were made to put across the ideas of equal rights for women – which many communists neither believed in, nor acted upon. As late as 1940 Tito addressed a meeting about its errors in this field. 'It not infrequently happens,' he said sternly, 'that even party members have an uncomradely attitude towards their wives, and even beat them. Others are still inclined to marry several times. Some of the women comrades have a petty bourgeois attitude towards men. All this greatly impairs the prestige, both of the comrades themselves, and of the party.'

A friend of Dedijer's, a communist who had served a three-year gaol sentence and who, after he came out of gaol, was known as the Goat, or Buck, because of his sexual prowess, illustrated one of the reasons for Tito's complaint. 'I belong to the old generation of communists who believe in free love,' he said, knotching up a mark on the table leg to indicate his latest conquest. 'I know that the present Party line is different – puritanism, revolutionary puritanism. I think I should adopt the Victorian custom and cover the legs of my table . . .'[17]

In spite of such backslidings, the Yugoslav Communist Party had a special significance for women as it had for young people. Neithe group had freedom or recognition in a contemporary society in which older men had all the power and were supposed to have all the wisdom. Young men had to wait until they were old; women had to be submissive and obedient – content with petticoat influence. Neither young people nor women had the vote. Other political parties made little use of them, though there were youth organizations among the Croat Peasant Party, the Frankovci in Croatia and the clerical parties of Slovenia. So work of both groups in the Communist Party offered an escape into a modern world, away from the inhibitions of what seemed like a static society. The party made use of these feelings and the recruitment of women and youth was to be invaluable in wartime.

Tito's own attitude to women seems to have combined orthodox communist theory with certain attitudes prevalent both in communist practice and in the society he lived in. In the communist movement, as his speech had shown, women had equal rights in theory, but none had a position in the topmost hierarchy, though a small number reached positions of secondary importance. In private life Tito was very attractive to women, and enjoyed their company; he had several close women friends during his career. But he never allowed his personal relations to interfere with his job; his private life was always subordinated to his duty to the party and he did not wish his women friends to be associated with the risks of his career.

\*     \*     \*

Tito was proud of the fact that he was the first General Secretary to make the Yugoslav Communist Party financially independent. This eliminated one major cause of friction with the Comintern, and between individual workers. It also weakened the hold of the Comintern over the Yugoslav party. The income from Moscow had to be replaced by a levy on members, by donations solicited from Yugoslav communists abroad – especially in the United States and Canada – and by donations in money or services from rich party

137

members or sympathizers in Yugoslavia. As the party's membership increased, its income grew.[18] Subscriptions were paid according to means. One member might pay fifty dinars, others who could not afford this could pay ten, but were encouraged to find four other members who also would donate ten dinars, and this was accounted to their credit.[19] Even so, the party experienced severe financial need in the early days of Tito's stewardship. When Gorkić had been General Secretary in 1934, the Yugoslav Communist Party had received from Moscow the equivalent in Yugoslav or foreign currency of 400 gold roubles per month with an additional monthly sum of 200 gold roubles for youth organization. Extra payments were also made to people whom the Comintern required for special duties. Though 400 roubles was a considerable sum at the current rate of exchange, it had to cover a wide variety of expenditure – renting and running a large and busy office, post and telephones for couriers and other staff. There were also travel costs and personal living expenses for staff. Gorkić's office also had to support many visitors and a number of dependents. His budget did not in theory (though it sometimes did in practice) include the dependents of political prisoners in Yugoslavia who were cared for by a special Moscow agency known as Red Help. Another charge on Gorkić's budget in Vienna had been the cost of printing propaganda material which had been written in the Comintern offices and was often quite valueless for use in Yugoslavia. Very little of these printing costs could be recovered, though up to 1939 some money was received from sales to party members in the United States and Canada. In fact Gorkić had not always found his income sufficient, nor paid with enough regularity to leave him free from financial worries.

The normal scale of payment to members working full-time for the party had not been lavish, though some had perhaps done well out of travelling expenses. In 1929, for example, monthly payments to include rent and subsistence had been 500 dinars; payment for a courier had been 100 dinars. Some comrades with special duties had sometimes received sums varying between 1,300 and 1,800 dinars per month, which had been about the contemporary wages of a school-teacher.[20] When the value of money changed in the nineteen-thirties, payments had been stepped up and the normal monthly allowance was raised to 600 dinars. This had been the sum that Tito had been authorized to offer when he had recruited party workers in 1934. But in 1937, after the Moscow subsidy was stopped, monthly payments for party workers in Yugoslavia were reduced to 300 dinars, which was only just enough for the barest subsistence.[21]

When Tito became General Secretary he told Dimitrov that the Yugoslav party would provide its own finances, but certain international activities were still paid for by the Comintern. These included any jobs undertaken specially for the Comintern, as for instance, Tito's journeys to and from Moscow, certain activities of SKOJ, and possibly some publications. Tito's own living expenses when he was in Yugoslavia were not paid by the Comintern, although his elaborate cover as a prosperous engineer with a house, car, telephone, piano and other perquisites of the bourgeois life must have been quite costly. Many expensive items – travel by plane, the chauffeur for his car and expensive clothes – were obtained cheaply through the wide network of party connections. At this time, as indeed throughout his life, Tito enjoyed this kind of luxury. It impressed people including members of his own party and justified itself by the fact that it provided both successful cover and satisfactory relaxation for a very active undercover agent. If his communist conscience was troubled at his brief spells of bourgeois existence – and there is no evidence that it was – there was also the other side of his existence to be taken into account; he had to spend many night-sharing hide-out rooms with poorer comrades, and had long spells of dangerous and humiliating duty in Moscow where conditions of life were more rigorous, though even there he was adequately paid and had privileges appropriate to his position.

\* \* \*

The approach of war provided an atmosphere of frustrated apprehension which made it much easier for Tito and his colleagues to work for a Popular Front policy as prescribed by the Comintern. As the Communist Party was still illegal it could not try to organize open coalition with legal parties in opposition to Prince Paul's government; but the communists initiated negotiations with various political leaders to try to arrange some kind of working coalition. None of these arrangements was very successful because opposition parties in Serbia, Croatia and Slovenia were organized on a regional basis and were not in any case anxious for communist support. In the election held in December 1938 none of the parties would accept communist-sponsored candidates since they believed – quite rightly as it turned out – that the united opposition would receive communist votes. In Serbia the Popular Front policy had some success in gaining support from left-wing people outside the main parties. Dr Ribar, sympathetic to many of the communist policies anyway, was expelled from the Democratic Party in March 1938 and formed a shortlived pro-communist party of the Democratic Left. A professor of Belgrade university, Dr Dragoljub Jovanović, also formed his own party – the People's Peasant Party, which for a time worked with the communists. But these formed a slender basis for a Popular Front.

In Slovenia and Croatia, the main opposition parties also refused to have any dealings with a Popular Front, but communists were successful in joining cultural and educational groups and social clubs. Once accepted in membership they were very active, and were able to recruit members for the Communist Party. In Croatia, they dominated the Independent Democratic Party which they claimed only existed by means of their support. They also worked closely with the youth and student organizations of the Croat Peasant Party (HSS), and had control in some of its committees. When Maček, the party leader since the murder of Radić in 1927, joined the government just before war broke out, he was in a position to take a fearful revenge on the communists who were at that time opposed to the war. In Serbia and other parts of the country political prisoners were released from gaol as the Germans were about to take over the country. Maček refused to release communists from Croatian gaols so that most of them were killed when handed over to the Germans. Vladimir Bakarić only got out of gaol because of his father's influence. He led the unsuccessful delegation that went to Maček to plead for the release of communists. Maček's refusal to save these communists from the death which eventually overtook them, was one of the many reasons why he had to escape from Yugoslavia to save his own life when the Germans had been defeated.

Tito also stepped up Party work in the many non-communist trade unions, and managed to increase the party's much desired working class support. As in the earlier period trade union activity was most successful in Croatia, Dalmatia and in some unions in Slovenia. But among the steel workers and miners at Jesenice and Trbovlje as late as 1940, the Communist Party only had twenty-two members out of 5,000 workers. There was also similar resistance to communist activity in industries in Serbia where Tito had earlier found union work difficult. The number of party workers in many

Serbian towns could be counted on the fingers of one hand even in 1939.[22]

The vast majority of the population in Yugoslavia up to the outbreak of war lived on smallholdings in the countryside, most in conditions of great poverty, many below subsistence level and near starvation. Yet the Communist Party also had difficulty in gaining support in the countryside, except in Montenegro where there was a strong fighting radical tradition, and an old link with Tsarist Russia had been carried over to support for the Soviet Union. By 1941 the party claimed it had the backing in Montenegro of 12,000 men – 1,800 party members, 3,000 in SKOJ and the rest sympathizers – out of a total population of 400,000. But elsewhere peasants remained conservative, mistrustful, cautious.

In many parts of the country there was still a marked tendency to regional independence which lasted until after the outbreak of war. This was evident in all the major regions in Croatia, Slovenia, Serbia, Montenegro and Macedonia. The achievement of a united, monolithic, unanimous party eluded even Tito. He continued to have difficulties with Croatian separatists and Macedonian nationalists, with independence and disobedience in Dalmatia. Some writers in the party refused to accept the deadening directive of socialist realism and fought against the Stalinist control that more fanatical leaders such as Djilas tried to impose. Tito's friend Krleža was one who fought for literary freedom, denouncing Djilas and two fanatical associates as 'the three rams', and refused to accept orders on what and how he should write.

But in general Tito could claim with truth that he had more than fulfilled the task that the Comintern had rather reluctantly assigned to him. What was not so obvious at the time was that the Popular Front policy changed the international basis of the Communist Party in Yugoslavia. For the first time it had allowed communists to mix freely with other political groups in the country, to appeal to people on matters of national self-interest. It was this national appeal that helped recruitment to the party, and weakened the hold of the Comintern on the Yugoslav Communist Party for the first time since the nineteen-twenties.

# 9 PREPARING FOR WAR

Tito's reactivation of the Yugoslav Communist Party was carried on against the background of German territorial expansion that eventually led to war. For Yugoslavia, as for other European countries, the danger became imminent with Hitler's march into the Rhineland in March 1936 and the annexation of Austria a year later. Up to this time it had been possible for Yugoslav politicians to accept the policy followed by King Alexander until his death in 1934. This had been that Italy, because of her territorial claims, was Yugoslavia's main enemy. Germany, with no direct interest in the Adriatic or eastern Europe was regarded as a potential ally. But after the Munich agreement in 1938 it was impossible to ignore the threat of Nazi expansionist policies. With the German invasion of Czechoslovakia and the Italian invasion of Albania in 1939, Yugoslavia's position was desperate. The Yugoslav leaders were faced with the insoluble task of trying to find a policy that would defend the country's independence and territorial integrity, and at the same time avert the still undefined German aims to make Yugoslavia into some form of puppet state.

In 1935, before the German danger was clearly spelled out, Prince Paul the Yugoslav Regent had appointed Milan Stojadinović prime minister. Even at this time Stojadinović was known to support the earlier theory that Germany as an enemy was less dangerous than Italy. 'If it comes to a choice between Italy and Germany, there is no question at all as to which we would prefer,' his foreign minister Bogoljub Jevtić told Sir Nevile Henderson, 'Germany recognizes Yugoslavia and would be willing to work with us.'[1]

Stojadinović also had personal motives in preferring Germany as an ally, since he hoped that German protection would give him a special position of power in Yugoslavia. He went to great lengths to cultivate German friendship, laying on lavish parties for visiting Nazis and the German diplomatic corps. At one such hunting party, which was witnessed by an Austrian diplomat, von Wimmer, he provided 'sleighs, flourishes and fanfares, and silver and linen bearing the coat of arms of the Archduke Frederick. On the day after the hunt, trumpets summoned the guests to a great tent and a banquet table laden with wines and food. In high spirits generated by his native plum brandy, Stojadinović began to dance the *kolo* with the German minister's wife. As the dance gathered momentum he became more and more excited, and soon jumped on the table laden with food. With a crash, the table collapsed and Stojadinović and Frau von Heeren rolled among the wines, tea, ham, salami, cheese and fruit compote now carpeting the banqueting tent. 'I cannot say what people thought', von Wimmer ended his report. 'One old footman crept towards me and kissed my hand.'[2]

The Germans repaid the hospitality with more formality. When Stojadinović visited Berlin in February 1938, Hitler staged a massive military parade, and declared his policy to be that Yugoslavia should be strong and independent. But he did not offer any real protection against the territorial claims of Hungary, Bulgaria and Italy, nor elucidate Germany's own intentions. After a general election in Yugoslavia in December, in which in spite of intimidation and bribery, the heavy opposition vote showed the unpopularity of pro-German policies, Dragiša Cvetković replaced Stojadinović who was arrested in May 1940 on suspicion of planning to make himself a pro-German Führer in Yugoslavia. When war between Germany and the western Allies broke out on 1 September 1939, Yugoslavia's role in Germany's war plans was still unknown, and it was to be another agonizing eighteen months before her fate was decided.

The general attitude of the Yugoslav Communist Party to international developments before the summer of 1939 had been laid down by the Comintern in 1934 and was determined by the Soviet Union's assessment of dangers threatening its own continued existence. The policy was one with which Tito was fully familiar. It was to popularize the Soviet Union as the only country which stood for peace. 'It was our principal activity, it commanded the bulk of our funds,' he said later.[3] This was made easier up to 1939, because of the unequivocal stand taken by Russia in denouncing Nazi and Fascist aggression at a time when Yugoslavia itself was threatened. Support for Russia could thus be presented by the communists as identical with Yugoslav national interests.

The new muted attitude of the Comintern to the idea of world revolution also helped Tito to popularize communist policies. Even in countries as antidemocratic and politically unstable as Yugoslavia,

**143**

the Comintern did not want any armed revolt. As long as Russia was preoccupied with dangers from Hitler trying to accomplish his messianic mission against communism, she could not give aid to, or be distracted by communist revolt in eastern Europe. This relieved Tito of the impossible task the party had had under Comintern orders in 1929. It left him free to show communists and others that duty and self-interest lay in friendship and alliance with the Soviet Union.

Before the outbreak of the second world war, Russian leaders were obsessed by the fear of a possible German alliance with countries of western Europe, or the danger that in event of war, the West might be defeated and then harnessed for a war against Russia. Munich had convinced the Russian leaders that England would not make a real stand against Hitler, and even when Churchill took over from Neville Chamberlain they still feared British intentions. For them the name of Churchill had sinister associations with Archangel and the anti-Bolshevik invasion of Russia in 1918 and 1919. The Russian leaders were also acutely aware of their country's internal weaknesses. In 1939 Russia was in the second year of the Third Five-Year Plan and production was still sluggish. The purges of the previous three years had seriously weakened the Red Army and there had not been time to train up new officers to replace the thousands who had been liquidated. It is probable also that the Soviet leaders, in common with most western governments, overestimated both the Germans' active war potential and their rate of armaments production. All this was part of the complex background to the Nazi–Soviet Pact signed on 23 August 1939.

The pact was a ten-year non-aggression treaty with a secret protocol providing for the partitioning of eastern Europe, allowing the Soviet Union the military annexation of eastern Poland – put into effect late in 1939 – a free hand in Finland, Estonia, Latvia, Romanian Bessarabia and, by a later amendment, in Lithuania. It led to Russia's winter war in Finland in 1939–40, and to all the other territories, including also another part of Romania, the northern Bukovina, being incorporated into the USSR. It thus regained for Russia a large part of the territory lost at the end of the first world war. It was an instrument of Russian national expansion and strategic defence in line with aims of foreign policy followed since the time of Peter the Great.

We know now that negotiations between Soviet and Nazi leaders had been protracted, though this was not generally known at the time. The pact was a complete reversal of previous Soviet policy, of the ideological line against Nazism and Fascism that communist parties had been instructed to follow ever since 1934. It came as a great shock to communists all over the world, especially in Yugoslavia. 'We accepted the pact like disciplined communists,' Tito explained later, 'considering it necessary for the security of the Soviet Union, at that time the only socialist state in the world. We were ignorant at that time of its secret clauses, countenancing Soviet interference in the rights of other nations, especially small ones.'[4]

The incorporation of small states into the Soviet Union was not an issue for Yugoslav communists. They had still not faced the long-term implications for themselves of the policy they had to accept. In Yugoslavia their problem was how to reconcile party members to the idea that Russia had made allies of the capitalist aggressors, the anti-communist, anti-Slav, racist and bestial Nazis. The policy could only be understood as a desperate measure to buy time, to stave off the Nazi attack on Russia as long as possible. But it could not be publicly announced to Yugoslav communists in this way, and there was always the tiny hope that it might prevent war coming to Yugoslavia in a totally destructive form. Communist propaganda was in any case ambivalent about war – the Soviet Union genuinely did not want it as its final successful outcome for them could certainly not have been foreseen. For Yugoslav communists on the other hand, war offered the only opportunity for social and political revolution and therefore might be welcomed. Yet their foreign policy was determined by the Russian leaders, and alliance with the Nazis had to be accepted and justified as long as Russia demanded it.

\*　　\*　　\*

Early in the summer of 1939, Tito received an order from Dimitrov to return to Moscow. The Comintern Paris office which dealt with travel arrangements to Russia, wrote a letter on 10 June asking for Tito's entry visa for Russia to be valid to the end of July.[5] Tito's personal instructions from Dimitrov were written on small pieces of paper hidden in the back of a book, and taken by courier to Lola Ribar for personal delivery to Tito who was at that time in Belgrade. Tito went to Dedijer's flat in Zemun outside Belgrade, to receive the secret papers. But Dedijer's wife and her friends were in the flat when he arrived, and as Engineer Babić he had to spend nearly an

145

hour discussing music and literature with the guests before he could receive the book. Tito opened it in front of Dedijer in his study, and told him that the message had been written by Dimitrov, and it meant that he, Tito, was going on a long journey.[6] He spent the night at Dedijer's flat and set off the next day. He left Split towards the end of June on an Italian ship the *Francesco Morosini* which sailed to Genoa; from there he travelled overland to Paris. He then took a Soviet ship from Le Havre to Leningrad. Travelling with him on the same ship was another Yugoslav Comintern agent who did not recognize Tito and denounced him as a spy to the captain of the ship, who was fortunately able to vouch for him. When the announcement was made of the signing of the Nazi–Soviet non-aggression pact on 23 August, he had reached Moscow.[7]

He spent four months in Moscow again working as an employee of the Comintern whose offices were still in the Lenin hills sector of Moscow, but were shortly to be moved again to the Ostankino Pushkinkoye suburb. Most of his work was in the Foreign Languages Publications department and there he at last completed his task of seeing the Yugoslav translation of Stalin's *History* through the press; copies were then despatched by the Russians to Yugoslavia through their secret channels, possibly by diplomatic bag. Tito said later that this period in Moscow was the worst time in his life. 'Even during the war [second world war, *ed.*] it was easier,' he said, 'because at least during war you knew where your enemies are.'[8] 'When I went to Moscow I never knew whether I would come back alive. And while I was there I never knew that I would not wake up in the middle of the night to hear the fatal knocking at my door.' Tito was afraid that the Russians might decide to keep him in Russia, as they later did to Dimitrov and other east European leaders.

The reason why they decided to let Tito go back to Yugoslavia is as obscure as the mystery of how he managed to escape Stalin's purge. By the end of 1939 Tito had proved himself an obedient Comintern employee, but always at a local level which was regarded as low in the Comintern hierarchy. He had carried out the tasks assigned to him earlier in the year, and this included the removal from active work in the party of Yugoslav communists who had been in Spain or Paris who were accused of being Trotskyists. His work on reorganizing party organization in Yugoslavia had been inspected on orders from the Comintern by a Czech communist called Schwerm, and he had reported favourably in Moscow. Tito may also have deliberately created the impression of being insignificant, his working-class origins – so much praised in communist thought – were in fact a protection because they made him less likely to be feared as a possible leader than if he had been an intellectual. Being apparently insignificant he was also expendable, could be considered as easily replaceable by any other obedient and disciplined working man of mediocre talents. It was a long time before the Russians accepted the fact that they had greatly miscalculated. It is evident that Tito on his side had judged correctly the kind of person the Russians would accept as their appointed leader in Yugoslavia – and that he had throughout and in most difficult circumstances, played the part convincingly.[9]

In January 1940, when he at last obtained permission to return home, he had 'flu – one of the few occasions when he is known to have been ill. Yet he took a Soviet merchant ship from Odessa to Istanbul. He was now travelling on the Canadian passport of Spiridon Mekas, a naturalized British subject, and hoped to make his way to Yugoslavia by train. The first hitch occurred when he got off the Soviet boat and was met by journalists who wanted to know his impressions of Soviet Russia. Refusing to answer questions he escaped their attentions and took a room at the expensive Park Hotel. His stay in Istanbul was much longer than he had reckoned on as he discovered that in wartime he needed a visa to enter Yugoslavia from Turkey. He sent a message to Zagreb asking for a courier to bring him a new passport containing a forged visa. While awaiting its arrival he spent his time visiting the tourist sights around the city. It was probably at this time in Istanbul that he bought the diamond ring which he still wears. It could be changed into currency in any country and was a useful insurance in wartime. He never needed to sell it.

The first courier to arrive was Vladimir Velebit, member of a distinguished Serbian family in Zagreb, whose father was an army general. Tito was not satisfied with the crudely forged passport he brought. At this stage in his career, having escaped alive from Moscow, and with so much at stake, Tito was determined not to be caught when entering Yugoslavia. He had an expert's experience of forged papers, an instinctive apprehension of danger, and he trusted no one. He knew that he had many enemies in the Party both in Yugoslavia and in the Comintern, and was not yet sure that they had all been completely eliminated. He sent to Zagreb for another more expertly forged passport. This was eventually brought by a young Slovene girl. This too he rejected as unsatisfactory. Both time and money were now running out, and he felt that the Turkish police were already suspicious of him. He reverted to the original passport of Spiridon Mekas, and with the help of the girl – an architectural student – managed to forge a visa for transit through Yugoslavia. 'Finally, when the Turkish police were hot on my trail,' he recounted later, 'I took a ticket for the United States on the Italian ship *Conte di Savoia*, then anchored at Naples.' This gave him a valid reason to travel through Yugoslavia to Italy on the Orient Express train. The danger point on this journey was when the train crossed the Yugoslav–Greek frontier at Djevdjevlje. His passport was collected by the frontier police who saw from it that he had been in the Soviet Union, and came to cross-question him about his business there. He had been working under contract as an engineer, Tito replied, and was now on his way home to Canada. As he was a British subject the police accepted the story and gave him back his passport. 'It's a pity he's a British subject,' Tito heard one of them say, 'otherwise we could have run him in.' When the train reached Zagreb two days later, Tito got out and quickly disappeared. It was by now the end of March 1940. The journey back had taken three months.[10]

While he had been away the party had carried on as best it could with routine work in most parts of the country. But in many parts – especially in Zagreb – it had been very disorganized. It had had the embarrassing propaganda job of reversing its successful policy of the Popular Front years. For most communists it was a bitter task, so traumatic that Yugoslav communists are reluctant to talk about it even today. The party line, transmitted from Moscow, was that the war was a fight between imperialists; that it threatened the USSR, the bastion of communism, behind which all progressive people and non-committed countries must rally as being the only country able to secure peace – her pacific intentions being shown by the non-aggression pact with Germany; moreover, Russia was the only country able to protect the small countries of the Balkans. It was not easy to show Soviet policy as simultaneously high-principled and expedient, but party propagandists did their best and instructions and leaflets went out with this message.

'Hitler's war against the English and French imperialists does not mean the Communists should fight Hitler,' said a Party pamphlet, 'rather it means that the English and French imperialists are the *avant-garde* of imperialism in its struggle against the working class, and the USSR.' The Russian invasion of Finland, the Ukraine and White Russia it described as a 'triumph for revolutionary war against capitalism'.[11] The non-aggression pact between the Soviet Union and Germany was in the spirit of the previous policy for peace followed by the USSR, of the tremendous efforts made by the USSR to defend peace and the rights of small nations. The USSR had made the non-aggression pact to protect itself from warmongers, to limit the war in Europe, and keep it away from small nations.[12] Some of the communist propagandists went even further, carried away in a fervour of trying to find a scapegoat that would exculpate the Soviet Union. One leaflet, typed on poor paper, clearly a local production, denounced the English financial oligarchy who with the help of social democrats such as Citrine, Attlee and others were fighting to protect their aggressive hegemony over colonial people. 'The second world war will be like the first,' said another leaflet, 'the British and French wish to force Germany to its knees so that they can maintain their imperialist sway in the world. It is all lies and fables that the English and French are fighting for democracy, for the freedom and independence of small nations. The Finnish war was provoked by English imperialist agents with the aim of bringing the Soviet Union into the war and using Finland as a base for operations against Russia, as they did twenty years ago.'[13]

On Tito's return after an absence of eight months he found the party in considerable disarray, for the Nazi–Soviet pact had shocked most of its members and many could not make the ideological somersault required by the new propaganda line. Tito accepted it as a matter of political expediency. His experiences in Russia had not shaken his determination to work for communist revolution in Yugoslavia. An independent communist movement was still at this time inconceivable, and Soviet policy which could not be changed must be accepted. He had the difficult task of trying to condemn the capitalist western Allies without condoning Nazism. Yugoslavia was not yet directly involved in the war, but he was convinced that it would come there too, and he intended to use war in Yugoslavia as a springboard for revolution. He concentrated on practical arrangements for ensuring that party organization was efficiently established on a countrywide basis. He held regular Politburo meetings at the party headquarters in Zagreb. He travelled about the country contacting leaders and addressing small groups of party members. He was careful to report all his activities back to the Comintern via the secret radio set that with the aid of Velebit had been assembled and installed in a house in Zagreb where it was operated by a Comintern employee, Ivan Kopinić (also known as Valdes). When the Russian secret service in Belgrade recruited some of Tito's own workers for their purposes, he grumbled but did not make an issue of it. For the first time since he had begun working as party secretary in Yugoslavia he felt relatively independent and free to get on with his work in his own way.

He decided to hold a party conference for the whole country before Yugoslav became directly involved in the war. As Hitler's troops overran one country after another it was clear that this was only a matter of time. The last congress – the party's fourth – had been held in November 1928 in Dresden just as Tito had been starting his long term of imprisonment. It had been organized by the Comintern, and Gorkić had been the new young secretary appointed there. Tito intended now to show that he had done far better than Gorkić. During the summer he sent orders to communist groups in each area to hold meetings to elect or appoint representatives to attend regional conferences that in their turn would choose delegates for the general conference. He himself attended most of these local meetings – in a private house in Belgrade; in Sarajevo, the main town of Bosnia; in a hamlet outside Split in Dalmatia, on the Žabljak mountain in Montenegro. He flew there by plane and was then taken by chauffeur-driven car from the tiny airport to the rendezvous. One meeting was held in a café in Zagreb, another was in a villa in a vineyard in Vojvodina, north of the Danube. When all had been successfully completed he was ready to make arrangements for the general conference.

The Fifth Communist Party Conference was held in a small house on the outskirts of Zagreb from 17 to 19 October 1940.[14] It was just a week before Mussolini launched his attack on Greece. Preparations for the conference had been made by a working party which included Tito, the secretary of the party in Croatia, Rade Končar, two other members and the party chauffeur, Branko Malešivić. Everything was treated with the utmost *konspiracija*; 101 delegates had to be provided for, and it was essential that neither the neighbours nor the police should become suspicious. Arrangements had to be made for hiring a house, pulling down a wall inside to make a large room with a platform at one end – decorated with huge pictures of Marx, Lenin and Stalin – finding communist workmen to make lightweight chairs, and transporting them camouflaged to the house. Women communists were responsible for the catering arrangements but delegates were told to bring their own bread as none could be baked in the house. Most important of all were travel arrangements. Orders were sent to delegates in all parts of the country to journey to Zagreb in small groups, at times that were staggered, so that organizers could meet them at appointed places – the station, bus stops, the Trade Union Hall – and take them to the meeting place which was only known to a few. They must all be able to prove their identity. Not surprisingly there were some minor mishaps. The Montenegrins characteristically nearly shot up their contact before he had identified himself, the Bosnians arrived at the railway station where they were not met and, nervous of attracting suspicion by hanging around too long, spent a cold night in the wooded countryside outside the town. Delegates arrived on 17 and 18 October and were crammed into the house. The conference took place from 8.30 a.m. to 4 p.m. on Saturday, 19 October.

Each delegate had had to fill in a form giving his particulars – number and place of party registration, age, length of membership of party and positions held, whether gaol sentence had been served for political work; social category – worker, peasant, intellectual, craftsman or other. The information was analysed carefully by the party officials. Out of 101 delegates fifty-three described themselves as workers – the communist élite category – fourteen peasants, twenty-nine intellectuals and five employees. The average age was thirty-three, average service with the party nine years. Eighty delegates had at some time in their lives been arrested by the police, and forty-two had served gaol sentences for an average two-year sentence. Delegates were instructed that before they left the house at the end of the meeting, all notes of the conference had to be torn up and the pieces handed over to an official at the door. Comrades were on duty patrolling the area throughout the meeting. The precautions were successful. No one was arrested and the police only learned about the conference later.[15]

In the history of Tito's leadership of the Yugoslav Communist Party, the Fifth Conference came to be considered as an historic occasion marking the beginning of a new phase in which the party was, for the first time, independent and controlled by its own national leadership – by what, in party language, was described as 'the best and most revolutionary cadres'. No representative of the Comintern was present.

Moša Pijade, who had recently finished his fourteen-year prison sentence followed by several months in the notorious political prisoners' concentration camp at Bileca, opened the conference with a speech of welcome. He was one of a twelve-man Presidium occupying the platform. Among the others were Tito, Kardelj, Lola Ribar, and a Macedonian, Metodije Šatarov (Šarlo) who had been sent from Moscow on Comintern orders and with whom Tito was later to have harsh disagreement over wartime policy.[16] It was customary procedure that the leaders' speeches should deal with developments since the previous conference. The twelve-year gap meant that a lot of painful and controversial history had to be covered. Tito himself handled the most delicate questions – the account of the power struggle within the party, the difficult orientation of foreign policy, and the somewhat easier subject of consistent opposition to the regime in Yugoslavia throughout the previous twelve years.[17] He also dealt at some length with his own reorganization of the party including the 'cleansing' of unreliable people. He repeatedly stressed the importance of 'cadres' – that is committed and loyal men and women and especially young people. He was trying to close the door on the past and concentrate on the future.[18] In the prepared discussion which followed his address twenty-five delegates spoke, representing all the areas of the country.

In contrast to all previous party conferences, it is obvious that Tito was aiming to create an impression of federal unity in which the separate regions – and peoples – had their own identity. Croatia and Slovenia already had their own Party organizations and the other regions, Serbia, Bosnia-Herzegovina, Dalmatia, Montenegro, Macedonia and the Vojvodina had area committees. Kosovo-Metohija and other smaller regions had district committees. An alternative to the centralist conception of the state, imposed by King Alexander and Prince Paul throughout the interwar period, was already being worked out. No other party had any such constructive plan.

The subject of federalism lay at the heart of all political life in the Yugoslav state, and in the Yugoslav Communist Party. It had been the matter at issue in the Vidovdan constitution, the subject on which Stalin had spoken and for which Sima Marković had been disgraced in the nineteen-twenties. Tito had fought over it in the thirties and it was still to be an issue in the 'sixties. The unity of voting and opinion that Tito brought about at the Zagreb conference in 1940 was neither final nor as total as it appeared. The question of relationships between the regions and the centre, between one region and another, was to remain one of the most important unsolved problems of Tito's life.

Under the threat of war Tito's strong and confident leadership gained enthusiastic support; but it did not mean that Croat-Serb hostility was eliminated, or that Macedonian separatism and pro-Bulgarian proclivities of some Macedonian communists had all been abandoned. Unity was still more a declaration of intent than a factual achievement. The conference ended in euphoric enthusiasm – increased, no doubt, by the satisfaction of knowing that it had been completed without being detected. It was the last conference held under conditions of illegality. 'Comrades, we are facing fateful days,' was Tito's final exhortation, 'Forward for the final struggle. We must hold our next conference in a country free from aliens and capitalists.'[19]

\* \* \*

The conference marked a change in Tito's policy towards preparations for war. At the outbreak of German hostilities in the west, and under the influence of the shock of the Nazi–Soviet non-aggression pact in the summer of 1939, the party had followed a line opposing conscription and call-up of reservists for the Yugoslav army. It had encouraged strikes in armaments and aircraft factories in Kragujevac, Valjevo and Zemun and antiwar demonstrations had been organized in Belgrade, Zagreb and other towns. In this policy it had had some strange bedfellows, for the extremist Croat separatists, the Ustaši, and Serbian extreme nationalists, who were strongly opposed by the communists, had also been against war and had taken part in communist organized strikes and demonstrations.

In the months after the Fifth Conference, as the inevitability of war became more and more obvious, a changed attitude to military service was introduced. It was necessary to encourage communists to join the Yugoslav army in order to have military training themselves, and because it was recognized that this was the only way to increase communist support among the service men. Work in the forces was now of primary importance because of the part the army could play in suppressing revolt or in turning the scales in favour of rebels, as had happened in 1917 in Russia. Tito was realist enough to know that if no communists went into the army it would be difficult to influence the soldiers and make party capital out of the many causes for dissatisfaction. At the time there were in the army only a few cells of three to five men, and these were not able to be very active.

On the eve of war the Yugoslav army was still run largely in the same way – and by many of the same people – as the Serbian army in the first world war. The army was not mechanized and had very few modern weapons. It had twenty infantry divisions, one guards division and three cavalry regiments and, for the most part, relied on horsedrawn transport. It was trained for trench warfare totally unsuited to the Nazi tactics of tank blitzkrieg. Army discipline, harsh and discouraging to initiative, was also a cause of discontent. It was besides an instrument of discrimination by Serbian officers and NCOs against other nationalities, especially against Croats.[20] This helped the work of the communists and contributed to the sense of alienation which led many Croats to disassociate themselves from the fighting when Germany invaded Yugoslavia in 1941.

In the final months before war, Tito had to carry out the policy outlined in his speech at the conference. He had to set up a strong central headquarters staff for the Communist Party, to select reliable regional leaders and to establish a network of communications strong enough to function in spite of police, military and other forms of surveillance. He needed trusted personnel in a wide variety of jobs. In addition to party officials, couriers were required in large numbers, and men, women, even children were used. He needed illegal printing presses and a host of backroom workers, including skilled craftsmen to produce forged passes, *legitimacije*, membership cards, etc. It took at least two days to produce a good forged passport as equipment was scarce and crude. There had to be reliable agents – informers in government offices, service establishments, police and intelligence departments – and someone to collate, analyse and store their information. It took a long time to get organized and there was considerable confusion.

During the months before the outbreak of war, other political parties in Yugoslavia besides the communists were affected in different ways by the difficulties of the times, and the uncertainty about how to react to or make use of Nazi and Italian ambitions. The role of Maček, leader of the Croat Peasant Party, was particularly ambivalent. His party had always been dissatisfied with Croatia's position in the Yugoslav state. He saw the encroachment of German power in central Europe as the opportunity to gain some kind of autonomy for Croatia – either by making a private deal with Italy or Germany, or by using the threat of Axis expansion to exact belated concessions from Prince Paul's government.

It is known that Maček made overtures to the Nazis and that, when they were not interested, he made contact with the Italian government through an Italian who lived in Croatia, engineer Amadeo Carnelluti. According to Ciano's diary and Carnelluti's own testimony, this was instituted by Maček himself. Though he later denied this, available evidence so far is against him. First negotiations took place in November 1938, when Italy was not yet interested in the possibility of backing an independent state of Croatia. By May 1939, after the Italian invasion of Albania, the situation had changed. Discussions took place between Carnelluti – for Maček – and Ciano, about the possibility of an independent Croatian state, with widened frontiers under Italian protection, and possibly as a part of a group of Catholic states in central Europe, Hungary, Poland, Ruthenia and Slovakia being mentioned, or as an independent state within a Yugoslav confederation.

These negotiations came to nothing when Maček's simultaneous negotiations with the central government resulted in him obtaining very broad concessions which were incorporated into an agreement on 26 August 1939, five days before the beginning of the second world war. Maček then became Vice-Premier in a broadly based government under the premiership of Cvetković. It is known that Maček also promoted discussions about the future state of Croatia with political figures in other European capitals – London, Paris, Berlin, Budapest – including talks with Winston Churchill. It is not impossible that British influence, which was already being exercised in Yugoslavia by a number of special emissaries trying to effect a stable government in case she could be persuaded to become an ally, may have had some influence on Maček's joining the Yugoslav government just before the war.[21]

The Yugoslav government was also engaged in complicated diplomatic manoeuvres to preserve its neutrality, to keep in with both Germany and Great Britain, and at all costs to prevent Mussolini developing his known ambitions to dismantle Yugoslavia. Even before the outbreak of war the Yugoslav government had deposited the greater part of its gold reserves in England and the United States.

The destroyer *Beograd* unloaded 7,344 gold ingots at Portsmouth on 20 May 1939, and later $47 million worth of gold was sent to the Federal Reserve Bank in New York. The numbers of British intelligence agents in Yugoslavia were also greatly increased. Yet this was easily offset by the economic stranglehold Germany had obtained over Yugoslavia through her control of exports and monopoly of all valuable copper and lead output of the British and French owned mines. German agents were also numerous and influential especially among the native *Volksdeutsche* population of northern Yugoslavia.

As Hitler's victories in the west mounted – Poland, September 1939; Norway, April 1940; Holland and Belgium in May of the same year, and the collapse of France in June – the destruction of Britain seemed inevitable, and the Yugoslav leaders began to take desperate measures to avoid a similar fate. They sought friendship with their old enemy Bulgaria, offering frontier concessions that were immediately nullified by bigger offers to Bulgaria from Germany. On 25 June they established diplomatic relations with the Soviet Union, with whom relations had been broken off ever since the Bolshevik revolution. In the interwar period the Yugoslav government had allowed a representative of 'Tsarist' Russia to maintain an embassy in Belgrade; but in 1940, when the Soviet Union declared in favour of the *status quo* in the Balkans, a Yugoslav Minister, Milan Gavrilović, was sent to Moscow.

Throughout the summer of 1940, after his announcement on 10 June that he had entered the war to support the Axis, Mussolini was eager to attack Yugoslavia and was only restrained from a September campaign by strong German resistance.[22] Rash action at the wrong moment, Hitler pointed out, might set the Balkans ablaze, provoke Russian intervention, or even give Britain a common cause with Soviet Russia. Instead, and against the advice of his general staff, Mussolini attacked Greece on 28 October 1940. The failure of Italian troops to gain a quick success seemed to avert immediate danger from Yugoslavia's southern frontier. In fact it brought the much greater danger of increased German pressure to allow passage of war supplies through Yugoslavia, in breach of neutrality, and insistence on Yugoslavia joining the Tripartite Pact. 'Without being sure of the Yugoslavs', Hitler wrote to Mussolini, 'we cannot risk a war in the Balkans.'[23] At the same time Great Britain was also putting pressure on Yugoslavia not to join the Axis – through letters from King George VI to Prince Paul, from Churchill to the Premier, through Sir Ronald Campbell, British Minister in Belgrade, and via a special US emissary, William Donovan, whose cipher the Germans had acquired and whose conversations with the Yugoslavs were known to them. In February 1941 German troops began to occupy Romania and in the following month, Bulgaria. The ring was closing round Yugoslavia.[24]

Hitler now believed – and said as much to the Japanese ambassador – that the Yugoslav government would accept collaboration with the Axis, and summoned Cvetković, the Yugoslav Premier, to see him on 14 February 1941. This was followed by a visit by Prince Paul to Berchtesgaden on 4 March, three days after Bulgaria had joined the Tripartite Pact, the alliance of Germany, Italy and Japan signed 27 September 1940. After a five hours' talk Hitler was convinced that with some show of reluctance, Prince Paul would agree to sign. At a cabinet meeting held on 6 March in Belgrade, after Prince Paul's return, the eight ministers voted unanimously for Yugoslavia to sign the pact.[25]

It was some time before this decision was implemented. Prince Paul and his government were still under strong British pressure not to sign away their neutrality, but to join the Allies and fight with them in Greece, where British forces could give help to the Greeks fighting against Mussolini's invading army. The Yugoslav government maintained discussions with both sides, and continued to postpone signature of the pact. They knew by this time that Hitler had preparations well advanced for an attack on the Soviet Union and there was still a last desperate hope that, if this came in time, they might yet avoid having to make a choice.

The Yugoslav military attaché in Berlin, Colonel Vladimir Vauhnik, a most successful intelligence agent, had obtained information about this proposed attack from a number of different reliable sources. 'My friend, this means the end of Germany,' one of his perspicacious German informants had said. Vauhnik – who also made his information available to Britain, who in turn through their envoy in Moscow, Sir Stafford Cripps, notified the Russians – had been told that an attack by 200 German divisions on Russia would be made in the second half of May 1941.[26] Vauhnik's information relayed to both military and political leaders in Yugoslavia was never acknowledged, and it cannot be certain what effect it had on official Yugoslav policy. It certainly explained why Hitler was determined to consolidate his position in the Balkans. On 23 March 1941, the German ambassador in Belgrade told the Yugoslav government that Hitler wanted the pact signed within forty-eight hours. On the afternoon of 25 March, Cvetković and his foreign minister Cincar-Marković, signed Yugoslavia's adherence to Hitler's Tripartite Pact.

When the news was released there were immediate demonstrations – both spontaneous and organized – against it in Belgrade. In Serbia, opposition to the pact was very widespread – '*bolje rat nego pakt*' ('better war than the pact') chanted the crowds – and came from people of all parties, including the communists, as well as from the majority of ordinary people. Opinion was not so unanimous in other parts of the country, especially in Croatia. A small group of people, among them British secret service agents, had made their dispositions about what to do if the pact was signed. Do not 'neglect any alternative to which we may have to resort if we find present Government have gone beyond recall' cabled Churchill to the British Minister in Belgrade. Hugh Dalton, head of Britain's secret service department known as SOE, signalled his agents to 'use all means to raise a revolution'. For this, he said, 'all was well prepared beforehand'.[27]

On 26 March, a speech by Leopold Amery was broadcast to Yugoslavia by the BBC's European network. It was a passionate appeal to Yugoslavs – especially to the Serbs – to renounce the pact. 'If the [Yugoslav] people clearly show that accession to the Axis pact is regarded by them as a betrayal of honour and independence, then surely it is the duty of the government to consult the people before the pact is ratified. No, it is not too late for that. The whole future for Yugoslavia is on the razor's edge.'[28]

Most of the Serbs, at any rate, needed no encouragement. On 23 March, before the signing of the pact, General Dušan Simović, commander of the Yugoslav air force, called on Prince Paul to repeat a warning he had already made several times – that if the pact were signed he could not guarantee that his officers would not mutiny and overthrow the regency. This was exactly what happened. On the night of 26/27 March 1941, a group of military and air force officers carried out a successful *coup d'état* overthrowing the Regent and his government. Only one person was killed, an officer who refused to hand over the radio station. Prince Paul was deposed and forced to leave the country. A new government took over in the name of the young King Peter. A broadcast to the country was made in his name, by someone with a similar voice. The King himself heard it on his radio at 9 a.m. that morning, and did not officially give it his approval until several hours later.

The moving spirit behind the coup had been Brigadier-General Bora Mirković who had opposed Prince Paul's government for a long time, and for many different reasons. In preparing the coup he had approached a number of officers who had refused support, but General Simović had promised to act as political head once the government had been overthrown. Support for the coup had come from many Serbs who disapproved of the inglorious dictatorship or pro-German policies of the Regency, or had suffered personal disappointments from it. It also came from a number of genuinely Yugoslav-minded people, Croats, Slovenes and others as well as Serbs, who believed that joining the pact would lead to the country being dismembered by the Germans – the end of Yugoslavia. The British had also been in touch with General Mirković through the British military and air attachés and through Mirko Kosić, a friend of General Simović. They were believed to have influenced people to join the plot.[29]

The communists had no part in the conspiracy itself, but they organized demonstrations in Belgrade and other Serbian towns on the morning of 27 March. Communists demonstrated with characteristic slogans demanding *Pakt sa Rusijom* (Pact with Russia), *Bolje grob nego rob* (better a grave than slavery), *Bratski Sovietski Savez* (Brotherly SovietUnion), *Beograd–Moskva Savez* (Belgrade–Moscow Alliance) and in line with Tito's new policy, *Braničemo zemlju* (we will defend the country).

It could not be said that the government returned to normal after the success of the coup was assured, because the main question of Germany's reaction was still unanswered. The foreign minister in the new government, Momčilo Ninčić, who had been fetched from his bed, where he was convalescent after an operation, 'deathly pale, and as deaf as a post', attempted to carry out a policy approved by the new prime minister, General Simović, the vice-premier Maček and an all-party cabinet. This was to try to appease German wrath by not denouncing the previous government's signature of the Tripartite Pact. Simultaneously conversations were being held with the British. The British Chief of the Imperial General Staff, General Sir John Dill, visited Belgrade in civilian clothes on 1 April. Other talks took place in Greece with General Wilson and Anthony Eden to see what practical aid could be expected. Neither of these approaches was at all reassuring.[30] At the same time discussions with Russia for a military and political pact produced only a Pact of Friendship and Non-Aggression.

Hitler had been furious at the Yugoslav coup. At 2.30 p.m. on 27 March he released his Directive 25 with the order that Yugoslavia should be attacked, defeated with all speed, and Belgrade subjected to exemplary punishment by air bombardment. This was followed by feverish activity of German personnel in Yugoslavia, and withdrawal of diplomatic staff. The Germans made overtures to Maček through their agent, Herr Derffler, to see what his reaction would be to German offers of independence for Croatia. On 1 April Ribbentrop sent a message to the German consulate in Zagreb: 'In answer to Dr Maček's request for our advice, which has reached us by various channels, please tell him the following. . . . We would strongly advise him and other Croat leaders not to cooperate in any way with the Belgrade government. The fact of our giving such advice must be treated as secret. Should he follow our advice we would remain in touch with him. He would have to make communication secure on his side by means of suitable intermediaries.'[31]

Through another intermediary Maček informed the Germans that he felt he must join the Yugoslav government to prevent hostilities breaking out between Serbs and Croats. He complained that though he had asked for arms for a Croatian Home Guard, the Germans had not supplied them. Maček, as the Germans were well aware, was negotiating with both sides.

Time was very short for everyone. Colonel Vauhnik, in Berlin, as usual had reliable and correct intelligence about the attack ordered on Yugoslavia. On 1 April he heard that it was fixed for 6 April. He sent this information to Belgrade by three different routes, but had no confirmation of its receipt. On the night of 2 April at 2 a.m. his telephone bell rang three times. This was a signal to pick up documents from a slit in the wall by his garage. Passing two sleeping Gestapo agents he found the message which said, 'Conference ended now. Attack on Yugoslavia definitely fixed for 6 April. Surrounding attacks from Bulgaria in the east and Hungary in the north. May God's blessing and my sincerest wishes accompany you in this terrible ordeal.' Vauhnik sent telegrams and despatched his assistant personally to convey the warning to the government in Belgrade. The officials there paid little attention to the warnings for they did not believe in Vauhnik's sources. In fact he had the best possible intelligence source, none other than Admiral Canaris, chief of the German High Command's foreign and counter-intelligence office, who was in touch with Vauhnik through his own assistant, Major-General Hans Oster. So unmoved was Simović by Vauhnik's warnings – if they ever reached him, and this is not certain – that he had arranged for his daughter's wedding to take place in Belgrade on 6 April.[32]

At 5.15 on that morning, Sunday, 6 April 1941, German bombers flew in wave after wave to attack Belgrade, which was almost totally undefended. They killed some 10,000 people and destroyed great areas of the city. Simultaneously the German army, aided by Bulgarian and Hungarian units, invaded Yugoslavia. The Yugoslav army, in conditions of utmost confusion, put up very little resistance. The total German casualty figure was 558, including 151 killed, 392 wounded and fifteen missing. On 15 April the King and his government fled the country, first to Greece, later to the Middle East. On the same day, on his instruction, Yugoslav representatives met German General von Weichs in Belgrade and agreed to surrender. Signature of the document of capitulation took place on 17 April. The document was signed for Yugoslavia by General Janković and by the former Foreign Minister, Cincar-Marković, who had signed the Tripartite Pact. Yugoslavia had been defeated and occupied in exactly ten days.[33]

# PART III
# REVOLUTION THROUGH WAR

# 10 PARTY SECRETARY
# INTO ARMY COMMANDER

It had never been part of the Nazi's long-term plan to invade Yugoslavia and it is probable that it was a military error, undertaken to indulge Hitler's fury at the coup of 27 March. Although the German army had contingency plans for invading the Balkans, the *ad hoc* character of the Yugoslav campaign was shown by its code name – 'Operation Punishment'. The disposal of the conquered lands also had to be decided hastily; implementation of promises to Yugoslavia's hostile neighbours competed with Germany's own strategic needs. Decisions were taken in a series of meetings at the German Foreign Ministry and Hitler's headquarters in the second half of April. Hitler was still enraged because he had been forced to delay his 'Operation Barbarossa' against Russia, first for a month, then for a further two weeks. In characteristic diatribes he blamed this on the Serbs – the coup, he said, had been organized by the Black Hand, the secret Serbian military organization that had been responsible for the murder of King Alexander Obrenović of Serbia in 1903, of the Sarajevo murder in 1914 and the start of the first world war. It was Hitler's personal decision that Yugoslavia as a state must be destroyed, and Serbia punished, though he accepted the view of his experts that Serbia as an entity would have to remain in existence. Influenced by his first world war memories and garbled knowledge of history, he remained anti-Serb throughout the war, and this attitude was exacerbated by Tito's early successes against the German occupation forces in Serbia.[1]

Apart from this, Hitler's general view, frequently repeated, was that Germany had no political interest in the Yugoslav lands but was greatly interested in their food and raw materials, especially copper from Serbia and bauxite from Croatia.[2] The whole of the area was also of vital importance for military communications, since it lay across the north–south route to Greece and the Aegean, and the east–west routes from central Europe to the Black Sea. Hitler wanted to control it with as little trouble, as little expenditure of troops and manpower as possible.

The Yugoslav state ceased to exist. It was divided between eight different occupying authorities and fragmented into ten different regions. Germany took over the northern two-thirds of Slovenia and the greater part of Serbia – about the area of the pre-1912 kingdom. This gave her control of communications through the Balkans and along the Morava and Danube valleys. She had Belgrade as a 'German fortress, and German garrison'. Though a Serb General Milan Nedić, was put as nominal head of government from the end of August, Serbia remained German-occupied territory throughout the war. Italy received the southern third of Slovenia, including Ljubljana and access to the sea south of Rijeka, with the islands of Krk, Losinj and others in the northern Adriatic. She also received a long-coveted part of the Dalmatian littoral, with its offshore islands, from north of Zadar down to and including Split, as well as the islands of Vis and Korčula. She obtained a small part of Bosnia and the whole of Montenegro with its coastline and the valuable port of Kotor, as well as a part of Kosovo-Metohija and the Sandjak of Novi-Pazar which was largely inhabited by Albanians and was annexed to Italian-controlled Albania. The lion's portion went to create a large Independent State of Croatia stretching to the sea north of Zadar and again from Split to south of Dubrovnik. It was supposed to be a kingdom but remained without a king, since the Duke of Spoleto, nephew of King Victor Emmanuel III of Italy, who was offered the throne, preferred to remain in Rome. 'He is living with a well-known woman and takes her about in his private car. He frequents bars and night clubs and gets tight', wrote Ciano scornfully.[3] Macedonia was given to Bulgaria who made haste to occupy and Bulgarize it. Hungary obtained parts of Bačka, Baranja with the western Banat and other lands west of the Danube, while the Banat east of the Danube was given a *Volksdeutsche* administration. The divided territory was meant to give Germany strategic control over the whole region and political control through a policy of divide and rule. It left all recipients other than Germany dissatisfied and quarrelling with each other about frontiers. The rulers of the Independent State of Croatia were particularly bitter about the parts of Bosnia and Dalmatia which they had reluctantly agreed should go to Italy.

The number of different authorities, their different systems of occupation and conflicting interest, ultimately complicated and weakened German control of the economic wealth and strategic communications in the Balkans. They were later criticized by some Germans as having facilitated resistance operations. Tito's resistance movement was often able to exploit these differences, and the fragmentation of the country probably helped towards the creation of a renaissance of national Yugoslav feeling which was one of the strengths of his movement as it developed during the war.

At the time of the German invasion, Tito, still known as Engineer Babić – though the Yugoslav sculptor Augustinčić and perhaps others knew him as Engineer Tomanek, was living with Herta Has and their baby son Alexander (born in 1941), in a small house in the suburb of Zagreb. He took a plane to Belgrade on 29 March to discuss communist policy towards the *coup d'état* with other party leaders and to see the situation for himself. He was soon back in Zagreb for he had to remain near his secret radio link with the Comintern. He heard of the German bombardment of Belgrade from a neighbour who had been listening to the German radio. He immediately contacted communists in the town and gave them the hopeless, but at least concrete task of going to the local commander to ask that workers be given arms to defend their country. In Zagreb the situation developed dramatically, but predictably. On the evening of 10 April, Colonel Slavko Kvaternik gained control of the radio station and proclaimed an Independent State of Croatia under the Ustaša leader, Dr Ante Pavelić, at that time still in Italy. Maček, who had a large following throughout the country, was not opposed to the idea of an independent Croatia and had been in touch with Pavelić. Kvaternik, like many extreme nationalist Croats – including, so the Germans had been informed, the Croatian Franciscans – had been in touch with the Ustaši for some time, and Pavelić entered the city unopposed in the early hours of 15 April.[4]

People were stunned by the speed with which events had developed, by fear and uncertainty for the future. During these terrible days Tito was galvanized into activity. It was typical of the man that danger, as on other occasions in his life, brought out all his fighting instincts and talent for leadership. He had to work desperately to prevent the party organization which he had built up with such difficulty in the past few years from falling to pieces and being irrevocably lost in the chaos of war. The fact that the party had been based on a well-organized network of illegal communications was of inestimable value at this time. Luckily the party's headquarters with its illegal printing presses was in Zagreb, which experienced no bombardment or fighting, and it was possible at first to operate from there to re-establish contact with party members dispersed by the invasion. This was not easy in the chaotic conditions of war and occupation.

German, Italian, Hungarian and Bulgarian armies were on the move in different parts of the country. Roads were full of refugees, of people moving in all directions – Yugoslav soldiers trying to get rid of uniforms and weapons and return home or go into hiding before they could be arrested, people trying to join their families in different parts of the country before frontiers were closed, foreigners and political refugees trying to flee the country – including a party of British who made their way to Sarajevo and thence to the coast, where most of them were arrested by the Italians. Road transport had been requisitioned, petrol was almost impossible to obtain, telephones, railways and buses worked fitfully if at all.[5] The communist courier system, operating between villages and towns and along byways off the main road had to be adapted to the new conditions. Yet Tito managed to maintain contact with his most important colleagues. When the German army entered Zagreb on 10 April he was holding a meeting with a few of them in his house on the outskirts of the town.

The party's general line laid down by Moscow and transmitted by radio link to Tito was clear – the war was still a struggle between two bourgeois fascist opponents. The defeat of the Royalist government was no matter for regret. The party asked its members to oppose the Germans, but it could not call for uprising as long as the Nazis were allies of Russia. But the conflict between communist and national loyalties did not have to be resolved at this time since the party, without arms and disorganized by war, could not undertake any effective opposition to Germany and her allies who in spring 1941 were at the height of their success. Tito was prepared to let the situation develop and deal with immediate tasks. He was convinced that war had given him an opportunity to lead a communist revolution in Yugoslavia, that the Soviet Union must want this and would help to achieve it. He did not have to wait long.[6]

The committee that Tito summoned on 10 April decided that communists must be told to collect arms and hide them for future use. They must rebuild small local groups and give secret training in use of arms and first aid. They must collect intelligence about conditions in their own regions, about those who were working with, and those who were against the occupiers. They were to arrange communications links with each other, and with Tito's central headquarters. It was decided to set up a War Committee of which Tito was president. This, with the party's Central Committee, would eventually move to Belgrade, which was better placed for communications with all parts of the country. Tito personally was less well-known there, and less likely to be betrayed. The fact had to be accepted that Croatia was not likely to be a good centre for initial resistance or opposition to the occupiers since many Croats had welcomed the idea of an Independent State of Croatia. It was only later, when this state's brutal fascist character and lack of real independence had been demonstrated, that many changed their minds. For the time being Tito could expect to enlist more anti-German support and collect more arms in Serbia which had suffered from the German invasion, and where the tradition of resistance to foreign occupation of Turkish armies was still a living memory.

Another advantage of moving to Belgrade – though this could not be openly expressed – was that Tito would have more personal authority over the party. Since the Russians' secret service radio operating from a doctor's house in Belgrade, had been destroyed in the German bombardment, the only direct link with Moscow was by the Zagreb radio, whose operator Valdes-Kopinič was a Comintern employee not under Tito's orders, a situation which Tito found increasingly irksome. He accepted that he, too, was under Comintern orders, but he had no intention of allowing Kopinič to usurp his overall authority and give orders to the Zagreb party as was unsuccessfully attempted that summer after Tito had left Zagreb for Serbia.[7]

For the time being Tito continued to stay in Zagreb and made plans for meetings to be held by groups of communists in Montenegro, Croatia, Dalmatia and Slovenia. In Macedonia, which Bulgarian troops had begun to occupy on 19 April, the situation of the Communist Party was complicated by the fact that the Macedonian party secretary, a member of Tito's Central Committee, Šatarov-Šarlo, refused to take orders from Tito and decided to work with the Bulgarian Communist Party.[8] This started a dispute between the two parties about communist control and tactics in Macedonia which took a long time to resolve. News also came in from all parts of the country of the arrest and execution of many communists. In the same month, Pavelić had initiated his infamous policy of exterminating all Jews, Gipsies and Serbs who would not convert to Catholicism to make Croatia into what he liked to think of as a racially pure state.

\* \* \*

Tito's departure from Zagreb had to be undertaken hastily in the middle of May, when he narrowly escaped arrest. The town was full of Ustaši troops, German soldiers, Gestapo and police agents. To avoid drawing attention to himself by handing in his Ford car when all cars were requisitioned, Tito had had workmen in to brick it up in his garage. One of the men had informed the police who soon after were seen approaching his house. Tito, lucky as usual, was out in the town. A relative – his family are rarely mentioned as having been among his helpers – rushed out to warn him, and he was able to take the night train to Belgrade, a communist girl going ahead of him through the police controls at the station to make sure that no special checks or changes in papers were required that night.[9] He left Herta Has and his baby son behind in the charge of friends in Zagreb. He never lived in Zagreb again, and it was in effect the end of his family life with Herta.

Before the end of May, Tito knew that the Germans were going to invade the Soviet Union. The German troops that remained in Serbia after the Yugoslav capitulation – the 60th Motorized, 4th Mountain and 294th Infantry divisions and one regiment of the 183rd division – under their commander Field-Marshal von Weichs were removed at the end of April and early May, and replaced by three divisions made up of older men – class of 1907–13 – more suited to occupation than battle duties. German troop movements from Greece to Romania were also noted. The significance of these changes was clear, and was confirmed by a German officer's confidential remark to a White Russian, repeated to Tito, that Russia was to be liberated. Tito reported the intelligence to Dimitrov by radio telegram.[10] Tito knew that this would mean an end to the Comintern ban on armed activity and worked frenziedly to have people in all parts of the country ready to act when the time came.

The announcement of the German invasion of the Soviet Union on 22 June 1941, catastrophic news in one respect, was a matter for utmost joy and relief for Yugoslav communists. The tension of frustrating ambivalence and intolerable waiting was at an end; they were no longer alone. The attack on the Soviet Union released pent-up energies in the Yugoslav party which had been under constraint ever since the Nazi–Soviet Pact, and especially in the weeks since the Nazi invasion of Yugoslavia. Although still under the authority of the Comintern, its orders now coincided with national feelings, and allowed the party to appeal for patriotic support for immediate resistance. Conflict with Soviet aims now seemed out of the question. The party felt it would get Russian aid and approval if it carried out its orders satisfactorily. On 3 July Stalin issued a general appeal for guerrilla activities behind the lines of the German army.

'Grandfather' (Deda) – the pseudonym with which Dimitrov signed his signals to Tito – radioed a more explicit command a few hours after the German attack: 'Germany's treacherous attack upon the USSR is not only a blow against the country of socialism. It is a blow against the freedom and independence of all people. Defence of the USSR is also the defence of people of countries occupied by Germany. The peoples of Yugoslavia have now the opportunity to create a general liberation struggle against the German invader. It is a vital necessity to undertake all actions to assist and facilitate the just war of the Soviet people. . . . Such an endeavour is an integral part of the victory of the USSR. Remember that at present it is a question of liberation from Fascist domination and not a question of Socialist revolution.'[11]

Tito summoned the Politburo to a meeting that afternoon in the party's headquarters in a house in Dedinje, the upper-class suburb of Belgrade. As they discussed the new situation, Tito sat drafting a proclamation that was rushed to the secret printing press and issued that night. It was stirring, but still cautiously inexplicit: 'The fateful hour has struck. The decisive battle against the ancient enemy of the working class has begun. . . . Proletarians of all regions of Yugoslavia, to your places in the first fighting ranks. Close ranks around your vanguard, the Yugoslav Communist Party. . . . Do not allow the precious blood of the heroic Soviet people to be shed without your participation.'[12] It took some days to get the leaflets distributed throughout the country. It was clear that acts of sabotage – the Belgrade–Zagreb railway line was attacked on the night of 23 June – would need some form of direction and coordination to be most effective. Tito summoned the Central Committee to meet him on 27 June and it was decided to set up a General Headquarters of National Liberation Partisans' Detachments. Tito said later that the

171

name 'Partisans' was chosen because of its association with operations behind the lines in Napoleon's campaigns in Spain and Russia. Stalin also had used the name in his appeal to the Russian people. In fact it was some weeks before the word 'guerrilla' was dropped and the name 'Partisans' came to be used to describe Tito's followers. The meeting also decided to send twelve senior members of the Central Committee to the different regions of the country to supervise activities and raise Partisan detachments. A call for general uprising had not yet been made, and Yugoslav communists were not yet prepared for it. On 1 July, however, 'Grandfather' signalled new instructions: 'The hour has struck when communists must launch an open fight against the invaders. Without wasting a moment, organize partisan detachments and start a partisan war behind the enemy's lines. . . . Acknowledge receipt of these instructions, and notify facts to show fulfilment.'

Tito did as he was ordered. A new, specific proclamation was printed and issued on 4 July, and again on 12 July, repeating the Comintern appeal: 'Peoples of Yugoslavia: Serbs, Croats, Slovenes, Montenegrins, Macedonians and others'. Now is the time, the hour has struck to rise as one man for the battle against the invaders and hirelings, killers of our people. Do not falter in the face of any enemy terror. Answer terror with savage blows at the most vital points of the Fascist bandits' occupation.'[13] But for all its stirring words, this call for action passed virtually unnoticed by the outside world and for a time only achieved a major effect in Serbia and Montenegro where conditions were conducive to revolt. In Slovenia, Croatia and Macedonia there was as yet no general support for an uprising and the local communist parties were in varying degrees disunited among themselves. But there were plenty of individual acts of sabotage in all areas. On 7 July, in the village of Bela Crkva in Serbia, a communist who had fought in the Spanish Civil War, Zikica Jovanović, urged a crowd of peasants in the village street to join the Partisan resistance movement. When gendarmes tried to arrest him, he shot two of them and managed to escape – only to be killed the following year. This incident was later taken to mark the beginning of the uprising which was eventually to give Tito both military and political victory.

While Tito remained at headquarters in Belgrade with Alexander Ranković and a small staff, his other most capable and trusted lieutenants had dispersed throughout the country, mostly to their native regions. Reports from Croatia spoke of strong Croat nationalist feelings even among party leaders and said that the right spirit, that is, communist and all-Yugoslav, would not be enforced until a certain Andrija Hebrang – later to become notorious in party history had been removed from the region.[14] Kardelj went on to Slovenia to try to resolve doubts among members about the feasibility of uprising there. The Slovene revolt broke out about 22 July. Svetozar Vukmanović, known by his pseudonym 'Tempo', was working in both Serbia and Bosnia. Revolt in Bosnia-Herzegovina and Croatia started on 27 July. The whole movement had been given encourage-ment by events in Montenegro. Here, where Djilas was active, the country had risen on 13 July almost as one man. The Italians had been unable to occupy this wild mountainous country except along the scanty and difficult lines of communication. Djilas proved quite unable to control the ferocious violence of his countrymen, who were carried away at the thought of fighting again supported by their traditional allies the Russians. They raged through Montenegro burning, pillaging and slaying both Italians and any of their own people who were slow to support the revolt. They captured quantities of arms. By the end of the month the Italians had been pushed out of all except the garrison towns of Podgorica and Cetinje and it took them weeks before they were able to fight their way back.

Tito, too, had a Montenegrin problem on his hands, for Djilas and other party members, ignoring Grandfather's specific instructions not to make communist revolution, began to organize the most extreme form of government through soviets, killing off opponents and wreaking vengeance on enemies with a violence which greatly injured the communist cause – as Tito pointed out. He had to send Tempo to Montenegro to restore order and disband the revolutionary soviets.[15] By the end of July there were so many Partisans in Serbia mounting sabotage attacks against railway lines, telegraph communi-cations, isolated enemy positions, arms depots, local gendarme and police posts, that the Germans began to realize that they, as well as the Italians, had to deal with a general resistance movement.

Tito's original idea had been to fulfil the Comintern orders by organizing small groups who would live in the hills and woods out-side the main towns and away from the enemy-controlled lines of communication. It was high summer; the weather and heavy foliage, as well as the geographical configuration of a great part of Yugoslavia, aided guerrilla warfare. Much of the country was mountainous, a great part of it wooded, and roads very few, especially in the highlands.

From his operational headquarters in Belgrade Tito tried to keep track of the number of detachments formed, the numbers of men operating and the places where camps could be established to act as coordinating centres. Vladimir Dedijer, who kept a diary of the war, recorded some feverish movement around Tito in Belgrade at this time – the lulls of waiting interspersed with periods of intense activity. Intelligence reports came into headquarters by couriers, or by other impromptu methods such as messages written on the back of a cigarette packet; radio stations had to be monitored and a daily bulletin prepared. People were coming and going all the time, and every day reports were received of resistance workers who had been caught by the police or Gestapo: 'Vula Antić arrested at the National Bank. This morning Mitra [Mitrović Djilas's first wife, ed.] went from Dorcol to Dedinje by the busiest streets. I told her no sense in being so incautious, she would be caught', wrote Dedijer in his diary.[16] She was caught.

Tito's headquarters was in the house of a rich and well-known Belgrade figure, Vladislav Ribnikar, owner of the liberal newspaper *Politika* and secret member of the Communist Party. He had assigned rooms for Tito's use. In the bathroom a secret door in a cupboard behind the washbasin led to a hiding place under the roof where Tito could retire in event of police raids. Here he kept two revolvers and a supply of hand grenades in case of need. He still went about in the town, but as life became more dangerous he gave this up and spent most of his day working in Ribnikar's large and secluded garden.[17] He had to try to keep control of all military operations and make arrangements for distribution of arms and ammunition as they were captured or bought, or made in improvised workshops and factories. Intelligence reports of German troop movements and police and Gestapo activities also had to be kept. Reports about local informers and collaborators with the various German and Serbian quisling authorities were particularly important since these were the people through whom party members were most often captured. From the beginning Alexander Ranković became Tito's Intelligence Chief, a position in which he showed conspicuous professional ability.[18]

At the end of July 1941 Ranković's career was all but prematurely ended when he was organizing a plot to blow up Radio Belgrade. An informer told the Gestapo who were waiting for him when he went to meet an accomplice. Tito soon heard of his arrest and immediately

(*above*): **17. Slovenian delegation to AVNOJ, November 1943, led by Jaka Avšić followed by Herta Has.**

(*below*): **18. Tito in his HQ on Vis, June 1944.** *(Left to right)* **Vladimir Bakarić, Ivan Milutinović, Edward Kardelj, Tito, Aleksandar Ranković, Svetozar Vukmanović-Tempo and Milovan Djilas.**

(*above*): **19. Tito meets Churchill, Naples, 1944.**
(*below*): **20. Tito signing agreement with Stalin in Moscow, April 1945.**

ordered that he must be rescued at all costs. It was reported that he had fought the police and been clubbed into unconsciousness, but at first even his whereabouts were unknown. The Gestapo did not realize whom they had arrested and took him to the prison hospital in the middle of Belgrade to be restored to a condition in which he could be interrogated. Mitra Mitrović, who had been arrested as Dedijer had forecast, was detained in the same hospital. She managed to smuggle out a note, and a doctor provided a plan of the hospital showing the room where Ranković was in bed under close guard. The authorities had decided it would be five days before he was fit to be moved and interrogated.

At 10 a.m. on Tuesday, 29 July, forty Partisans armed with revolvers and grenades, and dressed in civilian clothes, surrounded the hospital in groups of three. Ten of them, with one in handcuffs to give the appearance of prisoners and escort, entered the hospital and passed the guard at the gate. When a policeman in the corridor challenged them, he was shot down. As they burst into Ranković's room and began to fight the four-man guard, Ranković himself jumped out of bed and was bustled out of the building and over a wall into the street, while Partisans covered his retreat with fighting and confusion. The car that should have been waiting to take him away was missing and Ranković had to take shelter in a nearby house. He removed his head bandages and hospital clothes and was given a suit that proved too small for his hefty figure. In tight trousers and shirt he was moved to another house and provided with a passable jacket and hat. He got away in a van and was driven out to a safe house in the suburbs of Belgrade to lie up and recover from his experience. Several Partisans who took part in the operations were wounded, but none was killed.[19] The incident gave a much needed boost to their morale, but it showed Tito the dangers of staying on in Belgrade. As soon as he had recovered, Ranković left town on foot. Dressed as a peasant he made his way to his native village, and then went on to join Partisan headquarters in western Serbia.

Tito left the city on 16 September. He did not return to it until he entered in triumph after the German retreat in October 1944. When he came back with the Red Army, but also as Commander-in-Chief in his own right of an army of 300,000 men and women. His departure from Belgrade had that element of musical comedy mixed with real danger and confident bravado that had characterized many of his escapades in the past. This time the danger of capture was very great indeed but, as before, courage and careful attention to detail paid dividends. It was considered safest to travel in company with other people who would make a convincing party of travellers. Tito, still in his identity of prosperous engineer Babić, met an Orthodox priest, Milutinović, known to be a Partisan sympathizer, at lunch at the Ribnikar's house. The priest agreed to furnish Tito – whose real identity he did not yet know – with travel permits, and offered to accompany him. A man called Jaša Reiter, a party member who was a *Volksdeutsche* and so had legal documents, was also enlisted as one of the group, and they were joined by a number of women to give the party a homely, normal appearance. They passed the checks at the railway station without event and travelled by train to central Serbia. Tito, it is recorded, was in high good humour, joking in German with Reiter and entertaining his companions.

When the train was approaching Kraljevo it was brought to a stop because, passengers were told, the bridge over the river Morava had been blown up by communist bandits. The travellers had to go from Stalac to Čačak on foot. At Čačak one of the girls saw a police agent who knew her by sight. He was successfully evaded and the party reached their destination, the small town of Požega, without further mishap. From here they took a horse cab to Krupanj, close to Partisan headquarters in the recently captured town of Valjevo. The cab driver told his passengers of the dangers of the journey because of the woods being full of bandits. 'I suppose you are not going to join the Partisans?' he asked shrewdly. 'Is it likely in clothes like these?' said Tito, well dressed as usual. The driver apologized but added that you never knew with people these days.[20] Tito was finally met by Ranković and arrived at his headquarters on 18 September. This journey saw the end of Engineer Babić. Tito was at last free to be himself and take on perhaps his most satisfying role – that of military commander in the field.

During the summer of 1941 Tito had taken certain decisions after deep discussion at least with his closest associates in the Politburo – and this meant with Kardelj, Djilas, Ranković and Lola Ribar. In retrospect these can be seen as having been vital to the whole pattern of military and political developments throughout the war. They were important also in bringing about the revolution of power which was Tito's long-term objective. Although there was in them an element of gambling with fate inevitable in any strategic political planning, they displayed that sure understanding of the basic requirements for political power which was the hallmark of Tito's greatness. The decision taken at the meeting in Belgrade on 4 July to transform the party leadership into a military General Staff was especially important. It was not implicit in the Comintern order, and Tito could have remained simply a party leader directing Partisan operations in different parts of the country.

The idea of creating an army to undertake guerrilla activity was uniquely Yugoslav and certainly germinated from Tito's own ideas. At the beginning of July 1941, when there were eighteen German, Italian, Bulgarian and Hungarian military divisions in Yugoslav lands, with an additional five divisions of local forces (Domobrani) in the Independent State of Croatia and some thousands of locally recruited quisling police units, it may have seemed somewhat ludicrous for Tito to have a General Staff without an army. The groups of threes and fives, even tens and fifties, of communist-led patriots without uniforms, ill-equipped and scarcely armed, widely dispersed throughout the country, could not in the wildest fantasy be called a fighting force. The creation of a General Staff was a declaration of intent to create an army. No one outside Yugoslavia, perhaps no one outside the small group around Tito, least of all the Russians, believed this to be a possibility. Within six months his General Staff reckoned it commanded about 80,000 men, theoretically under arms even if many lacked modern weapons. 'You could not call this a regular army,' said Tito later. 'You cannot have a regular army until you have conscription. These were all volunteers.'[21]

The second important decision, also taken in early July, and also perhaps attributable to Tito, though again it was worked out with his lieutenants, was that his forces should aim to clear the enemy from certain areas of the country and create operational bases which came to be called liberated territories. This was normal military strategy which perhaps owed something to experience gained from the Spanish Civil War, but it had the important political consequences which Tito had intended. It meant that for as long as the Partisans held such territory they were able to rule it as a small state – to deal with all matters of civil government, to impose their ideas on the population, and to begin to put into practice their political theories – within the very narrow limits imposed by war conditions. Liberated territories were fought over, won and lost during the course of the war, but a framework of local government was built up bit by bit from the very first months of the fighting.[22]

Another decision taken by Tito in July 1941, one which was in line with Comintern instructions, was that the appeal for armed resistance should be made to all the population, on the basis of a popular front. The Communist Party should provide the leaders for resistance, but should play down ideological extremism and not aim directly at socialist revolution. Tito's Partisan movement appealed to a popular front, appealed to patriotism and eventually to nationalism among the various Yugoslav peoples. It is doubtful whether he at first realized the forces that this would release. It is certain that Tito still felt that he was in charge of one small part of something that was an international movement of which Russia was the head. He dutifully transmitted all major decisions to the Comintern and did his best to carry out the orders that he received back. Yet simultaneously he was for the first time conscious that the Yugoslavs were on their own. 'I felt myself to be an independent leader from the very beginning in 1941', he recalled. 'I felt completely independent, especially when we saw that nobody would help us and we were on our own.'[23]

It was to be a long time before the consequences of this independence were to be recognized by either side. It is understandable that the Russians, battling desperately in 1941 for the defence of Moscow, should have been indifferent to what Tito was doing in Yugoslavia. Yet throughout the war, even when their situation was less threatened, they always underestimated Tito and denigrated his political and military achievements. This was in line with Stalin's attitude to foreign communist parties from the early days of the Comintern. Tito also at this time cannot have clearly understood the full implications of his own policy. He did not yet see the complete incompatibility of independence and national liberation with total acceptance of Russian authority. Farseeing as Tito was in his planning for communist revolution in Yugoslavia, he remained for a long time blind to the fact that it was relatively unimportant to, and in some ways unwanted by, the Russian politicians who directed Soviet strategy in world politics.

# 11 TITO AND MIHAILOVIĆ

Tito and the Partisans were not the only people to have the idea of resistance. As early as 15 or 16 April 1941 a number of officers and men of the defeated royalist army had taken to the woods in Serbia as their ancestors had so often done before them. They soon came to be called by the traditional name of Četniks, from the Serbian word *četa* meaning military company. 'The name Četnik came from the people, not from me,' said Mihailović later. One of their first leaders was Kosta Pećanac, a large ageing man with a commanding presence. He had been well known as a Serbian guerrilla leader behind the Bulgarian lines in the first world war and between the wars had kept his Četniks in being as a Serbian paramilitary force which was used against Croats, communists or any other supposed state enemies. There were other Četnik leaders – Ljuba Novaković, a tall man 'with greying hair and an air of worried preoccupation' and Keserović 'cruel, brutal and fanatically opposed to any suggestion of toleration to the Partisans'. The most important of them was Colonel Dragoljub – usually shortened to Draža – Mihailović. He went to west Bosnia at the time of the Yugoslav collapse and reached Ravna Gora in the wooded Šumadija hills in western Serbia sometime between 10 and 15 May.[1]

Born in 1893, Mihailović had also seen service in the first world war when as a young lieutenant he had taken part in the Serbian army's final breakthrough into Serbia from Salonika. His memories of how with Allied aid defeat had then been turned into triumphal success influenced much of Mihailović's thinking. After the first world war, his career as a regular officer had not been outstanding. He had been Yugoslav military attaché in Sofia and Prague, but had not reached a high rank in the army. Like many officers, he had been intensely pro-Serb and anti-Croat. At the time of the German invasion he was disgusted at the lack of defensive preparations and at the defection of the Croats.

In the summer of 1941 his headquarters at Ravna Gora became a centre for patriotic Serbs who were looking for some kind of lead in resistance. Unlike many of his followers – the giant Jovanović, for instance who had 'a chest like a bull and a golden beard reaching half way down it; shoulders like a gorilla's with red-gold hair falling about them almost like a woman's but with a voice that was far from womanly and a handshake that nearly cracked your bones' – Mihailović was a small man, giving a misleading first impression of being mild and insignificant. 'He struck me as a nice, pleasant-mannered  sort of man – a typical regular officer' was how he impressed Tito at this time.[2] He was described by an English officer who saw him later as 'A slight somewhat stooping figure, wearing a British battle-dress without badges of rank, a dark blue shirt buttoned at the collar, with no tie, and thick peasant socks pulled over the ends of his trousers. . . . The round head covered with a thatch of greyish hair was the head of a Serbian peasant. The grizzled beard did not conceal the sharp lines of the face, nor the hollows under the cheek bones. From behind strong glasses there looked out a pair of deceptively mild, pale-blue eyes.' Christie Lawrence, a British journalist who had escaped from Crete, had a similar impression in 1942. 'He looked an old man, though I knew his age to be between forty-five and fifty. He was small and slight with grey hair, a thin, lined face, and gold-rimmed spectacles.'[3]

Later events were to show Mihailović to be a man of complex character, but limited capabilities and outlook. Moulded by the old-fashioned military training and the archaic peasant society from which he came, he had charm and the vanity of his officer class. He was both cunning and shrewd – qualities which led him to undertake many involved intrigues. As a result he was often out-manoeuvred by more quick-witted adversaries or supporters, and was later used as a cat's-paw by the government in exile. He thought of himself as a soldier, but in an already outmoded concept of that vocation. 'I am a soldier;' he said at his trial in 1946, adding 'politics never interested me.'[4] Yet from the moment he reached Ravna Gora, most of his activity was concerned with politics. There could be no doubt about his courage, or his fanatical Serbian patriotism. He wished to restore Serbia to power in any postwar state and saw communist revolution as a threat. He seems to have had no understanding of the deeper issues underlying revolutionary feeling among all Yugoslav peoples during the war.

Mihailović had about thirty officers with him when he started what was at first called the Ravna Gora and later the Četnik movement. By June he had linked up with other Četnik leaders and soon his emissaries were out in the Serbian countryside setting up recruiting centres and contacting other leaders. The plan was to call up all Serbian males between the ages of twenty and thirty in country districts, to form an operational army divided into companies of fifteen to twenty men. Those between the ages of thirty and forty were to form groups of saboteurs, and the older men were to remain in the villages and maintain order. By the end of September 1941 there were 5,000 Četniks. Many of these were only very loosely under Mihailović's authority and some, like Kosta Pećanac, defected to the Germans before the end of the summer.

* * *

Tito's Partisans were also active in the countryside, especially after 22 June, trying to persuade the peasants to volunteer for their army. By the end of September they had mustered some 15,000 men. Thus the two leaders were in competition for Serbian support – Mihailović the intensely patriotic Serb, Tito the communist with an all-Yugoslav, radical and totally anti-German appeal. This rivalry grafted an element of civil war on to the already complex situation in Yugoslavia. While in 1941 no one could envisage the end of the war or its outcome, it is clear that both men were aware that their struggle for power would affect the character of any future state. For the time being they were both faced with a German occupation system which though highly organized was not at first designed to deal with large-scale resistance.

German rule for Serbia was divided between three major authorities. In theory, each had a different responsibility – military, administrative and local government. In the summer of 1941 military operations were under the command of General Bader who was subordinate to Field-Marshal List in Athens. Military administration for Serbia – corresponding to Allied Military Government in occupied territories later in the war – was under former SS Brigade-Führer Dr Harold Turner. This department was responsible for general security and for political and economic policy and had important sections dealing with the extraction of food, raw materials and labour required for the German war effort. Local administration, carried on largely through the same machinery, often with the same personnel as in prewar Serbia, was directed by a quisling Serbian government wholly controlled by the Germans but with Serbian ministers and, after 29 August, a Serbian head of state, former Yugoslav army General Milan Nedić. All three sections had their troops, security organs, intelligence agencies and different methods of operating to quell opposition and get the country working obediently and industriously for the German. Their efforts frequently over-lapped and conflicted as did those of the different intelligence and counter-intelligence services – the Abwehr, the security organs (SD) and security police (SIPO) which included the Gestapo. There were endless possibilities for Yugoslavs to have contacts or to collaborate with occupying authorities, and for informers or spies to become multiple agents. Yet in spite of this impressive organization of power the Germans only held in strength, the main lines of communication and a few key points in Serbia. In the summer of 1941 they were only just beginning to organize the locally raised Serbian forces to guard the interior of the country.

The Germans had not anticipated the Serbian insurrection that broke out in the summer of 1941. It was led by Partisans and joined by some Četniks, although Mihailović had ordered his followers not to attack the Germans. It was so widespread as to be clearly a spontaneous revolt of a great part of the people. By September the Germans had lost control of about two-thirds of the countryside. 'It is not only a question of dealing with communists', reported General Wisshaupt, 'but with a general national movement.' Dr Turner wrote a little later: 'The Partisan positions in the forests are such that it is virtually impossible to attack them frontally. The intensification of propaganda which says in effect that the Bolsheviks are not doing well in their fighting, is of little use. We have gained the impression that even news of Soviet capitulation would not lead to the surrender of these bandits who are resilient as fiends. Besides, their organization is excellent and could serve as an example of what a secret organization should be.'[5]

As the uprising spread, Partisans and Četniks, separately or together, were highly successful in attacking enemy positions – roads, railway lines, bridges, villages and even towns. Partisan detachments established control over certain areas, Četniks over others. The situation was extremely confused and there were frequent clashes of interest and authority between individual Četnik leaders, and in spite of many joint operations, between Partisans and Četniks, whose aims, organization and behaviour were so dissimilar. The Partisans were becoming increasingly disciplined, increasingly subject to central control; the Četniks on the other hand remained dependent on the personality of their often undisciplined and unprincipled local leaders. Rivalry between the two groups became more embittered when it came to the capture of sizeable towns offering valuable booty. On 24 September the Partisans captured Užice, a rich prize with a bank full of money – about fifty-five million dinars – and an armaments factory with a daily output of 400 rifles and large quantities of ammunition. Partisan forces also held Požega, Kraljevo and Čačak in the western Morava valley, while Četniks held Ložnica and a useful foundry.

Throughout the summer of 1941 Mihailović was trying in various ways to get support – or protection – for his movement. He did not wish to lose his forces in an abortive uprising before his plans were completed, or indeed before the Germans were weaker than he knew them to be at that time. He wished to preserve Serbian Četniks for the defence of Serbia and to prevent the Serbian people being decimated by German reprisals. One of his main objectives was to establish links with the royalist government in exile and with British forces in the Middle East. He tried a number of methods of contact and was first successful on 19 June 1941 when news of his guerrilla movement, taken by courier, reached Istanbul. Here there were royalist Yugoslavs as well as members of the British Special Operations Executive (SOE), an agency engaged in multifarious activities including propaganda, military intelligence and field operations. Mihailović also secured parts of a radio transmitter, and after nearly two months' repair work this was made operational and messages from it were picked up in Malta. By August he had established direct contact with SOE in Cairo. He also managed to get in touch with the royalist government through the American and Turkish Embassies in Belgrade.[6] He sent his first signal for the royalist government in London on 4 September and received a reply twenty days later.

His accounts of the Serbian uprising – with no mention of the Partisan's preponderant share in it – were the first news to reach the Allies of guerrilla activity in any part of occupied Europe. Coming after shattering German successes in western and eastern Europe, after the Nazi invasion of Russia, Rommel's successes in the Middle East and the *Luftwaffe* raids on London, it was most heartening news for the Allies and exiled Yugoslav government alike. The story of heroic Serbian resistance appealed to the imagination and emotions of people in the west wearied and depressed by unrelieved disaster. It is small wonder that it had a jubilant reception and that the Yugoslav government in exile should have been eager to make the most of it. It was especially welcome to the Serbs in the exiled government for it gave them a weapon they could use in internal disputes with Croats and Slovenes, and a potential lever for demanding aid which would go to Serbs in Serbia and be useful in any postwar struggle for power. Thus from the beginning Mihailović's movement became the subject of political intrigues and of a propaganda myth which soon bore little relation to actual facts. Mihailović became the centre, and in many ways the prisoner, ultimately the victim of this myth. It is impossible to know how much it altered his ideas. It certainly influenced all his subsequent actions.

At the same time as he was establishing connections with the British, Mihailović was in contact with the quisling Nedić government. He wished to get protection for his movement, and arms so that he could crush the communists and eliminate them as competitors, while Nedić on his side was not unwilling to have his own link with a patriotic Serb organization. The Germans approved of these contacts. They favoured the creation of 'legal' Četniks to prevent the development of a united Partisan–Četnik resistance movement. In early September a number of meetings were held in Belgrade between representatives of Mihailović and Nedić. Mihailović himself did not go. He said at his trial in 1946 that this was because in two years in which he had served under Nedić in the army 'he twice punished me with thirty days' detention. I had no respect for him and would not have gone'.[7] The results of the talks were that Nedić offered to stop his troops acting against the Četniks, and they on their side were to help him to fight the Partisans. It is possible that some arrangement was made for Mihailović to be financed from the National Bank in Belgrade. His intelligence officer Pipan set out from Belgrade taking a liaison officer of the Nedić government, Marko Olujić, to Ravna Gora. On their way both were captured by the Partisans, who learnt about these talks from the papers they were carrying. Olujić was executed as a traitor.[8]

A third line of negotiation being carried on concurrently, was through Mihailović's discussions with the Partisans. In spite of his hatred of communists and the belief that they were the ultimate enemy, Mihailović was willing to meet their representatives and hear what they had to say – perhaps an element of curiosity about the communists was added to his desperate determination to try every means of strengthening and securing his own movement. Urged by the Comintern to set up a wartime Popular Front, the Partisans were pressing for talks. In August Ranković had suggested to the party that it should consider the whole question of agreement with the Četniks about joint action. Arrangements were made through intermediaries, and on the night of 14/15 August, Partisan representatives Miloš Minić and Dragojlo Dudić went to Ravna Gora. They met Mihailović himself and two people whom he later described as his chief lieutenants, Dragiša Vasić, a writer known for his chauvinistic Serbian views, and Major Dragoslav Pavolović, a former army officer. Mihailović was very reserved in his reaction to Partisan proposals for joint operations. He said that German defeat was likely to take a long time, and that there was no need at that stage to press attacks against the Germans who would impose heavy reprisals on the Serbian population.[9] The talks were inconclusive and were followed by a number of other exchanges in August and early September, though relations between the two sides were deteriorating as disputes became more frequent. Tito believed that it was essential to come to some definitive agreement as soon as possible. The measure of urgency for him can be gauged by the fact that he went himself to see Mihailović on 19 September, the day after he had arrived from Belgrade at Partisan headquarters.

The meeting took place in the house of Alexander Misić, who had been one of Mihailović's emissaries to Nedić a fortnight before, in the village of Struganik near Ravna Gora. Tito arrived on horseback, accompanied by two lieutenants, Miloš Minić and Obrad Stefanović, with a posse of fifteen Partisans on foot. Mihailović sent a mounted guard to meet him. After handshakes and the traditional food and drink they sat down to talk. Mihailović was at the head of the table, his assistant Vasić on the right, Tito on his left, with Partisans and Četniks alternately standing round, armed and eyeing each other suspiciously. Vasić began by asking Tito if he was a Russian and it was obvious that Tito's brief account of himself as a Croat and a communist who had spent some time in Russia was considered little better and not very convincing. 'Because Draža Mihailović – for I do not know what reasons – both then and for a long time afterwards, took me for a Russian, he spoke very openly about Croats and all other peoples of Yugoslavia,' Tito said later when recalling this meeting. The difference of approach between the two leaders soon became obvious, Tito pressed for joint action, and

185

offered to put his forces under Mihailović's command. But Mihailović warned of the dangers of premature resistance, and emphasized the strength of the Germans. The possibility of help was almost negligible, he said, the Allies were far away and could not be counted upon. Neither leader was prepared to show his full hand – Mihailović already in touch with the British and, through Nedić, with the Germans, Tito in contact with Moscow. They parted at eight o'clock in the evening without reaching agreement.[10] Relations were not ruptured but before their next meeting six weeks later events had taken place which made agreement virtually impossible.

Mihailović's messages to Istanbul began to bring results by the end of the summer. On 25 August Prime Minister Churchill wrote to Hugh Dalton, British Minister of Economic Warfare, who was in charge of secret action of all kinds against the enemy: 'I am informed by General Simović that there is widespread guerrilla activity in Yugoslavia. They need allies, support and direction from abroad. Please make contact with those groups as soon as possible and do what is necessary to give them help.' SOE Cairo was ordered to send a mission to try to contact 'patriotic groups'.[11] The man chosen as head of mission was Captain D. H. (later Colonel and always known as 'Bill') Hudson. On 22 September, accompanied by two majors of the royal Yugoslav forces in exile, Ostojić and Lalatović, he was put ashore from a submarine on the coast of Montenegro, territory at that time held by Tito's forces. A young Partisan officer Veljko Mičunović – later to be Tito's ambassador in Washington – conducted them across Partisan liberated territory to Tito's headquarters at Užice.[12] Hudson thus had the opportunity to see something of the size and operation of Tito's movements from the start. A few days later Partisans conducted him to Mihailović's headquarters at Ravna Gora.

Hudson had taken two radio transmitters and cipher books for himself and Mihailović, but was unable to transmit further than Malta. By the time he arrived, fighting between Partisans and Četniks had become frequent and his first recommendation to Cairo was that no aid should be given to the Četniks until they had settled their differences with the Partisans. He also advised that a mission be sent to Tito. The first advice was not taken, and the second, for reasons that are still not clear as British documents have not yet been made available, was not acted upon for eighteen months. One explanation is to be found in the fact that no one in Britain or Cairo believed it possible that a group of communists led by a totally unknown man – even Tito's name was not known abroad at this time – could have raised a general resistance movement. Memories of the first world war coloured by romantic views of earlier Serbian history, plus the enthusiastic and almost certainly exaggerated accounts of Četnik activities given by Yugoslav government officials, and the direct contact with Mihailović, made a Četnik movement quite credible. Tito also came to believe, perhaps with reason, that anything favourable to him was likely to be suppressed by certain people in Cairo or London simply because his movement was communist led, and also in order to strengthen the royalist case for supporting Mihailović.

Shortly after Hudson arrived, and after he had sent the message suggesting an end to hostilities against the Partisans and a mission to Tito, he lost control of his own radio transmitter. One story was that Mihailović took charge of it, another that it was confiscated by the Germans who had broken his cipher. In either case his communications with Cairo for twelve months were subject to Četnik vetting; news favourable to Partisans was suppressed.[13] An emissary from Mihailović, Dr Miloš Sekulić, who left Belgrade on 25 September and reached London on 10 October, gave his version of Četnik activities. Thus neither the British nor the Yugoslav government was fully informed about Partisan activities, organization and strength. The Germans at this time had much better intelligence about the Partisans.[14] They also had a truer picture of Mihailović's potential strength and of his political manoeuvres, for they had a special unit which monitored his radio emissions and they had managed to break his cipher.

Archives of the Yugoslav government in exile show that there was intense activity in London about supplies to the Četniks during the month of October 1941. King Peter II had talks with Churchill on the 13th which were followed a week later by an *aide memoire* from his prime minister, General Simović, in which a request was put to Churchill for medical aid for 10,000 wounded, and arms for 80,000 to 100,000 guerrillas – figures that could only have been correct if they included the Partisans.[15] Churchill replied favourably on 26 October, though he pointed out the geographical and transport difficulties involved. Simović had meanwhile seen the foreign minister, Anthony Eden, on 20 October, and General Sir John Dill, Chief of the Imperial General Staff, on the 23rd. Another Yugoslav minister, Branko Čubrilović, saw the British ministers Amery on the

28th and Hugh Dalton on the 29th. On the 28th he also saw Maisky, the Soviet Ambassador in London, to enlist his support. Maisky showed interest in the kind of aid needed and asked about the possibility of it being dropped by air.[16] On 29 October General Dill wrote a Top Secret letter to Simović saying that in a few days Mihailović would be sent '30 guns, 20 automatic [rifles], 90 automatic revolvers, 1,000 bandages and 10,000 [sic, probably pounds sterling] gold,' with other supplies to follow later. He added that the British Commandant in the Middle East was in touch with the 'patriots' and would do all he could to supply their needs.[17] The favourable trend of these negotiations in London was radioed to Mihailović who had sent twenty-nine telegrams to the royalist government between 6 and 29 October. He must have been aware before his second encounter with Tito on 27th October that he would receive Allied aid.

This meeting was also affected by other factors which made it even less likely than the first to result in agreement. By October, Tito and his general staff had taken important decisions to widen the scope of their military organization. At a meeting held at Stolice in Serbia on 26 September, attended by Partisan leaders from all regions of the country except Macedonia, they had decided to set up separate military commands in each region of Yugoslavia, under the supreme command of Tito's General Staff. They now had a skeleton staff for an all-Yugoslav army, a general strategic plan for the whole country, and they agreed on a plan to set up military–civilian administrations in all places cleared of enemy troops.

On 16 September Hitler ordered three German divisions with air support, under the command of General Böhme, to start large-scale operations against resistance forces in Serbia. At the same time Hitler's chief of staff, Field-Marshal von Keitel, issued a directive on methods to be used against resistance in any occupied lands: 'In order to stop disorder from the beginning', it said, 'the harshest measures must be taken at once and without delay at the very first signs. . . . It should be kept in mind that in the countries in question, one man's life is often not valued so highly so that an intimidating effect can only be reached by cruelty. . . . In a reprisal for the life of one German soldier, the general rule should be capital punishment of 50–100 communists. The manner of execution must have a frightening effect.'[18] On 20–21 October this order was put into effect in the most terrible way at Kragujevac, in Serbia, in retaliation for a nearby Partisan raid two days previously in which ten German soldiers had been killed and twenty wounded. The Germans rounded up most of the males between the ages of sixteen and sixty, herded them into the town barracks and marched them out in groups of a hundred to be shot. The massacre continued all day until even the German execution squads were sickened and some broke down. The Kragujevac incident was on the indictment at the trial of war criminals at Nuremberg at the end of the war. The numbers of those executed vary in different accounts but are usually given as up to 5,000. Among them were many communist supporters, for the town was one of the few industrial centres in Serbia. The rest were ordinary people and many were children who were marched out of school to be shot. To Mihailović the massacre was an appalling illustration of the kind of reprisals he most feared, a backing for his argument that the time was not ripe for revolution. To Tito it called for more widespread revolt.

The second meeting between Tito and Mihailović took place a few days later on 26/27 October. It was again held in Četnik territory near Ravna Gora, in a large house in the village of Brajici. This time the Partisans arrived in two cars – captured from the Italians. Tito was accompanied by his adjutant Mitar Bakić, his former Comintern associate, now Staff-Officer Sreten, Žujović – known as Crni (the black one) and an eight-man bodyguard carrying sub-machine guns. Mihailović had with him an armed bodyguard and his close associates Dragiša Vasić and Colonel Pavlović. The contrast between the opposing sides facing each other across the table was as great as before – 'our chaps were young, clean-shaven with an occasional moustache, while Draža's men wore long beards', Tito recalled later. The Četniks were 'heavily armed, festooned with bandoliers'.[19] The atmosphere was more hostile, the talks less exploratory than before. Both sides were better informed about each other and the situation was more tense, for the German advance in Serbia was by this time well under way. Although Mihailović knew that he would get British aid, he did not know how much or when, and Tito on his side had had no favourable reply to his radioed requests to the Comintern for Russian aid. Hoping to get news of Partisan activity sent to London, Tito asked that Captain Hudson should be allowed to attend the talks. Mihailović refused and Hudson remained in the next room. He was allowed to join the party for supper, at which Mihailović with sly humour offered Tito a drink. Taking a deep draught Tito discovered it to be 'Šumadija tea' warm slivovica, or plum brandy. Mihailović burst into laughter as Tito choked over the fiery, alcoholic drink and wiped the 'tea' off his uniform.[20]

The talks, however, were no laughing matter. They were based on a note with twelve points for discussion sent by Tito to Mihailović on 20 October. These covered joint military operations against the enemy (Germans and Nedić's forces); a joint operational staff; equipment and supply; equal sharing of booty; joint local commands; permanent joint commissions to settle differences; organization of local authorities for civilian administration in liberated areas on a united front basis (the suggestion was that these should be the Partisan National Liberation Committees); voluntary mobilization rather than conscription; no free hand for local commanders, all to be subject to the two high commands which, to avoid clashes, should be in different places; intensification of work against fifth columnists, and joint courts martial to try to sentence traitors, but specifically no extra-legal judgments of such cases; joint action to stop quisling Četnik groups – such as Pećanac's forces fighting against Partisans; and finally Partisans and Četniks to stop issuing identity papers to 'fifth columnists and spies'.[21] Mihailović does not appear to have made any serious counterproposals, but in any case it seems likely that by now he had no intention of reaching agreement with the Partisans. For Mihailović the choice between working with German army officers and their collaborator, the Serbian General Nedić, and joining forces with Tito, a self-confessed Croat and communist, must have been so heavily weighted in favour of the former as to be no choice at all. Committing his supporters to what seemed like suicidal fighting before he had received Allied aid, and while the Germans were everywhere successful, also seemed to Mihailović to be courting disaster for his whole movement.

Predictably Mihailović rejected Tito's points about joint operations and operational staff and those about National Liberation committees which would have committed him to communist-controlled rule in liberated territories. He was in favour of conscription which might have given his Četniks an advantage over the Partisans' volunteers. Some agreement was reached on other points: separate staff headquarters – the Partisans at Užice, which they held, the Četniks at Požega – and joint courts to deal with disputes. An earnest of the Partisans' real desire to reach agreement was the fact that they offered Mihailović ammunition from the Užice factory and 1,200 guns – and in fact, gave him 500 before relations were ruptured. They agreed

(*above*): **21. Tito with wife at the time of the public announcement of their marriage, entertaining the British Foreign Secretary, Anthony Eden, 18 September 1952.**

(*left*): **22. Tito with old peasant woman, Slavonski Brod, May 1953**

(*above*): **23. Tito, Mme Broz, his second son Alexander and grandchildren Josip and Zlatka (children of Zarko, his eldest son), 1954.**

(*below*): **24. Tito on Brioni, June 1952.**

that each side should take five million dinars from the fifty-five million captured with the Užice bank.

During the discussions the Partisans in the egalitarian, comradely way of their as yet amateurish army, began to throw in their own opinions. Most of the talking on their side was in any case being done by Žujović; Tito was very quiet. The Četniks followed their lead. 'Draža Mihailović suddenly took off his glasses, pulled nervously at his beard, and snapped at them "Be quiet there, no one is asking you anything." This silenced the Četniks.' The talks concluded, the Partisans spent the night at Brajici. 'I did not sleep all night,' said Tito, 'and kept my revolver under my pillow.'[22] After some discussion next day they returned to Užice, having an unpleasant encounter *en route* with a group of Četniks who had mined a bridge on the road back. In retrospect it can be seen that the talks had no chance of success, and that neither side really expected agreement, though Tito may have felt at this stage that any military ally was better than none. Many years later Tito said that his efforts to reach agreement with Mihailović 'had nothing to do with the Comintern. Our idea, desire and intentions were to unite all forces in the struggle against the invaders. Mihailović was an intelligent and very ambitious man. I offered him the supreme command. It was clear, however, that he would not accept it.' Had he accepted it, Tito said he would not have served under him, but would have 'dealt with other matters'.[23]

\* \* \*

After this second meeting, relations between Partisans and Četniks rapidly deteriorated into civil war, and each side blamed the other for starting it. On the night of 1/2 November, Četnik forces attacked Užice and other Partisan positions at a number of places, including Požega, Čačak and Ivanjica. Although Mihailović later denied personal responsibility for the raid on Užice, the simultaneous attacks bore every evidence of a synchronized plan. Major Radoslav Djurić, at that time one of Mihailović's close collaborators, said later that he had been opposed to the plan. Captain Hudson, an independent observer and certainly no supporter of Tito wrote: 'Mihailović, grossly underestimating the Partisans' hold on their followers, unsuccessfully attacked Užice.'[24] Hudson was in a position to know what happened since, for reasons that have not yet been elucidated, he was himself actually in Užice at the time.

The Partisans mobilized all their forces, including workers from the arms factory, to repel the Četniks. On 3 November Mihailović's Chief of Staff Colonel Pavlović, telephoned Tito in Užice and offered a truce if the Partisans would cede Požega. Tito refused. As fighting continued, the Četniks were slowly driven back.

During the fiercest fighting, Mihailović had sent urgent messages to London pressing for immediate aid. 'Situation demands aid most urgently', he radioed on 4 November. On the following day he sent three long signals giving the reasons for urgency: 'The leader of the communists in Serbia under the false name of Tito cannot be considered as a leader of resistance. The fight of the communists against Germans is a fraud. . . . The Partisans have taken arms from the people, I cannot follow that road. They have the arms factory at Užice from which we get nothing, and they still want English arms. If they get them we are finished for ever.'[25] On the following days he radioed information about landing grounds. On 9 November he received his first parachuted supplies and asked that the Allies should request Radio Moscow to denounce all hostilities between Partisans and Četniks. By 12 November the Partisans had approached within one kilometre of Ravna Gora, and Četnik reinforcements called up from Bosnia had not arrived. The Četnik radio stations had to go off the air in case it was captured by Partisans. Četnik headquarters was preparing for hasty evacuation, destroying papers, packing vital supplies and records. In the general panic and fear, Vasić was in tears – he wept like a child. 'Do you realize?' he cried, 'Draža and I will both be condemned to death.'[26]

In this critical situation Mihailović turned to the Germans for help against the Partisans. He made contact through an Abwehr officer, Hauptman Josef Matl, who had already been to Ravna Gora for discussions. A meeting was held on the night of 13/14 November in the inn at Divci near Valjevo. This explains why Mihailović was absent from Ravna Gora at the height of the panic. With three of his staff he had ridden nine hours on horseback to the meeting. Three German officers arrived by car – Matl, Dr George Kiessel, deputy to Dr Harold Turner at the German Administrative Headquarters for Serbia, and Dr Kraus, a Gestapo officer. Mihailović proposed joint operations against the communists and after their liquidation the withdrawal of German troops from Serbia which could then be taken over by the Četniks. But his immediate need was for arms. 'My main aim,' he told the Germans, according to Matl, 'is to save the majority of the people from annihilation.'[27] Mihailović agreed to hand over to the Germans 365 Partisans captured by the Četniks. The Germans were prepared to use Mihailović, though they did not trust him, believing as their intelligence reports stated – and Hitler frequently reiterated – that the Serbs were 'fundamentally anti-German'. They were not prepared to give him arms, and ordered him to disarm his men. When Mihailović left the meeting greatly disappointed he said to Matl 'Tell your officers that I am not nearly such an Englishman as they think I am.' A German report shortly after this meeting described him as no longer having 'a numerous following behind him, but even so, should not be underestimated as there are many thinking Serbs who sympathize with him. In present circumstances he does not present any acute danger, especially as he has become an enemy of, and is fighting against, the communists with whom he worked at the beginning. But from a long-term point of view, he could be dangerous.'[28] When Mihailović returned to Ravna Gora he heard that he had been made 'Commander-in-Chief of Yugoslav forces in the Fatherland'. This was announced by the BBC on 15 November.[29] The appointment made a deep impression on his character. It was the culmination of all his thwarted military ambitions, and gave him an exaggerated view of his own importance and the prospects of his movement, now certain of the support of the government in exile and all the Allied resources it could command. This, and his belief that he had neutralized the Germans, made him more convinced than ever that he did not need to work with the Partisans and that his immediate task was to annihilate them.

The Partisans did not press home their attack against Četnik headquarters. It seems probable that Tito was restrained by orders from Russia whose leaders were still at this time urging him to come to agreement with Mihailović, even to make arrangements for joint command. Royalist government officials were also very active on this account. Their Chargé d'Affaires in Moscow saw Vyshinsky on 17 November and Sir Stafford Cripps, British ambassador to Russia, on the following day, emphasizing the urgency of their request for Russian aid in forcing Tito to accept Mihailović as leader. Russian orders and the German advance with tanks and air support in western Serbia caused Tito to continue his efforts to reach agreement with Mihailović, even though he had heard by this time that the Četniks had handed over the 365 captured Partisans for execution by the

193

Germans. Mihailović said later that they had been sold to the Germans 'at so much per head'.[30]

While Mihailović was parleying with the Germans, his officers, Majors Djurić and Lalatović, met Partisan representatives Ranković, Petar Stambolić and Lola Ribar and reached a nine-point agreement about cessation of hostilities. Further meetings took place on 18, 24, 26 and again on 27 November, when Tito's military expert Koča Popović took the place of the political expert Ranković.[31] Before this series of talks was concluded the Germans had brought up reinforcements, the 113th Infantry Division from the Eastern Front and part of the 704th Division, and were investing the towns of Čačak, Požega and Užice. It was clear the Partisans could not hold out in Serbia. In the middle of the meeting on 27 November, Tito telephoned the negotiators. Major Djurić answered the telephone and Tito asked him to make an urgent request to Mihailović for joint operations. Djurić replied that he would contact his leader. He said later that when he did so Mihailović replied that joint leadership was out of the question as he personally was the only recognized leader of resistance forces in Yugoslavia.

The Partisans had already (25–30 November) evacuated Užice where the arms factory had been blown up by a saboteur some days previously. They were now burdened by many wounded. Tito, carrying a sub-machine gun and accompanied by Captain Hudson, left the town twenty minutes before the Germans arrived, and lost touch with his staff for several hours. On 28 November, with his forces in full retreat, Tito again telephoned Mihailović and asked for help to hold up the German advance. Mihailović replied that it was not possible to engage in open war against the Germans, that Četnik and Partisan forces should each withdraw to their own territory.[32] This was the last personal contact between the two leaders; Tito's attempts to negotiate joint operations had failed. Mihailović had taken his decision to remain inactive against the occupying armies and to commit his forces to fighting with Germans and Italians in an attempt to exterminate his internal political opponents, the communists.

Tito ordered Partisan forces to retreat across the high Zlatibor range into the bleak inaccessible mountain country on the borders of Serbia. Mihailović's policy was less clear. While some Četnik leaders continued to fight the Partisans, Mihailović was concerned to preserve his forces and explored ways of 'legalizing' Četniks to give them protection from the Italians, as well as from German and Nedić forces whose offensive in Serbia was now mounting to a successful climax. With the onset of severe winter, it looked as if the Partisan movement could be broken. From this time on a welter of evidence – captured Četnik documents, reports from British liaison officers with the Četniks, and many German and Italian documents taken by the Allies during and after the war – shows that many Četnik leaders received arms and payments from Germans, Italians and the quisling Serbian régime. Četniks supported Italian troops in all their major operations against the Partisans and some fought alongside the Germans, yet Mihailović continued to receive Allied aid for at least another eighteen months, in spite of the anomalous fact that he condoned cooperation with enemies of the western Allies.

Mihailović's irrevocable decision to make agreements with the occupiers and to fight only against the communists was taken before the end of 1941 when the Germans were still advancing in Russia and the Middle East. Ultimate German victory seemed in sight, and it must have appeared probable that with German and Italian help the Partisans could not fail to be destroyed. In the unlikely event of an Allied success, or a landing in the Balkans, Mihailović still had a strong place in the Allied camp, and was prepared to switch sides – as the Germans so shrewdly suspected. The Yugoslav government in exile, which was certainly a party to Mihailović's policy, was in good relations with the British and Soviet governments and for a time managed to conceal from them the true facts of the situation in Yugoslavia. In the event, Mihailović and the Yugoslav government miscalculated about the strength of Tito as an opponent, about the strength of Yugoslav nationalist feeling against the occupiers, about German invincibility, about Churchill's realistic approach to military issues, and they were mistaken in believing that once they had the true facts the British would continue to be complaisant about Četnik collaboration with Britain's enemies.

It is clear from Hudson's reports that at least some sections of British military intelligence knew about Partisan activity and Mihailović's collaboration before the end of 1941. But it was either not known at the top level in Britain, or doubted and discounted. In Russia it was known to the Comintern through Tito's daily telegrams, and therefore it must be assumed was known to higher Soviet authorities. But even in Russia the evidence that Tito supplied was doubted. Radio Moscow, to Tito's incredulous fury, attributed Partisan successes to Četniks, and when Radio Free Yugoslavia began to broadcast from Soviet territory from 11 November 1941 its accounts of Partisan successes were interpreted in the west as propaganda.

One important factor in this situation was that events in Yugoslavia in late 1941 and early 1942 were only of minimal importance to Britain and Soviet Russia, both still in retreat before the impetus of the first German advances. The Balkans was not an important region of military operations and other theatres of war had priority. For this reason neither country gave close attention to major policy decisions about events in Yugoslavia. This was not so obvious to Tito, who saw Mihailović with a British liaison officer at his headquarters, aided by the British even when Četniks were helping the Germans. There was also the – to him – sinister fact that the Četnik attack on Užice came shortly after the British mission had joined Mihailović. Short of arms, food, medical supplies, it seemed to Tito that the Partisans, who were really fighting the Germans, should have been receiving aid rather than Mihailović. That they did not appeared as a typical example of perfidious British policy, based on anti-communism, which was what Tito had long been taught to expect from this capitalist country. This view coloured his attitude to Britain and the British for a long time.

# 12 FIGHTING ALONE

For Tito, as for the Allies, 1942 was the most crucial year of the war. It was perhaps the most critical of his career as a leader in Yugoslavia, for it was during these months of tremendous hardship that he transformed the Serbian uprising into a national movement, still communist-led but with popular support in all parts of the country. Although many different factors contributed to this development, it is certain that Tito's own personality, his planning and leadership, were vital to it. The transformation which was the essential groundwork of revolution took place although conditions of warfare were at their worst, in spite of defeats, and in the face of disappointments about receiving Soviet aid and Allied recognition.

At a staff meeting in Foča at the end of February, Tito stressed the importance of political work both in the army, and among civilians through the National Liberation Committees. He said that Partisan leaders must do everything possible to gain peasant support for the Partisan movement, and that even Četnik sympathizers could be persuaded to join the Partisans. But it was evident that in the winter of 1942 life with the Partisans was so hard and dangerous that it was only likely to appeal to those who were inspired by great idealism.[1]

Partisans and civilian populations, especially in country districts in Bosnia and Croatia, suffered terrible losses. There were many deaths from starvation and endemic typhus as well as from enemy operations. Thousands of Yugoslavs also died as a result of civil war, of the fighting between Partisans and Četniks, or against local forces who helped the foreign occupiers. Many others died as a result of religious and national rivalries, always present among the people of Yugoslavia, that had been whipped up and exploited by occupying powers and other forces released by war. In the Sandjak and south Serbia, Četniks slaughtered Muslims to try to create a homogeneous Serbian population in regions they claimed as their Serbian homeland. In Bosnia and Croatia great numbers of Orthodox Serbs

were killed on account of their religion. Pavelić, ruler of the Independent State of Croatia, saw himself as the defender of Catholic
Christianity against the Eastern Orthodox religion. In Croatia
massacres of many thousands of Serbian men, women and children
were carried out by special Ustaši bands with atrocities so bestial as
to be incredible were they not attested beyond dispute. A frequently
repeated story was of Ustaši who collected eyes or other parts of their
victims' bodies and boasted of the tally. A British doctor wrote that
he himself saw such grisly trophies. 'Stepping forward I took the bag
lying on the table and opened it. At first I thought it was a bag of
shelled oysters, then on looking closer, I saw they were human eyes.'[2]
There are many such accounts. Some people were driven into churches
which were then locked and fired, others had their throats cut or
were thrown into swift running rivers. Others, more fortunate,
managed to escape by agreeing to forced conversion to catholicism.[3]
Most Muslims in Croatia were spared the same fate as Pavelić
regarded them as being of pure Croatian race.

Archbishop Stepinac, Catholic Metropolitan of Croatia, and
members of the Catholic hierarchy of Croatia who first supported
Pavelić's state began to have doubts about this policy of extermination or forced conversions. The massacres, begun in the summer of
1941, continued through the winter. In early 1942, as the Partisans
moved from Montenegro into Bosnia and Croatia, they passed
through burnt out and pillaged villages, each with its own frightful
tragedy. Tito had to exert his strongest authority to prevent retaliation
in kind. The Ustaši were hunted down and executed when caught,
but he would not countenance atrocities. 'When the Ustaši were being
led to execution', wrote Dedijer in his diary, 'a peasant woman rushed
into their midst and began scratching and beating them, screaming
all the time. The Partisans had difficulty in getting her off them. . . .
When the rifles rang out, she once more rushed forward, now among
the corpses, dancing in the blood. We were told that the Ustaši had
slaughtered all her sons.'[4]

In the end the horrors of Ustaši massacres boomeranged against
Pavelić's state. Thousands of people from villages in Bosnia and
Croatia – among them a girl who was later to become Tito's wife –
fled from their villages and joined the Partisans. Many of those who
remained welcomed Tito's army when it moved into Croatia in the
summer of 1942. It was support that might not otherwise have been
given so readily at a time when the Partisans had not had major or

lasting successes. It added a strong Croat (including Serbs from Croatia) and Bosnian element to the Partisan movement which up to now had been preponderantly Serbian in the south and Slovene in the north. By the end of 1942 Tito's movement was in the process of becoming all-Yugoslav, in fact as well as in theory. New recruits more than made up for Partisan losses. Until November 1943 there was no conscription in Tito's army. Recruiting was by volunteers, but there is no doubt that patriotic and crusading zeal was such that in areas occupied by the Partisans it was difficult for the population to avoid involvement or to remain neutral. Once joined, it was for the duration; those who were not with the movement were judged to be against it.

Throughout 1942 Tito and his Supreme Command were trying to create and train a professional army, with a formal structure on regular military lines. In the Serbian uprising in the summer of 1941 peasants had fought to defend their homes. But Tito needed a mobile army. From the men who retreated with him out of Serbia, he created on 22 December 1941 the First Proletarian Brigade. Its founding members were 1,199 volunteers from Montenegrin and Serbian units, its first commanding officer the Serb communist who had fought in Spain, Koča Popović. Four other Proletarian Brigades of about 1,000 each, and predominantly based on one region, were founded in the next six months.[5] They went into action as shock troops available for use on any front. They became the equivalent of guards regiments, the core of Tito's army which by the end of the war had over 300,000 soldiers and five army groups.

Tito judged that fighting the enemy was an essential preliminary to, and simultaneous part of, political revolution. He used the Proletarian Brigades unsparingly in operations against Germans and Italians. Statutes were published in the Army Bulletin during February and March 1942: iron discipline, it said, was to prevail with severe punishments for disobedience. There were to be 'comradely relations' between officers and men, but on duty army discipline must prevail. Each brigade had a headquarters with a commander and political commissar, their deputies, shock battalions, escort companies, artillery, medical and motorized units. They had their own red banners with five-point Partisan star in the middle and a hammer and sickle in the top righthand corner. At first much of this – except personnel – existed only on paper, for the Partisans had only the arms and transport they managed to capture.[6]

199

The communist character of these brigades was openly proclaimed, to the annoyance of the Russians, who would have preferred it to be hidden. 'Why did you need to form a special proletarian brigade?' cabled Dimitrov to Tito on 5 March, 'Surely at the moment the basic, immediate task is to unite all anti-Nazi movements, defeat the invader, and achieve national liberation.'[7] Tito believed, and replied with some indignation, that he was doing both and carried on as before. Communist propaganda was instilled into army and civilian population alike by every possible means – newspapers, leaflets, books and, for the many people who were illiterate, thousands of meetings, endless talks, songs, poems. Almost every aspect of life became a vehicle for the message. As in any community in wartime, there was no alternative to official propaganda. But when Partisans lost 'liberated' territory, its inhabitants had the opportunity of seeing how their enemies behaved and comparing them with the Partisans.

From the beginning the Partisan code of discipline was extremely strict, especially about the treatment of civilians, whether friendly or hostile, and about sexual relations between men and women who were living and fighting in close proximity in the forces. Their Spartan behaviour was commented on with wondering admiration by all Allied officers who were assigned to Partisan units in the latter part of the war.[8] Even in the terrible conditions of 1942 Tito did not intend to allow his movement to be ruined by its weaker members. Looting and theft – even in the smallest degree – were punished, after summary trial, by execution. There are stories of Partisans who were shot for what seemed negligible offences – the theft of a few potatoes, a pair of shoes or socks. Couples who broke the sexual code were separated; it is said that for persistent misbehaviour some were even shot.[9] But the resulting discipline created a proud tradition and brought tremendous advantages in the respect and trust of the civilian population towards the Partisan army, and made it possible for Tito to get support and the all important supplies which would otherwise have been withheld.

It would, however, be wrong to think of the Partisans only in terms of military divisions. Tito recognized that his army could not exist in a vacuum, and Peoples' Liberation Committees had been set up in liberated areas to deal with civilian government. By the end of 1942 there were thousands of these committees in local government areas. Some of them – like the military units – were very small *ad hoc* groups. A special section of Tito's headquarters had been set up to coordinate their activities and great care was being taken to get broad-based support and to see that their work was efficient and in the communist spirit of the Partisan movement. 'It is essential to build up close relations between army and civilians so that the people feels itself one with the military. . . . The correct functioning of even the smallest organs of government is the very basis for success in the war of liberation; without this the greatest victories in the field are built on sand.'[10]

The People's Committees in villages, towns, larger country districts, countries and provinces such as Slovenia, Croatia and Serbia were designed as a prototype of communist government in which all who supported the Partisans – and this meant many who were not communists – could participate. Important positions were usually held by communists. As in the Communist Party, many women and young people held responsible jobs. There were also tasks for old people and others who for one reason or another could not be in the army. Committees dealt with basic local matters. Feeding and housing were especially important. Most liberated areas had many refugees so that welfare and social assistance had to be improved. Health and hygiene were essential. 'Wash your clothes, cut your hair, keep free from lice and you will not get typhus' were among the many slogans painted up on walls – but when over-enthusiastic comrades went into action to cut hair by force, Ranković stopped them. Consideration for the population was basic to winning their support. There was a moratorium on debts, but taxes had to be levied and collected, wages and prices fixed, transport and communications repaired, burnt-out villages rebuilt, and local industry and agriculture put into some kind of working order. Local committees had to find their own finances, but in cases of emergency cash grants were made from resources of the Supreme Command.[11] The distribution of food supplies, both for the civilian population and for armies, required complicated liaison between National Liberation Committees and local staff headquarters in all parts of the country; a special commissariat unit in the army took charge of this. The basic problem was to move food from areas where there was a surplus into regions where there was a deficit. This meant buying food from peasants and despatching it often great distances, sometimes across enemy territory. The food was sometimes paid for by Partisan IOUs – promises to pay after the war, which at the time must have seemed of doubtful validity, but were paid up between 1946 and 1948.

For the greater part of the war shortage of money was not a problem for Tito, though evidence seems to show that the Partisans received no financial help from Russia before 1944. In a telegram sent to the Comintern in mid-March 1942, in reply to a query from Dimitrov as to what their financial resources were, Tito stated that they disposed of a great variety of currencies which were valid in different parts of the country. He explained that the Supreme Command had eight million dinars and 500,000 marks left over from the money captured at Užice. He added that to feed his military units some requisitioning was necessary and some confiscations from various 'agents of the occupiers'.[12]

Another important field of work by National Liberation Committees and in the army was that of education, both in the narrow sense of the word, with classes in reading and writing for young and old, and political education to win people's support for the immediate and long-term objectives of Tito's movement. When Tito controlled a large liberated area in Bosnia and Croatia towards the end of 1942, he issued a directive explaining its importance. 'This territory', he wrote, 'and our military force concentrated there, open up broad prospects for us. It is now necessary to organize this base politically, to consolidate our military successes, broaden and deepen our influence among the people, and preclude all influence by the enemy and their collaborators.'[13] When the Partisans had to abandon a territory all old prewar and war archives that were found were destroyed, to make it more difficult for the old system to be restored. Wherever possible, they took their own papers with them on retreat. This was grass-roots revolution carried out systematically with great attention to detail, under Tito's supervision, with the strong central authority imposed by wartime conditions and backed by an army. Equally important was the fact that it was associated with a liberating, patriotic all-Yugoslav movement. Tito may have felt bitter about being ignored by the Allies in 1942, but he made full use of the opportunity to carry out the groundwork of his social and political revolution unobserved and unhindered by Allied – and especially by Russian – interference.

\*　　\*　　\*

During the early weeks of 1942 Tito was very hopeful that he would receive aid from Russia. He was very punctilious about sending full reports to Dimitrov for transmission to the Russian leaders. The messages were addressed to Dimitrov and signed by Tito with his Comintern name of Valter. They were written in Russian usually in his own hand – mostly in pencil, with his own corrections and careful punctuation, on sheets from an ordinary notebook which he kept in his satchel. They gave detailed information about Partisan activities, with periodical round-ups of military engagements, information about political and military decisions, about German and Italian troop movements, and much information on Četniks' activities, atrocities and collaboration. Tito replied with care to Dimitrov's questions, furnishing details about those communists he had appointed to General Staff positions, those who had been arrested by the Germans and Italians, his relations with Macedonians, and his contacts with Greek, Bulgarian, Hungarian and Albanian communists. He gave information about the range of the Soviet-based Radio Free Yugoslavia, and a lot of material about Četnik contacts with the Yugoslav emigré government in London.[14]

The most important of Tito's signals were those in which he informed Dimitrov in detail, quoting copious documentary evidence, about the collaboration of Četniks with Italians and Germans, and the telegrams in which he asked for aid. As far back as August 1941 he had told Dimitrov of his soldiers' need of arms; at the end of December he named a place where parachute drops could be made. In early February 1942 he received a reply: 'There is a possibility of our sending men to you in the near future. Send details of landing ground for planes . . .' On 17 February Tito replied: 'We urgently require medicaments, particularly anti-typhoid serum. . . . Send munitions, automatic arms, boots, material for uniforms for the men . . . parachute to us at Žabljak at the foot of Mount Durmitor in Montenegro. Here snow has fallen and airfields unfit for landing unless aircraft fitted with runners. . . . Anything you send will be of great moral and material assistance. . . .'[15] As a postcript a second message on the same day added 'the site is completely safe on totally liberated territory. . . . To enable large aircraft to land at a future date, urgently send reasonable quantity various automatic weapons, machine guns, signals materials, rockets, light machine guns and ammunition.' He added the latitude and gave identification instructions, stating they would expect Soviet planes any time after 23 February. The landing ground had already been prepared and Moša Pijade, fifty-two years old, ardent communist, who could be relied on to see that everything was efficiently carried out, was sent to supervise arrangements. 'I reached Žabljak on the evening of 22 February', Pijade wrote later, 'the day before the aircraft were due to arrive, so that I had time to check all preparations. The extensive plateau at the village of Jundja Dol where we waited for those planes on 23 February and for thirty-seven subsequent nights, was covered in six feet of snow. We used to wait on that bleak and snow-covered plateau just over four miles from Žabljak, tramping there every night and back again at daybreak.' Eventually they built a snow hut – 'it looked like the quarters of a polar expedition' – for the men to shelter in. Couriers stood by for communication with Tito in Foča.

On 25 February Tito wrote to Pijade saying that Dimitrov had suggested that the Partisan Supreme Staff should issue a proclamation in the name of the people of Yugoslavia to the people of Europe. Tito had replied immediately with a draft proclamation in glowing terms which he thought would please. It was never published, and from the beginning of March a cooler tone was noted in Dimitrov's messages. Tito kept up his flow of information and requests for arms. British planes had parachuted two Yugoslav and two British officers, but they had been captured by the Germans, he signalled. Ribar's house in Zagreb had been raided. Herta Has had been arrested. A second Proletarian Brigade had been formed and direct radio communication established with Bulgarian communists. On 5 March 'Grandfather' issued his rebuke about the Proletarian Brigades and said: 'Study of all the information you have sent gives the impression that members of the British and Yugoslav governments have some [justification? word could not be deciphered, ed.] for suspecting the Partisan movement of taking on a communist character aiming at the Sovietization of Yugoslavia. . . . Are there really no other Yugoslav patriots – apart from communists and communist sympathizers – with whom you could join in a common struggle against the invaders? . . . We earnestly request you to give your tactics and your actions completely serious attention.' Tito replied with a strong justification of his policy saying that 'the establishment of the Proletarian Brigades was an indispensable step when the Partisan movement was in danger of being disrupted by fifth columnists'. They were not fighting for Sovietization but by their heroism 'are an example to our people'. . . . In another message on 9 March he said tartly, 'We need arms and ammunition. That is the best way of creating a National Liberation Front. In this country we have huge numbers of people anxious to fight the invaders, but they have no weapons.' He also went over to the attack – Why had the Soviet radio not told the world the truth about Četnik activities against the Partisans? Dimitrov hastened to soothe him. 'Unfortunately you misunderstood our telegram. We did not reproach you. . . . You enjoy our complete unbreakable confidence. . . . Seeing that Soviet foreign broadcasting – for reasons of policy – for the present makes no mention of the Četniks, it is not right to mention that the struggle is mainly against the Četniks. World opinion must first and foremost be mobilized against the invaders; mentioning or unmasking the Četniks is a secondary matter. . . . We firmly grip your plucky hand.'[16]

Tito was not mollified; he was not interested in any handshakes except the one that meant aid. 'We are in a critical situation for lack of ammunition. Please do all possible to send us arms and military supplies. Tell us if we can expect anything and when', he radioed on 19 March. A week later he wrote to Pijade, still waiting in the snow on Durmitor, that he believed political reasons were the cause of the hold-up in aid. 'The Yugoslav government and not our policy is the main bar to our obtaining assistance', he wrote. It became apparent later that sometime in the last week in February or early days of March, the policy of sending aid to Tito had been vetoed. The Russians have not published their version of the story, and in the absence of full evidence it is only possible to surmise that Stalin himself had reversed an earlier decision to help Tito. We do not know when this decision was communicated to Dimitrov. On 29 March Dimitrov began to break it gently that aid was not going to be sent. 'All possible efforts are being made to help you with armaments. But technical difficulties are enormous. You should not, alas, count on our overcoming them in the near future. Remember to do all you can to try to get arms from the enemy and to make the most economical use of what arms you have.' To Tito this was a fatuous statement of the obvious. The whole experience was highly traumatic as was revealed at the time of Tito's break with Stalin six years later.[17]

In the first half of 1942, Tito and the Partisans were fighting for survival. It was the most critical stage of the war. The movement was still being transformed from a local uprising into a general, liberating, revolutionary movement; the army was barely organized, popular support not yet entirely won. Refugees were joining Četnik bands as well as Partisans units – and British aid to Četniks was a powerful draw for uncommitted peasants. The Germans and Italians had brought up reinforcements of their own and local troops. Tito did not give up his pressure to try to make the Russian leaders appreciate the seriousness of his position. In message after message he hammered home three points – the collaboration of Četniks with Italians and Germans, the association of the Yugoslav government with this policy of aiding the enemies of the Allies, and the desperate realities of the way the Partisans were fighting Germans and all who fought with them. On 24 May he signalled 'Grandfather': 'Since 20 May I have been on the Montenegrin front. The situation is critical. Incessant fighting has left our Partisans exhausted . . . they have no ammunition left. The whole people curse the Yugoslav government in London which through Draža Mihailović is aiding the invader. On all sides the people are asking why the Soviet Union does not send aid. . . . Is it really impossible to do anything in London against the present treacherous policy of the Yugoslav government?' A few days later he complained about the BBC talking about 'the common fight' of Partisans and Četniks against the invaders. 'That is a horrible lie. Please do all you can to expose this terrible treachery and tell the whole world about it. . . . In a few days we propose to issue a proclamation against the Četniks and Yugoslav government. Please communicate your opinion.' He replied carefully to all Russian enquiries, trying to show that his movement was, as the Russians wanted, based on broad national support even if he had not concealed its communist leadership.[18]

We do not know in what form or how much of this information reached the Soviet leaders, but by the summer of 1942 there were signs that it was having at least some effect on their relations with the royalist émigré government, which was keeping up its diplomatic pressure in London and Kuibishev to force Tito to put his army under the command of Mihailović. Some of the information requested by Dimitrov was clearly required as background for their negotiations with royalist Yugoslav ministers. The situation was complicated by the fact that Mihailović had been made Minister of War – army, sea and air forces – in the Yugoslav cabinet on 5 January 1942. In August the Soviet government presented the Yugoslav premier, Professor Slobodan Jovanović, with detailed information about support Mihailović's forces were giving to the Italian army. But still the Russians moved very cautiously indeed. They were afraid of doing anything to offend the western Allies and delay preparations for a second front; they were also still haunted by the fear that the

Allies might make a deal with the Germans and support a joint anti-communist crusade against the Soviet Union. Aid to Tito, or indeed the survival of his movement, was unimportant compared with this danger.

On 14 September Dimitrov cabled Tito to send authenticated documents about Četnik collaboration, adding a warning that the Germans had good reason to foment dissension among Yugoslavs and some papers might be forged. Tito had a great deal of documentation which he knew to be quite genuine. Much of it has since been corroborated from official German and Italian archives.[19] The Russians were now proposing to send their own observers to Mihailović. A 'Top Secret' telegram addressed to him from the royalist premier Jovanović on 30 November said: 'The Russians have suggested sending high-level officers to your staff to make contact with you and from squadrons of your people in Russia to get assistance to you and develop joint broadcasting. Have rejected proposal. We are insisting first on immediate cessation of radio and press campaign against Yugoslav army under your command, secondly on Partisans being told not to attack our army forces, thirdly for Partisans to be placed under your command. Only when this is done can there be talk of further cooperation.'[20]

Other telegrams in December repeated the same arrogant and unrealistic views, but by this time the Allies – including the Russians – were convinced beyond a shadow of doubt of Četniks' collaboration with the enemy. Yugoslav royalist government sources reported that a British official, Major Peter Boughey, in conversation with the Chief of the Royalist War Cabinet, Major Ž. Knežević, had said that Mihailović was a quisling, just like Nedić.[21] The Allies, however, still sent aid to Mihailović and did not help Tito until mid-1943, while a Russian mission – and then with limited aid – was not sent until 1944. Tito eventually won his struggle for Allied recognition and aid, but only, as it appeared to him, after some of the worst fighting was over, and too late to prevent the heaviest losses and most terrible sufferings of the war.

\* \* \*

In summer 1942 Tito decided to withdraw the major part of his army from Bosnia to Croatia, 200 miles to the north, where enemy forces were less concentrated and there was a possibility of clearing a liberated territory. The 'long march' as it came to be known among Partisans, started on 24 June. It took over three months to move an army of 1,000 men – recruits replacing those killed on the march – accompanied as before by their wounded. It was Tito's firm ruling that if the injured could not be left in a safe place, they must be taken along with the army. They were not recognized as combatants and when captured by the enemy they faced extermination. This had happened after the retreat from Užice when German tanks had moved backwards and forwards over wounded Partisans lying in the fields, until all were dead.

As Tito moved his headquarters steadily forwards – to Kula, Prozor, Glamoč, Bosanski Petrovac, and eventually to the small Bosnian town of Bihać, he made contact with bands of Partisans which were now operating with some success in most parts of the country. On 12 November Tito radioed Dimitrov: 'So far we have formed eight divisions each with three full brigades in Bosnia, Croatia and Dalmatia. . . . We are now setting up something like a government to be called the National Liberation Committee of Yugoslavia. This committee will include representatives of all nationalities of Yugoslavia and some representatives of former parties.' He received a cautious reply telling him 'to give the committee an all-party, anti-fascist character both in personnel and programme of work. Do not look upon the committee as a kind of government, but as the political arm of the national liberation struggle. At this stage do not raise the question of the abolition of the monarchy. Do not put forward any republican slogans. The question of the regime . . . will come up for settlement after the German–Italian coalition has been smashed and the country freed from the invaders.'[22]

Tito went ahead with arrangements for a big meeting at Bihać. It was held on 26/27 November 1942 and was attended by representatives of Partisans and their supporters (civilian and military) from most parts of the country. The Anti-Fascist Council of Yugoslavia (AVNOJ) as it was called did not appoint a government – in deference to Russian orders – but it did elect a National Liberation Executive Committee which had virtually the same purpose. The Council was held in the great hall of a convent, decorated by banners and Allied flags, under streamers with the Partisan slogan *Smrt Fašizmu; Sloboda Narodu* – 'Death to Fascism, Freedom for the Peoples'. The former Yugoslav politician Dr Ivan Ribar was chairman; the meeting generated enormous enthusiasm and was a piece of psychological warfare aimed at internal and international opinion. 'We agree to the advice you gave . . . and shall observe it,' Tito signalled to Dimitrov after the meeting, 'but I must warn you that . . . the whole body of people present condemned the Yugoslav government as traitors. Although we do not look on this executive committee as a kind of government, it will nevertheless have to look after all state business and occupy itself with the war, in which it will have the support of the People's Liberation Committees. . . . There are no other authorities in Yugoslavia outside these committees and the military authorities conducting the war . . . who enjoy immense authority through Yugoslavia.'[23]

A new tone of pride, authority and perhaps defiance is apparent in this message. Even though this moment of triumph was shortlived, Bihać can be seen as a turning-point in the Partisan movement. It served notice on the Russians that Tito now considered he had both an army and a state. It marked Tito's political coming of age. Though he continued to keep the Russians fully informed and asked for advice on many matters that were not sovereign decisions, he had now claimed a new independent status. Had the Russians chosen to send aid in 1942, and especially if they had sent a military mission, it is difficult to see how Tito could have prevented them exercising some control over military and political strategy and ousting him from his position of undisputed leader. This would almost certainly have prevented the evolution of the Partisan movement into the independent national movement it became, and it would have changed the whole character of Yugoslav communism and Yugoslav postwar development.

# 13 ALLIED RECOGNITION

The year 1943 brought great changes in the military situation of the Allies. With the German forces routed in North Africa, the Russians moving over to the offensive on the eastern front, and Allied invasion of Italy leading to an Italian unconditional surrender early in September, the eventual defeat of Germany could be foreseen as inevitable. Changes in Tito's situation were also dramatic. Before the end of the year he had received Allied aid and recognition. He had also assumed the title of head of a Provisional Government for Yugoslavia which challenged the authority of the royalist government in exile.

When the Allies began to plan an invasion of Italy they had to consider the military situation in the Balkans. The more divisions the Germans were forced to use to protect their lines of communication from guerrilla attacks in this now important strategic region, the less there would be available to oppose Allied advances in Italy. This meant that for the first time the Allied leaders had to make determined efforts to discover what was the real situation among insurgents in Yugoslavia. Between the summer of 1941 and June 1942 SOE Cairo had made eight attempts to send missions into Yugoslavia. One parachuted mission had been killed by Croat soldiers – the Domobrani – on arrival in the mountains above Sarajevo; some members of another arriving by sea were captured by the Italians at Korčula.[1]

This mission which was led by Major Terence Atherton has been the subject of considerable mystery. In January 1942, with two other Englishmen and two Yugoslavs he was sent by SOE to Yugoslavia, it is presumed with orders to contact Mihailović, and landed on the coast of Montenegro. He established contact with Partisans who controlled the territory and was taken by them to Tito's headquarters at Foča in Bosnia where they arrived at the beginning of March. The mission was well received by Tito, who was anxious to have good relations with the British with a view to obtaining recognition and aid for his own movement. Atherton had lost his radio equipment and Tito's own radio communications system had only just been established. It was some time before arrangements could be made for Atherton to move on. He stayed some weeks in Foča during which time he made contact with a former royalist Yugoslav general, Ljuba Novaković. Atherton knew the area well since he had spent several fishing holidays there in previous years, and it cannot be excluded that he had a personal reason for wishing to go on that mission. He evidently decided not to wait for the Partisans to arrange his safe conduct across their liberated territory and through the various occupied areas to get to Četnik headquarters. He made his own secret arrangements with the help of two anti-Partisan Yugoslavs, Spasoje Dakić and Radovan Blagojević. Novaković only agreed to be associated with the escapade on condition that Atherton gave him a letter ordering the operation. On the night of 16 April Atherton and the rest of the group slipped away secretly from Foča with the intention of joining Mihailović. After conducting them for a certain distance, Novaković handed the mission over to local guides, but continued with them. When the guides realized that Atherton was in charge of a large sum of money, mainly in gold pieces, they sent Novaković away and killed the whole mission, making off with the money and other valuables. When news of the murder became known in the west, pro-Četnik people accused Tito of having engineered it and used this as a means of undermining confidence in Tito and his movement. Tito was very angry indeed. He instituted a hunt for the identification and apprehension of the murderers. Dakić was later a commandant of Četniks in East Bosnia and was killed the following year in fighting with the Partisans. Novaković was imprisoned, and Blagojević was executed. This incident made Tito for a time very suspicious of British agents.[2]

By early 1943, however, the British had succeeded in sending several other liaison officers to the Četniks. On 25 December 1942 Colonel S. W. Bailey had taken over the post of head of mission at Mihailović's headquarters in the Sandjak; other British officers visited Četnik groups in Croatia, Bosnia, and Montenegro in the following months. Colonel Bailey's reports and information the British obtained from the royalist government made Četnik policy quite clear. It was that Mihailović was not prepared to use his forces against the Germans and their allies until such time as an Allied invasion of the Balkans would enable Serbs to go into action alongside Allied armies. He refused to allow his forces to undertake even sabotage operations. By 1943 Allied authorities had reliable intelligence about other factors limiting Mihailović's activities, his arrangements with German and Nedić's officials, and the close integration of various Četnik groups with the Italians.[3]

Between November 1941 and June 1943 the British sent twenty-three tons of supplies to Mihailović, including arms, gold, radio equipment, clothes and medical supplies. Yet he and royalist leaders became increasingly importunate for more aid while refusing to carry out the Allies' requests.[4] Colonel Bailey reported that Mihailović had accused the British of wanting 'to fight to the last Serb', and relations between the British and Yugoslav government officials became increasingly strained.[5]

Tito's situation was very different. By 1943 the British knew that he had considerable forces actively resisting in many parts of Yugoslavia. They knew by this time that Tito was no myth and that he was not a woman as had once been rumoured. They were aware that he was a communist, and thought he was probably Yugoslav and not Russian, but they had little detailed information and did not even know where his headquarters were at any given time. They had sent him no aid. When Colonel Bailey failed to get cooperation from the Četniks it was decided early in 1943 to make direct contact with the Partisan leadership. This was a military decision taken on the advice of SOE and AFHQ Middle East, and not without some opposition. Its political implications were important for it meant possible recognition of communist insurgents engaged in bitter fighting with Četniks whose commander-in-chief was war minister in the exiled government. The royalist government was informed of the decision and the reasons for taking it.[6]

British policy was later to be denounced by both sides as Machiavellian, the Četniks and royalist government claiming to have been betrayed by perfidious opportunists, the Partisans convinced that Britain as a capitalist country was only making use of them, and was really supporting Mihailović with a view to restoring a pro-Serbian clique to power after the war. It seems likely, however, that British policy about postwar Yugoslavia had not yet crystallized. The British government had actively supported the 1941 coup in Belgrade and this, together with the general policy of support for governments exiled from Hitler's Europe, gave them an obligation to back the royalist government and their minister of war. Had Mihailović cooperated with the British by fighting against the Germans and

Italians in Yugoslavia, it is difficult to see how British aid for Tito could have developed as it did.

Following the decision taken by Churchill and his advisers, SOE in Cairo received authority on 23 March to make official contact with the Partisans. On 21 April two teams of Canadians of Yugoslav origin were parachuted 'blind' into areas where Partisans were known to be. One group of men made an easy landing and were picked up by car and taken to Croat headquarters; the others, who came down in eastern Bosnia where the Partisans were in action, ran into some difficulties. The first group which included a middle-aged Canadian, Major W. Jones, arrived at Partisan headquarters in Croatia in mid-May. After negotiations with Tito, agreement was reached for a British mission to join his headquarters.[7]

Allied interest in the Partisans came at a crucial phase in Tito's military situation, for during the first six months of 1943 the Germans mounted two consecutive operations with the object of annihilating his main army, breaking the Partisan movement and freeing the German lines of communication from Greece through Yugoslavia to Italy and central Europe. Plans were drawn up for what the Germans called 'Operation Weiss' (White) and the Partisans recorded as the 'Fourth Offensive'. The operation aimed in its first phase to encircle Partisan positions in the Bihać area where Tito had his headquarters, then, in the second phase, to penetrate Partisan held territory in Bosnia and destroy most of the Partisan army. In the third phase, which was never reached, the Germans intended to disarm the Četniks and reduce them to auxiliary duties.

Over 18,000 Četniks were mobilized to take part in the operation. Some 12,000 of these, under their leader Colonel Stanišić, were in Montenegro; in Herzegovina the Italian Murge division took up positions to the south and south-east to cut off the Partisan retreat.[8] Tito decided with his military advisers that it was in this direction the Partisans must attempt to break through. It was to be a fighting retreat with surprise sorties by Partisan shock brigades covering the withdrawal of the main forces and the large numbers of wounded and refugees who accompanied them. It took the main Partisan army three weeks to withdraw across the central uplands of Bosnia towards the Neretva river which had to be crossed if they were to break out of the enemy ring. The sick and wounded, over 2,000 to start with and increasing all the time, were divided into those who could walk those who could ride, and stretcher cases. Dedijer, helping with the columns of wounded, wrote up his diary in the frequent stops on the march: 'I went to inspect the typhus cases . . . sunken faces, bones not arms, huge burning eyes. . . . The whole bare mountain dotted with stretchers right across the Dinaric range. . . . At Stipanici four hundred wounded and no transport.'

Ten days after the offensive began Tito radioed Dimitrov: 'Am obliged once again to ask you if it is really quite impossible to send us some kind of assistance. Hundreds of thousands of refugees are threatened by death from starvation. Is it really impossible after twenty months of heroic, almost superhuman fighting to find some way to help us? . . . Typhus has now started to spread and we are without drugs. People are dying like flies from starvation. . . . Do your utmost to render assistance.'

Eleven days later on 11 February 1943 he got the usual answer from Dimitrov: 'The Soviet people and its leaders are totally on your side. Josip Vissarionovitch [Stalin, ed.] and myself have many times [? group indecipherable, ed.] discussed ways and means of helping you. So far, unfortunately, we have not been able to find a satisfactory solution to the problem on account of insuperable technical difficulties. . . . The moment there are conditions we shall do all that is most urgent. Can you possibly doubt this?'[9] Tito's comment had to be suppressed, but he allowed himself a sharp reply a few weeks later during an interchange of telegrams with Dimitrov on the subject of Partisan negotiations about an exchange of prisoners with Germans and Ustaši. The Partisans were trying to get the release of a group of people which included Herta Has, and the Croat communist Hebrang – who was later accused of having agreed under torture to spy for the Ustaši if he was released. When Dimitrov complained about these negotiations, Tito snapped back: 'If you cannot understand what a hard time we are having, and if you cannot help us, at least do not hinder us.' Thirty Partisans, including Herta who joined the Partisan army in Slovenia, were exchanged for two prominent Ustaši.[10]

On 22 February the Second Division had captured Jablanica and thrown back the Četnik attack, while the First and Third Divisions reached Neretva near Konjić, securing their flank from enemy attack from the Sarajevo direction. The advance troops cut their way through Četnik units on Mount Prenj routing the entire Četnik forces. By 15 March Tito knew that his main army had escaped and gave the order for withdrawal into the heart of Montenegro. Here in the uplands of Montenegro were fought some of the most savage Partisan–Četnik battles of the whole war. It is arguable that Tito allowed his military judgment to be influenced by political considerations when he saw the opportunity to destroy large Četnik forces and liberate great areas of Montenegro. One result was that the Četniks were never again to be assembled in numbers that were a major threat to the Partisans, though their units regrouped and continued to fight the Partisans and to operate with the Germans to the end of the war. Another result of the pursuit into Montenegro was that Tito's forces were concentrated and were not well placed when it became apparent that the German offensive was to be maintained.

Operation Weiss had merged into Operation Schwarz (Black) – a new and more dangerous offensive because the Partisans had had no time to recuperate, regroup or choose their terrain. Tito said later that the mountains which had once been a hiding-place proved in this campaign a disadvantage to the Partisans, whose mobility was so restricted that they almost failed to make good their escape.

Partisan troops engaged in the Fifth Offensive, as they came to call it, were only a small proportion of Tito's total forces, which were distributed in different parts of Yugoslavia, linked by radio through regional headquarters with his Supreme Command, but operating with considerable dependence on their own resources and often in very small units. They numbered in all about 150,000 over the whole country. Figures for the Partisan army at this stage of the war and for a considerable time later can only have been approximate. They were kept by commanders in the field whose many duties left them neither means nor staff for recording the daily fluctuation of numbers. In mountain warfare, it was always difficult to count dead and wounded. It is probable that Tito's forces in the field were much more heavily out-numbered than the six to one ratio of official figures.[11]

Tito had intended to move his main forces south-eastwards towards South Serbia and Kosovo-Metohija on the borders of Serbia and Montenegro. Here again he combined political with military considerations, for this would have activated support in an entirely new area. His representatives had been in touch with Albanian, Greek and Bulgarian communists, as well as with Macedonians. Tito, with his usual long view, was probably already thinking in terms of coordinating a movement of all Partisans in the southern Balkans. Yet he rejected the idea of a joint Balkan

215

Headquarters. He was unable to withdraw in this direction because of rapid German advances from the south-east.

On 6 May, in the middle of these operations, Tito received a message from Dimitrov informing him of a proposal to disband the Comintern as being obsolete and asking urgently for comment from the Yugoslav Communist Party's Politburo. Preoccupied with the dangerous military situation, and with all members of the Politburo engaged as officers in the field, Tito did not reply immediately and the message was repeated on 22 and 23 May. He eventually gave the required assent on 26 May, well aware that it made no difference. The Comintern had been disbanded on 15 May and Stalin had already published his reasons – that it had become an obstacle to the creation of united fronts of 'progressive forces in the common struggle against fascism', and that it encouraged the belief that Moscow interfered through communist parties in internal affairs of other nations.[12] It was one of many Russian moves to placate Allied opinion in preparation for political bargaining in the later stages of the war.

The demise of the Comintern at first made little difference to Tito's formal relations with Russia – as had no doubt been the Soviet leaders' intention. To the end of 1943 he continued as usual to report fully to Dimitrov, informing him of military and major political developments, about negotiations for receiving British missions, about the supplies they brought and asking advice about relations with them. From the evidence so far available, it seems that he received only general directives in return, for the Russians were preoccupied with military campaigns and content for the time being to allow Tito his head in Yugoslavia, as long as he did nothing to alienate Allied goodwill.

Tito's consolidation of the political independence which he had had since the German invasion of the Soviet Union was imperceptible and extremely cautious. He was certainly convinced at this stage of the war that – whatever his disappointments about Soviet aid – he would still be dependent on Russian support if he were to bring about communist revolution in Yugoslavia. He did not intend to cut this lifeline and it seems likely that he did not yet have a clear idea of what form a postwar communist state of Yugoslavia would take.

By mid-May, when arrangements were being made for him to receive a British mission at his headquarters, his military situation was deteriorating. German forces closing in all round had secured a commanding position on the slopes of Mount Maglić overlooking the Sutjeska river and a deep gorge with its exit at Suha where Tito's forces had to make an east–west crossing if they were to extricate themselves. Time was vital, yet Tito delayed his own departure for thirty-six hours to wait for the arrival of the British Mission. This consisted of six men, including Major William Stuart, and Major W. F. Deakin, a friend of Churchill's. When they arrived, dropping by parachute against a forty mile an hour wind, on the night of 27/28 May 1943, they had to set off almost immediately with Tito and his staff before the German ring closed. Had they been twenty-four hours later it is doubtful if they could have landed. After several days on the march the party managed to cross the narrow Sutjeska river. They were climbing the wooded slopes on the other side when on 9 June, as the weather cleared, they were sighted and bombed by planes. Major Stuart and Djuro Vujović, Tito's bodyguard, were killed. Tito received a piece of shrapnel in his left arm, Major Deakin was injured in the foot.[13] Tito's escape was again a matter of extraordinary luck, for when he threw himself to the ground, his dog Lux, lying close to his master's head, was killed by a bomb fragment which might otherwise have struck him.

By the end of June, the headquarters staff and remnants of the main Partisan army had made good their escape across the Zelengora – green mountains – towards the Foča–Kalinovik road into the relative safety of east Bosnia. Their losses had been terrible, both of fighting men and of sick and wounded. Tito's main armies were never again in danger of annihilation but the Germans proved a tenacious and resourceful enemy to the end, and there was much desperate fighting still to do.

\*    \*    \*

Supplies and air cover were Tito's most immediate needs, and at first he was bitterly disappointed that the British mission was not able to make these available with the speed and in the quantities that he wished. He was never free from the suspicion that supplies were being held back for political reasons. Some of the hold-ups in sending supplies to Tito may have been caused by deliberate delaying tactics from individuals in the Allied chain of command, but the main difficulty was shortage of aircraft at the disposal of SOE Cairo, which was at first responsible for moving supplies. This the Partisans found difficult to believe. When Churchill became fully informed about Tito's active fighting policy, he took a personal interest in speeding up supplies. General Sir Henry Maitland Wilson, Supreme Allied Commander, Mediterranean, was 'in favour of a really wide channel of supply to Tito' and did his best to help.[14]

The 65 tons of supplies that went in after the first missions to Tito were largely for the purpose of aiding sabotage operations against the Germans' north–south communications through Yugoslavia. When the Partisans showed that they used them quickly and effectively for this purpose – in contrast to Mihailović – other supplies followed. On 23 June Churchill decided that these should be sent at the rate of 500 tons per month. To aid in this operation, and to observe the results, British officers and technical staff were permitted by Tito to be attached to Partisan formations all over the country. In August Brigadier Fitzroy Maclean was appointed head of mission at Tito's headquarters with responsibility direct to Churchill, and with all British liaison officers under his command.[15]

Tito's relief at getting supplies at last and his confidence in the British were marred by the fact that supplies were still being sent to Mihailović. He was also annoyed that the new British Chief of Mission, sent in September 1943 to Četnik headquarters, Brigadier Armstrong, had had his rank raised to equal that of the head of mission to Tito. Tito suffered a further blow which both enraged and disappointed him – emotions which he did not attempt to conceal from the British mission. The Allies gave him no advance information about the unconditional surrender of Italy on 8 September. His chagrin was increased because he believed – erroneously – that Colonel Bailey had leaked the information to Mihailović.[16]

At the time of surrender, Italy had in Yugoslavia fourteen divisions and four divisions under strength. It was vitally important to Tito to get control of the areas they occupied, and of their armament, before these could fall to Germans or Četniks. He ordered his forces to race to occupy the Dalmatian coast and islands, especially the embarkation ports of Split and Šibenik, to prevent Italian escape and to take over stores stockpiled there. Partisans succeeded in disarming ten Italian divisions and acquired great quantities of armament and stores. They also gained a complement of some 80,000 men to their armed forces. Some of these were Italian prisoners who chose to join special units formed for them in the Partisan forces – the Garibaldi, and Garibaldi Natisone divisions.

By the end of the year Tito's army numbered about 290,000 men and women. The Germans at this time had more troops than ever before in Yugoslavia – 200,000 of their own soldiers and 160,000 Bulgarian and quisling Serb and Croat forces.[17] They were still afraid of an Allied landing in Dalmatia and could not afford to let Tito keep control of the Dalmatian coast. Within a matter of weeks they had ousted Partisans from most coastal positions and all the islands with the exception of Vis, the one nearest to the Italian mainland. From the end of September 1943, throughout the exceptionally cold winter – in 1943 and 1944 – they continued to harry the widely dispersed Partisan forces, especially in Bosnia, making use of new fluid anti-guerrilla tactics and using air support which the Partisans still lacked.

Tito now knew he had the manpower to deal with the Germans if only he could continue to be supplied with sufficient weapons, food, equipment, air support and medical aid. He lost no opportunity of making his requests known, and was given permission to fly out his own military mission to Allied Headquarters in Cairo to discuss them. Lola Ribar was appointed chief of the mission, but on 27 November he was killed by a bomb from a single German raider, just as (impatient at repeated delays in the arrival of British planes) he was boarding a captured enemy plane to fly to Cairo. Vladimir Velebit was appointed to replace him, and in December flew to Cairo with Brigadier Maclean who went to report to Churchill, then passing through Cairo on his way from the Teheran Conference with Stalin and Roosevelt.

The Big Three had agreed at Teheran 'that the Partisans in Yugoslavia should be supported by supplies and equipment to the greatest possible extent, and also by commando operations'. While Velebit stayed behind to discuss details, Maclean was able to return to Yugoslavia with a reassuring letter from Churchill to Tito: 'From Major Deakin, who is a friend of mine, I learnt all about your valiant efforts,' it said. 'It is my most earnest desire to give you all aid that is humanly possible by sea supplies, by air support and by commandos to help you in the island fighting. Brigadier Maclean is also a friend of mine and colleague in the House of Commons. My son, Major Randolph Churchill, also a member of parliament, will soon be serving with him at your Headquarters.

'One supreme object stands before us – to cleanse the soil of Europe from the vile Nazi taint. You may be sure that we British have no desire to dictate the future government of Yugoslavia. At the same time, we hope that all will pull together as much as possible for the defeat of the common foe, and afterwards to settle the form of government in accordance with the will of the people.

'I am resolved that the British government shall give no further military support to Mihailović and will only give help to you, and we should be glad if the Royal Yugoslavian Government would dismiss him from their councils. King Peter the Second, however, escaped as a boy from the treacherous clutches of the Regent Prince Paul, and came to us as the representative of Yugoslavia and as a young Prince in distress. It would not be chivalrous or honourable for Great Britain to cast him aside. Nor can we ask him to cut all his existing contacts with his country. I hope therefore that you will understand we shall in any case remain in official relations with him while at the same time giving you all possible military support. I hope that there may be an end to polemics on either side, for these only help the Germans.

'You may be sure I shall work in the closest contact with my friends Marshal Stalin and President Roosevelt; and I earnestly hope the Military Mission which the Soviet government are sending to your Headquarters will work in similar harmony with the Anglo-American Mission under Brigadier Maclean. Please correspond with me through Brigadier Maclean and let me know anything I can do to help, for I will certainly try my best.'[18]

From this time on, help for the Partisans was steadily increased. Churchill's policy in the Balkans as well as his aid to Tito was not at first endorsed by, or acceptable to, the United States military and government authorities. They suspected Britain's motives for inter-ference in the Balkans, seeing it as an offshoot of British colonialism or an attempt to gain a special position in eastern Europe. They did not wish to be 'embroiled in the Balkans' and were at first unwilling to aid communists even though they might be fighting the Germans. They were in principle more prepared to support existing governments and were unwilling to withdraw support from the royalist government and General Mihailović. For a long time Roosevelt himself was inclined to be pro-Serb, and the strong royalist lobby in Washington, led by the Yugoslav royalist ambassador Fotić, was highly successful. This attitude changed only slowly, and after the Teheran conference. At the same time they were jointly involved in Mediterranean strategy and saw the importance of the operations of Tito's Partisans against German lines of communication which were specially important when it became obvious in the second half of 1943 that defeat of the Germans in Italy was going to be long drawn out. They wished to have their own sources of information about what was going on in Yugoslavia, and a number of United States missions were sent there in 1943 and 1944. An American officer, Captain Walter Mansfield parachuted to Četnik territory in southern Serbia in mid-August 1943, and joined Mihailović's headquarters. He was followed in September by Lieutenant-Colonel Albert Seitz, who joined Mihailović about the same time as the British mission was taken over by Brigadier Armstrong. Both these American officers left Mihailović in January 1944, and were replaced by Lieutenant George Musulin, who stayed until May of that year and left Mihailović at the same time as Brigadier Armstrong. Although the British decided to break all contact with Mihailović, the Americans sent Colonel McDowell to Mihailović in August 1944 on an intelligence mission. The exact purpose of his mission has not been made clear, but the Partisans believed he had been sent to try to arrange that the German surrender – when it came – should be made to Mihailović rather than to the Partisans; it is known that McDowell did in fact go with Mihailović's officers to meetings with the Germans. McDowell was not dealing with air crew rescue operations for US fliers as has been sometimes suggested, since this was the responsibility of a separate mission headed by Colonel Nicholas Lalić, who went into the territory at the same time. When Churchill complained to Roosevelt about the ill-will that McDowell's mission was causing, especially in relations with Marshal Tito, the mission was withdrawn in November 1944.

At the same time, the Americans also had missions with the Partisans, both at Tito's headquarters and at regional headquarters in the field. The first US officer to arrive at Tito's headquarters was Lieutenant Melvin O. Benson, who parachuted in during the same moon period as the first US officer to Mihailović. Benson was followed a month later by Major Linn Farish, who was with Tito for several short periods (returning several times to Italy) up to April 1944. He was responsible for a very favourable report about Partisan activity which was thought to have influenced the decision to aid Tito that was made at Teheran. When Tito moved his headquarters to Vis in the summer of 1944 another American mission was sent under Colonel Ellery C. Huntington. All the American missions took in supplies – though not on any large scale – and Americans were also associated with the medical aid, air transport and air cover that were organized from Italy to help Tito's forces in the later stages of the war.[19]

\* \* \*

Aid for the Partisans was mainly a British responsibility because it was in the Mediterranean theatre of war. Russia gave token help with a small group of six Dakotas under Allied command at Bari. But the main Russian aid arrived in the terminal stages of the war when the Partisan forces were moving over from guerrilla to frontal warfare. According to Soviet sources this totalled 20,528 rifles, 68,819 machine guns, light machine guns and automatic weapons, 3,797 anti-tank rifles, 3,364 mortars, 170 anti-tank guns, 898 varied types of guns, 491 aircraft, 65 tanks, 1,329 radio stations, 7 base hospitals, 4 surgical field hospitals and other items of various kinds.[20] It is very difficult to calculate the full extent of western aid, since British records are not yet all open to inspection and Partisan records are of necessity incomplete and in many cases non-existent. Supplies were parachuted into most parts of Yugoslavia; they were also taken in by plane and by small boats of all kinds. At first about a dozen or more special British units of all three services were sending supplies.[21] In an attempt to coordinate these activities a new authority, Balkan Air Force, was created in June 1944 under the command of Air Vice-Marshal Elliot, with headquarters at Bari on the east coast of Italy. But many of the eccentric individualities of the special units still remained, and there was no uniform or central system of recording despatch of supplies. During 1944 'something like' 9,000 tons of supplies were dropped to Partisans in Yugoslavia, including 100,000 rifles, 50,000 machine guns, 1,400 mortars and one million mortar bombs and handgrenades, and 100 million rounds of small arms ammunition.[22] This did not include supplies that went by sea, among which were food and medical materials, trucks and quantities of fuel, as well as 107 tanks and 346 planes, a number of landing craft and small boats. In addition two squadrons of Partisan pilots were trained by the RAF. An aspect of Allied aid which was immensely helpful to Tito – and gratefully acknowledged by him – was the evacuation of sick and wounded to Italy, and their treatment in special hospitals which the British established for them. In 1944 alone 11,842 wounded were evacuated in this way and the total figure ran into tens of thousands. The British also helped by sending doctors and surgeons to work in Partisan field hospitals in Yugoslavia.[23]

Whatever the total amount of help received it was never enough to satisfy Partisan needs and demands, and their quite genuine gratitude was always tempered by the thoughts that it should, according to their calculation, have been more, and that had they instead of Mihailović, received help earlier, they would have been saved some appalling losses. The great majority of Partisans, including until 1944 Tito himself, were unaware of the overall supply problems of the Allied global war. Their terrible experiences and lack of information made them myopically obsessed with their own problems. They were also victims of their own propaganda system which concentrated on informing their peoples of the suffering, the heroic fighting and successes of the Soviet armies, and gave little information about the struggles Britain had had, to contain and throw back Axis forces in the Middle East. They did not see that their own struggles, and those of the Soviet Union could have been nullified and might have had a totally different issue but for the Anglo-American campaigns in the west.

Tito's personal relations with Allied missions were good. These were the first British people he had had the opportunity of knowing well, and he soon found it possible to establish human contact based on mutual respect and a common task. There was no friction in the personal relations between Tito and the Head of the British Mission, and many British officers found Tito an impressive, likeable, highly intelligent and human character. They appraised him more objectively than his followers, whose hero worship was by this time an integral part of the Partisan movement. 'Tito stood head and shoulders above his fellows', wrote Brigadier Maclean, who had plenty of opportunity of observing Tito as a leader. 'He brought to the war against the Germans . . . leadership, courage, realism, ruthless determination and singleness of purpose, resourcefulness, adaptability and plain common sense. Where there were important decisions to be made, whether political or military, he took them . . . calmly and collectedly, however precarious the situation. . . . When the Partisans were on the move, he moved with them, covering immense distances on horseback or on foot. . . . He believed in seeing all he could for himself at first hand. Having dealt with the immediate problems requiring his attention he would join the members of his headquarters staff in a convivial meal or a game of chess, or simply

223

lie down on the ground and go to sleep. He had the gift, when he chose, of putting his cares aside and relaxing completely. Then he would laugh and joke as if he had not a worry in the world.'[24]

Dr Lindsay Rogers described his first impression of Tito: 'I looked at his rugged strong face. Yet this was not the face I had seen portrayed in every village thoughout the country. This face was kindly in its strength; the merry blue eyes which looked at you with every word he spoke.'[25] Sir John Slessor, Air Force Chief of Staff for the Middle East Allied Command, first met Tito shortly after he arrived in Bari after his gruelling experiences at Drvar. 'I was immediately impressed with him and have since had good reason to return to the opinion I then formed of him, that he was much more than a guerrilla leader – an outstanding personality and potentially a statesman of no mean order. . . . A fine looking man he was also very intelligent. Though one frequently had cause to be irritated beyond measure by the intransigence of some of his subordinates, it was always possible by some direct speaking to get a commonsense solution of our difficulties with them out of Tito himself.'[26]

Inevitably there were misunderstandings and difficulties between Allied missions in the field and Partisans, and especially with some of the suspicious, and fanatically indoctrinated political commissars. Nor were the difficulties all on one side, for some members of mission staffs found it difficult to accept the Partisans' austere rules of life and their narrow political indoctrination. Members of Allied missions, well fed, well equipped and adequately clothed, went into Partisan held areas of Yugoslavia like beings from another planet. They found themselves among guerrillas who had come to terms with a life of extreme privation and frequent danger. 'A piece of bacon fat here, and a crust of bread there, and everywhere a welcome. . . . No boots, no socks, no vitamins, no overcoats, little ammunition, poor obsolete guns. . . . Yet everywhere such deep enthusiasm and such a burning belief that one day freedom would come. . . . Every bandage was threadbare for all were washed at least ten or twelve times until they rotted and fell into dust.'[27] 'The necessary filth to be lived in was never allowed to uproot the belief that Partisans need not be clean if they could. . . . The primary need and duty was to lessen the insect population that you inevitably carried; this could be done with due respect to Partisan convention by retiring into the shelter of the trees and stripping to the waist . . . nothing could reduce the plague of lice except personal attention every day.'[28] Yet in spite of these conditions all Allied officers commented on the indomitable spirit, the cheerfulness, the endless singing of old ballads and new songs commemorating Partisan achievements or glorifying Tito. Allied personnel in their turn, often elicited admiration for their expertise, courage and their cheerful acceptance of strange circumstances. On the whole relations between Allied missions and Partisans were workable, sometimes even friendly, especially so in the outlying units where people were less self-conscious about political considerations and ideological attitudes.

# PART IV
# REVOLUTION ACCOMPLISHED

# 14 TRANSITION TO PEACE

Tito called a second session of the Anti-Fascist Council as a kind of wartime parliament to meet in Jajce on 29–30 November 1943. Even more than the Bihać meeting it was a brilliant move in political strategy, designed to define and consolidate his position before it came to bargaining over postwar government for Yugoslavia. In retrospect it can be seen as the beginning of a vital phase in the political revolution. It was early to make such a move. Tito did not know that the Allied conference at Quebec in August 1943, called to coordinate plans for 'Overlord', the invasion of Normandy the following year, had agreed that limited aid by air and sea transport and minor commando forces was to be given to 'Balkan guerrillas', but he knew of the change in the British attitude towards his own activities.[1] He expected a possible Allied landing in the Balkans, and he wished to be associated with it, not superseded by it. He knew that it had been the policy of the royalist government and Mihailović to remain inactive till they could be restored to power by joining in with Allied troops in the final phase of the war. He did not intend to lose the position his movement had won in Yugoslavia by being out-manoeuvred in the international field.

When he heard about preparations for an Allied leaders' conference he radioed Dimitrov asking him to inform the government of the USSR that the Partisan movement would recognize neither the Yugoslav government in exile nor the King. 'We shall not permit them to come to Yugoslavia, for that would mean civil war.' He said that the sole lawful authority of the people at the present time was the National Liberation Committees.[2] This was the basic decision to be taken at the Jajce meeting. He did not give Dimitrov prior information about the detailed resolutions that were being prepared, nor ask for Russian permission, though he was careful to ask for views about questions of organization.[3] He intended to face the Russians as well as the western Allies with a *fait accompli*. This was not difficult, for both were preoccupied at this time with preparations for the Teheran Conference which was to take place almost at the same time.

The second session of AVNOJ was one of the most triumphant

moments of Tito's career, euphoric with a sense of achievement and impending success, and uncomplicated by Allied interference or any expression of political opposition. It was spiced with a feeling of successful defiance of the Germans, for Jajce was officially at the time part of the satellite state of Croatia. Tito and a large staff had been in the town for two months preparing for the conference. His headquarters were in a wooden shed with underground rooms prepared nearby to be used as an air-raid shelter when the Germans, aware of the conference preparations, stepped up their bombing raids. He was now fifty-one years old and very thin after the rigours of two years on the move and long periods of inadequate food. The skin, stretched tight over the bone structure of his face, was parchment coloured from exposure to all weathers, alternating with long periods of office work often done in dugouts and improvised shelters. Yet he was still extremely vigorous, capable of working longer hours than almost any of his staff, and of waking refreshed after short snatches of sleep – a faculty which he was to keep into old age. He had already become a legend to his followers, a legend cultivated as a wartime inspiration and symbol of unity, celebrated in marching songs and heroic ballads wherever there were Partisan units. It also had a basis in fact and real achievement; he was the undisputed leader, a man of quite exceptional qualities.

Delegations appointed or elected from Partisans and their supporters were sent from every part of the country except Macedonia. Some delegations – like the one from Slovenia which included Herta Has, the mother of Tito's second son – walked several hundreds of miles, a journey of several weeks, and reached Jajce only after the conference had begun. When they all met, people were reunited who had been separated since the beginning of the war; some had not seen each other since fighting together in Spain. Many but not all of the delegates were communists, all were associated in some way with Partisan resistance. Among the men and women in a motley collection of improvised uniforms were a few in civilian dress, and care had been taken to see that all religious faiths – Catholic, Orthodox and Muslim – were represented at the meeting.[4]

The speech Tito made from the platform of the Jajce town theatre to a packed and wildly enthusiastic audience was designed not only for their ears and for the people in occupied Yugoslavia, but for the attention of the Allied leaders gathering in Teheran, and of the royalist government in exile. Its main purpose was to reaffirm the

Partisans' war aims to liberate all Yugoslav lands and to announce the formation of a provisional government for the whole country. It was to have its own Presidium and Executive Committee with full powers. It declared itself to be the legal government of Yugoslavia, taking the place of the King and royalist government whose legal right to represent the Yugoslav people was declared null and void. These decisions were incorporated into a resolution that was passed unanimously.[5] Members of the Anti-Fascist Council which was to act as government were elected immediately. Tito became President, Secretary for Defence and was created a Marshal. He now had the status he felt necessary before he could negotiate as an equal with other heads of state and military leaders. But he still had to have these decisions accepted by the Allied leaders.

At the end of the AVNOJ session, on 30 November, just as the Allied leaders were beginning their meeting at Teheran, Tito sent a signal to Moscow giving details of the decisions that had been taken. It had a very hostile reception. 'The boss [meaning Stalin, ed.] is extremely angry. He says it is a stab in the back for the Soviet Union and the Teheran decisions', Manuilsky told Vlahović, the Yugoslav who was in charge of the Soviet based 'Free Yugoslavia' radio, and he forbade him to broadcast details of the AVNOJ resolutions.[6] Stalin was afraid it would annoy the Allies and prejudice his negotiations with them. By the time the Teheran discussions were concluded, however, he discovered that the Allies were determined to help and recognize Tito, and were not opposed to the decisions he had taken. They hoped it would assist their policy of persuading him to agree to work with a reformed, broader-based royalist government. It seems probable also that they knew nothing about Stalin's anger and were convinced that Tito's action was inspired by the Soviet leader. They were engaged in preparations for the Normandy landing; the United States was also seriously preoccupied with strategic planning for the terminal phases of war in the Pacific. Both Allies were therefore very anxious to keep on good terms with the Russians. Tito thus profited for a time from the desires of the western Allies and the Soviet Union not to oppose each other in a lesser sphere of interest before the major victories had been won. His advantage was thus aided by the lack of understanding between the Allies; it was not at this stage the result of a deliberate policy of playing off one side against the other. But an element of this was not lacking even at this time, especially in relation to aid and supplies.

Although it is possible that unofficial Soviet emissaries had been parachuted to Tito's headquarters in September 1943, the official Soviet mission finally arrived on 23 February 1944; it was clearly not intended as a high-powered military or political mission to supersede Tito's leadership. Its chief was ex-Army Group Chief-of-Staff Lieutenant General Korneev, of whom Stalin said contemptuously, 'The poor man is not stupid, but he is a drunkard, an incurable drunkard' – a fact which was to be borne out by the quantities of liquor the Russians had flown in.[7] Because of the severe weather, the Russian mission arrived in ski-equipped gliders for which special air-strips had been prepared, secured from German attacks, and repeatedly cleared of heavy snowfalls. This mission travelled first to Algiers, then to Bari in Italy before crossing to Bosnia.[8]

Glorification of the achievements of the Red Army, added to long years of idolatry of Russia as the home of communist revolution, made the arrival of the Soviet mission a tremendous occasion for the Partisans, and they had arranged a warm welcome. But their frenzied enthusiasm was not entirely reciprocated. General Korneev descended from the plane 'a plump, amiable-looking elderly gentleman' resplendent in new Red Army uniform with its heavy gold-embroidered epaulettes and many decorations, his immaculate top-boots polished to perfection. Tito wore the unadorned field-grey uniform of a soldier in the field. Korneev was accompanied by eight officers of the rank of major or above, including a second-in-command, General Gorshkov, who was an expert in Russian Partisan warfare – which he was soon to learn was very different from that of the Yugoslavs' Partisan warfare. An army doctor, political intelligence officers and a number of technical staff and aides completed the party. They retired to quarters which had been specially prepared, and which they immediately pronounced to have inadequate lavatory arrangements so that these had to be hastily built to specification.[9]

Except for a brief period during the German attack of Drvar a few months later the Russian mission mixed little, and then only on formal occasions, with other missions. This was on official instructions from Moscow which Tito had received earlier. Like the Anglo-American mission they had their representatives at Croatian and Slovene Partisan Headquarters, but few soldiers in the field. They acted as Tito's line of contact with Moscow.[10] By adding a new channel of communication they almost certainly increased Soviet lack of understanding of developments in Yugoslavia. At the same time this very lack of understanding encouraged Tito to act with greater independence. British officers formed the impression that the Russians regarded the Yugoslavs as lesser Slavs whose culture was in every way inferior to their own. From May onwards their planes – Allied lease-lend Dakotas which the Russians flew from British bases near Bari – brought in supplies for the mission and some aid for the Partisans. But this never reached anything like the quantities that were now being sent in by the western Allies – a fact which Tito noted dryly at his formal weekly meeting with heads of missions.[11]

Tito sent his own military mission to Moscow a few days after the arrival of the Russians. Its purpose was to ask for aid, especially for a loan of $200,000 to cover the expenses of Partisan representatives in London and the missions which Tito was proposing to send to the west – and, even more important, to try to get Soviet support for his demand that Allied postwar aid for reconstruction which was under discussion with the newly formed United Nations Relief and Reconstruction Agency (UNRRA), should be administered by his officials and not by nominees of the royalist government or Allied military government. The mission also had party political objectives of trying to re-establish direct contact with Soviet Communist Party officials, which it was felt had been lost after the abolition of the Comintern.[12]

Milovan Djilas, one of Tito's most trusted colleagues, and a member of the Politburo, was appointed head of mission and was to make contact with Dimitrov. According to Djilas's own account he was also hoping to receive the approbation and praise of the Soviet leaders for the Partisans' war effort, and for the great contribution to communist history which the Yugoslav Party was convinced it had made. Djilas's raptures over Soviet Russia were not yet dimmed by his failure to find adequate appreciation of the Yugoslav war efforts, nor by his discovery that the main Soviet purpose of the meeting was to warn Tito not to 'frighten' the English by revealing his revolutionary intention to establish communist control in Yugoslavia. Stalin told Djilas that Partisans did not need to wear red stars in their caps; he repeatedly warned him about the duplicity of Churchill, who was he said 'the kind of man who will pick your pocket of a kopeck if you don't watch him'. Roosevelt was almost as bad. He warned him to beware of the British Intelligence Service and possible English attempts on Tito's life. 'They were the ones who killed

General Sikorski in a plane and then neatly shot down the plane – no proof, no witnesses,' he said. He insisted that Tito must compromise with the royalist Yugoslav government saying: 'You ought to talk with Šubašić and see if you can reach a compromise somehow.'[13] With this advice, which coming from Stalin himself carried great weight, Djilas returned in early June to Partisan headquarters, recently established on the island of Vis.

*　*　*

While Djilas was away a dramatic incident occurred which underlined the Partisans' need for increased aid, especially for air support. This was the German parachute attack on Tito's headquarters in Drvar in Bosnia on the morning of 25 May 1944. Inspired perhaps by the success of the parachute drop by which Mussolini was captured in September 1943, the operation with the code name of *Rösselsprung* – Knight's Move – had been planned in the utmost secrecy. The 500 SS parachute battalion was to be the main force. This consisted of men who had been under some army charge and were given the chance of redeeming themselves in specially dangerous operations. Each was provided with a picture of Tito who was to be captured alive if possible. To ensure surprise even the officers were not told of the place or time of attack. The Partisans had, in fact, on 11 November 1943, received from an agent in Zagreb a warning that the Germans were preparing parachute drops to wipe out their headquarters at Jajce, but nothing worse than ordinary air attacks on the town had happened, and Tito's headquarters were moved to the small industrial town of Drvar in Bosnia early in 1944.[14]

With its two cellulose factories, railway line and Partisan tradition, Drvar seemed a good site for the new headquarters. It lay in a valley with the Jasenovac mountains rising steeply to the north and high wooded hills to the south. Partisan units were stationed at a distance all round in the surrounding hills. A Cadet Military Training School was established in the town, and arrangements had been made for the Partisans' youth movement – Anti-Fascist Youth – to hold a conference at which Tito was to give the opening address on 23 May.

Tito's headquarters had developed greatly during the past year with the increased work brought by his new Allied military and political contacts. It now had the busy almost sophisticated organization necessary for a commander-in-chief who was also head of a provisional government. The British mission, where the British premier's son Randolph Churchill was stationed, was situated in a peasant's house on the outskirts of the town. An independent American mission, including some meteorological experts, was near by. But the chiefs of both British and American missions were not present at this time. The Russian mission was in a hamlet further away. There were many other visitors including Allied officers, British and American journalists, some dancers from the Zagreb ballet and members of the Executive Committee of the new provisional government who had arrived to confer with Tito. The town had a gay busy atmosphere as it prepared to celebrate Tito's fifty-second birthday on 25 May. Two days earlier he had sent by courier with his mail to Croatia, a confident greetings postcard to the people of his native village, Kumrovec, at that time still in Pavelić's enemy state.[15]

Tito's own quarters were in a protected, well-nigh impregnable position just outside the town. They were approached by a path along the river Unac with hills on one side and steep cliffs on the other. In a natural cleft in the rock three flights of wooden steps led to a place where the opening widened into a natural cave, inside which rooms had been constructed with a veranda in front commanding a fine view across the valley. Great wooden beams supported the construction and inside in Tito's office the walls were lined, and the windows curtained with parachute silk, while a huge British military map of Yugoslavia covered a wall behind his desk. German reconnaissance planes had been noted in the district for several days, and on 23 May a single plane spent some time flying up and down the valley obviously taking photographs. The British warned Tito that the Germans were preparing to attack. In spite of this no extra defensive precautions were taken and it is impossible to escape the conclusion that the whole headquarters staff, including Tito himself, had become relaxed to the point of over-confidence in their own capacity to deal with any German threat.

About 6.35 a.m. on 25 May just after Tito got up he saw from his window German bombers and fighters coming in. They immediately began to bomb targets in the town and many fires were started. At 7 a.m. they were followed by forty big Junker 52 planes dropping parachutists who grouped as they landed and rushed off to special targets. Ten minutes later gliders were towed in, machine gunners pouring out as they touched down. By 9 a.m. the Germans had captured most of the town including the radio communications centre, but had failed to establish positions on the right bank of the Unac which was being defended desperately by the Supreme Staff's defence corps with officers and students from the Cadet Training School. Urgent appeals for help had been sent by courier and radio to the four Partisan divisions within reach. The British mission managed to get messages out to Bari asking for air support which was sent the following day. The nearest Partisan unit, the 6th Lika Proletarian Division were 12 kilometres away; they arrived about 9 a.m. having run most of the way. Other Partisan units came in during the rest of the day. German parachutist reinforcements were dropped at noon and ferocious fighting continued until nightfall with severe losses on both sides. It was not until 3.30 a.m. that it became clear that the Germans had failed in their objective.

Tito and all his main headquarters' personnel had escaped. He got away shortly after midday by an escape route ingeniously contrived by cutting a hole in the floor of his office and dropping a rope to the bed of the stream below; thirty yards, further along it was possible to cross into the orchards on the other side. Most of Tito's personal staff got away, including Kardelj who had the narrowest possible escape as the Germans passed within feet of his hiding place. Tito's girl secretaries Zdenka and Olga went ahead, and he, with his personal bodyguard and dog Tiger – which had to be lowered by rope – followed. They managed to make their way through the woods to Potoci where the Partisans had a few huts sheltered by trees. From here they were able to take a train along a little line through the woods. All the important Partisan leaders got away; most of the foreign visitors also escaped, though an American photographer and English journalist were captured by the Germans.[16]

The British and Russian missions joined Tito and for several nights they were on the move trying to evade the German motorized forces converging from Banjaluka, Jajce, Livno and Knin, combing the district with air support. During the week from 25 May, Allied fighter and bombing planes from Italy flew over 1,000 sorties to aid the Partisans. Tito himself, with great coolness, directed the survival operations. The party was short of food and ammunition but they managed to receive one parachute drop of RAF supplies.

For some time past there had been discussion of Tito establishing a permanent headquarters on the island of Vis where with Allied air cover and ground support he could be free from the need for continual movement and safe from attack. The matter now became urgent as there was great danger of the party being captured. The Soviet mission pressed Tito to escape to Italy. He eventually agreed, although for obvious political reasons he was extremely reluctant to leave the country even for a brief time. On the night of 3/4 June Tito, accompanied by some of his staff, Tiger, a British officer and the Russian Mission, was flown out to Bari in Italy from an airstrip near Mliniste. They were piloted by a Russian in a Soviet Dakota plane operating under British control from Bari. The others were evacuated in British planes.

Tito stayed two days in a villa outside Bari – long enough to negotiate with the British Air Chief-of-Staff Sir John Slessor, about the supplies he needed. Though tired and for once a little depressed, he was able to point out the lesson of his recent experience. The *Luftwaffe* had freedom of the air in Yugoslavia; it was necessary for the Partisans to have strong air support if they were to be able to aid Allied operations in Italy. Three days later he crossed by night to Vis in HMS *Blackmore*, a Hunt class destroyer. Under the influence of the convivial atmosphere of a wardroom dinner and the immeasurable relief of being alive, neither prisoner nor refugee, delighted to be returning to Yugoslav territory where he would again be in control of his own fate, Tito ended the evening reciting 'The Owl and the Pussycat' in broken English to an admiring audience.

\* \* \*

In the summer of 1944, British policy in relation to Yugoslavia was concentrated on trying to persuade the royalist government and Tito's provisional government to come to a compromise agreement. It was hoped that this would put an end to civil war, and increase the military cooperation which Tito's armies could give the Allies, by holding down German forces in the Balkans until the Russians arrived. It was also believed that if real agreement could be reached it would be a first step towards establishing the basis for an all-party, democratic government in postwar Yugoslavia and would help to prevent what Churchill called 'the communization of the Balkans'. A number of members of the Yugoslav politicians in exile supported this policy, especially the former Ban – or Governor – of Croatia, Dr Ivan Šubašić. In May Tito sent his representative Dr Vladimir Velebit, who had been in Cairo, to London to inform both the

British and royalist Yugoslav governments of his basic conditions for negotiations. These were: recognition of the AVNOJ government and its proclaimed aims, and abandonment of support for Mihailović. The return of the King was to be left an open issue.

The crisis in the royalist government brought about by the whole situation was bitter and prolonged, but eventually the prime minister, Božidar Purić resigned, and the way was open for the compromise which Britain and Stalin had advised. Šubašić travelled to Vis in early June, and on 16 June the Tito–Šubašić Agreement was signed. It incorporated all Tito's basic demands. It was agreed that when a new royalist government composed of 'progressive democratic elements' was formed, its main task would be to organize aid and supplies for Tito's army; that final decisions about the postwar form of state and the return of the monarchy must be left to the Yugoslav people. It was accepted that an interim government composed of representatives of the new royalist government and of Tito's National Committee should be formed. Šubašić was then appointed prime minister of the new government; Mihailović was dismissed as minister of war, and King Peter broadcast a message to Yugoslavia denouncing collaboration and urging support for Tito and the National Committee.

In retrospect it can be seen as a major political breakthrough for Tito; he had gained for his movement the support of the royalist government and added its claims to legality to his own. Yet Tito was very uneasy. 'We had to consent to this as it was the Allies' condition for recognition of the new state of affairs in Yugoslavia . . . because the western Allies stubbornly insisted on it.'[17] He was still afraid that the British would manage to trick him, and especially he feared that they would use their troops in some way to try to restore the King. He was now moving into the field of interstate relations in which he had no previous experience.

Earlier in 1944 there had been repeated suggestions that Tito should himself visit Allied leaders in Italy. These had been treated with great caution – and some suspicion, especially from extremists among his colleagues. Djilas had brought back Stalin's warning from Moscow. The help Tito received from the British after the German descent on Drvar, and his successful negotiations with Šubašić helped to clear the air. In early August 1944 he flew from Vis to Allied headquarters at Caserta near Naples, taking with him his Deputy Commander-in-Chief, Žujović, his Chief-of-Staff, Arso

(*left*): **25. Tito and Krushchev, a reconciliation visit, 26 May 1955.**

(*below*) **26. Tito shows Krushchev and Bulganin an archaeological exhibit, Brioni, 1956.**

(*above*): **27. A non-alignment meeting: Tito with Nehru and Nasser, Brioni, July 1956.**
(*below*): **28. Tito with West German Foreign Minister, Willy Brandt, 1968.**

Jovanović, and the heads of his military intelligence, medical and supply services. He was accompanied everywhere by his personal bodyguard and his dog Tiger. In his personal entourage was his elder son, Žarko Broz, who had only recently returned to Yugoslavia from Russia, where he had been brought up.[18] He had lost an arm fighting in the Red Army and was convalescing.

Clothes conscious as always Tito wore a new tight-fitting grey uniform with a scarlet stripe down the trousers and gold braid and insignia of his rank of marshal. Churchill later called it his 'gold-lace strait-jacket'. Tito did not wish to be patronized by capitalist leaders as merely a guerrilla leader from the backwoods, and was determined that the status and achievements of his Partisan movement should not be underrated. He wanted to get greatly increased aid from the British; some of his advisers who had little understanding of the Allied supply position had grandiose ideas of the numbers of planes and tanks they believed they needed and felt they deserved.

General Sir Henry Maitland Wilson, Supreme Allied Commander in the Mediterranean theatre of war, was determined that everything should be done to make the visit a success. His first encounter with Tito was on 6 August and a meeting took place with General Alexander, Commander-in-Chief of the Allied armies in Italy, the following day. A week was spent discussing aid, visiting supply depots and the British front in Italy, giving Tito a better understanding of the Allied war effort and allowing both sides to take the measure of each other. It was understood that the British prime minister, Winston Churchill, would himself be coming to Italy to see Tito.

The meeting between Churchill and Tito took place on 12 August in General Wilson's villa overlooking the Bay of Naples. Tito was formally dressed in his splendid uniform; Churchill arrived wearing his white boiler-suit. But both status and appearance soon became irrelevant, for the two men took to each other from the start, in spite of their widely divergent backgrounds and political beliefs. They were of the same generation – both had taken part in very different circumstances in the first world war. They shared certain warm human characteristics, both enjoyed the pleasures of life and the power of office, both were pragmatic leaders, confident that they were using their positions as a force for good in a war against evil. They spoke to each other through Tito's interpreter Olga Ninčić, communist daughter of a former Yugoslav foreign minister, but they

R

managed to make direct human contact and the meeting was marked by frankness and plain speaking on both sides. Conversation was relaxed, ranging over the military situation in Normandy after the recent Allied landing and the slow moving position in Italy. They discussed the position of the Germans in the Balkans and the role of Tito's forces. Churchill asked Tito whether his forces would cooperate if the Allies established a bridgehead near Istria and invaded central Europe through the north of Yugoslavia towards the Ljubljana Gap. 'Yes,' replied Tito, 'we have our troops in Slovenia and Croatia who would certainly assist.' This, as both leaders knew, was a very delicate proposition, for Tito was afraid that if Allied troops landed in Yugoslavia they might be used to prevent him taking over power, or to restrict his claim to Trieste and its hinterland as well as Istria and other areas occupied by the Italians after the first world war.

The conversation then turned to Partisan fighting in Yugoslavia. Churchill asked Tito about fighting between Četniks and Partisans. 'Yes, there is very fierce fighting,' Tito said. 'We had much rather see our bullets used to kill Germans,' replied Churchill. He then went on to explain that it was the reports of his liaison officers Deakin and Maclean which finally convinced him that he must withdraw British support from Mihailović. 'I hope we shall see as little fighting as possible between Yugoslavs,' said Churchill, to which Tito replied 'We have always been against a civil war and consider the Germans to be our main enemy. We only fight Četniks when it cannot be avoided. If we had considered Mihailović our main enemy the Partisans could not have become so popular in our country.'

Churchill then turned to the question of Serbian peasants, suggesting that they would not wish to see a communist system introduced after the war, and spoke of the sufferings that Stalin had imposed on Russian peasants by his collectivization. Tito answered that in Yugoslavia the problem was not quite the same. 'We do not intend to impose any such system. I have often stated this publicly,' he said, adding that his movement only recognized two classes of Yugoslavs – quislings and patriots and that the Russian mission in Yugoslavia had never tried to exert their influence towards introducing a communist system. Towards the end of the meeting Tito said that Churchill had done much for the Yugoslavs and the Partisan cause. Churchill then returned again to the question of civil war; Tito replied that it was not likely to take place in Yugoslavia. 'It really depends on what backing the Allies give,' he added pointedly. Churchill asked if Tito would allow individual freedom in Yugoslavia after the war. 'That is our basic principle – democracy and freedom of the individual,' was Tito's answer. And to Churchill's question if workers' strikes would be allowed, Tito replied, 'Not while war lasts'. After some dicussion about the terrible devastation of war in Yugoslavia, Churchill asked if Tito wished to say anything more. Tito's reply was that he was concerned about statements being made about the introduction of communism in Yugoslavia after the war. He emphasized that Yugoslavia would have a democratic system – but he did not specify of what kind, and he refused Churchill's request that he make a public statement about communism. He said that they could profit from Russian experience, and look for help from the Allies. It was important for Yugoslavia that relations between the Allies and Russia should be good. The exchange of views had been direct and friendly, but it is clear that the two leaders did not always speak the same political language and each put a different interpretation on the word 'democracy'. Churchill with his long career as a parliamentarian in the British two-party system saw it as one thing, Tito with his varied experience in the communist world saw it as another. The meeting cannot have been entirely reassuring for Tito because of the hint of possible Allied landings in Istria and of Churchill's views on future political developments in Yugoslavia.

There has been much comment about the 'friendship' established between the two leaders as a result of this meeting. Both appreciated the qualities of greatness in the other, but their basic political ideas remained unchanged. Tito had more understanding thereafter of the Allied war effort, he was impressed by the easy comradeship at all levels of Anglo-American cooperation – so unlike relations between allies in the communist world; and above all, he had been very impressed by Churchill. He said later that it had helped to remove some of his suspicions of British ploicy. 'When I met Churchill in 1944 I had a very frank discussion with him, and I myself saw that England had suffered very much and realized that they wanted to use all Allies to end the war. Churchill and I understood each other very well. The only thing was that Churchill thought the Serbian people were for the King, and I said that the Serbian people were very disgusted about the King leaving the country, and not even *they* were for the monarchy.'[19]

It can hardly have been a coincidence that a meeting between

Stalin and Tito was arranged to take place shortly after Tito had returned from seeing Churchill. Stalin had already shown that he was determined that Tito's relations with the British should not become friendly, that he did not wish any weakening in Tito's ties with Moscow. The arrangements made for Tito's visit to Moscow were designed to demonstrate this. In circumstances of great secrecy he was flown with General Korneev in a Russian plane to the headquarters of the Red Army in Romania on the night of 18/19 September 1944, and travelled on to Moscow two days laters. To fly off by night from the British controlled airport in Vis and evade its security guards without informing the British had required considerable *konspiracija*, and was difficult to explain away so soon after Tito's warm reception in Italy. Churchill was very angry, saying that Tito had 'levanted'. Molotov later blamed the secrecy on Tito. It was 'all you could expect of a Balkan peasant', he said. But the incident had the hallmark of Stalin's malicious methods of setting one ally against another.[20]

Tito's first visit to Stalin marked the highest point in his relations with the Russian leader. He still accepted without question the Soviet right to lead international communism and was very conscious of the honour of being received by Stalin. He did not query his duty to report to Moscow. At the same time he felt immensely proud of his own and his party's war record, convinced that 'the Yugoslav Communist Party had brilliantly passed the test, and uniquely so'.[21] He expected to be praised. Stalin received him very warmly, embracing him so vigorously that he was literally swept off his feet. 'I had the impression that he appreciated our efforts,' Tito said much later, adding with hindsight, 'Perhaps it was only apparent, not real.'

In the discussion that followed with Stalin, Molotov and other Soviet leaders, Tito's new authority was evident in the confident way he spoke. It did not endear him to other Soviet leaders. But he convinced Stalin that his army was strong enough to undertake occupation duties in Yugoslavia, that it should remain under his command, that the Soviet army should only enter Yugoslavia for the limited campaigns necessary for its advance through central Europe, and that Yugoslav forces should undertake operations simultaneously and join the Red Army in the advance on Belgrade. It was also agreed that the Soviet forces should have no administrative or civil powers in Yugoslavia. Tito had rightly seen that these concessions were immensely important for the conditions in which any postwar revolutionary transfer of power would take place. He was confident of succeeding without the aid of the Red Army, and did not wish to appear to be beholden to it. It was the only agreement of this kind made between Russian leaders and a resistance movement.

Stalin clearly did not attach the same importance to these concessions though he did not agree easily to them. He saw Tito as another puppet who could be used and discarded if he did not obey. As the Red Army approached Berlin and the Americans prepared to step up their forces in the Far East, he had more important issues to deal with than Yugoslavia, which he confidently believed could be manipulated as he wished when he was ready to do so. Stalin was ignorant of the changes that had taken place in Yugoslavia during the war in spite of all Tito's telegrams and the assessments of the Soviet mission; he and his advisers did not consider the Partisan war as very important and as Molotov's remark showed – thought of Tito as a Balkan peasant, no different from the Valter who had been in Moscow in the 'thirties. They consistently devalued all his reports with a monumental lack of understanding which was to turn to their own disadvantage in 1948.

Some of this ill-will and lack of understanding was dimly perceived by Tito in the discussions with Stalin about political change in Yugoslavia after the war. Stalin's characteristic advice was for Tito to work with royalist politicians, even the King. 'You need not restore him for ever. Take him back temporarily. Then you can slip a knife in his back at a suitable moment,' he said. He also added a bit more fuel to Tito's suspicions of the British, telling him at one stage that a news agency had reported a British landing in Dalmatia. When Tito failed to rise, and explained that he had been promised British artillery support in this area, Stalin enquired what Tito would do if the British were to land forces in Yugoslavia, 'We should offer determined resistance,' answered Tito.[22] This was sufficient for Stalin for the time being and the rest of the visit was spent in the feasting and heavy drinking with innumerable toasts in wine and vodka that characterized Stalin's barbaric entertainment of his guests.

For Tito the visit had been a qualified success in that he had got the practical arrangements he wanted, if not the adulation. For Stalin, to whom it was an occasion of less importance, it was also a success. He had made concessions which suited his convenience and he had ensured that Tito's relations with the British would remain suspiciously hostile. Tito returned to Yugoslavia on 5 October via

Craiova in Romania, where he spent several days and met representatives of the Bulgarian Partisans. He then flew to Vrsac in the Banat and after a wait of some days as Soviet and Partisan troops fought their way towards Belgrade, he flew to the air-strip outside Belgrade and entered the city by car on 27 October 1944.

On 9 October, shortly after Tito's departure from Moscow, Stalin had another meeting of Allied leaders at the Kremlin. This time with Churchill and Averell Harriman, President Roosevelt's representative. It was at this meeting that the future of eastern Europe was discussed, and Stalin agreed with Churchill's suggestion – written in a pencilled note pushed across the table to him by Churchill – that Yugoslavia should be shared as a sphere of influence between Great Britain and the Soviet Union on a fifty-fifty basis. This was designed as an interim measure until the peace conference and had been discussed with American leaders who were still suspicious of Churchill's Balkan policy. It raises the question whether Stalin had already had some such compromise in mind when he had seen Tito only a few days earlier. It was of fundamental importance to all Tito's future policy, but he had not discussed the matter with him, nor given him any hint of its possibility. Nor did he inform him after it had taken place, but left the Yugoslav communists to pick up the news much later from other sources. Although Tito was very angry indeed when he eventually learnt about the fifty-fifty agreement – which was never, in fact, put into effect – the idea that Yugoslavia should belong to neither political camp in the postwar world was one that Tito eventually accepted and turned to Yugoslavia's great advantage.[23]

The deterioration in Tito's relations with the British before the end of the war was not, as it turned out, entirely due to Stalin's influence. It arose in the first place from differences over the occupation of Trieste and its hinterland, as well as Zara (Zadar), Fiume (Rijeka) and Istria, areas that had been given as a reward to Italy at the end of the first world war. Tito had already informed the British during his visit to Italy that Yugoslavia would claim these as ethnically and historically Yugoslav lands. The decision, he had been told by Churchill, would be one for the peace conference. Both leaders knew that capture and military occupation would greatly strengthen any claim to possession. Military cooperation for simultaneous operations against German positions in northern Yugoslavia and Venetia Giulia was agreed between Tito and General Alexander in meetings in Italy and Belgrade. While the Allied Eighth Army fought its way across northern Italy, Tito's Fourth Army was to attack the Germans in the region inland from the Adriatic north of Zadar. Squeezed between the two, the Germans fought tenaciously, hoping to be able to surrender to the British. By the last week in April 1945, both armies were within striking distance of Trieste. On 27 April as Churchill was cabling President Truman, 'The great thing is to be there before Tito's guerrillas are in occupation', Tito gave orders that Trieste must be 'liberated' immediately.[24] The Yugoslav 9th Corps abandoned its attempts to break through a defence position of the German 97th Army Corps, outflanked the Germans and raced to Trieste, entering the city on 30 April and occupying it in strength the following day. Units of the 2nd New Zealand Division fighting with the British Eighth Army entered the city from the other side on 2 May and were there in strength by 3 May, so that for a time both armies occupied the city.[25] General Alexander believed that Tito had gone beyond the terms of their agreement. Tito was convinced the Allies were taking steps that would effectively prevent Yugoslavia's claims being realized. There was angry deadlock for some weeks.

In the end, and in spite of some representations by Stalin on his behalf, Tito failed to get Soviet support and had to agree to withdraw his troops from Trieste behind the so-called Morgan Line which divided the disputed region into Zone A including Trieste, which was occupied by Anglo-American forces, and Zone B, which excluded parts of Istria and the Slovene littoral; this was occupied by the Yugoslavs. The Russians had had to take into account their relations with the Allies as well as the possibilities of repercussions from Italian communists had they backed Tito's claims to Trieste. Tito was convinced that, because of great power politics he had been cheated of areas to which his country had a rightful claim. He knew by this time of the fifty-fifty agreement, and believed this was a result of it. He gave vent to his spleen in a speech in Ljubljana. 'We do not wish to be used as small change in international bargaining,' he said. Throughout this crisis, Tito did not behave as a docile satellite, and did not show understanding of the overriding importance of Soviet interests which the Russian leaders expected. He behaved with a belligerent nationalism that gained him the support of many Yugoslavs who were not communists. It was noted in Moscow with strong disapproval.

# 15  INTERNATIONAL STATESMAN

In 1945 Tito's movement came to power and Yugoslavia was reunited as a federal republic with a communist government. Tito was immediately faced with the complex problems of establishing the new state and of protecting its position in a hostile world. The two tasks were interdependent. He needed peace and security to carry through the revolutionary changes that had been his distant objective throughout the war. To protect Yugoslavia's interests abroad he had to have internal stability. In the end he accomplished both aims; for over a quarter of a century he remained head of state, becoming with the passage of time a venerated symbol of unity at home and an Olympian figure on the international scene.

In all aspects of government he always worked with a team of colleagues whose members changed over the years; but in foreign policy his personality and influence were specially important. He showed qualities of statesmanship that gave Yugoslavia prestige such as it had never had since its foundation as a state, and won for himself respect and – sometimes reluctant – admiration throughout the world. In 1945 he was a novice in the wider fields of foreign affairs his experience limited to what he had learnt during the war. He still accepted Soviet leadership in international communism; but Yugoslav foreign policy could be seen as an extension of the foreign relations he had begun to develop during the war. Yet there is no doubt that once he was prime minister of an autonomous state, Tito believed his relations with Russian leaders had moved on to a different plane and considered that he was entitled to behave with an independence unthought of when he had been only a communist party leader dealing with Comintern or Soviet party officials.

At first there seemed no fundamental contradictions in this situation. The Yugoslav party was the first communist party in Europe to gain power for itself since the Bolshevik revolution. Its leaders naturally turned to the Soviet Union for advice and example. On Yugoslav request, Soviet experts flooded into the country to advise on military matters, to found joint stock companies for transport, to help with technical matters such as industrial reconstruction 'We had great confidence in the USSR until 1947,' Tito said much later, 'and the Russians had a great deal of influence on the organization of our state because we took them as our example.'[1] Yet in foreign affairs conditions were somewhat different since there was no precedent to cover Yugoslavia's national interests and it had never been foreseen that they might clash with those of Russia. Tito and his colleagues had to find a policy that would protect Yugoslav interests and at the same time they felt that Yugoslavia deserved a special position in the communist world because of the Partisans' remarkable achievements during the war. Accepting the idea of hierarchical authority in the communist pyramid, they believed their rightful position was only just below that of the Soviet Union, whose general lines of foreign policy they willingly agreed with.

Yugoslav leaders, including Tito, threw themselves with characteristic vigour into the truculent attitudes of the cold war that had already started to develop between east and west. They cut themselves off from former western friends, and relations became very strained, especially with the United States. Until 1947 at least, and perhaps even later, they were greatly afraid of Allied attempts to restore a royalist government to power. British documents about this period have not yet been made public and we do not know exactly what British contingency plans were – especially if fighting had broken out over the Trieste question – but there were certainly influential people in Britain and the United States who would have pressed for intervention had the opportunity arisen. There were plenty of border incidents to feed Yugoslav suspicions. The many provocative flights over Yugoslav territory by American military planes from bases in Italy and Austria aroused Tito to fury. When diplomatic protests failed to stop them, Yugoslav anti-aircraft defences were ordered to fire on intruding planes. On 9 August 1946 two American planes were brought down, killing the crew of one plane.[2] On hearing that two American planes had been shot down, Molotov 'almost embraced' the Yugoslav foreign minister Kardelj – even though it had demonstrated Yugoslavia's independence; but he warned him not to shoot down any more.[3]

When Tito visited the Soviet Union for the signature of a Treaty of Friendship and Alliance on 11 April 1945 he was treated with full honours and seated at Stalin's left hand at the celebration dinners. But an indication of the true Russian attitude could be seen in

247

Stalin's malicious jokes at Tito's expense. The Bulgarian army was better than the Yugoslav, he said, adding that the Yugoslav soldiers were still Partisans 'unfit for serious front-line fighting'. He recalled how one German regiment had broken up a division of Partisans the previous winter. Considering that the Bulgarian army had been occupying part of Yugoslavia throughout the war and that the Bulgarian Partisans had not been very active until aided by Tito's forces, these were bitter insults. Tito had borne the first remarks in silence, but was finally provoked into an angry shout that the Yugoslav army would quickly rid itself of its weakness; he still had not reached the point when he could contradict or answer Stalin in kind.[4] The incident could be shrugged off for the time being, and Tito's personal relations with Stalin were still cordial when he visited Moscow again in the spring of 1946.

Following the Soviet pattern Yugoslavia signed treaties of friendship and mutual assistance with the countries of eastern Europe as one by one Stalin was able to put communist governments in power.[5] When, in 1947, the United States offered Marshall Aid to war-destroyed countries, Yugoslavia refused to accept it, in spite of the terribly hard postwar conditions the people were experiencing. Tito was afraid it would be used by the capitalist Americans for subversive purposes against him. Twenty years later he was still prepared to defend this decision. 'Our rejection of the Marshall Plan was our own idea, and we were right,' he said, 'in this way we kept ourselves free from American influence.' He was convinced that decisions about Yugoslav foreign policy were taken independently. 'We did not accept Russian influence or direction,' he said, the 'policy was taken on our own initiative, and no one forced us to it.'[6]

Given some identity of interests, the truth about Soviet policy was not apparent to the Yugoslav leaders. In 1945 and 1946 Stalin was dealing with more urgent problems and was not disposed to interfere with Tito's efforts as long as they followed the general Soviet line. Stalin's major preoccupation after the war was security. His intention was to establish a protective zone of puppet communist states in eastern Europe under his own control. He had no intention of allowing satellite leaders to follow independent lines of policy – and Yugoslavia was intended to fit into this pattern. The Yugoslav leaders, including Tito himself, were not yet sufficiently detached from their prewar indoctrination and romantic wartime ideas about communist brotherhood and unity to recognize the brutal truth of the dichotomy between Soviet theory and practice. They had already had plenty of evidence of the real situation, but were blinded by their wish to believe in Soviet friendship, by overconfidence and perhaps by a naïve optimism that stemmed from their remarkable wartime success.

When Stalin suggested a new international organization of communist states along similar lines to the defunct Comintern, Tito supported it; it seemed to offer a possibility for Yugoslavia to play a 'leading role' as it was called in communist language, in eastern Europe. 'We were at first in favour of it. It seemed a good idea to have an organization for consultation between communist states, and at the Warsaw meeting we were for it,' he said later. 'A soon as we saw what it was really like we turned against it.'[7] The Cominform – or 'Informburo' was founded in September 1947; on the Russian suggestion its headquarters was to be in Belgrade. It sounded like a compliment to the Yugoslavs but was actually intended by Stalin as a means of controlling Tito and gaining more information about what he was doing.

By this time there were a number of matters, both important and trivial, in which there had been trouble between the Yugoslavs and Russians. One of these had been an injudicious remark by Djilas on the subject of violence, rape and drunkenness by Soviet officers as they passed through Yugoslavia; he had pointed out that British officers behaved better and did not 'indulge in such excesses'.[8] Stalin never forgave him although the matter was patched up later. Tito had also incurred displeasure by his independence over Trieste – and his outspoken speech at Ljubljana. He had visited most of the countries in eastern Europe and had been given a hero's welcome. But perhaps his most dangerous move towards leadership in eastern Europe could be seen in his ideas on Balkan federation. This was an old idea in the communist world and had not originated with Tito, so it was understandable if he thought it was acceptable to Russia. During the war Tito, with Soviet agreement, had had close contacts with Bulgarian and Albanian Partisans; and after the war Albania was virtually run as a Yugoslav dependency.[9] When this arrangement was later criticized, the Yugoslav leaders pointed out that they had given Albania far more generous treatment than they had themselves received from the Soviet Union even though the aid – food, experts, investment, joint stock companies – had been along the same lines. Stalin declared to Djilas when he visited Moscow early in 1948 that he had no objection to Yugoslav–Albanian federation. 'We have no special interest in Albania. We agree to Yugoslavia swallowing Albania,' said Stalin, gesturing with his fingers to his mouth. When Djilas, rather shocked by this unusual frankness, demurred and said, 'It is not a matter of swallowing, but unification!' Molotov interjected, 'But that is swallowing.'[10]

Stalin was more concerned about the question of federation between Bulgaria and Yugoslavia though it was some time before his policy crystallized. This had been discussed between Yugoslav and Bulgarian leaders as far back as 1944 with Soviet approval, but no agreement had been reached.[11] It was raised again between Tito and Dimitrov after the latter had at last been allowed by Stalin to return to Bulgaria in January 1947. In July of that year Dimitrov went to meet Tito at Bled in Slovenia. The two men were old friends who understood each other well; even so the problems of federating the two countries were too great – Dimitrov was eager for federation but unwilling for Bulgaria to become simply a seventh republic along with the six that already formed the Yugoslav state. He also had some ideas of a possible wider federation to include Romania. It was not possible to reach agreement on how Bulgarian Macedonia should be joined to Yugoslav Macedonia though Dimitrov was prepared to allow this to take place eventually. There was also the matter of the part of Macedonia that still belonged to Greece where an anti-communist regime was in power. The two leaders agreed that federation must wait, but close cooperation in trade and cultural matters could be started right away.[12] Angry at this show of independence Stalin summoned the two leaders to Moscow. Dimitrov went, Tito sent Kardelj and Djilas.

Although Stalin had earlier urged federation, he now changed his mind and after bullying Dimitrov said playfully to Kardelj, 'What about waiting a while with the federation with Bulgaria? Perhaps in the meantime the USSR could join the Yugoslav federation?'[13] This was a sinister suggestion. It was impossible to be sure whether Stalin was serious or not, but Kardelj knew that at an earlier stage Stalin had been considering the possibility of grouping the east European states in federation with the USSR. The idea had been considered that Yugoslavia and Bulgaria should form one group, the Ukraine, Romania and Hungary another; Poland, Czechoslovakia and White Russia would be a third, but it never reached the stage of a concrete proposal.[14] Before Kardelj returned to Yugoslavia he had to sign a document promising that Yugoslavia would consult with the

USSR on all matters of foreign policy. Tito had by this time angered the Russians in other matters of foreign policy – he had sent Yugoslav troops to Albania to strengthen defence on the frontiers with Greece, where a civil war was already in progress. On their own initiative the Yugoslavs had started to give considerable help to the Greek communist rebels. This was an embarrassment to Stalin who had agreed with Churchill that Greece should be within the British sphere of influence; he did not at this time wish to go back on this agreement for he was not yet ready for any confrontation with the western Allies. True though it was, no one in the west would believe that Yugoslav support for Greek rebels was Tito's independent policy. Stalin decided it was time to teach Tito a lesson.

The news of the break between Tito and Stalin was announced to an astonished and incredulous world on 28 June 1948, by a simple statement in a Czech newspaper that Yugoslavia had been expelled from the Cominform. This was followed by the Russians publishing a few selected excerpts from correspondence they had had with Tito and Kardelj as senior officials of the Yugoslav Communist Party. Tito retaliated by publishing all except two – which have never been published – of the letters that had preceded the break.[15] They made fascinating reading for the outside world which had been unaware of any deep rift between Yugoslav and Soviet leaders. As these were private letters, not intended originally for publication, they gave a remarkable picture of the attitude of the Soviet leaders to satellite states, and an unusual insight into Tito's character and beliefs. The correspondence exchanged between 20 March and 22 May had started when the Russians suddenly withdrew all their military and civilian experts from Yugoslavia, stating that they were 'surrounded by hostility'. This opened a flood of complaints and recriminations on both sides revealing pent-up grievances that went back to the war period and had obviously been accumulating since 1945. Trivial and important issues were argued indiscriminately, the tone of the letters becoming increasingly hostile. The Soviet leaders accused Yugoslavs of having first asked for many military experts, then later requested them to be reduced in numbers because of their very high cost.[16] The Russian letters alleged that Yugoslavs – unnamed – had described Soviet military experts as unnecessary, their rules hidebound, stereotyped and inappropriate to the Yugoslav army. Their economic experts had been refused information; they had been followed by Yugoslav secret police. 'Leading Yugoslav comrades' – again unspecified – had said that 'great power chauvinism is rampant in the USSR . . . the Cominform is a means of controlling the other Parties by the CPSU' (Soviet Communist Party).

Yugoslav communists were also accused of having claimed that Yugoslavia was the only exponent of revolutionary socialism. 'It was naturally laughable to hear such statements about the CPSU from such questionable Marxists as Djilas, Vukmanović, Kidrić and others', the Soviet letter said scornfully. Another letter also tried to sow dissension between the Yugoslav leaders, especially between Tito and Kardelj who had jointly signed their letters – by trying to show that Kardelj had been anxious to federate Yugoslavia to the Soviet Union. The Russians said that Yugoslav criticisms of the Soviet Union were 'both underhand and dishonest and of a hypocritical nature'. They compared Yugoslav leaders with Trotsky – the final insult in Soviet terms. They added detailed attacks on the Yugoslav Communist Party – it was undemocratic, secretive, was merged into the wider political movement called the Peoples' Front; it had not held a party congress for twenty years, was divorced from the masses, had a wrong attitude to the peasants, was under the domination of Ranković's secret police.[17]

The correspondence was supposed to be a fraternal one between two communist parties. Tito and Kardelj replied for the Yugoslav party after they had obtained the consensus first of the Politburo and later of the whole Central Committee. One member, Sreten Žujović, disagreed with taking a strong line in replying to the Russians. The Yugoslav replies, in which the hands of both Tito and Kardelj can be detected, said that the Russians had received information – some of it from Žujović and Hebrang – that was inaccurate, slanderous and tendentious, coming from 'anti-party elements and dissatisfied persons'. They added a comment that has since become world famous as the essence of Tito's political credo – 'No matter how much each of us loves the land of socialism, the USSR, he can, in no case, love his country less, which is also developing socialism.' This was a far cry from the denationalized international communism which Tito as a young man had once accepted, and which the Russians now wished to reimpose.

Tito and Kardelj took up the Russian charges and refuted them one by one, defending those of their colleagues who had been attacked – these were men, they said, 'who have performed invaluable services popularizing the USSR in Yugoslavia and won priceless renown in the war of liberation. . . . Love for the USSR did not come of itself. It was stubbornly inculcated into the masses of the Party and the people in general by the present leaders of the new Yugoslavia, including in the first rank those accused in the [Soviet] letter.' They refuted criticisms of the Yugoslav party with heat; accusations of remains of capitalism in Yugoslavia were untrue – 'nowhere in the world have there been such firm consistent social changes as in Yugoslavia. . . . The great reputation of our Party, won not only in our country but in the whole world, on the basis of the results it has obtained, speaks for itself . . . there are many specific aspects in the social transformation of Yugoslavia which can be of benefit to the revolutionary development of other countries, and are already being used . . . we study and take as an example the Soviet system, but we are developing socialism in our country in somewhat different forms. . . . We do not do this in order to prove that our road is better than that taken by the Soviet Union . . . but because this is forced on us by our daily life.'[18]

All this was only further proof to the Soviet leaders of what they most disapproved of in Tito and his associates – exaggeratedly ambitious they called it in their reply – creating an alarming situation in the Yugoslav party, showing that the Yugoslav leaders were 'intoxicated with success'. All other communist parties of eastern Europe, said the Russians, in an attempt to deflate the Yugoslav pride in their war effort, had had successes to equal those of Yugoslavia, but they had been more modest, they 'do not boast about their successes as do the Yugoslav leaders, who have pierced everyone's ears by their unlimited self-praises'.[19] The Soviet leaders summoned Yugoslavia to a meeting of the Cominform which had already moved its seat to Bucharest; all its members received copies of the Russian letters and accusations. Yugoslavia refused to attend on the ground that the matters at issue had been prejudged. This in fact proved to be the case and a unanimous Cominform resolution condemned the Yugoslavs, quoting the detailed accusations that had appeared in the Soviet letters. It ended with an appeal to the Yugoslav leaders to recognize their mistakes openly and rectify them – 'to break with nationalism, return to internationalism; and in every way to consolidate the united front against imperialism'. Should they prove incapable of doing this, the resolution called upon the Yugoslav Communist Party to replace them with 'a new international leadership of the Party'.

'I will shake my finger and there will be no more Tito,' said Stalin confidently to his cronies. On his orders the satellite countries stepped up their propaganda; Tito was denounced as a paid British Secret Service agent, an insolent dwarf (he was in fact rather taller than Stalin) a 'troubadour of Wall Street'; agents were sent into Yugoslavia to cause revolt, to assassinate Tito. A strict economic boycott by all communist countries aimed to bring about collapse of the Yugoslav economy and turn the people against the régime. Soviet troops were massed on the frontiers ready to act at the first sign of popular revolt. All these things failed. Tito received the support of the greater part of his Communist Party including all the top leaders, except Žujović, Hebrang and Tito's former Chief-of-Staff, Arso Jovanović. But the Russians had calculated without the great support that Tito received from communists and from ordinary non-communist Yugoslavs. Support came from those who backed his government and from those who preferred it to a more extreme form of Soviet-led communism, which they feared was the only other alternative. Tito had again shown that his claim to be a leader of the whole Yugoslav people was justified. The break was not healed during Stalin's lifetime. 'Stalin envisaged us as being his satellites after the war. We did not even think of it as a possibility,' he said later. 'Still in 1948 he was clever enough not to attack us when he saw what the consequences would be and he saw that we were ready to fight. He did everything possible to provoke a fight and he had his forces massed on our frontiers in case the opportunity should arise. But he recognized what the situation was in our country and he came to the right conclusion.'[20]

For Tito personally, as for many of his colleagues in the party, the break with Soviet Russia was a wrench that tore at the roots of political commitment. A deeply felt desire to work for a better life for his fellow countrymen had been the driving force in his life, and he had always believed that this was identical with the purposes of the Soviet leadership. Over the years he had frequently rationalized evidence to the contrary to fit in with the language and theories of communist indoctrination. In 1948 he could do this no longer and had to face the truth. He had always been, like Dimitrov, 'a revolutionary who did his own thinking'. His resilient and aggressive character as well as a powerful personal will to succeed helped Tito. He was a shrewd and experienced judge of people, and had had to learn to make careful appraisal of factual circumstances. When he was at last able to use these faculties in judging Soviet leaders and their

29. Mme Tito and the President, 1969.

30. President Tito

policies, the truth was terrifying; but there was still a chance for him to win through by playing a lone hand. He could not have carried on without the support of his colleagues – who refused his offer to resign – and if he had not been confident of the support of the Yugoslav people. Since 1948 he has remained outside the Soviet dominated communist world, interpreting socialism in ways adapted to Yugoslavia's needs and circumstances.

\* \* \*

Although it did not appear so at the time, the Yugoslavs were fortunate in being obliged to face the realities of relations with the Soviet Union so soon after the end of the war when the Russians did not yet feel strong enough to provoke a conflict with the west. They were fortunate too, that Yugoslavia's geographical position was on the strategic frontiers of the west, giving access to the Mediterranean and Italy. It was not a position that the United States and Britain could let go to Russia by default, and the interim fifty-fifty agreement between Churchill and Stalin, which the Yugoslavs hated so much, had recognized this; it now proved a protection for Tito's régime.

Tito tackled his new situation with typical vigour and pragmatism. His first objective was to see that Yugoslavs did not starve, that their economic development was not destroyed by the withdrawal of Soviet aid, and the loss of the trade with eastern Europe which had made up fifty-five per cent of the country's total trade turnover. He had to have relations with the west, so swallowing his pride he at once began trade talks; as Yugoslavia's rich minerals, including copper and iron, need no longer be committed to the Soviet Union, he had something to bargain with. The first urgent need was for wheat, bread, and coal for industry; credit was required to pay for them and loans to buy machinery for factories and mines.

From late 1949 Britain began negotiations with Tito believing that if he was overthrown Soviet influence was bound to prevail, with disastrous consequences for western Europe, where communist parties in France and Italy were still strong. The United States was at first more cautious, some people still believing that the whole Cominform affair was a Yugoslav–Soviet plot to get financial assistance for world communism; but eventually they too came round to the view that aid was necessary 'to keep Tito afloat'. It was notable that even in these dire circumstances he was never a humble suppliant, and he made it quite clear that he would accept no aid unless it was completely free from political strings. In order to emphasize that he was not a capitalist lackey, as Russian propaganda so often described him, he remained proud and distant and his officials were difficult to deal with. 'No one can buy us!' he proclaimed in reply to a Russian jibe that Yugoslavia could be bought for $100 million. But in the end the Yugoslavs received western aid in many different forms and on a considerable scale. In the ten years between 1949 and 1959 Tito obtained about 2·4 thousand million dollars' worth of aid – it took the forms of loans, of credit for buying heavy machinery for industry, of fertilizers, seed and stock for farmers, of American surplus wheat and flour for bread, medical supplies, military equipment, service aircraft, naval and merchant ships and many other vital needs for a modern state. A novel feature was the offer for Yugoslav specialists to be trained in the United States, Great Britain, and other western countries.[21] The greater part of the aid programme came from the United States, but Great Britain also made a substantial contribution, and France gave token assistance. It was argued in the west that this was the cheapest way of keeping a defence force ready for action against Soviet aggression. For some years Yugoslavia kept over 300,000 men mobilized and spent twenty-three per cent of its national income on defence. Tito was aware that benefits did not flow only one way and pointed out firmly that western aid only amounted to four per cent of Yugoslavia's national income. At the same time, however, he said 'it would be an improper and senseless attitude on our part if we were to deny the great significance of the aid we received at a time when things were at their worst for us'.[22]

Besides accepting aid he recognized the need for Yugoslavia to find friends and allies to strengthen her isolated position. This also required serious reorientation from extreme cold-war attitudes towards capitalist states. The time for ambitious schemes for communist grouping in south-eastern Europe was over. The question of Balkan federation was closed and has so far not been reopened. If Tito was disappointed that difficulties had been too great for the achievement of this ambitious dream, he wasted no time in regrets. He had a supreme gift for closing doors firmly on the past when necessary. Yugoslav aid to Greek rebels was stopped in 1949 and the revolt which it had sustained, collapsed.[23] He set about patiently to improve relations with the governments of Greece and Turkey, and in 1954 was able to sign with them a Balkan Pact which gave some security on Yugoslavia's southern frontier, even if it did not mature into any great friendship.

He gave his attention to the unsatisfactory situation on the country's northern frontiers which were vulnerable to possible Soviet attack from Hungary. He concluded that it was unrealistic to continue hostile relations with Austria and that Yugoslavia must accept the decisions of the peace treaty which had awarded all the territory she claimed in Carinthia to Austria. From that time relations between the two countries slowly improved, trade increased and Tito himself paid a state visit to Austria in 1965.[24] The Austrian President was given a warm welcome when he visited Yugoslavia in 1968.

Relations with Italy were more delicate because of the unsolved problems of Trieste and Zones A and B. In 1952 and 1953 the Allied Military Government, without Tito's agreement, began to hand over military and civilian control in Zone A to the Italians and it looked as if Tito would lose the possibility to negotiate about his claims in this area. Weak as Yugoslavia was, Tito threatened to use force if the Italians were infiltrated into the administration of the disputed territory without his agreement. He managed to get acceptance for his view that the problem was basically one for settlement between the two claimants. The matter was eventually resolved in this way: Yugoslavia abandoned her claim to Trieste and its hinterland, but received Zone B with a slightly improved frontier with Zone A, and part of her claims in Gorizia. It was perhaps the most favourable settlement that Yugoslavia could have achieved – a triumph for Tito's tough policy and realistic negotiations. After this, and in spite of difficulties with exchange of populations in areas that changed hands, relations with Italy improved rapidly until she became one of Yugoslavia's strongest trading partners.

With these problems out of the way and the increase in contacts with the west, the cruder anti-capitalist attitudes of prewar and immediate postwar years began to disappear. After his war experiences they had never come very naturally to Tito himself, though he had admitted to being under considerable pressure from some of the more extreme and less mature among his colleagues. Tito himself was not prepared to let ideological differences with the west interfere with the policy of cooperation and coexistence which he knew to be necessary for Yugoslavia's security and prosperity. He worked hard to improve relations with Great Britain and the United States, visiting

England in 1953, and dining at Buckingham Palace with Queen Elizabeth II. 'You think your way is better, we think ours is,' he said mildly at a press conference at this time. 'However, we must leave it to the future to decide because we cannot say yet which is the better in practice; we have not yet had a chance to prove it.' When Anthony Eden, as Britain's foreign minister, accepted an invitation to visit Yugoslavia, Tito took pleasure in using the occasion of the first formal reception to break the news that he had married again.

In his relations with the United States Tito had always been aloof. He had specially resented the American contacts with Mihailović which continued to the end of the war, and the American hostility to his régime in the immediate postwar years. He did not visit America until 1960, when he had talks with General Eisenhower and addressed an Assembly of the United Nations. On this occasion he made a more dignified and statesmanlike impression than Khrushchev who appeared at the same session and slapped the podium with his shoe to emphasize an angry point.

Reconciliation with Russia came at last in 1955, two years after the death of Stalin and on the initiative of the Soviet leaders. Khrushchev was facing opposition at home and a challenge in the communist world from Mao-tse-tung in China; he needed Tito's support to consolidate his position among the communist states of eastern Europe. He was prepared to make concessions to get it, and mistakenly thought that Tito would be easy to win back. But by this time the Yugoslavs were on the road to recovery and had learnt to appreciate the benefits of independence. Tito had no intention of throwing these away. When the Soviet premier, N. A. Bulganin, and Khrushchev in his official position of Secretary of the Soviet Communist Party, arrived at Belgrade airport at the end of May they had a chilly reception. Tito unsmiling and grim, listened to Khrushchev's warm greeting and apology for Soviet mistakes and waved the Russians brusquely to the waiting Rolls-Royce. Khrushchev, refusing to be put off, continued to act his part with verve and brio, drinking and clowning at the public receptions to give an impression of uproarious fraternal celebration. Behind the scenes negotiations were tough, but eventually he had to give in to Tito's basic conditions.

In the joint *communiqué* that was issued at the end of the visit the Russians agreed that 'questions of internal reorganization or differences of social systems and of different forms of Socialist development are solely the concern of the individual countries'. Tito insisted all along that the negotiations were between independent states, not between communist parties, and he insisted that Bulganin as premier, not Khrushchev as party secretary, should sign the *communiqué* to show this. It was the biggest triumph of Tito's career and a milestone in the history of communism. He had obtained recognition not only of Yugoslavia's right to independence, but acceptance of the principle of independence for all states within the communist world. It seemed to mark the end of the theory of Soviet pre-eminence and authority over other communist states. Yet one year later its application to states other than Yugoslavia was shown to be illusory by the Soviet invasion of Hungary, and fifteen years later the same bitter lesson was demonstrated when the Russians repeated the same tactics in Czechoslovakia and followed it up by the Brezhnev doctrine which denied independent sovereignty to smaller communist states.

In 1955, however, Tito would have been less than human had he not been exultant over this success for Yugoslavia, but it was not in his character to gloat. His reaction as usual was practical, and he tried to win the maximum advantage from his position. He had demanded that the Cominform be disbanded and this was done on 17 April the following year; he had asked for economic cooperation with Russia and her satellites, and this was restored. He gained a lot of other less spectacular concessions such as the return of Yugoslav citizens who had been kept in the Soviet Union since 1948, and repayment of debts that had been withheld. But his most important demand was for the 'de-Stalinization' of communist governments in countries of eastern Europe. This gave Tito an opportunity again to try to extend his influence to the communist world outside Yugoslavia.

For a very short time he had the satisfaction of seeing Khrushchev influenced by his ideas. Khrushchev now tried other methods of winning Tito to his side. For a few months in 1955 and 1956 the two leaders appeared to have a special relationship. Khrushchev gave Tito a wonderful reception when he visited Russia in April 1956 – the first time for ten years. It was even said that it was Tito who persuaded Khrushchev to make his famous speech to the Twentieth Soviet Communist Party Congress in which he revealed the evils of Stalin's career. Stalinists began to be deposed in countries of eastern Europe and were replaced by more liberal communists. But opposition to these ideas of 'independent communism' remained strong in some parties, especially in Hungary, in spite of Tito's demand that the obdurate, hated Stalinist Hungarian leader Rákosi must go. In the summer of 1956 Tito seemed to be in almost permanent consultation with Soviet leaders over the problems in Hungary. Khrushchev, Malenkov and Mikoyan visited Tito at his summer residence on the Adriatic island of Brioni in July. Tito then went to visit Khrushchev at his holiday resort of Sochi on the Black Sea in October, and there at last it was agreed that Rákosi should be replaced by Gero, whom Tito still thought to be too right wing to satisfy the demands for change in Hungary. As soon as he returned to Yugoslavia he heard that the Hungarian revolt had started. The invasion of Soviet troops and tanks into Hungary on 24 October was condemned by Tito as unnecessary and inexcusable – a demonstration of brutal Soviet force against a small communist state, the kind of situation he had been struggling all summer to avoid. Yet after the first Soviet invasion, Hungarian revolt escalated further until the whole communist position was endangered and on 4 November the Soviet Union invaded Hungary for a second time. Tito was put in the humiliating position of having to agree that this was necessary. Had communism been overthrown in Hungary, his own revolution in Yugoslavia and communist governments in all other countries of eastern Europe might have been endangered.

The Hungarian revolt provided ammunition for people like Molotov in the Soviet Union who had consistently disapproved of Tito's liberal form of communism and had watched with undisguised hostility Khrushchev's flirtation with anti-Stalinist change. It marked the end of Tito's direct influence on Soviet policy. For a time relations with Russia were very strained and since then his relations with Soviet leaders have fluctuated between cool and only cautiously friendly. The Russian leaders could never afford to ignore the important influence of Tito's independent communism on all other communist countries and parties, but they have been divided among themselves as to what methods to use to neutralize this influence.

Although after 1956 Tito was unable to play a direct part as a leader of communist eastern Europe, he did his best to make sure that other communist countries understood what was happening in Yugoslavia and could draw their own conclusions. It was a continued challenge to the Russians. He refused to be drawn back into the Soviet camp; would not send official representatives to Khrushchev's conference of communist states in Moscow in 1957. Kardelj attended only as an observer and was subjected to some pressure from Mao-tse-tung who did his best to persuade Yugoslav communists to return to the fold, saying that China had suffered more from Stalin than even Yugoslavia but still had not refused to accept Soviet leadership of international communism.[25] Tito refused to join the Soviet defence system of the Warsaw Pact, and although Yugoslavia had increased economic relations with Russia and communist countries of eastern Europe, he resisted attempts to draw Yugoslavia into the Russian-dominated economic community known as COMECON.

In 1958 the Yugoslav Communist Party held its seventh congress in Ljubljana and took the opportunity to stage a public declaration of the principle of separate roads to socialism, and of the practical methods which were being applied in Yugoslavia.[26] In the middle of a challenging speech by Ranković, observers from the Soviet Union and all east European communist states except Poland walked out to demonstrate their disapproval.

Refusing to accept Soviet leadership and prevented by ideology from close association with the American-dominated west, Tito had to find some other way out of isolation. His solution was to build up a movement of non-alignment. He aimed to gain support from all non-committed countries, great or small or weak, and all who did not wish to line up with one or other of the great power blocs. The non-alignment movement was Tito's own creation, and he worked hard to gain support from countries in Asia, Africa and the Middle East. Even before 1956 he had started travelling abroad to make friends. In the decade from 1958 to 1968 he visited more than thirty countries. At first he travelled in his yacht *Galeb*, then, when visits became more distant and extended, he overcame his personal aversion to aeroplanes and travelled by air. Tito and his wife, who travelled with him, were received with all the honours appropriate to his position as head of state. They were banqueted, garlanded with flowers, paraded through town and country, given rides on elephants. They received many exotic gifts which were later presented to museums in Yugoslavia or used to decorate Tito's residences. Livestock that he was given – deer, lion cubs, giraffes – formed the nucleus of a private zoo near his villa on the island of Brioni.

The journeys may have satisfied Tito's desire to make contacts in other states, but they imposed a considerable physical strain. When he was seventy-eight Tito was still travelling in the cause of non-alignment. His visits won respect for Yugoslavia in parts of the world where it had been virtually unknown before. They opened up new markets for commerce. Yugoslavia sent out experts to aid other countries; they helped to build ports in Syria, hydroelectric power stations in India, factories in Argentina.[27] Tito's visits were returned and foreign rulers visited Belgrade and toured the country. Yugoslavia gained prestige and standing in the world as never before. Tito had the satisfaction of seeing his country leading an international movement that embraced half the world. Two non-alignment conferences were held – one in Belgrade in 1961 was attended by twenty-three countries, but its opening was marred by Russia exploding a nuclear bomb on the day the conference began. The second, held in Cairo in 1964, was attended by forty-seven nations, but there were difficulties in persuading some of the members to put aside their national policies and keep to the subject of non-alignment. On both occasions Tito was the dominating figure. He had achieved a world platform for his foreign policy ideas – peace, coexistence, non-alignment, disarmament and conciliation through the machinery of the United Nations. Yugoslavia became a leader among the small nations in the United Nations, showing an independence in voting that pleased neither the Soviet Union nor the United States.[28]

Although the non-alignment movement never became a powerful world force, able to challenge the great powers or to act as mediator between them, it gave Yugoslavia an unprecedented place in world affairs, and Tito a unique prestige as an international statesman. President Johnson's emissary went to consult him in 1967 when sounding world opinion about peace in Vietnam. After the Israeli–Arab war in 1967 Tito produced his own formula for peace. He was handicapped from the start by having broken off relations with Israel at the beginning of hostilities. This was one of the few occasions in his career when he acted without full consultations with his government officials. His own association with Nasser in non-alignment movements had led to close friendship between the two men. This destroyed from the start his potential as a mediator, but he was able to use his influence with Nasser to counsel moderation. In all these activities Tito advised common sense and peaceful compromise solutions to the world's problems, but in common with other statesmen he found it easier to preach peace than to ensure it.

Tito's greatest achievement in foreign policy was his successful challenge to Soviet authority in the communist world, his assertion of the principle of the right of communist states to independence and autonomy. He exposed the naked Russian imperialism and nationalism that lay hidden behind the phrases of communist internationalism. This led to an irreversible trend in world communism and to demands in all communist parties in eastern Europe for greater freedom. Events in Hungary in 1956 and in Czechoslovakia in 1968 showed the dangers that these developments posed for the Soviet Union, and the lengths to which Russia was prepared to go to defend her own national interests. They demonstrated too the real weakness of Tito's position and that of all small countries when faced by the total force of a world power.

'It is quite clear,' said Tito prophetically in 1949, 'that every military occupation even though it be by the Red Army, has inherent unsocialist elements in it, so that national oppression and enslavement is inevitable, all equality is lost and unconditional subordination is given to the occupier. The irony is greater in that today that sort of occupation is considered as help.'[29]

Tito was able to defend Yugoslavia from this fate because of its geographic position and because of the remarkable support he had won from Yugoslavs who accepted him as their national leader. But ruefully he had to acknowledge that in the final issue what mattered most was the knowledge that the Yugoslavs would fight to defend their freedom. 'Every foot of our land is saturated in blood,' he said in 1951, 'but if it is necessary we will saturate it again, and it will remain ours. Yugoslavia will never be conquered except over the dead bodies of its peoples.'[30] This had been his view in the bitter days when Russian invasion seemed a possibility. In 1968 he denounced the Soviet invasion of Czechoslovakia. It is said that he told the Soviet Ambassador that Yugoslavia would fight if attacked. It was the last card that even the most successful leader of a small country could play.

# 16 HEAD OF STATE

From the end of the second world war Tito had the opportunity to create a state based on the beliefs he had accepted when he became a communist, 'a state that was new not only in form but in content as well . . . a socialist state'.[1] It was an opportunity which few people have had, and even fewer have, like Tito, lived to see their own creation develop for more than a quarter of a century. Lenin, after the Bolshevik revolution, had the same power and authority, but he only lived for a few years and he never had during his lifetime the personal popularity and general acclaim that were Tito's at the end of the war, nor the special authority and veneration that Tito has had because of continuing success into old age.

At the end of the war Tito faced formidable problems, but this was nothing new. He had always in the past won through in the end and he was confident he could do so again. The country was in ruins, thousands of villages burnt out, the houses charred and roofless; roads were destroyed and hardly a bridge in the country remained intact. One in nine of the population had died, very many of them in fighting between Yugoslavs. As the Germans retreated in 1945 they fought doggedly and inflicted still more casualties – 'the peasants bought back the dead to their villages. Horse- and ox-carts were the only vehicles moving on the long roads; they waited at the station to receive the coffins from the trains, then carrying no other freight.'[2] Those whose dead were long since buried, also turned back to their former homes to see what could be saved from the wreckage, to struggle to build up their lives again. In later years those who had experienced the war and its aftermath found it impossible to explain to younger generations, for whom it was only another episode in history, how deeply they had been affected by the compound of sadness, hope, fear and triumph that was present at the end of the war.

In these conditions the difficulties of peace were only an extension of those of the war, and Tito's leadership was accepted as natural and unquestioned. There was no other leader with an all-Yugoslav following inside or outside the country. Prewar political parties seemed outdated and irrelevant; politicians who had spent the war years abroad were discredited – and for most Yugoslavs this included the King – since they had not shared the nation's transforming and cathartic experiences. Tito was determined that no other political group should reap the rewards of the Communist Party's success. By 1945 the revolution was more than half accomplished; no opposition was to be allowed to interfere with its completion. He was prepared to be quite ruthless. In 1944, under heavy pressure from the western Allies, as he said bitterly later, he accepted three royalist representatives, Šubašić, Grol and Šutej, into a Provisional Government. They were so confident of joining some kind of united front in which they would have popular support, that they took the royalist government's files to Belgrade with them. But they grossly underrated Tito as an opponent. 'They had illusions about who would beat whom; but we had no such illusions, we knew how the whole thing would end – to the detriment of our adversaries,' Tito explained later. 'We knew the cooperation with Šubašić, Grol and Šutej would not last long, because we had to go quickly along our clearly defined road.'³ The royalist representatives were not allowed to organize their own political platform in the election campaign, and finding themselves powerless all resigned before the election was held.

Although the communists were confident that the Partisan movement would gain widespread support at a general election, they were afraid of outside interference against them, and were nervous and insecure till they had an undisputable legal mandate. They kept tight control of all government machinery throughout the country. Partisans, armed with tommy-guns, trigger-happy and seeing potential spies in every unfamiliar face, protected all government offices and zealously patrolled towns and villages. Known collaborators – and Rankvoić's intelligence system had been collecting dossiers throughout the war – were routed out, many were tried, many were killed. Even those who had been against the Partisan movement, or seemed likely to oppose the new state – and this by definition meant those of the small class of prewar bourgeoisie who had not already shown their support for the Partisans – were penalized, intimidated or imprisoned. Some disappeared, for a lot of old scores were paid off in these months.

At the general election on 27 November 1945, the electorate had a choice of voting for or against a single list of communists and their supporters. Few wished to vote against the party which had won the war and had such evident power; fewer still dared to put their voting disc in the opposition polling box. Tito's movement obtained ninety-six per cent of the total votes cast, and there were not many abstentions or spoiled papers. Though everything possible had been done to persuade people to vote for the communists, and though it can be presumed that the percentage for it would have been less had opposition parties been allowed, there is no doubt that Tito and the Partisans had massive genuine support at this time, and that they would in any case have obtained a majority. Tito now had a legal mandate and an obedient parliament which, following the practice for parliament in the Soviet Union, was allowed neither initiative nor freedom of action. It became a rubber stamp for decisions first taken by the small Politburo which met under Tito's chairmanship, and then endorsed by the larger Central Committee of the Communist Party.

On 29 November parliament abolished the monarchy and made Yugoslavia into a Federal Peoples' Republic.[4] Industry, banks and all commercial businesses were nationalized, and taken over without compensation, leaving craftsmen who could work alone without employing labour, as the sole remnants of private industry. Land was not nationalized but permitted holdings were limited to 60 acres. The land made available in this way, or confiscated from collaborators and dispossessed Volksdeutche, was distributed among landless peasants who had supported the Partisans. The many who were allotted land were obliged to join collective farms – cooperatives as they were called. House property was restricted to owner-occupiers and much accommodation was commandeered because of the terrible housing shortage. These and many other radical changes were incorporated into a constitution passed on 31 January 1947. It was based on the Soviet constitution of 1936 and guaranteed many rights that were in practice virtually disregarded in the new state, as, for example, freedom of the press, association, assembly, freedom to hold public meetings and manifestations, inviolability of person. These were no more than paper guarantees. The truth was that the new republic was a centralized, coercive state in which power was in the hands of the Communist Party, and within the party in the hands of a small group in which Tito had unquestioned authority. Tito and his colleagues in the party leadership believed they had a right to rule because they had received a mandate from the people, whose sovereignty they exercised; that they were going to create a new world, far better than anything Yugoslavia had ever known, that the people would be grateful and give their support. After the remarkable wartime success the mood of the leaders, including even Tito – pragmatic and cautious though he had shown himself to be – was that for Yugoslavs who knew how to work and endure, anything was possible.

One important matter had to be resolved before Tito could feel that his revolution was safe. This was the problem of Mihailović, who after the war became a fugitive in the mountains on the borders of Bosnia and Serbia. Tito was determined that he should be captured alive and brought to public trial so that the facts about his wartime collaboration and pro-Serbian policies could be made known to the world, and the whole Četnik movement could be descredited. Mihailović had had many opportunities in 1945 to flee from Yugoslavia as so many of his supporters had done. He refused. A proud Serbian patriot to the last, he retained the delusion that had been his undoing during the war – that some day he would be able to lead a national Serbian uprising which would exterminate the communist menace and restore Serbian power. After months on the run, abandoned by all but a handful of his followers, half-starved and suffering from exposure, he was finally captured in early March 1946. Tito, on his way to Russia for his second visit to Stalin received a laconic telegram from Ranković – 'Plan completed'. Mihailović's trial began on 10 June and lasted for a month. He said in court that he had been well treated in prison, and this was accepted by independent witnesses as true. The outcome of the trial was never in doubt, for the evidence of Mihailović's collaboration was overwhelming, and he freely admitted it. In court he was far from cowed and his final speech in his own defence, which lasted for four hours, was a remarkably clear and detailed analysis of his wartime career and the 'whirlpool of events' which had overwhelmed him. He was less explicit about his own motives. He felt he had been the victim of changes in Allied policy and of a 'merciless fate'. 'I wanted much, I began much,' he concluded, 'but the gale of the world carried away me and my work.' He was executed together with other condemned Četniks on 17 July 1947.[5]

At the beginning of the war the Yugoslav Communist Party had had 12,000 members; only 3,000 survived and these veterans, with the aid of some 300,000 men and women who had joined the Party during and after the war, had to direct the multitudinous operations of government and carry out tremendous changes in the new state.[6] To say that communists who had been expert in preparing and distributing illegal pamphlets before the war now became heads of ministries or local government, directors of enterprises, state planners, housing, land reform, or food administrators, would give a misleading impression; most communists of any calibre – and they had been chosen for this quality – had had experience of planning and administration, of local government and many other public services during the war. But the complex operation of a peacetime state and planning for a stable future proved to be very different matters. The communists themselves excluded the assistance of almost all people with technical, administrative or political experience in the prewar state who had not joined the Partisan movement. They were barred on ideological grounds because they were by definition part of the capitalist bourgeoisie and enemies of the new state.

We know very little about the details of how policy was made and political decisions taken by the leaders at this time. The Communist Party – as the Russians were to point out scornfully in 1948 – retained its prewar conspiratorial character, partly through old habit and partly to mask the narrow basis of real power. There is plenty of evidence that a small group took joint decisions and that Tito himself retained the same authority and personal power as he had had before and during the war. Most of Tito's close associates had survived the war, but Ivan Milutinović was killed when a ship on the Danube struck a mine in 1945, and the greatest loss had been that of Ivo Lola Ribar, the dynamic young man who had been so close to Tito and who, had he lived, would probably have been the most likely person to be his deputy and successor.

The men most closely associated with Tito in the policy-making innermost circle – the Politburo as it was called – were a group of four or five, varying according to the matters being discussed, but including in the central core Edward Kardelj, a Slovene, Moša Pijade and Alexander Ranković who were Serbs, and Milovan Djilas, a Montenegrin. There were others close to this inner circle – Vladimir Bakarić, a Croat, Boris Kidrić, from Slovenia and Vukmanović-Tempo also a Serb, but an expert on Macedonia.[7] All these were communists from prewar days. They represented a rough balance between the different national groups in the country. A more careful balance was maintained in the much larger Central Committee of the Party, which discussed policy, made suggestions on many minor matters, but always – at this stage – accepted major decisions of Tito's inner group as final. We know that discussions about methods of establishing government and planning were lively and argumentative, that there were many disagreements especially on planning and about the continued existence of private property in land. Tito had always encouraged discussion, but persistent opposition had to be abandoned once a decision had been taken. The leaders had long experience of this method of working together, and most of the basic principles of revolutionary change had been decided on by them well before the end of the war – many of them before the AVNOJ meeting at Jajce in 1943. Once the leaders were agreed on strategy, tactics had to be decided between them on an *ad hoc* basis and meetings were held several times a week. They were a close-knit team. Tito, as chief, had a special position, and a special authority which was accepted by his closest associates and most members of the wider circle of government officials who were all communists subject to strict discipline. Those who did not accept it – the enigmatic Croat, Andrija Hebrang, was one – must have concealed any doubts they had about the party's leadership, for doubts were tantamount to treason.

Tito had his own special relationship with each member of the team; it is difficult to know how far any of these could be called friendship. Tito was some twenty years older than all his closest colleagues except Moša Pijade with whom he had a long established friendship. But others treated him as a man apart, as their reverential descriptions of him show, and it can be taken as certain that this also was how he thought of himself. This did not prevent him relaxing, joking, hunting, playing chess and other games with them. He had the advantage of age plus a youthful appearance. Perhaps because of his physical and mental vigour, he had always enjoyed the company of younger men and he had a special affection for the two liveliest of his associates, Djilas and Kidrić. Both were men of manic energy and abundant ideas, eloquent conversationalists, and highly intelligent. Neither was the prototype working-class communist. Djilas came from a poor – but by no means the poorest – family in Montenegro; his father had been a subaltern in the royalist Yugoslav army, but had died during Milovan's childhood. The family history, as Djilas was to recount later, was a typical Montenegrin saga of feuds, murder

269

and violence in every generation, and Djilas contributed his own share to the story. 'My father's grandfather, my own two grandfathers, my father and my uncle were killed as though a dread curse lay upon them. . . . It seems to me that I was born with blood on my eyes. My first sight was of blood.'[8] This explains something of Djilas's character, his wholehearted committal to communism and later violent reaction against it, his emotionalism and undisciplined idealism. Boris Kidrić was very different. The son of a Ljubljana professor, he had become a communist while still a student. He had been imprisoned and then gone to work for the party abroad, in Prague, Vienna and Paris, but he had preferred to return to underground work in his native Slovenia, rather than go to Moscow in the 'thirties to be trained in the Comintern.

In 1945 the change from Supreme General Staff that had exercised complete control in wartime to the group of people who controlled government in the new state required little adaptation as the personnel was, in the main, the same; the party organization was unchanged and the Politburo gave continuity of authority. Each member of the Politburo specialized in a particular field – as they had done during the war. Moša Pijade continued the work on constitutional matters the theory and legal bases of the state, which he had dealt with since 1943. Ranković retained control of the all-important job of security. He organized the various intelligence and counter-intelligence agencies, and the dreaded secret police.[9] He was ruthlessly efficient and successful in protecting Tito and the new revolutionary state; over the years he built up what eventually came to be considered as a dangerous personal empire based on secret information about everyone of any importance in the land. Djilas became a Vice-President with special responsibilities in literary and propaganda work. Kardelj developed the speciality for foreign relations which he had begun to work on during the war. His responsibility was for day to day foreign business, with occasional special missions. Tito himself dealt with interstate relations and, as prime minister, coordinated the work of his team and had overall responsibility. It is clear, however, that he could no longer oversee in detail all the executive work that was going on simultaneously in so many different fields. Details of home affairs had to be delegated to others.

In addition to his preoccupation with foreign affairs, Tito also had a very heavy programme of public engagements – receiving foreign visitors, opening parliament, making speeches on anniversaries in different parts of the country, or when people needed to be spurred to greater efforts and reassured that things would be better in the future. He was seen wearing his Marshal's uniforms – white in summer, field-grey in winter – resplendent with war decorations (he received a decoration from the Soviet Union, but none from Great Britain or the United States) and gold braid, impressive enough to satisfy even Tito's sartorial pride. As the war receded, uniform seemed to be an anachronism except for military occasions, and Tito appeared more often in impeccably tailored civilian suits.

One of the most serious immediate problems facing the leaders was to ensure that people were fed. Tito had eventually accepted UNRRA aid on the understanding that his own people – and not the western Allies – should be responsible for its distribution. Much of this aid was sent in food supplies or seed, stock and implements to help the farmers to get the land under cultivation again.[10] Peasants were under great pressure to produce as much food as possible, but Marxist ideology prevented them getting the kind of incentives they wanted. Landholdings had been limited, the government forced the peasants to sell most of their surplus food at strictly controlled, low prices. Black market activities were punished severely. Peasants retaliated by passive resistance and refused to produce more than they needed for themselves; propaganda, fines and imprisonment failed to break them and there was an acute food shortage.

To reorganize the country's economy after nationalization, an ambitious Five-Year Plan was drawn up. Based on Soviet models, it aimed to develop the country's industrial potential. This appealed to doctrinaire communists for it promised goods from new factories, a higher standard of living, jobs for workers and an industrial proletariat which, in theory, would provide those cadres of comrades who would become the flower of the Communist Party of the future. This was a reflection of the romantic Partisan view that even if adequate investment was lacking, heroic endurance, improvization and Yugoslav communism would bring success. Even among Yugoslav communists there were considerable differences over this plan, and eventually Boris Kidrić was put in charge. He worked tirelessly but abortively to make it a success, and when he died of leukaemia in 1953 his colleagues believed that his death came from overwork.

The Five-Year Plan was broken down into yearly plans, plans for one month, for a week, even for a day. Plans were assigned for each republic, each works, each department. Factories were told what to make, where to sell and at what cost. It was said that the annual plan alone on paper weighed some 3,300 pounds. Two hundred and seventeen federal and republican ministers gave orders to hundreds of directors who gave orders to their men, and themselves had to send back about 600 to 800 reports each year. Unfortunately the plan which appeared so neat and comprehensive in theory had dire results in practice. Planners forgot many essential items such as needles, combs and pins which at once came to have an enormous black market value. The need for certain articles – slippers for instance – was grossly overestimated. Since all the emphasis was on increased production and special rewards went to those who exceeded the norm, quantity was all that mattered and shops were flooded with shoddy goods that no one wanted. Above all, the country itself could not produce the major investments needed for the heavy industry envisaged in the plan.[11]

During the postwar years everyone was working inhumanly hard – often doing two jobs in twenty-four hours – to make ends meet and to get the basic needs of life – food, clothing, fuel and shelter – or simply out of idealism. As the people slowly realized they were to get few material rewards their mood changed to discontent. They became tired of overwork, dirt and discomfort, tired of endless exhortation to greater efforts with promises of a better future. From foreigners who came into the country they saw that others who had not suffered so much during the war had better clothes, food, medicaments, more luxuries and an easier life. Yugoslavs were no longer willing to accept that this was the result of belonging to a chronically underdeveloped state which had experienced four years of total war, nor were they interested in Marxist doctrine and theories of planning for a still hypothetical rosy future. It all seemed the fault of the leaders and they were disillusioned with socialist government; but this could not be said too openly for Ranković's police informers were everywhere, criticism of socialism was considered as sabotage and those who uttered it went to gaol. A police state for an overworked population was far from the happy dream of socialism, equality and plenty that the communists had hoped they could realize.

Tito himself, in spite of his other preoccupations, cannot have been unaware of the mood in Yugoslavia. He read newspapers, but they were so censored as to contain no criticisms. He spoke at many meetings, but always to enthusiastic audiences who gave him a hero's welcome. His portrait hung in every office, shop or inn and he was almost worshipped. He was more insulated from public opinion than he had ever been before. Yet political intuition had been one of his strongest characteristics and it could hardly have ceased to function. At this stage in his career Tito was trapped in a political dilemma. Communist theory and the lines of practice laid down in the Soviet Union must be right. It was true that Soviet leaders had criticized the economic plan – 'What do you need industry for?' a Soviet representative had said 'In the Urals we have everything you need.'[12] They had also criticized the Yugoslavs' organization of their army, the fact that peasants were allowed private property in land and many other aspects of the new state. But to have accepted these criticisms would have meant integrating the Yugoslav economy and armed forces with those of the Soviet Union. Collectivization of the land would have led to a bloody battle with the peasants and mass starvation, as had happened in the Soviet Union in the 'thirties. Tito was not prepared to subordinate the Yugoslav state to the Soviet Union, nor was he willing to do battle to the death with the Yugoslav peasants who had provided much of the support for the Partisan movement.

In spite of all that had been said in the letters he received from the Russian leaders early in 1948 he was still convinced that he was a good and obedient communist, that he had carried out his tasks as a party man successfully, and in the true spirit of Marxism – and what had been the result? Both the Yugoslav people and the Soviet leaders were dissatisfied with him. The record needed examining to see what had gone wrong. It was at this stage that the dispute with Russia came to a head and the Yugoslav Communist Party was expelled from the Cominform. Stalin had decided that Tito was too independent, too ambitious, too Yugoslav, and above all too successful to be the kind of docile satellite leader he wanted in Yugoslavia. Tito must be got rid of and replaced by someone who would owe his position to the Russians and take his orders from them. Stalin's lack of understanding of the real situation in the Yugoslav Communist Party – and among ordinary Yugoslavs – is shown by the fact that he believed that Tito could be easily overthrown. We do not know whom Stalin had in mind as a replacement for Tito, but it has often been suggested that the Croat Andrija Hebrang had been groomed by the Russians for the part. Credence is given to this theory by the fact that a Russian letter about the Five-Year Plan had been addressed to Hebrang and

Tito. The other senior Yugoslav communist who had almost certainly made some kind of secret arrangements with the Soviet leaders was Arso Jovanović, Tito's former Chief-of-Staff. No one who knew Jovanović was surprised that he had sided with the Russians. A saturnine, fanatical, Montenegrin and former royalist army officer who had become a communist only after the beginning of the uprising, he had been obsessed by hatred of the west. When he accompanied Tito on his visit to Italy to meet Churchill in 1944, he had shown himself in all his contacts with the British to be suspicious, ill-natured, intransigent and incapable of compromise. It seems probable – but cannot be proved on present evidence – that he would have attempted to take the Yugoslav army over to the Russian side and against Tito. He never had the opportunity. At the beginning of the Cominform quarrel, he was shot – it was officially said, while trying to escape across the frontier to Hungary.

For Tito personally the Russian move against him was a terrible blow and he was stirred to the depths of his being. It was all the more shattering because he was being rejected in spite of his long years' service to communism. He was not at first consciously aware of the basic cause. A feeling of injustice remained with him for the rest of his life. 'It was very hard for me,' he said many years later, 'the more so as I had gained the impression during my earlier conversations with Stalin that he had appreciated my integrity.'[13] At the time, however, he behaved with characteristic resilience. He knew that his life's work, and indeed his own life, depended on his gaining and keeping the loyalty of his colleagues and of the majority of members of the Yugoslav Communist Party – people whom he himself had trained to admire the Soviet leaders. It had never seemed possible that they would have to choose between him and them.

As in earlier crises in his life, Tito's reaction was to plunge into purposeful activity. 'Life had taught me that the most dangerous thing at such critical moments is not to take a stand, to hesitate. In such situations, reactions must always be bold and determined.'[14] Even before the actual expulsion from the Cominform was announced in June, Tito had put the whole problem of Soviet criticisms before a full meeting of the Central Committee of the party on 13 April. All had supported the independent line agreed by the Politburo except Hebrang and Žujović, who were arrested shortly after the meeting – unanimity was essential at this stage, open support for Russia so dangerous as to be accounted treasonable. The quarrel and the leaders' reaction to it were then expounded to party organizations down to the smallest cells. Members of the party still remember the terrible shock they experienced on hearing that Soviet leaders whom they had been taught to venerate were criticizing Tito and withdrawing their support from Yugoslavia. It was at first very difficult for Yugoslav communists to reorientate their views about Russia, and the idea of facing the future without Soviet aid or the comradeship of other communist parties seemed to foreshadow certain disaster.

The eighteen months that followed the expulsion from the Cominform were a supreme test of Tito's qualities as a leader. During this time, in addition to the threat of Soviet invasion – which Tito believed would have come if the internal situation had broken down and offered any opportunity for intervention – there were internal dangers. There was the threat of counterrevolution from the few who still believed in obedience to the Soviet leaders, or thought that the Yugoslav revolution could not survive without Soviet support. About 12,000 people were imprisoned for being Cominform supporters, and it is probable that there was a considerable number who evaded arrest by maintaining silence. But this was a very small proportion of the 400,000 party membership, and the rest rallied behind Tito in spite of their disappointments about life under socialism. Once he had support from the leaders, the majority of the party and the general people, Tito knew he had a fighting chance to win through – even against Russia. And it is evident from his actions that for some time he still could not believe that Stalin would be implacable.

It is interesting that in the first eighteen months the Yugoslav leaders tried to meet those Soviet criticisms that they felt could be justified. The Russians had complained that the Yugoslav party was too conspiratorial and had not held a Party Congress for twenty years. On 21 July, within a month of the explusion, the Fifth party Congress was held in Belgrade. Tito's official report, covering the history of the party since the last congress in 1928 and showing signs of hasty drafting, took several hours to deliver.[15] In spite of the Russians' deflating remarks about Partisan pride, Tito devoted a major part of his speech to the triumphs and tragedies of the Partisan war. This was what most party members wished to hear, for all except a few had joined the party through the Partisans and Tito owed his popularity and following to his wartime leadership. The war was fact and myth, a unifying element for party and people; to undervalue it as history or experience would be to undermine the pride of the Yugoslav people and the roots of communist revolution. This Tito was not prepared to do even at Stalin's behest, though he had not yet completely understood that the real purpose of the Russian policy was destruction of his revolution. After Tito's speech, other party leaders delivered their reports on various aspects of party work – Ranković, Djilas, Kardelj, Kidrić – on organization, propaganda, foreign affairs and economic planning. None hurled defiance at the Soviet Union, all stressed the orthodoxy of Yugoslav communism. They still believed that they could win their passage back if they showed they were good communists.

Six months later they were still working on these lines. By 1949, steps had been taken to meet the Soviet criticisms about the continued existence of private landholders. An organization was set up to force peasant landholders to join their farms into cooperatives and thus get rid of private land tenure. Savage pressure was used to accomplish this. Teams of communists toured the country preaching the advantages of cooperative farms; peasants who opposed too violently were imprisoned. The numbers of cooperatives rose from 1,318 in 1948 to 6,075 in 1950, when they included more than a quarter of cultivable land. But the policy was not a success. It made no impression on the Russians and it brought the Yugoslav economy near to collapse. The peasants fought back with sullen and effective passive resistance, refusing to work more than necessary for their own wants. Land went out of cultivation; stock was killed and eaten, harvests slumped and were made even more disastrous by bad weather so that the country faced the danger of famine.

During these months it took all the drive and vigilance of Ranković's efficient security service to deal with Soviet agents infiltrating from Hungary, Bulgaria, Romania and Albania. There were rumours – but details were never released – of plots to kill Tito. Satellite countries denounced their treaties of friendship with Yugoslavia, stopped their trade, ceased to make reparations payments and maintained virulent and abusive propaganda campaigns against Yugoslavia. Trials were rigged of communists thought to have been favourable to Yugoslavia. Rajk in Hungary, Kostov in Bulgaria and a number of others were executed on such charges which were later admitted to have been false.[16] As a realist Tito had to face the fact that his efforts to win a way back into Stalin's favour had no chance of success; it was necessary to find another road to survival. It was also apparent that he was faced with another dilemma – and one which, though he did not know it at that time, he would have to live with for the rest of his life – how to accept aid from capitalist countries without compromising his communist position, and how to remain divorced from the rest of the communist bloc and yet prove that he was a good communist?

Tito's solution to the Yugoslav dilemma evolved gradually and painfully in the process of dealing with critical problems. For three years after 1948 he was totally preoccupied with problems of survival – survival of his revolution and of Yugoslavia's independence. His personal survival as leader was only incidentally bound up in these greater issues; but it was clear that he would stand or fall with the system he had created. At this time, practical considerations were all important; the political theories explaining them came later. The first essential was to prevent breakdown through starvation. To do this, Tito had to reverse his earlier decision to take no aid and to have no economic relations with the capitalist west. He had to balance his suspicions of western counterrevolutionary intentions against his knowledge that Russia had exactly the same aim; it was evident that the west was the lesser danger. As has been shown above he made trade agreements with the west, accepted western food, armaments, loans and grants for a revised industrialization programme.

Reorientation to close economic relations with the non-communist world came slowly, allowing both Tito and western leaders time to dissipate their suspicions of each other. There can be no doubt that this policy was very popular with the great majority of Yugoslavs – not only because it gave them food and work, and eventually goods in the shops, but also because it restored their connections with the western world whose culture and traditions they felt they shared. Very few Yugoslavs felt strong attachment to the Soviet Union – most of those who did came from Montenegro which had had a long tradition of association with Russia.[17] Support for the Soviet Union, so strong during the war, had been artificially created by intensive propaganda. Once the first shock of disillusionment was over, it collapsed like a pricked balloon. But Tito's personal popularity and standing, based on real achievement, remained and was enhanced by his change of policy. With immense vitality he travelled the country making speeches, received delegations, urged the Yugoslavs to save themselves by their own efforts. Looking strong, and well-dressed as

ever, he inspired them with confidence. They tightened their belts
and responded. Yugoslavia's recovery was a joint effort of leaders and
people – but it was a triumph for Tito's leadership.

\* \* \*

The break with the Soviet Union and reopening of relations with the
west precipitated a re-examination of the fundamental character of
the new Yugoslav state. This would have come in any case, as it did
much later in the other states of eastern Europe. Stalin's implacable
hostility made it possible – even essential – for Yugoslav communists
to examine the Soviet inspired practices that had been followed in
Yugoslavia since 1945, in an uninhibited way that would have been
impossible had they remained in the Soviet orbit. This was the
supreme test of the character of Yugoslav communism – was it a
means for achieving a better life for Yugoslav people, or an end in
itself? Tito and his colleagues chose the national and more human
alternative. The centralized coercive state and enforced cooperatives
had brought dissatisfaction and economic disaster. They were
abandoned. Cooperatives were allowed to be disbanded in 1953.
Peasants rushed to regain their private holdings and thereafter,
although they were heavily taxed and for a long time not given
adequate incentives to production, they were allowed to remain an
important element of private enterprise in a communist state.[18]

The problem of disbanding the coercive state was more difficult.
Some degree of centralization was essential for security, for economic
development, and, it was at first believed, for the continuation in
power of the Communist Party. After 1949 Party theoreticians began
to consider how the system of government could be democratized in
a way that would allow the Communist Party to retain power, and
could at the same time be reconciled with Marxist–Lenin doctrine
which, it was now admitted freely, provided little detailed guidance
for contemporary Yugoslav conditions. The first change proposed
was a system of workers' self-management in factories. This was
introduced by law in 1950. Workers' councils were to be elected and
take part in all decisions of factory management including the disposal
of profits. At first the councils were hedged in by so many restrictions
that workers' participation in management was not effective.
Communists appointed for their political beliefs or services remained
in control of all important positions. But the institution of self-

management was incorporated into successive constitutions and became an integral part of Titoist socialism.[19] By nineteen-seventy many changes had been introduced into the original system, and workers had a greater share in the responsibilities of management. Opinions inside and outside Yugoslavia differed on how far it was successful in practice, but as an institution it appeared to have taken root and was studied with interest as a solution to problems of management and labour, both by other communist states and by capitalists.

Between 1950 and 1970, with western aid and Yugoslav effort, an industrial revolution took place which affected every part of the country, even though the more backward parts of the southern areas developed less rapidly and successfully than the already more advanced regions of Slovenia, Croatia and the part of Serbia near Belgrade. Slowly and painfully the country moved towards a prosperity such as the people had never known before. Yugoslavia was sharing in the postwar economic development of western Europe in a way that she could not have done had she remained in the communist bloc, limited by the demands of Soviet development, defence and industrial programmes. A better life for the poor had been the simple slogan of many of the pamphlets that Tito himself had drafted in the days of illegality before the second world war; this was in the process of being achieved. It became evident as the years passed that this was the essential basis for a successful socialist state, a fundamental necessity if Tito and the Communist Party were to retain power. Thus economic development came to be an all-important factor in political change.

To encourage trade and industrial development, many pre-conceived communist theories had to be abandoned. New methods of planning were introduced which abolished the old centralized methods; decentralization of economic planning and emphasis on making profits and reinvesting accumulated capital for further development and further profit became accepted practice. Economic decentralization led to political decentralization so that by the late nineteen-sixties the most important functions of government were carried on in the six federal republics, with only coordinating and residual powers left to the central authority. Regional independence was jealously guarded and it became obvious that even among many communists, local patriotism – in the republics and regions – was stronger than any feeling of Yugoslavism, even though all agreed that republics could not exist independently of the federated Yugoslav state. The clash between local interests and economic needs, especially the needs of the backward areas compared with those of the more advanced regions, promoted recurring crises.[20]

It was not easy to reconcile these developments with the continued existence of an unchanged monolithic, centralized Communist Party exercising total power. The party itself had to change with the changing times, and with the rise of a new generation of members for whom illegal prewar activities and Partisan warfare were only stories from party history, a legend which they had been brought up on, but which had no personal meaning for them. It became in the end a legend which formed an irritating barrier to understanding between the party's old generation which retained power from 1945 into the 'sixties, and the new generations, educated and brought up in postwar Yugoslavia. Young members began to press for change and modernization of a party they felt was being ossified in an old image. The situation was complicated by the fact that most of Tito's colleagues had achieved power at an exceptionally young age; when Tito was seventy in 1962, most of his oldest associates were still in their fifties, many even younger, not yet ready to relinquish power or fade into retirement. This conflict of the generations, and the inescapable fact that Tito was getting old and must inevitably die one day leaving a serious problem of succession, added complications to an already complex situation inside the Communist Party.

In the early years after the war, it had been accepted as axiomatic that party members should provide a ruling caste in the new state. They were the trusted members who filled all responsible jobs and were obedient to the ruling hierarchy in the party. In return they received high pay and privileges that marked them off from the rest of the community, and made them envied and sometimes hated. It was this glaring inequality as well as aspects of the police state that went with it that roused Djilas's criticism – although he himself had taken part in its excesses and profited largely by its privileges – in the early nineteen-fifties. It spurred him to write a crude short story attacking the selfish and vulgar social *mores* of party members and their wives.

The attack was the immediate occasion of his expulsion from the party, but the deeper reason was that in spite of his long association with Tito, and the friendship there had once been between them, Djilas had flouted Tito's authority and published in the press opinions of Yugoslav communism which he could perhaps have held with impunity had he voiced them only in private. It was a personal betrayal which Tito never forgave. Two years later, embittered by disgrace and imprisonment, Djilas wrote more thoughtfully about his criticisms of contemporary Yugoslav society in *The New Class*.[21] He came out against communism which had been his fanatical creed for so long, and in favour of multi-party democracy of western style. His attack was the more virulent because of his own previous extremism. He did not show how this could have been made to work in Yugoslavia. Djilas's idealism had turned sour on him. He was not a practical politician, was not content to accept compromise or wait for results. It was his tragedy that he chose to denounce his former colleagues and become a martyr just at the moment that liberal change, which he was later to approve, was beginning in Yugoslavia. These changes, once begun, continued at first slowly but with gathering momentum.

In 1952, when Djilas first attacked Yugoslav communist society, Stalin was still alive and Yugoslavia's position weak and insecure. After the death of Stalin, and after Khrushchev's visit of reconciliation to Belgrade, Yugoslavia was at least for some years able to go ahead with her own 'road to socialism' safe from the fear of Soviet interference. The police state was abandoned, many political prisoners were released and communists' privileges and powers curbed.[22] As trade and new industries expanded, and contacts with the west developed, communists were no longer the only people earning high salaries in the state. At the Seventh Party Congress in 1958 the Yugoslav Communist Party changed its name to League of Communists to mark its change of role – no longer a leading élite, it was to work as an influence on society from within. Another class had replaced Djilas's new class; these were the technocrats, the educated professionals and experts who earned high salaries and privileges because of their qualifications. They might be party members but were not necessarily so. The most affluent people in society could be craftsmen, workers in heavy industry, or people engaged in foreign trade. By the late nineteen-sixties it was possible for anyone to become a party member who wished to do so; but once joined, he had to accept limitations to personal freedom, and the knowledge that responsible jobs would only be given to those with the appropriate qualifications.

Concurrent with these changes was the development of increased regional feeling in Yugoslavia and this was reflected in relations within the League of Communists where members disputed with each other over investment funds for their own particular republic, over the official status of the different languages and other cultural and economic issues. Communists themselves were divided over whether liberalization and decentralization had weakened the party or strengthened it. It was in danger of being split between those in favour of change and openly voiced discussion of different views – including some form of expression for opposition – and those who believed that such changes would themselves bring the destruction of the régime. Throughout all these developments Tito himself maintained a central position above and outside the conflict, intervening from time to time to curb excessive change, and always condemning demands for institutionalized opposition in the form of other parties, but at the same time in favour of liberalization within certain limits. Tito's pronouncements were often conservative, but it was well known that his authority was such that the considerable changes that were made could not have been introduced against his wishes.

A major crisis occurred within the party in the summer of 1966 when Tito had to part company with one of his oldest and most valued colleagues – Alexander Ranković – the man who had been security chief throughout the war and during the most difficult years of the foundation of the postwar state and the attempt by Stalin to overthrow it after the Cominform break. During all these years Ranković had been at the very centre of all party councils. He was one of the few men of real working-class origin besides Tito in the party leadership. Inscrutable and in the shadows, he had carried out the most unpopular job of eradicating the enemies of the communist revolution with a ruthless efficiency which earned him for a time an unenviable reputation. During the liberalization of the 'fifties he changed his official job and with it his public image until he was thought to be in line with Kardelj as one of a small group who could succeed to power had Tito died at that time. By the 'sixties he was thought to have outstripped Kardelj and to be personally in line for the succession to Tito. It was, however, known that unlike Tito, he was opposed to liberal changes and to decentralization. On 28 June 1966 a full meeting of the League of Communists' Central Committee was suddenly summoned to meet Tito on his private island of Brioni in conditions of secrecy and crisis. Members were transported by plane in groups from Belgrade; army units were moved from their normal location.[23] The meeting had been called to consider serious charges against Ranković who was accused of having opposed party reform over many years and of having kept his own personal authority over the widely ramified state security system. This had allowed him to control decisions in economic and political life throughout the country, not only in regional government but even down to local government at commune and even factory level. Investigations had revealed that Ranković had kept control of an empire of power which had private files on everybody of importance in the land – he had the reputation of never destroying any papers. His employees had even tapped the telephone of Tito himself. Ranković admitted that he had used his power to oppose policies which had been agreed at the highest level.[24] How much support he had had from other members of the party or in his own republic of Serbia has not yet been revealed; but it was not sufficient to allow him to challenge Tito's position, nor to avert his own disgrace. This crisis, like the Dijlas affair, but in a less traumatic way because Ranković had not turned against the revolution as such, was a sad blow for Tito. But he refused to allow his old colleague to be imprisoned. Ranković was stripped of office, but not expelled from the party. He went into complete but obedient retirement and continued to watch developments from the wings.

The fundamental issue between Ranković and his colleagues was not settled by his demotion. The real question was how was the Yugoslav League of Communists to retain power and authority and at the same time meet the demands of both party and public for greater democratic freedom? How to give greater democracy and not destroy the whole basis of the postwar socialist state? Pressure for changes of all kinds posed a critical situation for Tito, and the solution was not yet apparent when in the summer of 1968 the Soviet Union brutally invaded Czechoslovakia in order to suppress liberal change which would have gone even further and faster than Tito had been prepared to allow in Yugoslavia. Tito denounced the invasion in categorical terms, but the moral for Yugoslavs – communists and other – was obvious. The Soviet Union was not prepared to allow communist government to lose power in central Europe, and Yugoslavia itself was in danger unless the communists retained power. It underlined the fact that Tito's policy of controlled liberalization had been wise and realistic in view of Yugoslavia's position and the Soviet attitude to changes in communism in eastern Europe. This feeling seems to have prevailed among leading members of the League of Communists when it met for its Ninth Congress in March 1969. There had been many proposals for reforming the party and bringing it more into line with economic and social change that had taken place since 1958. There had even been some talk of making provision within the party for expressions of dissent. In the event, the congress did bring in some sweeping reforms. Many of the old Partisan generation who had had a monopoly of power in party and state since 1945 failed to get re-election to party office. The congress for the first time since the war was dominated by a new generation. The work of the congress was open and there was much expression of different views – especially on economic matters and on the nationalities question. Party institutions were changed in order to effect democratization and some decentralization of power such as had already taken place within the state system. It was decided that the congress was to meet every four (instead of five) years, and party conferences at republican and federal level were to meet every year.[25] A new party programme was issued incorporating these decisions and it was stated that in future party members would have the right to dissent from decisions taken, but must accept the will of the majority. These changes, designed as part of a general movement to introduce self-management into political life, had the support of Tito. But it was clear that he, in common with a number of other party leaders, was afraid that they might lead to excessive decentralization and weaken the national Yugoslav character and authority of the party. In view of external threats – primarily from Soviet Russia – and internal centrifugal tendencies of the nationalities in the different republics, many people thought the changes could undermine the unity of the state. Tito himself provided the answer to this dilemma with a compromise that illustrated his unique political gifts. Shortly before the conference opened he saw the leaders of each republican party and discussed with them – and gained their agreement to – his solution. In his speech on the opening day of the conference, he announced the creation of a new institution, the Executive Bureau of the Central Committee of the party. It was to be a small committee composed of two representatives of each republic, one each from the Vojvodina and Kosmet, and Tito himself as President of the federal state. This was to be a unifying and integrating institution, a small committee where decisions could be taken in which all republics took equal responsibility. It was clear that it could also be used as an all-Yugoslav organ to provide stability in a difficult period of interregnum in event of a successor having to be found for Tito himself.

After nearly twenty-five years of power in the postwar state, Tito could look with understandable pride and satisfaction on his achievements. By 1970 Yugoslavia had been modernized and developed to the extent that her rate of growth no longer qualified her for the title of underdeveloped country. In spite of backward areas, poverty, unemployment and inequalities, the Yugoslav people were in general well-pleased with the changes brought by Tito's revolution. Modern blocks of flats, washing-machines, televisions, new roads, motor-cars, traffic jams, an unfavourable balance of payments, rising prices all proclaimed Yugoslavia at one with many contemporary developments in modern industrial society. In spite of some limitation on political activity and on publication of political views, Yugoslavs were in no doubt whatever that their situation was far easier, freer and more prosperous than that of the inhabitants of other communist states including the Soviet Union.

After a quarter of a century of rule the League of Communists had achieved many of the material goals that had been promised. The heroic age of tragic suffering and exalted success had disappeared into the past and, to those who had shared Tito's revolution, the present seemed in comparison flat and ordinary, lacking in inspiration. The new generation, interested in consumer goods, travel and enjoyment, seemed to older generations to lack the ideals and endurance of their fathers. Some questioned whether they would have the understanding or the capacity to retain the revolution intact. After 1968 the future was again menaced by the shadow of Soviet aggression. In these conditions Tito remained for all Yugoslavs a figure of supreme importance, legendary leader, symbol of success, a guarantee that there would be no return to the tyranny of the earlier phase of the Yugoslav revolution. He could also be trusted if the worst came to the worst, and Russia attacked Yugoslavia, to lead the people in a renewed struggle to defend their independence.

# 17 TITO THE MAN

What kind of a man was Tito as he developed from maturity into old age? How did his character withstand the highest test of all, the possession of great power over a long period of time? He was fifty-three years old when he became prime minister of Yugoslavia in 1945, fifty-six when he was excommunicated by Stalin, sixty-two when Khrushchev sued for peace, almost seventy before he could look at conditions in Yugoslavia and feel that some of the material conditions that he had wanted for ordinary people were being achieved. At seventy-six he had to face up to renewed Soviet threat to Yugoslav independence, and later, even in 1970, he was still the lynchpin of the Yugoslav state, the one man whom all Yugoslavs looked on as leader. He had outlived most of his generation of Yugoslav communists, and was one of the last remaining witnesses of the Bolshevik revolution; he was the last of the great national leaders who had grown up in the early years of the century and had come to power as a result of the second world war. He was also the first and only great man – in national and international terms – to be produced by European communism outside the Soviet Union.

In his later years, in periods of crisis as well as relative calm, his basic character remained essentially the same as it had been in earlier years. In some ways he had mellowed and softened; his political attitudes were certainly less intolerant, less naïve, less romantic than they had been as a young man. He had learned by experience that human nature did not change even in a socialist society, that communist ideals could be aspired to, but the ideal communist state 'did not exist anywhere, least of all', as he said himself, 'in the Soviet Union', and that it was unlikely to be achieved anywhere in a fore-seeable future.[1] With a realism that had always been present, that increased with age, and allowed him to accept partial achievement without bitterness, Tito had come to terms with his idealism. During the immediate postwar years lack of appreciation of Yugoslavia's war efforts had made him aggressively resentful; but by the nineteen-sixties he had all the appreciation and acknowledgement that he could wish for. He accepted, indeed appeared to expect, the full honours due to his office, but he did not give the impression that he felt they were for himself alone. He clearly enjoyed being Yugoslav President and at the same time set himself exacting standards for fulfilling this position in a hardworking and responsible way.

One of the most remarkable aspects of his personality was that he never became drunk with power, was not corrupted by it even though he enjoyed it. His manner was neither pompous nor self-important. He was ruthless, but only when survival was at stake, and he was never wantonly cruel, never indulged in purges. The reason for this lay deep in his character and experiences of life and are difficult to define; but his development from childhood through manhood had shown many consistent features that throw light on his character. Though he had made enemies, he was a person who had always been loved – if not by everyone at least by many people – members of his family, colleagues of most diverse kinds, a number of women, and men of all ages. He liked to be popular, but he had never chosen popularity at the expense of integrity. He had a powerful drive to succeed which must have brought him to the top whatever career had come his way. The life-wish had always been strong in him, giving him a highly developed instinct for approaching danger which helped him to survive perils that might have destroyed another man. As boy and man, he approached unfamiliar circumstances with caution, but once sure of his ground he acted with superb self-confidence – which on all except the rarest occasions stopped short of the over-self-confidence with which some South Slavs were wont to endanger their lives. With these qualities he did not need to surround himself with Byzantine pomp. He accepted the trappings of office and of greatness – but never to excess. He had numbers of houses, powerful cars, yachts, aeroplanes, but these were no more than were available to most heads of state, though perhaps they were more luxurious than those that the heads of some other communist states allowed themselves. But for every Yugoslav who criticized this, there was another who considered it fitting for their President.

As head of state Tito's habits of work were similar to those he had always had. He liked to work with colleagues – not sycophants – and though he was often authoritarian in manner, as he had always been, he liked to discuss everything with independent-minded people who could speak for themselves. He was usually good-natured to work with, though he did not suffer fools gladly and he was capable of explosive shortlived anger if things went wrong through stupidity or inefficiency. He was efficient and disciplined himself. Even in old age he followed a strenuous daily regime which kept four or five personal aides and their staff employed to the limit. Rising about 6 a.m. it was his habit to make his own coffee and read the daily papers before his staff came on duty. He went to bed at midnight or after, the eighteen-hour day having been divided into three or four periods of intensive work interspersed with breaks for a walk or rest. He had the gift of complete relaxation so that he could switch from work to entertainment, or go to sleep at will for brief periods and wake up refreshed whenever necessary.

After the war, Tito managed to build up again a normal private life which he had not been able to enjoy since he had lived with his first wife, Polka, in the early 'twenties. He established a satisfying and enduring relationship with a former Partisan, Jovanka Budisavljević, a Serbian girl from Croatia, nearly thirty years his junior, who became his wife in April 1952. He was young for his years and had remarkable physical vitality, so that the discrepancy in age – not so unusual among South Slavs as it is in western Europe – appeared to be of little importance. Jovanka Broz proved to have the right qualities to become a splendid consort for the Yugoslav President, and an excellent wife for Tito, the man. Coming from a humble peasant background, and having missed through the war what would in any case have been a very simple education, she had a lot in common with Tito's early origins. Like him she was very intelligent and made the most of her later opportunities for advanced education. When she took an honours degree in arts at Belgrade university her professors found it quite unnecessary to make allowances for her special position. Her work was of high quality by any standards. Accompanying her husband on his many journeys abroad in the nineteen-fifties and 'sixties, she learnt foreign languages and made a careful study of the history and customs of the countries they were to visit. She made herself a welcome and interested guest. She cultivated the simple elegance that her husband favoured, and her broad smile and good nature came to be regarded as assets for the Yugoslav image throughout the world.

It was characteristic of Tito that his wife remained essentially a private person playing no public role other than that of his wife and consort. Whether this was a reflection of a residual patriarchal attitude to women or not, it was a wise choice. It kept – as he had always kept – his private life out of politics and gave him friendship and a warm intimate family life during the years when he was isolated by success and at a time when he had outlived most of his contemporaries. He never lacked companions either in work or relaxation, but his special position above political conflict made it impossible for him to have close and intimate friendships which could have given rise to intrigue and suspicion. He had no children by Jovanka, but she helped to bring up Tito's son by Herta Has – who had married another husband after the war; and Tito's grandchildren, the son and daughter of his eldest son, were adopted into his household after the break-up of Žarko's marriage with their mother. Tito kept his family strictly in the background, and used his authority to protect them from publicity while letting them make their own way in the world. He had always been careful to look after his relations, but gave them neither outstanding wealth nor great privilege. There are no signs whatever of a Broz dynasty, and in any case, inherited power or riches are alien to the beliefs Tito has stood for.

As head of state for over a quarter of a century, he met many of the outstanding personalities of the second half of the twentieth century. Almost without exception they commented on his charm, directness of manner, and intelligence. He could draw on aspects of his many-sided character, or bring into play some of his wide variety of interests to make contact with the most varied personalities. Just as he had won the admiration and liking of Churchill, Alexander, Maclean, Lindsay Rogers and many others during the war, so he was to arouse the same sentiments in a wide variety of postwar personalities including Nasser, Nehru, Hailé Selassie, Eleanor Roosevelt, Averell Harriman and Aneurin Bevan. He could be serious and humorous – even broadly humorous – in the right company. He could also be savage and biting when roused. His capacity to feel human emotions deeply or to enjoy human company did not seem to blunt with age; and his love of outdoor life and activities remained unchanged.

Today he receives many of his guests, both official and private, on the island of Brioni, at the head of the Adriatic, which is his favourite among a number of official residences. The beautiful subtropical island – about seventy acres in extent – forms a special estate. In addition to his private house there are villas and hotels for official personnel and visitors. His own villa is quite modest; it is furnished with pictures of the Partisan war, with trophies from other phases in his life and with gifts he has received from all over Yugoslavia, and from many parts of the world. Since he has retained such an enduring interest in affairs of state, and the workings of the League of Communists, and because he has always been conscientious about giving interviews to many different people, he has very little time to himself. In an attempt to gain a privacy that even Brioni could not offer, he had built another house on the tiny island of Vanga beyond Brioni. Here he has facilities for relaxation – a dark room where he himself develops the pictures he takes on his journeys, for he is a passionate amateur photographer. He has his own workshop where he keeps his hand in at the metal work in which he was trained so long ago. He also works in a small garden which drops down through the cypress and palm trees to the blue-green sea. In material things he has surpassed his boyhood dreams. He has all the elegant clothes he could want, suitable to every occasion and made by the best tailors. He has kept his love of good clothes as an outward sign of success, and laughs at himself for admitting to such a weakness. He still wears the diamond ring he bought in 1940 with the money earned for translating Stalin's *History of the Bolshevik Party*. Is this too a symbol of success? A talisman against ill-fortune? A trophy of another life?

And what about the courageous and ardent young communist who shouted defiance against society in the Zagreb court in 1928? How much of him has survived after forty years of communist experience and a successful revolution? Looking back on that particular experience, Tito cannot have failed to conclude that though his behaviour may have seemed foolhardy at the time – even to many communists – and though its lack of caution was in some ways out of character, it unleashed a chain of events that set him on the career that led to his final exalted position. After his prison sentence Tito became totally committed to the communist cause and, though his interpretation of what this meant changed during his life, he remained in his own estimation a convinced communist for the rest of his life. 'From the beginning I was a disciplined communist,' said Tito in his seventies, but I always tried to avoid disagreements, and right up to the present I have not really changed. I am still a disciplined communist, even today.'[2]

By the time he said this, Tito's period of disciplined acceptance of the Russian interpretation of communism – cruel, stupid and ineffective as it had so often been – was over. After 1941 Tito's discipline and obedience had been to his own communist principles and code of behaviour. By this time also, he had evolved pragmatically and with considerable aid from others, his own communist system which the world called Titoism. This is a term that Tito himself does not like. The political system that he has helped to evolve in Yugoslavia has been determined by specifically Yugoslav conditions. Tito is aware that it is not communism, and prefers to call it socialism indicating thereby that it is a stage in the evolution towards communism which, in maturity – in contrast to his beliefs as a young man – he admitted was an ideal for the future. Perhaps he felt that communism could never be more than an ideal. He did not say this, but he came very close to it when Eleanor Roosevelt asked him to classify himself in government philosophy. 'I suppose I might call myself a social democrat,' he replied.[3] Democratic socialism was in many ways a suitable description for the ideas behind the Titoist state of Yugoslavia. It had become a state in which nationalization and private property, strong central powers and decentralization, workers' self-management and state control, economic planning and market economy, lived side by side in an amalgam that has produced many satisfactory results; and when the results have not been satisfactory Titoism has shown the flexibility to go into reverse, or to allow the mixture to be varied, uninhibited by preconceived doctrinal concepts. When the doctrine proved unworkable, it could be reconsidered.

The explanation of why Tito became a communist, which he was not allowed to give in court in 1928, emphasized the miserable conditions he had witnessed among the majority of people in his youth. He became a member of the Communist Party to try to change those conditions and in doing so accepted the hardships and risks that went with the life of a revolutionary. The material rewards that he obtained towards the end of his life could never have been foreseen and played no part in his political ambition. He enjoyed them when they came, but for the greater part of Tito's life the ideal was his inspiration and justification; and its partial achievement must stand as the justification for Tito's political career. No one could doubt that the Yugoslavia of today is a far more prosperous, more equitable, more estimable a society than that of his youth.

It is not possible to distinguish exactly how much of this change has come from the ineluctable processes of history, how much has been due to Tito's intervention. But it is beyond doubt that he personally has played an important part in directing these developments of Yugoslav and communist history. It may even be doubted if, had there been no Tito, the Yugoslav revolution would have been successful. This raises the question of whether the present state of Yugoslavia can continue to exist without Tito? To give it permanent stability and ensure that its independence and basic socialism – principles to which Tito remained unchangingly committed – should not be lost, has been a major problem of Tito's later years. It is a problem whose solution he knows he will never be able to see.

The instrument which brought Tito to power, by means of which the revolution has been achieved and the new state ruled, was the Communist Party. Though it changed its name, its role and its organization, Tito has been convinced that its continuation in undisputed power is the *sine qua non* of the continuation of the socialist state of Yugoslavia that he had done so much to create. Tito is not one of those people who believes it should continue unchanged; he is aware that change is necessary to survival. He has supported liberalization policies which divested the Party of automatic control. But he has never accepted the ideas of multi-party government, believing that these would result in a splintering of political life into regional and factional interests that could destroy not only the socialist system but the state as such. This might lead to western-type democracy, or to Russian intervention to impose Soviet-type communism. He would regard either as a disaster. These considerations, especially the fear of Russia, explain why Tito has received such universal support in Yugoslavia. He has been a guarantee of stability, of fighting leadership and political sense; someone who has won, and kept, people's trust, someone to whom difficult problems of political life can be referred, with the confident knowledge that he would do his best to find a just and equitable solution.

If Tito ever brooded over the cost of his revolution, he did not show it. He has been realist enough to know that every revolution exacts its victims, in death, imprisonment and injustices. He has felt that he did his best to limit the excesses of the revolution and that he has restrained some of his colleagues who would have gone to greater extremes.[4] Though prepared to be ruthless in elimination of enemies when it came to a question of survival, Tito himself remained an essentially human man, normal and in many ways quite ordinary.

At the same time, he is far from ordinary because he has both the necessary qualities that produce greatness, and the indefinable gift of good fortune. He himself has denied that random chance was responsible for his escape from Stalin's purges, saying it was due to his own understanding of what was happening in Russia and what measures to take to evade it.[5] It is possible that many of his apparently lucky escapes may have been due to his own qualities, but there is no doubt that he has been exceptionally lucky. He has also had the supremely valuable capacity to recognize the qualities of the times and grasp opportunity as it rushed past. He has had foresight and always believed in appraising a situation well in advance and making preparations accordingly, in order to be ahead of his enemies. He has combined caution and careful preparation for long-distance targets with a capacity to gamble for high stakes when the opportunity arose. Failure tended to rouse him to anger rather than self-pity, but he has never been intoxicated by success. When faced with a crisis he has always been bold and decisive. These qualities were notable during the war; to be able to use them against the Russians after the war, he had to unlearn painfully and at first reluctantly, his habit of obedience to the Russian leaders. However, once learnt he has deployed his gifts to Yugoslavia's advantage. He has been both revolutionary and conservative. 'I have not raised my voice against modernization in general,' he said in 1963 when there were great pressures for change, 'but against the modernization that is harmful to our correct socialist development, both in literature and in general.' Above all, he has shown even in old age the capacity to learn and the will to change with the times.

It is small wonder that this extraordinary man, who has lived through enough experience for several full lives, should have become a legend in his own lifetime. To be a living myth may have its disadvantages, leaving Tito a majestic figure, isolated and alone; but this position has its compensations, and his achievements must have given him profound satisfaction. When asked if he would have acted differently if he were to have his life again he answered: 'I think I would go the same way. Perhaps I would do some things better. I can only say that I am sorry I could not achieve even more.'[6] When asked what he would like to be remembered for, he answered 'That is not my business. It is up to history to decide what has been positive in my life, and the people will remember me for it. History will also say what has not been good. As far as I am concerned, I have tried to devote my life to the good of the people and the country, and I shall continue to do so as long as I am able.'[7] He knew that he was assured of a place in the history of his own country, of communism and of his own times.

# NOTES AND SOURCES

Full details of books listed in the Bibliography (*pp.* 321–329) *are
not repeated in the Notes.*

CHAPTER I. *Child and youth*

1. The story of this trial has been retold many times. See V. Dedijer,
   *Tito Speaks* (hereafter referred to as Dedijer, *Tito*), 62–8; F. Maclean,
   *Disputed Barricade* (Maclean, *Barricade*), 53–7; *Tito Život i Rad* 54,
   55, 56; Zilliacus, *Tito* 81–3.
2. Tito was born on 7 May 1892 (V. Vinterhalter, *Životnom Stazom
   Josipa Broza* – hereafter Vinterhalter, *Broz* – 51). An entry in the
   school register exhibited in the house in Kumrovec where Tito was
   brought up gives this date when he was first registered at school.
   Military papers when Tito was conscripted into the Austrian army
   (quoted in *Tito Život i Rad*, Zagreb, 1962, pp. 9, 10) and various
   police documents exhibited in the Kumrovec Tito Museum give the
   dates 5 and 12 March. Another police file compiled for the Germans
   in 1943 (German documents in the British Foreign Office Library,
   6136/E458407), gives 7 March. Tito's official birthday is celebrated in
   Yugoslavia on 25 May. See also Dedijer, *Tito* 6.
3. Dedijer, *Tito* 9.
4. Szabo, *Kroz Hrvatsko Zagorje*, gives an excellent almost contemporary
   account of Zagorje in the time of Tito's childhood.
5. Among many accounts of conditions of peasant life in Croatia in Tito's
   childhood as well as before their liberation from serfdom, see Bićanić,
   *Kako Živi Narod* (How Our People Live) and his 'Oslobodjenje
   kmetova u Hrvatskoj 1848' (The freeing of the serfs in 1848) in *Delo* 3,
   Zagreb, March 1948. See also Tomasevitch, *Peasants, Politics and
   Economic Change in Yugoslavia* 60, 86 and *passim*. Out of a population
   in Croatia in 1906 of two and a half million, there was an electorate
   of 43,381.
6. Dedijer, *Tito* 16; Szabo, *Stari Zagreb* 189, 190.
7. Dedijer, *Tito* 7–8.
8. A brief account is given in Dedijer, *Tito* 3–4. Another account can be
   found in Crnja, *Cultural History of Croatia* 247–55, from which this
   quotation is taken. See also discussion about the revolt by N. Klaić

and B. Grafenauer in *Jugoslavenski Istorijski Časopis*, no. 2, 1963, 68–87.
9. Crnja, 250.                                                                10.
10. Ibid.
11. Dedijer, *Tito* 4.
12. E. I. von Tkalac, *Jugenderinnerungen aus Kroatien*, 1749–1823, 1824–1843; Verlag von Otto Wigand, Leipzig, 1894.
13. Dedijer, *Tito* 5.
14. There is a large literature about the *Zadruga* and there are some interesting studies of *zadrugal* survivals in the twentieth century. See Mosely, 'The Peasant Family: The *Zadruga* or Communal Joint-Family in the Balkans and its recent Evolution', in *The Cultural Approach to History*, ed. C. Ware, 95–108; Halpern, *The Zadruga, a Century of Change*; Erlich, *Family in Transition*. See also Auty, 'Yugoslavia', in *Contrasts in Emerging Societies*, ed. D. Warriner.
15. Dedijer, *Tito* 6; Vinterhalter, *Broz* 52–3.
16. Zilliacus, *Tito* 17.
17. Dedijer, *Tito* 8; Maclean, *Barricade* 16.
18. Dedijer, *Tito* 10; Zilliacus, *Tito* 19–20.
19. Zilliacus, *Tito* 21.
20. Letter in Kumrovec Tito Museum.
21. Dedijer, *Tito* 12; Tomasevitch, *Peasants* 154, gives higher figures for total emigration from Croatia with an estimate of 400–450,000, which included people who emigrated to avoid military service and would not be included in official statistics.

CHAPTER 2. *Boy into man*

1. Tito gave accounts of his early life to a number of biographers and journalists. The story was always basically the same, though some accounts have different detail and anecdotes from others. This chapter has made most use of three accounts which have to be used by a biographer as original sources. These are Dedijer, *Tito*; Maclean, *Barricade* and Zilliacus, *Tito*. There are also newspaper articles and published interviews which contained additional detail, of which Sir Fitzroy Maclean's interview with Tito, 14 December 1963, published in *Borba*, 12 May 1964, is most important. Notes and interesting photographs of Tito's early life have been published in *Tito Život i Rad*, entries 14 to 24. There are numerous photographs, documents and other exhibits in Tito museums at Kumrovec, Sisak, Zagreb and elsewhere. Some new details are to be found in Vinterhalter, *Broz*. Mr Vinterhalter is at present working in an institute in Belgrade especially devoted to assembling the materials for an exhaustive biography of President Tito. The interview with Karas quoted in this

chapter is collated from Dedijer, *Tito* 13; Zilliacus, *Tito* 22–3, and an interview with Walter Lippman, 9 February 1950.

2. Maclean, Interview 1963; Vinterhalter, *Broz* 60.

3. Dedijer, *Tito* 20–1.

4. Ibid., 23; Vinterhalter, *Broz* 62. The factory was at Jinec-Cenkov in Bohemia.

5. Martin Broz (1884–1964) was the first of his parents' children to survive infancy. He was eight years older than Josip; another brother Dragutin (1885–1932) came in between together with three sisters, Anka, Marija and Janica who did not survive. Other siblings were Stjepan (born in 1893), Matilda (1896), Vjekoslav (1898), Tereza (1902) and Franjica (1906).

6. From Tito's account to Sir Fitzroy Maclean in the 1963 interview, it appears that he had hoped to do his military service in the artillery which would have meant being based in Vienna, but he found this meant being stationed with Austrians and cut off from his own Croatian-speaking countrymen, so he asked to be transferred to Zagreb, and was posted to the 25th Domobran regiment.

7. Dedijer, *Tito* 26. The Petrovaradin fortress was an ancient fortress of striking appearance on the river Danube, near Novi Sad, north of Belgrade. Built in medieval times it was later strengthened by the Austrians for use against the Turks and vice versa. Today it is a national monument housing archives and a museum.

8. Dedijer, *Tito* 28–30; Zilliacus, *Tito* 38; Maclean, Interview 1963.

9. Josip Broz qualified for an Austrian war medal for his service in this campaign but did not receive it due to the confusion following the break up of the Austro-Hungarian empire at the end of the war. He was offered the medal when, as President of Yugoslavia, he made an official visit to Austria in 1965, but he gracefully declined it.

10. Dedijer, *Tito* 30–5; Zilliacus, *Tito* 39; Maclean, Interview 1963.

11. 'Cadets' was the name given to the Constitutional Democrats, the party that predominated in the Russian government in 1917. See Carr, *The Bolshevik Revolution* 1917–1923, vol. i.

12. Dedijer, *Tito* 30–5; *Borba*, 10 May 1964; Zilliacus, *Tito* 50–1.

13. J. F. N. Bradley, 'The Czechoslovak revolt against the Bolsheviks', in *Soviet Studies*, xv, no. 2, October 1963, 124-51.

14. Zilliacus, *Tito* 51–3.

15. The exact date of Josip Broz's marriage has not been made known. The place is noted in the 1928 police dossier exhibited in the Kumrovec Tito Museum, which states the marriage took place in 1918. This date appears to be a mistake as all other evidence suggests that it cannot have been as early as that. Vinterhalter gives the date as January 1920, *Broz* 75.

16. There were some 40,000 South Slavs – Serbs, Croats and Slovenes – among the prisoners of war in Russia in the first world war (Vinterhalter, *Broz* 82).

    The exact date and circumstances of Tito actually joining a communist party are somewhat obscure. It is sometimes said that he became a member of the Russian Party (Bolshevik) in the Omsk region in January 1919, and that this information was sent as confirmation for his application to join the Yugoslav Communist Party when he returned home in 1920. But Omsk was in the hands of the White Russians at this time, and this date seems open to doubt. Tito himself regarded his party membership as dating from his enrolment on return to Yugoslavia in October 1920. See below, Chapter 3.

17. The existence of the new South Slav state was proclaimed on 1 December 1918, with the name of Kingdom of the Serbs, Croats and Slovenes. It came to be called Jugoslavia eleven years later (*jugo* means south), and this name in its anglicized form Yugoslavia, has been used throughout this book.

CHAPTER 3. *Evolution of a revolutionary*

1. Conversation between Wickham Steed and Pašić quoted in Ostović, *The Truth about Yugoslavia* 88–9.
2. Lederer, *Yugoslavia at the Paris Peace Conference* 309–12.
3. The International Macedonian Revolutionary Organization (IMRO) was founded in 1896 by Damian Gruev and Gotse Delchev, both nationalistic Macedonians. It was divided over its aims, one section working for autonomy, the other becoming increasingly associated with Bulgarian aims to annex all Macedonia.
4. Tito, *Political Report of the Central Committee of the Communist Party of Yugoslavia* 14.
5. Dedijer, *Tito* 40.
6. *Pregled Istorije Saveza Komunista Jugoslavije* 60–2 (hereafter *Pregled*).
7. Ibid., 63; Avakumović, *History of the Communist Party of Yugoslavia* 29, 32. Topalović was a Social Democrat who supported union with the communists in 1919. Later he was opposed to the Comintern's domination of the Yugoslav Communist Party. He continued to be active as an intellectual Social Democrat, his activities being more Serbian than Yugoslav. His Serbian nationalism explains in part why he joined Mihailović's Četniks during the second world war. He was the prime mover in Mihailović's abortive St Sava Congress, held in January 1944.
8. Radical and revolutionary feelings remained latent among Yugoslav

peasants in spite of many conservative attitudes, and were strengthened by the disastrous economic conditions of the interwar years. During the second world war the major part of support for Tito's Partisan movement came from the peasants.

9. Institut za Radnički Pokret (Institute for the Archives of the Croatian Workers' Movement) Zagreb, ZB. VIII, L3/32.
10. Dedijer, *Tito* 40.
11. Tito, *Political Report* 32.
12. Dedijer, *Tito* 40. See police report 1928, Kumrovec Tito Museum, and the dossier compiled about Josip Broz from police files in the possession of the authorities of the Independent State of Croatia for the German Embassy in Belgrade. The dossier was sent to the embassy from Pavelić's office, 13 February 1943. It is document 6136/E458406–411 (the latter number being the British number for the microfilm frame) of captured German war documents. These can also be inspected in Washington and Bonn; other copies are in Moscow.
13. Article in the Yugoslav daily paper *Politika*, 25 May 1957; Dedijer, *Tito* 42–3.
14. Ibid., *Politika* and *Tito*. Šabić was exterminated in a concentration camp in Yugoslavia in the second world war.
15. The arms were not discovered until they were unearthed for use by Tito's Partisans also during the second world war. Dedijer, *Tito* 44–6.
16. Article in the Yugoslav communist daily paper *Borba*, 25 May 1949. Interview of author with Dr Pavle Gregorić in Zagreb April 1968. *Tito u Zapisima Suvremenika*, ed. M. Bekić, 12.
17. Dedijer, *Tito* 52; Vinterhalter, *Broz* 111–12.
18. *Borba*, 8 July 1959; Dedijer, *Tito* 53–6.

CHAPTER 4. *Political prisoner*

1. The Croat Peasant Party refused to accept the Vidovdan constitution and retained the word 'republican' in its title until July 1925 when Radić made an agreement with Pašić and finally recognized the constitution and dynasty. Maček, *In the Struggle for Freedom* 105.
2. The Frankovci were followers of Dr Josip Frank (1844–1911), who in 1896 had founded in Croatia an extreme nationlist party known as the Party of the Pure Right. Its programme had been to make extensive claims for Croatian lands and it did not support the idea of a Yugoslav state. After this state was created and Serbian leadership was established, the Frankovci worked for the break up of the state and the establishment of an enlarged, independent Croatia. Their territorial aims were largely realized with the establishment of the Independent State of Croatia for a short time during the second world war. This so-called

independent state was, however, a German satellite without real independence.

3. Avakumović, *History of the Communist Party of Yugoslavia* 74 n.; Maček, 100.

4. *Pregled* 61, 122. How far these figures were accurate it is impossible to tell. They were based on local secretaries' reports often compiled in the most difficult conditions, but the trend they show seems likely to be correct.

5. See below, pp. 137–9 and footnote.

6. *Pregled* 121, 122.

7. Avakumović, 61 n.

8. *Pregled* 91–7, 113–16.

9. Ibid., *Istoriski Arhiv*, ii, 424–9.

10. Tito, *Political Report*, 28.

11. Ibid., 28, 29; Vinterhalter, *Broz* 122–3; *Istoriski Arhiv*, 11, 138–9.

12. IRP, Zagreb, ZB. XVIII, LI/3, 4, 5.

13. Dedijer, *Tito* 60–1.

14. FO 6136/E458407.

15. Zilliacus, *Tito* 78; Institut za Radnički Pokret KI/VIII/73; *Tito Zivot i Rad* 55.

16. Zilliacus, *Tito* 78.

17. Kumrovec Tito Museum, typed sheet of police copy of Broz's notes written in exercise book. Numbered headings were:

(1) The internal and external situation: civil war in China. Defeat of the people in France, England and other capitalist states.

(2) Persecution of communist parties; completion of first phase of fight and beginning of a new one; persecution of Yugoslav Communist Party, yet its continuing strength.

(3) Bloody battles going on in India and Greece.

(4) Fight against Fascism in Italy and discontent of masses; persecution and draconic sentences against communists.

(5) Orgies of White terror in Balkans – Hungary, Romania, Bulgaria, Greece, Yugoslavia.

(6) Struggles of communist parties in England, Germany, France and Poland.

(7) Consolidation of the USSR and her preparations for wars to be made against her.

Under a second major heading 'The Political Situation in Yugoslavia' topics were listed:

(1) The Vukičović–Davidović government comes to power; fight between upper and lower bourgeoisie.

(2) Convention of Nettuno; events of 20 June; demonstration in Zagreb and position of YCP.

(3) Open Letter of the KKI (Executive Committee of the Comintern, *ed.*); new approach in Party politics, activation of members and strengthening of Party.

18. The trial is described in all major accounts of Tito's life including Dedijer, *Tito* 62–8; Maclean, *Barricade* 53–7; Zilliacus, *Tito* 78–83; Vinterhalter, *Broz* 127–34. The *Novosti* article describing the trial is printed in *Tito Život i Rad*, entry 56. An account of the trial was printed in *Borba*, 8 July 1958. Contemporary court records of the trial have not been preserved. It was only one of many such trials that took place in the interwar years. A report of the sentence on the prisoners was sent to the Comintern, IRP, Belgrade, CKKI 1928.

19. Maclean, *Barricade* 59.

20. *Politika*, 29 November 1959; Zilliacus, *Tito* 90–1.

21. Moša Pijade writing in *Politika*, 25 May 1952.

22. Dr Gregorić to this author in interview, April 1968.

23. R. Čolaković to this author, April 1968.


CHAPTER 5. *Illegal communist at large*

1. Tito's own account of his activities between his release from gaol and his departure for Moscow is given in Dedijer, *Tito* 79–91. Other accounts are given in Maclean, *Barricade* 63–73; Zilliacus, *Tito* 91–3; Vinterhalter, *Broz* 156–62, and Damjanović, *Tito na Čelu Partije* 17–38. Information about his contacts with Nikola Cikara is mentioned only in FO 6136/E458407–8. His aunt was his mother's sister.

2. Zilliacus, *Tito* 91–3.

3. FO 6136/E458407–8; Čolaković, *Kazivanje o Jednom Pokoljenju*, ii, 290.

4. Pribicevitch, *La Dictature du Roi Alexandre* 99–127, gives an opposition view of the circumstances that led up to, and the character of King Alexander's proclamation of personal rule.

5. In 1939 Yugoslavia's *per capita* income was the lowest in Europe with the exception of Romania.

6. Tomasevitch, *Peasants, Politics and Economic Change in Yugoslavia*, 248–9, 426–7, 675–80.

7. According to the official Yugoslav party history, Djaković and N. Hecimović were arrested in Zagreb, tortured and then taken to the Austrian frontier to be executed so that the story that they had tried to escape could be fabricated, see *Pregled* 156–7. Tito's figures for party members at this time are given in *Večernje Novosti*, 18 April 1967.

8. The leaflet is quoted from IRP, Zagreb, ZB. VIII. L1/11 (1931). Tito's denunciation is from Tito, *Political Report* 33.

9. This account of Gorkić was told to the author in April 1968 by R. Čolaković who knew Gorkić well.
10. Boris Kidrić was released in 1930, Kardelj in 1933, Blagoje Parović in 1934 and Dr Pavle Gregorić in 1935.
11. FO 6136/E458408.
12. *Borba*, 29 November 1962.
13. Dedijer, *Tito* 83–4.
14. Josip Broz's attendance at Central Committee meetings of the Yugoslav Communist Party held in Vienna on the dates quoted is based on party documents quoted in Damjanović, *Tito* 23. The official use of the name Tito at this early stage of Broz's political career disposes of some fanciful theories current during the second world war which supposedly explained the origins of the pseudonym. One of these was that Broz had been in the habit of ordering people to different jobs and used the familiar first person singular form of address 'ti to', meaning 'thou that'.
15. Damjanović, *Tito* 24–5.
16. Dedijer, *Tito* 87.
17. Ibid., 88 and article by E. Kardelj in *Borba*, 29 November 1962, quoted in *Zapisi* 26.
18. Damjanović, *Tito* 28–30.
19. Tito himself qualified the description of the Yugoslav government as a 'war-fascist dictatorship' (Tito, *Political Report* 33) saying that he did not know why this term had been used for King Alexander's government, since this had been 'an ordinary dictatorship of the most reactionary part of the bourgeoisie personified by the king as representative of the bourgeoisie'.
20. The French premier M. Louis Barthou was assassinated at the same time.
21. Dedijer, *Tito* 90; Zilliacus, *Tito* 99–100.
22. Gorkić was known as 'Somer'. Other members who attended were Ivan Maček, Joze Brilej, Franc Hocevar, Tone Sustarčić and Franko Otokar.
23. Tito, *Political Report* 34.
24. *Pregled* 193–4; Dedijer, *Tito* 90–1; Damjanović, *Tito* 36–8.

CHAPTER 6. *Comintern trainee in Moscow*

1. The murder of Kirov is described in Conquest, *The Great Terror* 43–54, and its consequences are dealt with throughout the book.
2. Maclean, *Barricade* 73.
3. Ibid., 82.

4. After the failure of the Hungarian revolt Bela Kun had first escaped to Vienna. The Austrian government had allowed him to proceed to Russia in exchange for some Austrian banners captured by the Russian army when it had helped the Austrian government to put down the Hungarian revolt of 1848. He was one of the earlier foreigners to be liquidated in Stalin's great purge being arrested at the end of May 1937. See Conquest, *The Great Terror* 431.
5. This account of Tito's activities in Moscow is given in all his biographies. See Dedijer, *Tito* 95–104.
6. I. Gošnjak, 'Na Tečaju u "Leninskoj Skoli" ', in *Borba*, 29 November 1962; Čolaković, *Kazivanje* 80–1.
7. Vinterhalter, *Broz* 164–5 and all other biographies, mention the foreign communists in Moscow. Tito himself commented on his relations with Manuilsky to the author of this book in an interview on 8 October 1968. See also Čolaković, *Kazivanje* 135.
8. Damjanović, *Tito* 40.
9. McKenzie, *Comintern and World Revolution, 1928–1943*, 16–43; the organization of the Comintern is described in pp. 24–33.
10. Dedijer, *Broz* 97–8; Damjanović 42–3; Vinterhalter, *Broz* 167.
11. Maclean, *Barricade* 82, 83; *Pregled* 198; McKenzie, *Comintern* 146, 325 n.
12. McKenzie, *Comintern* 43.
13. Damjanović, *Tito* 46–7.
14. Dedijer, *Tito* 99–100; *Politika*, 29 November 1959; Damjanović, *Tito* 48–9; Vinterhalter, *Broz* 170–2.
15. Dedijer, *Tito* 100; Damjanović, *Tito* 49–50.
16. *Pregled* 216–17; FO 6136/E458409.
17. *Komunist*, 1 October 1946, 69; Tito, *Political Report* 34–5.
18. Dedijer, *Tito* 103; Tito, *Govori i Članci*, viii, 101–2; *Večernje Novosti*, 18 April 1967.
19. Dedijer, *Tito* 103; *Večernje Novosti*, ibid.; Tito, *Govori*, viii, 101–2. Quotations about Manuilsky and Dimitrov are from this author's interview with Tito, 8 October 1968.
20. Dedijer, *Tito* 104; *Komunist* 69–70.


CHAPTER 7. *International experience*

1. Ciliga, *The Russian Enigma* 282–3; Conquest, *The Great Terror* 428.
2. Tito has given many accounts of his relations with the Comintern from 1936–40, including those to his biographer Dedijer, to Sir Fitzroy Maclean and to K. Zilliacus. He also spoke of them in a number of his important political speeches including his Political Report to the Fifth Congress of the Yugoslav Communist Party in

1948 (*Political Report*); his speech to the Fifth Conference of the Yugoslav Communist Party in November 1940, printed in *Komunist*, 1 October 1946, 71–4; his interview with members of the editorial board of *Komunist*, 11 April 1959, printed in Tito, *Govori*, xiv, 202–10; and his speech to the Tenth Conference of the Communist Party of Belgrade, printed in *Večernje Novosti*, 18 April 1967. See Tito, *Govori* 204–5; Dedijer, *Tito* 104; Damjanović, *Tito* 59.

3. *Pregled* 229.

4. J. Joll, 'The Front Populaire after thirty years' in *Journal of Contemporary History*, i, 1966, 30–1.

5. R. Čolaković in interview with this author April 1968 gave these addresses; general facts about the Yugoslav Communist Party in Paris are to be found in all biographies, see Dedijer, *Tito* 104, 107.

6. IRP, Zagreb, ZB. S952/342.

7. Dedijer, *The Beloved Land* 215–22.

8. *Komunist*, 16 April 1959; *Politika*, 29 November 1959; Dedijer, *Tito* 108 CKKI 1937/26; Damjanović, *Tito* 61 n. Different figures are given for the number of volunteers which the ship was expecting to pick up. Dedijer wrote 'a thousand or so'; Damjanović says 500, and this is the figure given in Tito's letter to the Comintern, *q.s.*, CKKI 1937/26.

9. CKKI 1937/26, 31.

10. *Pregled* 234–7.

11. CKKI 1937/? 1, 3, 51; Damjanović, *Tito* 61–7.

12. Dedijer, *Tito* 111–13.

13. Damjanović, *Tito* 67–9; *Pregled* 226; CKKI 1937/51.

14. *Borba*, 25 May 1952; also printed in *Tito u Zapisima Suvremenika*, ed. M. Bekić 31–40.

15. Damjanović, *Tito* 71.

16. Dedijer, *Tito* 109–10.

17. CKKI 1937/70, 73.

18. Quotation from interview with author, 8 October 1968.

19. *Večernje Novosti*, 18 April 1967.

20. Damjanović, *Tito* 75.

21. Conquest, *The Great Terror* 428.

22. Damjanović, *Tito* 74. Tito expressed gratitude for the help of Dimitrov and Pieck in his interview with this author, 8 October 1968.

23. Damjanović, *Tito* 82.

24. There are many accounts of the Miletić story including Damjanović, *Tito* 76; *Večernje Novosti*, 18 April 1967; Tito, *Govori*, xiv, 206. The quotation is from *Borba*, 17 March 1957. See below, pp. 130–1.

25. FO 6136/E458410. Ana Grzetić (wife of Ivan Grzetić) was arrested by the Yugoslav police on 3 March 1938 and under interrogation had

given them information about the Communist Party and its leading members, but the information about Tito's impending arrival is not stated in the police report as coming from her. It seems more likely to have come through someone in Paris who knew details about Tito's future movements.

26. Dedijer, *The Beloved Land* 251–3.
27. Ibid.
28. Damjanović, *Tito* 90–1.
29. Burmeister, *Dissolution and Aftermath of the Comintern* 7, 14.
30. Tito, *Govori*, xiv, 207–8.
31. Tito, 'Fifty Years of Revolutionary Struggle by the Communists of Yugoslavia', an address given at the opening session of the Ninth Congress of the League of Communists of Yugoslavia, 11 March 1969 (official English translation, 34). See also Press Service of the Federation of Yugoslav Journalists, vol. xiii, no. 617, 12 March 1969. The quotation Djilas referred to is *Conversations* 35. Djilas added: 'There was no one to stand behind the Yugoslavs; on the contrary, they dug graves for one another in their race for power in the party, and in their zeal to prove their devotion to Stalin and Leninism.' This statement was written after Djilas had broken with his former colleagues. Djilas had no personal experience of work in Moscow during the time of the purge. Testimony of those who had does not indicate that the Yugoslavs were particularly disloyal to each other. It does indicate that they tried to be loyal to the Comintern. See Djilas, *Conversations*, Chapter I. Čolaković, *Kazivanje* 11, 79 *et seq.* There is overwhelming evidence that the irrational character of Stalin's purge – which superseded all previous rules of conduct in the Comintern – was the dominant factor; see Conquest, *The Great Terror; passim.*
32. Interview with this author, 8 October 1968.

CHAPTER 8. *General Secretary of the party*

1. Tito's first biography written by Vladimir Dedijer and published in 1952, dates Tito's appointment as General Secretary of the Yugoslav Communist Party sometime between late December 1937 and early 1938 (Dedijer, *Tito* 109–11). This dating has until recently been followed by all subsequent writers. Early in 1968 Pero Damjanović published his short study of Tito's rise to power, *Tito*. This is based on documents made available since Dedijer's biography. On their evidence Damjanović dates Tito's visit to Moscow in 1938 instead of 1937, and gives the date of his visit to Dimitrov in which he was

offered the position of General Secretary of the Party, as 20 October
1938 (Damjanović, *Tito* 92–5). The evidence cited by Damjanović
seems conclusive and I have accepted it as correct. It is also the dating
that is used by Vinterhalter, *Broz* 218–25. Vinterhalter's book
published in the summer of 1968 uses the same recent sources as
Damjanović. The sequence of events followed by both these authors
clears up some of the confusion resulting from Dedijer's dating. One
of the problems in Dedijer's narrative was that if Tito was appointed
in 1937 how could Dimitrov have referred to the dissolution of the
Polish Party as having already taken place (Dedijer, *Tito* 110) when
we know that this actually happened in the summer of 1938? If Tito
saw Dimitrov in October 1938, as Damjanović states, this fact might
well have been referred to in Dimitrov's conversation with Tito.

2. Djilas, *Conversations* 34; *Pregled* 252.
3. Interview with this author, 8 October 1968.
4. Maclean, *Barricade* 103; Dedijer, *Tito* 125–6.
5. Tito, *Govori*, viii, 104. Jovanović was reported to have been released
   from gaol in Russia in 1941 in order to fight in the Red Army.
6. Damjanović, *Tito* 93. It is not clear exactly when the historic meeting
   with Manuilsky took place and it may have been after Tito's interview
   with Dimitrov, possibly as late as December. It was attended by other
   Yugoslav communists besides Tito, and all argued strongly for the
   retention of the Party under Tito's leadership.
7. There are many accounts of this story, see Dedijer, *Tito* 110; Maclean,
   *Barricade* 99; Damjanović, *Tito* 94; Vinterhalter, *Broz* 222.
8. Maclean, 'Interview';*Večernje Novosti*, 18 April 1967.
9. *Večernje Novosti*, ibid.; Tito, *Govori*, xiv, 206; Tito, *Political Report*.
   The rumour of Miletić having been seen in Moscow in 1945 is
   unconfirmed hearsay. The exact dating of Tito's investigation on
   charges of Trotskyism has not been given, and it is not certain whether
   it took place before or after his chance meeting with Miletić on the bus.
   It seems more likely to have been some time before the meeting, since
   the account of events given by Tito (qvs) describes Miletić as
   disappearing immediately after Tito had seen Damianov.
10. Vinterhalter, *Broz* 225.
11. *Pregled* 271, 272, 274. The figure of 12,000 was given by Tito in his
    speech to the ninth Congress of the Communist Party, 11 March
    1969, op. cit., 22.
12. Dedijer, *The Beloved Land* 251, 253, 268.
13. Avakumović, *History of the Communist Party of Yugoslavia* 139 n.
14. Dedijer, *The Beloved Land* 217.
15. IRP, Zagreb, ZB. Kom. 10/208; *Pregled* 229–30.
16. Avakumović, 165 n.

17. Dedijer, *The Beloved Land* 205–6; Avakumović 147.
18. *Pregled* 252; *Večernje Novosti*, 18 April 1967.
19. Aleksander Ranković, 'S. Drugom Titom' in *Četredeset Godina* Book 3, Belgrade, 1961. Also printed in *Zapisi* 46.
20. IRP, Belgrade, CKKPJ/1929/2; CKKI 1934/101, 1938/43; FO 6136/E458408. Between 1 April 1934 and 26 October 1936 the gold rouble was worth 0.15 pounds sterling ($0.87), so that 400 gold roubles were worth £60, which was a considerable monthly payment at that time. After devaluation 400 roubles equalled between £12 and £18.
21. Djilas, ibid. 261.
22. *Pregled* 269, and personal accounts of party workers to author.

CHAPTER 9. *Preparing for War*

1. Hoptner, *Yugoslavia in Crisis 1934–1941* 110.
2. Hoptner, 112, quoted from v. Wimmer, *Experiences et Tribulations d'un Diplomat Autrichien* 221–4.
3. Dedijer, *Tito* 114.
4. Dedijer, *Tito* 124.
5. Vinterhalter, *Tito* 230.
6. Dedijer, *The Beloved Land* 265–6.
7. Vinterhalter, *Tito* 230.
8. Tito, *Govori*, xiv, 209.
9. Maclean, *Barricade* 103–4. One job assigned to Tito by the Comintern besides the internal organization of the Party, was to 'persuade our men abroad to return, in particular the comrades who had been in Spain and were interned in French camps. . . . Naturally we were concerned only with upright comrades.' See Dedijer, *Tito* 111, and for Tito's account of Schwerm's report to the Comintern on Yugoslavia, Dedijer, *Tito* 126.
10. Tito has on many occasions described his hazardous return journey to Yugoslavia in 1940. The different versions tally, though some have different detail from others. See Maclean, *Barricade* 108–10; Dedijer *Tito* 126–7; Vinterhalter, *Broz* 238–9 is based on Dedijer's account. The story of his visit to Istanbul with a passport for Tito was told to this author by Vladimir Velebit in an interview on 27 March 1969.
11. IRP, Zagreb, ZB. KOM 4/71.
12. IRP, Zagreb, KOM 6/87.
13. IRP, Zagreb, ZB. CKKPJ 1/15, 16.
14. The following account of the fifth Conference is based on Damjanović, *Tito* 109–49, and on reminiscences of people who attended it. No complete set of documents about this meeting has been published, and it is said that they did not all survive the war. There are no surviving

authentic pictures; one that is sometimes produced was a re-enactment in 1952 of the conference platform by those members of the Politburo who had survived the war. A partial account (mainly Tito's speech at the Conference) was printed in 'Materijali pete Konferencije KPJ Održane Novembra 1940 u Zagrebu', in *Komunist*, 1 October 1946, 59–122. In Yugoslav Communist Party organization, a conference was less important than a congress.

15. Damjanović, *Tito* 121. Herta Has, mother of Tito's second son Alexander (born in Zagreb the following year) was a delegate at this conference.

16. Ibid., 131.

17. The agenda provided for twelve main speeches: Tito on the subject of 'organization questions', Kardelj on political matters, Aleksander Ranković on the trade unions, Ivan Milutinović on agriculture and peasant questions. Nationality questions, i.e. the problem of the relations of the different peoples in the state, were dealt with by Milovan Djilas, propaganda by Boris Kidrić, youth by Lola Ribar, work among women by Vida Tomšić. Work in the army had a special delegate, Mitar Bakić. A talk on organization and *konspiracija* was given by Paul Pap and one on people's help by Dragan Pavlović. The final item, without a main speaker listed, was election of leadership. Damjanović, *Tito* 131–2.

18. *Komunist*, 1 October 1946, 99–100 contains Tito's remarks on 'Trotskyism' in the Yugoslav party 'and many other countries' and shows that Tito accepted at this time – or at least felt it necessary to appear to accept – the Stalinist view on Trotskyism which had been one of the excuses for the purge. He did not give names of Yugoslavs who had been purged, though many of these had been published in party papers.

19. Dedijer, *Tito* 128.

20. Tomasevitch, *Peasants, Politics and Economic Change in Yugoslavia* 241–3.

21. L. Boban, 'Oko Mačekovih Pregovora s Grofom Cianom', in *Istorija XX Veku, Zbornik Radova*, vi, Belgrade, 1964, 304–55; Churchill, *The Second World War*, v, 141.

22. Ciano, *Diaries 1939–43*, 281, 284, 295.

23. Hoptner, 188.

24. Ibid., 205; Churchill, v. 140.

25. Ristić, *Yugoslavia's Revolution of 1941*, 62–5; Hoptner, 238–40.

26. Hoptner, 232, 233 and notes.

27. Ibid., 241–3.

28. BBC News Release, 26 March 1941. No. 21 quoted in Hoptner, 242 n.

29. *The Times Saturday Review*, 23 March 1968.

30. Winston Churchill, who was Britain's prime minister at this time has given a brief account (quoting some official papers) of British official contacts with the Yugoslav government immediately before the attack on Yugoslavia. The *Second World War*, v, 152–5. A full account of these relations will have to wait until the British official papers are made available to the public in 1971 and until the publication of Yugoslav government papers (at the Vojna Istoriski Institut in Belgrade) has been completed.
31. Hoptner, 272, quoting German documents USMT. Doc. NG-3260.
32. Hoptner, ibid.
33. *Vojna Enciklopedija*, Belgrade, 1958, i, 189. Different figures varying between 10,000 and 30,000 have been given. Churchill, v, 153 gives 17,000. It is unlikely that an exact figure can be given because the total population of Belgrade at the time is not known, and the dead were not counted.

CHAPTER 10. *Party Secretary into army commander*

1. Churchill, *The Second World War*, v, 146–8.
2. German Documents, FO H.
3. Ciano, *Diaries 1939–43*, ii, 87.
4. German Documents, FO Pol. 3/H, 31057.
5. A vivid first-hand account of conditions in Croatia and Bosnia at the time of the German invasion is given in Kingscote, *Balkan Exit*.
6. Zilliacus, *Tito* 122.
7. Josip Kopinić was a Slovene communist who had been trained in Moscow and returned with Tito via Istanbul in 1941. He was sent by the Comintern to Yugoslavia to be in charge of the secret radio that Velebit had installed in his house in Zagreb – which operated throughout the war without being discovered. A woman travelling with him as his wife – who later in fact became his wife – was a trained radio operator. They left Istanbul before Tito and arrived safely in Zagreb. See above, p. 131. In spite of the dispute with Tito that summer (below, p. 169) Kopinić continued work in Yugoslavia and survived to hold an important position as director of one of the largest industrial works in postwar Yugoslavia.
8. *Istoriski Arhiv*, iii, 383; Plenča, *Medjunarodni Odnosi Jugoslavije u toku Drugog Svjetskog Rata* 64–5; Shoup, *Communism and the Yugoslav National Question* 82–3; CKKI, 1941/9, 3.
9. Dedijer, *Tito* 142–3.
10. Ibid., 143.
11. *Četrdeset Prva; Ustanak Naroda Jugoslavije* 67; J. Marjanović in *Komunist*, January 1951, 116.

12. *Zbornik Dokumenta i Podataka o Narodnooslobodilačkom Ratu Jugoslovenskih Naroda* (hereafter *Zbornik*), i, book 1; 12, 15, 17; *Oslobodilački Rat Naroda Jugoslavije*, i, 44.
13. Marjanović, *Komunist*, ibid, 117; CKKI, 1941/1.
14. BG. CKKI, 1941/33, 34.
15. B. Domazetović, *Revolucija u Crnoj Gori*
16. Dedijer, *With Tito Through the War; Partisan Diary* (hereafter *Diary*) 24.
17. Dedijer, *Diary* 25
18. Ibid., 25–6. Some of Ranković's reports to Tito are contained in party archives, e.g. CKKI, 1941/27 – but the bulk of this material is not of the kind that is normally made available to the public in any country. Ranković remained Tito's intelligence chief for some time after the war and even after he had officially relinquished that position his voluminous and detailed inside knowledge gave him a unique power in the party. This was the reason for his demotion in 1966. See below, pp. 282–3.
19. Dedijer, *Tito* 155–6.
20. Ibid., 157.
21. Tito to this author, 8 October 1968.
22. The first committees were founded in Serbia in July 1941 and were soon followed by others in Slovenia and Montenegro. See above, pp. 200–1.
23. Tito to this author, 8 October 1968.

CHAPTER 11. *Tito and Mihailović*

1. Lawrence, *Irregular Adventure* 96, 98, 104; *The Četniks: A survey of Četnik activity in Yugoslavia, April 1941–July 1944* 22; *The Trial of Dragoljub-Draža Mihailović: Stenographic record and Documents from the Trial* (hereafter called *Trial*) 109.
2. Maclean, *Barricade* 145. The description of Jovanović is from Rootham, *Miss Fire* 192–3.
3. Lawrence, 230; Rootham, 211.
4. *Trial* 131.
5. J. Marjanović, *Ustanak i Narodno-Oslobodilački Pokret u Srbiji* (hereafter *Ustanak*) 220; *Zbornik*, i, book 1, 159.
   J. Marjanović, 'The German Occupation System in Serbia in 1941; in *Les Systemes d'Occupation en Yugoslavie 1941–1945*.
6. Sweet-Escott, *Baker Street Irregular* 40–3; F. W. Deakin, 'Britanija i Jugoslavija 1941–1945, in *Jugoslovenski Istorijski Časopis*, ii, 1963, 44–5. See also *Kniga o Draži*, i and ii. Četnik supporters have always claimed that Četnik forces rose in revolt before the communist-led

insurrection. The argument about who was first, Četnik or Partisan is impossible to solve; both forces were active in the summer of 1941; Tito's policy was one of active revolt, Mihailović's was not to encourage revolt though many Četniks were fighting at that time in spite of his commands. See Branko Lazitsch, *La Tragédie du Général Mihailovitch*, Paris, 19. Fotich, *The War We Lost*; Marjanović, *Ustanak* 184 *et seq.*

7. *Trial* 155.
8. Marjanović, *Ustanak* 192.
9. J. Marjanović, 'Prilozi istoriji sukoba NOP i Četnika DM', in *Istorija XX Veka Zbornik Radova*, i, Belgrade, 1959, 185.
10. Tito told this author (8 October 1968) of his offer to put his forces under Mihailović's command. Marjanović, *Ustanak* 226–8; Tito, *Govori*, i, 188.
11. Deakin, 45.
12. V. Mičunović to this author, August 1966.
13. Deakin, 45–6; Marjanović, *Ustanak* 306 n, 307; Zilliacus, *Tito* 150; *Trial* 124.
14. Professor J. Matl to the author, 18 June 1969.
15. Marjanović, *Ustanak* 304–7. Professor Marjanović has been able to use Yugoslav royalist government sources including secret and confidential letters received from British ministers with copies of the Yugoslav government's replies and of its communications with Mihailović. These papers (the British copies and originals will not be able to be made public until 1971 under the thirty-year rule for British archives) are deposited at the Vojna Istoriski Institut in Belgrade. They were taken to Belgrade by Šubašić when he joined the Provisional Government in 1944; see below, pp. 238, 265.
16. Marjanović, *Ustanak* 305.
17. Ibid., 306.
18. *Zbornik*, i, book 1, 159.
19. Marjanović, 'Prilozi . . .', 205–7; *Ustanak* 315–16; Maclean, *Barricade* 151–3; *Četniks* 9; Dedijer, *Tito* 161–4.
20. Dedijer, *Tito* 163.
21. Marjanović, *Ustanak* 315–18.
22. Čolaković, *Kazivanje* i, 203–5; Tito to this author, 8 October 1968.
23. Tito to this author, 8 October 1968.
24. *Četniks* 10 and footnote.
25. Marjanović, *Ustanak* 356 *et seq.*
26. Ibid., 352.
27. Ibid.; Marjanović, 'Četničko-Nemački Pregovori u Selu Divci 1941', in *Zbornik Filosofski Fakulteta Book X-1* 1968; J. Matl, *Das Dritte Reich und Europa* 158; Matl to this author, 18 June 1969; *Trial* 127–9.
28. Mihailović's remark was quoted to this author by Professor Matl in

the interview of 18 June 1969. Marjanović, *Ustanak* 354-5, 389 n.; FO H310467.

29. Marjanović, ibid.
30. *Trial* 129-30.
31. Marjanović, *Ustanak* 388.
32. Ibid., 387-8; Maclean, *Barricade* 154-5; Tito to author, 8 October 1968.

CHAPTER 12. *Fighting alone*

1. Čolaković. *Winning Freedom*, English translation of *Kazivanje*, i (hereafter Čolaković, *Freedom*), 205, 227-30. This book by a well-known communist and Partisan leader gives a vivid account of life and problems of Partisans in many part of the country.
   'Fočanski Prepisi' are printed in Geršković, *Dokumenti o razvoju narodne vlasti*, Belgrade, 1948, 29-35.
2. Rogers, *Guerrilla Surgeon* 46.
3. Maclean, *Barricade* 161-7, quoting F. Cavalli, *Il Processo dell' Arciviscovo di Zagabria* 210-22; Dedijer, *Diary* 163-5, 199-200; Rootham *Miss Fire* 55-6.
4. Dedijer, *Diary* 208.
5. The Second Proletarian Brigade was established on 1 March 1942, the Third on 5 March, and the Fourth and Fifth on 10 June 1942 Tito, *Political Report* 78-83.
6. Tito, *Selected Military Works* 240-4.
7. Pijade, *About the Legend that the Yugoslav Uprising Owed its Existence to Soviet Assistance* (hereafter *Legend*), 9. Tito's replies giving full details of Partisan activity, Četnik collaboration and British aid to Četniks are to be found in CKKI, 1942/31 *et seq.*
8. Maclean, *Barricade* 172; Davidson, *Partisan Picture* 30-1, 231; Rogers 109-12.
9. Rogers, 31-3, but for a case in which a British soldier was allowed to marry a Partisan, see ibid., 205-11; Jones, *Twelve Months with Tito's Partisans* 75-7, 81.
10. *The National Liberation Movement of Yugoslavia* 10. The comparatively long occupation by the Partisans at Užice in 1941 and Foča in 1942 gave experience in the problems of military government for civilians in wartime, and allowed Tito to be on the spot while policy was being hammered out. Edicts with general application were issued and are known as the 'Fočanski Prepisi' (note 1 above) and an accumulative body of law controlling civil government was built up from Supreme General Staff orders which were later ratified by the wartime government established at Jajce. Geršković, *Dokumenti*; Tito, *Political Report* 66-9.
11. Dedijer, *Diary* 105; CKKI, 1942/77; Tito, *Political Report* 68.

12. CKKI, 1942/41. In reply to a radioed query from Dimitrov (Deda) Tito replied that the Partisans had to use a great variety of different currencies – obtained from many sources. Kunars and Italian lire, in Croatia; new dinars and German marks in Serbia; Serbian, Croatian and Italian money in Bosnia; Italian lire in Montenegro and German marks in Slovenia. He said that feeding centres had had to be set up for starving people in many parts of liberated territories in Bosnia Montenegro and Sandjak.

13. *Zbornik*, ix, book 2; Čolaković, *Freedom* 254.

14. CKKI, 1942/101, 118.

15. Pijade, *Legend* 6–9; Dedijer, *Tito* 175; CKKI, 1941/3, 4, 31, 42, 55, 56, 61, 71, 80, 84, 95.

16. CKKI, 1942/31, 38; Pijade, *Legend* 9–12.

17. Pijade, *Legend* 13–16; CKKI, 1942/1, 4, 10, 14, 35, 86. See below, Chapter 15.

18. CKKI, 1942/109, 115, 147, 155; Pijade, *Legend* 13–21.

19. *Četniks, passim*; Ugo Cavallero, *Commando Supremo* 1948; *Hitler e Mussolini Lettere e Documenti*, Milan, 1946; German Foreign Office Documents (captured and microfilmed at the end of the war) H.310528, H.310565, H.312145, H.312233, H.312739, H.312731 are only a few examples among many from unpublished German documents. The order of battle of both Germans and Italians in the operations against Partisans is available and shows what Četnik units were used in these offensives.

20. Pijade, *Legend* 18–19.

21. Plenča, *Medjunarodni Odnosi Jugoslavije u toku Drugog Svjetskog Rata* 158, quoting Yugoslav royalist government document in Vojni, *Istoriski Arhiv*, vii, AVII, 173, 33/4–2.

22. Pijade, *Legend* 20; CKKI, 1942/269, 285, 289, 327, 329.

23. Pijade, *Legend* 20–1.

CHAPTER 13. *Allied recognition*

1. Deakin, 'Britanija i Jugoslavija' 49; Plenča, *Medjunarodni Odnosi Jugoslavije u toku Drugog Svjetskog Rata*, 124 and footnote.

2. I am indebted for material about the Atherton mission to Colonel V. Kljaković who supplied sources from the Vojna Istoriski Arhiv in Belgrade. When the British missions were sent to Croatia in 1943 (see below, p. 218) Tito warned Croatian Headquarters Staff not to be afraid that they would lead to some such 'provocation' as had occurred the previous year. When Atherton reached Partisan Headquarters in Foča in 1942, Tito had announced his arrival in one of his radio messages to Moscow (CKKI, 1942/46) and all evidence seems to suggest that he was anxious to have good relations with the mission. It was

clearly in his interests that Atherton should be able to report back to his superiors about the Partisans' active fight against the Germans. Alive he could have been useful to Tito, and his death in mysterious circumstances could only be a disadvantage. In his diary for 20 March 1942 Dedijer records Atherton's arrival at Foča and adds that he had been a newspaper correspondent in Belgrade for six years and had married a Muslim girl from Sarajevo (*Diary* 78). The accusation that Partisans had been responsible for Atherton's murder was made public in an article by C. Sulzberger in the *New York Times*, 4 February 1943. Tito was informed of this article in a telegram from Moscow. See *Borba*, 15 February 1943, for the Partisan reaction and for a short account of the affair, and *Zbornik* ii, book 2, 284.

3. *Četniks* 15 *et seq.*; Deakin, 46, 50–1; Plenča, 134. *Vojna Enciklopedija*, vi, 115.

4. Deakin, 50–3; Rootham, *Miss Fire* 49–50, 107. British proposals to Mihailović said to have been submitted by Colonel Bailey on 28 May 1943, and Mihailović's answer to the Yugoslav Prime Minister in London are quoted in Knezevitch, *Why the Allies Abandoned the Yugoslav Army of General Mihailovich – With Official Memoranda and Documents*, Documents, 10–13.

5. Knezevitch, ibid. The speech in question was made by Mihailović on 28 February 1942 at a local gathering and was very strongly anti-British. He said that the English, to suit their own strategic ends were urging Četniks to undertake operations without the slightest intention of helping them, either then or in the future, that the English were fighting 'to the last Serb'. When the British government protested, on receiving a report of the speech from Colonel Bailey, who had been present, the Yugoslav government denied that Mihailović had said these words and said that Colonel Bailey could not understand Serbian. In fact Bailey's understanding of Serbian was excellent. He had lived for years in Yugoslavia and still retained perfect understanding of the language many years later. There is no doubt that Mihailović uttered these words, and though extravagantly phrased, they represented his bitter disappointment at not receiving greater aid while still remaining inactive (Col. Bailey to this author, June 1969).

6. Ibid. The British Foreign Office documents and Yugoslav government replies and messages to Mihailović are quoted in full in the Knezevitch article.

7. Deakin, 52–3; Jones, *Twelve Months with Tito's Partisans*, Chapter 1 and *passim*.

8. *Vojna Enciklopedija*, vi, 117–18; *Oslobodilački Rat Naroda Jugoslavije*, 1941–1945 i, 362–8; B. Perović, 'Borba u Lici u toku operacije Vajs (Weiss) 1', in *Vojnoistoriski Glasnik*, xviii, May–August 1967; Fabian

Trgo, *Četvrta i Peta Neprijatelska Ofenziva*, Belgrade, 1968, 5–13; *Četniks* 45–62.

9. Dedijer, *Diary* 273; Pijade, *Legend* 21–2; CKKI, 1943/31, 49.
10. CKKI, 1943/73, 74; Maclean, *Barricade* 206.
11. Trgo, 53–81 (summary in English 84–6); *Vojna Enciklopedija*, vi, 117–18; Djonlagić *et al.*, *Yugoslavia in the Second World War* 116–21.
12. CKKI, 1943/140, 143, 150, 155.
13. Deakin, 52; Maclean, *Barricade* 231; Dedijer, *Diary* 195.
14. Slessor, *The Central Blue* 594. Interview with Air Vice-Marshal Sir William Elliot, August 1968. Butler, ed., *Grand Strategy* 78–9, 196.
15. Deakin, 53; Maclean, *Barricade* 232; Rogers, *Surgeon* 135–6 CKKI, 1943/161, 178.
16. Maclean, *Barricade* 242; CKKI, 1943/232, 276; *Trial* 211–12.
17. Deakin, 57; *Vojna Enciklopedija*, vi, 119 states that the Partisan army had about 300,000. The ferocity of Partisan fighting and severe conditions in Yugoslavia led many German soldiers to ask for transfer to the Russian front, reported General Rendulic, Commander of the German Second Mechanized Army (Rendulic, *Gekämpft, gesiegt, geschlagen* 210).
18. Churchill, *The Second World War*, v, 470–8; Plenča, 299–30. The original of this letter is in the War Museum in Belgrade (JNA 31/1a), Butler, 10.
19. I am indebted to Walter Roberts of the US Permanent Delegation to the European Office of the United Nations in Geneva for details about the US missions to Yugoslavia. See also Matloff, *Strategic Planning for Coalition Warfare, 1943–1944*, 424–5, 510; Murphy, *Diplomat Among Warriors* 187–8; Churchill, *The Second World War* v, 358; Howard, *The Mediterranean Strategy in the Second World War* 49–50; *Trial* 212, 255–8.
20. Djonlagić, 175 n., quoting Kolektiv autorov, *Sovetski voruzennie sili v borbe za oslobodzenie narodov Jugoslavije* 50–3.
21. Special units included the Desert Air Force (which had moved to Italy from North Africa), Coastal Air Force with its headquarters at Taranto, the US 15th Air Force, the British 334 Wing at Brindisi as well as special forces of Naval Command and various other British and American intelligence agencies additional to SOE.
22. Slessor, 21.
23. Djonlagić, 149; Tito, *Selected Speeches and Articles, 1941–1961*, 61–2.
24. Maclean, *Barricade* 234–5.
25. Rogers, *Surgeon* 83–4.
26. Slessor, 597.
27. Rogers, 57.
28. Davidson, *Partisan Picture* 165.

CHAPTER 14. *Transition to peace*

1. Butler, *Grand Strategy* 10.
2. Pijade, *Legend* 23–4.
3. Tito sent radio reports to Dimitrov in Moscow about the arrangements for AVNOJ on 12 October (CKKI, 1943/296) and further information later in the month (CKKI, 1943/350). The report in which he detailed four points of important political policy which had been decided on at Jajce was sent on 30 November (CKKI, 1943/350). These points were: 1. That no recognition would be given to the King and the royalist government. 2. They would not be permitted to return to Yugoslavia. 3. That the Jajce government as representatives of the majority of the people wanted a republic based on the National Liberation Committees. 4. That the sole authority in the country was those committees and AVNOJ.
4. Čolaković, *Freedom* 287–93.
5. *National Liberation Movement* 34; *Prvo i Drugo Zasjedanje AVNOJ – a* Zagreb, 1963, 206–8. The official text containing the four points mentioned above, also contained a provision that the Presidium of AVNOJ would review 'all international treaties and engagements entered into in the name of Yugoslavia by the exiled Yugoslav government with a view to their eventual abrogation or confirmation and approval', and that no future commitments of this government would be recognized by AVNOJ.
6. Dedijer, *Tito* 207; Djilas, *Conversations* 14.
7. Djilas, ibid. 103.
8. The fact that this route was necessary even in 1944 may lend support to the Russians' earlier claim that communications difficulties had made it impossible to get aid to the Partisans.
9. Maclean, *Barricade* 251–2; Rogers, *Surgeon* 96–7.
10. CKKI, 1944/29, 60, 62.
11. Maclean, *Barricade* 254; Slessor, *The Centred Blue* 604; CKKI, 1944/65.
12. Djilas, *Conversations* 18. The loan was granted and arrived by plane at the very last moment before Colonel Velebit left for London. The crates had to be rapidly off-loaded and opened up with bayonets. Colonel Velebit stuffed his brief-case with notes and wrote a hasty receipt as the engines of his plane were being warmed up.
13. Djilas, *Conversations* 70, 71.
14. CKKI, 1943/361.
15. Exhibit in museum at Kumrovec.
16. Sir Fitzroy Maclean was not present in Drvar at this time, but he accompanied Tito from Italy to Vis after the episode was over. His

account – which he obtained at first hand from Tito and others who were with him – is to be found in Maclean, *Barricade* 256–61. I am indebted to Colonel Vivien Street, Rodoljub Čolaković and others who were present at Drvar, for their accounts of the incident. See also *Vojna Enciklopedija* ii, 630–3; D. Jovanić, 'Drvarska Operacija', in *Vojno Delo*, June 1954; S. Odić, 'Desant na Drvar' in *Vojnoistoriski Glasnik*, April 1954; *Oslobodilački Rat*, ii, 96–104; Clissold, *Whirlwind* 184–5; Slessor, 596–9; Čolaković, *Freedom* 362–73.

17. Tito, *Political Report* 114–19; King Peter of Yugoslavia, *A King's Heritage* 160–6. See also K. St Pavlović, 'The Formation of the Regency', in *Glasnik SIKD 'Njegoš'*, Chicago, June 1962, 26–42; Fotić, *The War We Lost* 183 *et seq.*

18. Clissold, 190.

19. I am indebted to Stephan Clissold for permission to print this account of the interview between Tito and Sir Winston Churchill. Mr Clissold, who was present at the interview, had permission from the late Sir Winston Churchill to publish his account in *Whirlwind*. President Tito also spoke about the interview to me on 8 October 1968. It appears that the Yugoslav authorities have no verbatim text of the interview and if there is an official English text, it has not yet been released for public examination. See also Churchill, *The Second World War*, vi; *Triumph and Tragedy*, 79–85.

20. Maclean, *Barricade* 280.

21. Djilas, *Conversations* 18, and Tito's interview to this author, 8 October 1968.

22. Dedijer, *Tito* 234–5.

23. Churchill, vi, 198, 204. Anthony Eden, Earl of Avon, *The Reckoning*, Boston, 1965, 605; Cordell Hull, *Memoirs*, ii, 1451–9. See also United States, Department of State, *Foreign Relations of the United States: The Conference of Berlin, 1945*, Washington, 1960, i, 66, and ibid., *The Conference at Malta and Yalta, 1945*, 103–6. Royal Institute of International Affairs, *The Soviet–Yugoslav Dispute* (hereafter *Dispute*) 35. Tito, *Govori*, i, 276–80. Edward Kardelj to this author, August 1965.

24. Sir Henry Maitland Wilson. Churchill, vi, 482–7.

25. *The Alexander Memoirs* 1940–1945, 152; Churchill, vi, 482.

CHAPTER 15. *International statesman*

1. To this author, 8 October 1968.
2. Dedijer, *Tito* 260.
3. Djilas, *Conversations* 119.
4. Ibid., 103–6.
5. Tito, *Political Report* 129.

6. Tito, ibid., 128–9; to this author, 8 October 1968.
7. To this author, 8 October 1968. Djilas to this author in interview, 1951 described the uneasy atmosphere between Soviet and satellite representatives at the meeting to found the Cominform.
8. Djilas, *Conversations* 81–6; RIIA, *Dispute* 13, 20.
9. Shoup, *Communism and the Jugoslav National Question* 133–7; S. Skendi, ed., *Albania* 230; Dedijer, *Jugoslovensko–Albanski Odnosi 1938–49*, 69, 70.
10. Djilas, *Conservations* 130.
11. Edward Kardelj to this author, August 1965. See also *Zbornik dokumenata* ii, book 10, 361, and Shoup, 144–83 for detailed discussion of the Macedonian question.
12. M. Pijade in *Borba*, 29 December 1949; Djilas, *Conversations* 157–62; RIIA, *Documents on International Affairs, 1947–1948* 290–2.
13. Ibid., and Tito to this author, 8 October 1968; Mosely, *The Kremlin in World Politics* 231.
14. Kardelj to this author, August 1965.
15. RIIA, *Dispute; The Correspondence between the Central Committee of the Communist Party of Jugoslavia and the Central Committee of the All-Union Communist Party (Bolsheviks)*, Belgrade 1948; *Statement of the Central Committee of the Communist Party of Yugoslavia in regard to the Resolution of the Information Bureau of Communist Parties on the Situation in the Communist Party of Yugoslavia*, Belgrade, 1948.
16. *Dispute* 9–17; see also Ulam, *Titoism and the Cominform*.
17. *Dispute* 18 et seq.
18. Ibid., 27.
19. Ibid., 31–52.
20. To this author, 8 October 1968.
21. Campbell, *Tito's Separate Road* 22–7, 45–6. The total figure for Anglo-US aid to Yugoslavia varies according to what items are included. I have based my figures on statistics supplied to me by official US and British sources.
22. Tito, *Selected Speeches* 229. The quotation is from Tito's report to the Seventh Congress of the League of Communists of Yugoslavia held in Ljubljana, 22 April 1958.
23. In 1950 Yugoslav official sources said that during the fighting in Greece, Yugoslavia had received as refugees 10,000 Greek children and parents of 9000 of them.
24. It was on this occasion that Tito was offered, and politely declined as an anachronism, the Imperial Austrian decoration he had won during the first world war. See above, p. 297, footnote 9.
25. Kardelj to this author, August 1965. See also Auty, 'Tito's International Relations', in *Contemporary Yugoslavia*, ed. Vucinich.

26. Tito, *Collected Speeches* 229.
27. Campbell, 72–3.
28. Auty, in *Contemporary Yugoslavia* ibid.
29. Interview with Louis Dalmas printed in *Borba*, 28 December 1949
    See Tito, *Govori* 336–45.
30. News Conference in Belgrade, February 1951.


CHAPTER 16. *Head of State*

1. Tito, *Political Report* 119.
2. D. Warriner, 'Urban Thinkers and Peasant Policy in Yugoslavia 1918–59', in *The Slavonic and East European Review*, xxxviii, no. 90. December 1959, 67.
3. Tito, *Political Report* 121–2.
4. The six republics within the Federal Republic of Yugoslavia were Slovenia, Croatia, Bosnia-Herzegovina, Montenegro, Macedonia and Serbia, which included the autonomous province of Vojvodina and the autonomous region of Kosovo-Metohija (usually called Kosmet). This was incorporated in the constitution of 1947, see *Constitution of the Federative Republic of Yugoslavia*, Belgrade, 1947, 39–40.
5. *Trial, passim*; Dedijer, *Diary* 253–6.
6. Tito's speech to the Ninth Congress of the League of Communists of Yugoslavia on 11 March 1969, is printed in *Fifty Years of Revolutionary Struggle by the Communists of Yugoslavia*. Reference to party membership numbers is ibid. 22.
7. The affairs of the Yugoslav Communist Party were still kept very secret even after the war and membership of the Politburo was not published.
8. Djilas. *Land Without Justice* 25. The whole book is a most moving account of the terrible inheritance of Djilas and his generation of Montenegrins.
9. His control of intelligence material and staff was to remain even after he had left the office of Minister of the Interior and was a main reason for his demotion in 1966. See below, pp. 282–3.
10. The official UNRRA figure for aid supplied to Yugoslavia was 425 million dollars.
11. *Five Year Plan*, Belgrade, 1947. I am indebted to the late Professor Rudolf Bićanić for much critical material about the results of the Five Year Plan. See Bićanić, 'Economic growth under centralized planning: Jugoslavia a case study', in *Economic Development and Cultural Change*, vi, October 1957.
12. Dedijer, *Tito* 286.
13. To this author, 8 October 1968.

14. Dedijer, *Tito* 346.
15. Tito, *Political Report*. Shoup, *Communism and the Jugoslav National Question* 138 n. gives the ratio of party members to expulsions in some of the republics and points out the six to one ratio in Montenegro.
16. *White Book: On Aggressive Activities by the Governments of the USSR, Poland, Czechoslovakia, Hungary, Rumania, Bulgaria and Albania towards Yugoslavia*, Belgrade, 1951; also *The Trial of Traicho Kostov and His Group*, Sofia, 1949. Rajk, Kostov, Clementis and many others who were executed on charges of having been pro-Yugoslav spies were 'rehabilitated' by communist governments in their own countries after the death of Stalin.
17. Shoup, 138 and footnote. The author points out the high ratio of expulsions to numbers of party members in Montenegro at the time of the Cominform dispute. It was six to one, compared with twenty-three to one in Bosnia-Herzegovina, twenty to one in Croatia, and thirty-one to one in Macedonia.
18. See Bićanić, 'Dohodak Seljačkih Gospodarstava un FNRJ i NRH u Razdobluju od 1953–1955', in *Ekonomska Pregled*, no. 8–9, 1956.
19. Tito, *Workers Manage Factories*, Belgrade 1950; *New Fundamental Law of Yugoslavia*, Belgrade 1953, 53–4; *The Constitution of the Socialist Federal Republic of Yugoslavia*, Belgrade 1963, 13–18. *Workers' Management in Yugoslavia*, ILO, Geneva, 1962; *Deveti Kongres*, SKJ, Belgrade, 1969, 143–93.
20. A detailed discussion of economics and the national question is to be found in Shoup, 227–60. It was discussed openly and in detail in the economic commission at the ninth Congress of the League of Communists of Yugoslavia held in Belgrade, 11–15 March 1969. See *Deveti Kongres SKJ* 120–36, 137–93 and *passim*.
21. Djilas, *The New Class*, 1957.
22. See Neal, *Titoism in Action: The Reforms in Yugoslavia*.
23. The report of movements of army units was an unconfirmed observation at the time of the crisis.
24. *Komunist*, 7 July 1966 and 22 September 1966; Shoup, 257–8.
25. *Deveti Kongres SKJ*, 46 and *passim*.

CHAPTER 17. *Tito the man*

1. Tito to Eleanor Roosevelt in an interview in 1952.
2. To this author, 8 October 1968.
3. To Eleanor Roosevelt, 1952.
4. To this author, interview, 1951.
5. To this author, interview, 8 October 1968.
6. Ibid.
7. Ibid.

# SELECT BIBLIOGRAPHY

Archives of the Yugoslav Communist Party in the Institut za Radnički Pokret in Belgrade. These include papers of the Central Committee 1919–45, and correspondence with the Comintern (KI, 1919–41, and CKKI, 1941–43 and CK–KPJ).

Archives of the Croatian section of the Yugoslav Communist Party (mainly leaflets and poster) in the Institut za Radnički Pokret in Zagreb.

Archives of the Vojna Istoriski Institut in Belgrade (especially papers of the Royalist Yugoslav government in exile and some German documents).

Collections of unpublished German documents at the Foreign Office Research Department in London, especially the *Lösch Papers*. H310528–H312739, 6136/E458406–458411.

PRINTED SOURCES

*Istoriski Arhiv Komunistički Partije Jugoslavije*, vols. i–xxiv, Belgrade 1949–58.
*Zgodovinski Arhiv Komunističke Partije Jugoslavije*, vols. i–xi, Belgrade 1949–58.
*V Kongres Komunističke Partije Jugoslavije*, 18–21 Jula 1948, Belgrade 1949.
*VI Kongres Komunističke Partije Jugoslavije* (Saveza komunista Jugoslavije), 2–7 Novembra 1952, Belgrade, 1953.
*VII Kongres Saveza Komunista Jugoslavije*, Belgrade, 1958.
*Osmi Kongres Saveza Komunista Jugoslavije*, Belgrade, 1964.
*Deveti Kongres Saveza Komunista Jugoslavije*, Belgrade, 1969.
*Zbornik Dokumenata i Podataka o Narodnooslobodilačkom Ratu Jugoslavenskih Naroda*, i–xiv, Belgrade, 1950–60 (130 volumes).
*Documents on German Foreign Policy*, Series C, 1933–37, and Series D, 1936/7–40.
*Soviet Documents on Foreign Policy*, ed. J. Degras, Oxford U.P. for R.I.I.A., 1953.
*Documents on International Affairs*, ed. J. Wheeler Bennett, London, 1929.
*Documents on British Foreign Policy*, 2nd Series, 1929–38; 3rd Series 1938–39.

# SELECT BIBLIOGRAPHY

UNITED STATES DEPARTMENT OF STATE. *Foreign Relations of the United States, Diplomatic Papers: The Conferences at Cairo and Teheran,* 1943, Washington, 1961.
*Teheran, Jalta, Potsdam,* ed F. Epstein (Soviet Protokol of the conferences translated into German), Cologne, 1968.

## OTHER WORKS

ADAMIĆ,L. *The Eagle and the Roots,* New York, Doubleday, 1952.
ALEXANDER, A. R. L. G. (Field-Marshal, 1st Earl). *The Alexander Memoirs 1940–1945,* ed. J. North, London, Cassell, 1962.
AMERY, J. *Sons of the Eagle,* London, Macmillan, 1948.
ARMSTRONG, H. F. *Tito and Goliath,* London, Gollancz, 1951
AUTY, P. 'Yugoslavia', in *Central and South Eastern Europe, 1945–1948,* ed. R. B. Betts, London, Royal Institute of International Affairs, 1950.
—— *Building a New Yugoslavia,* London, Fabian Society pamphlet, 1954.
—— *Yugoslavia,* London, Thames & Hudson, 1965.
—— 'Yugoslavia', in *Contrasts in Emerging Societies,* ed. D Warriner, London, Athlone Press, 1965.
—— 'Tito's International Relations', in *Contemporary Yugoslavia,* ed. W. Vucinich, Univ. of California Press, 1969.
AVAKUMOVIĆ, I. *History of the Communist Party of Yugoslavia,* Aberdeen U.P., 1964.
EDEN, ANTHONY, Earl of Avon. *Memoirs, Part 2: Facing the Dictators,* London, Cassell, 1962.
—— *Memoirs, Part 3: The Reckoning,* London, Cassell, 1965.
BAERLEIN, H. *The Birth of Yugoslavia,* 2 vols. London, Parsons, 1922.
BARKER, ELIZABETH. *Macedonia: its place in Balkan Politics,* London, Royal Institute of International Affairs, 1950.
BEKIĆ, M., ed. *Tito u Zapisima Suvremenika,* Zagreb, 1965.
BELOFF, M. *The Foreign Policy of Soviet Russia, 1929–1936,* London, 1962.
BIĆANIĆ, R. *Kako Živi Narod,* Zagreb, 1936.
—— 'Economic Growth under Centralized and Decentralized Planning: Jugoslavia a Case Study', in *Economic Development and Cultural Change,* vi, no. 1, October 1957.
—— 'Interaction of Macro and Micro-Economic Decisions in Yugoslavia 1954–1957', in *Value and Plan: Economic Calculation and Organization in Eastern Europe,* ed. G. Grossman, Berkeley, Univ. of California Press, 1960.
—— 'The liberation of the serfs in 1848' and 'Attitudes to the Zadruga', in *Contrasts in Emerging Societies,* ed. D. Warriner, London, Athlone Press, 1965.
—— 'Effects of the First World War on the economics of Yugoslavia',

paper prepared for the Institute of Contemporary History Conference, October 1967.

BILAINKIN, G. *Tito*, London, Williams & Norgate, 1949.

BOBAN, L. *Sporazum Maček-Cvetković*, Zagreb, 1965.

BOBROWSKI, v. *La Yugoslavie Socialiste*, Paris, 1956.

BORKENAU, F. *The Communist International*, London, Faber, 1938.

—— *European Communism*, London, Faber, 1953.

BRAILSFORD, H. N. *Macedonia: its races and their future*, London, Methuen, 1906.

BRAŠIĆ, R. M. *Land Reform and Ownership in Yugoslavia 1919–1953*, New York, Free Europe Committee, 1954.

BRZEZINSKI, z. K. *The Soviet Bloc: Unity and Conflict* rev. edn. New York, Praeger; London, Pall Mall, 1963.

BULLOCK, A. *Hitler: A Study in Tyranny*, New York, Harper, 1962; London, Odhams, 1962.

BURMEISTER, A. *Dissolution and Aftermath of the Comintern: Experiences and Observations 1937–1947*, New York, 1955.

BUTLER, J. R. M., ed. *Grand Strategy*, vols. v, vi, London, H.M.S.O., 1956.

BYRNES, R., ed. *Yugoslavia*, New York and London, 1957.

CAMPBELL, J. C. *Tito's Separate Road: America and Yugoslavia in World Politics*, New York, Harper, 1967.

CARR, E. H. *The Twenty Years' Crisis 1919–39*, London, Macmillan, 1939; 2nd edn., 1946.

—— *The Bolshevik Revolution 1917–1923*, vols. i–iii, London, Macmillan, 1951, 1953.

CATTELL, D, T. *Communism and the Spanish Civil War*, Cambridge U.P., 1956.

*Četniks, The* (AFHQ Handbook), 1944.

CHURCHILL, W. S. *The Second World War*, 6 vols. London, Cassell, 1948–65, esp. v, *Closing the Ring*, and vi, *Triumph and Tragedy*.

CIANO, G. *Diaries 1939–43*, ed. H. Gibson, New York, Doubleday, 1946; London, Heinemann, 1947.

—— *Diary 1939*, trans. A Mayor, London, Methuen, 1952.

CILIGA, A. *The Russian Enigma*, London, Routledge & Kegan Paul, 1940.

CLISSOLD, S. *Whirlwind: The Story of Marshal Tito's Rise to Power*, London, Cresset Press, 1949.

—— ed. *A Short History of Yugoslavia*, Cambridge U.P., 1966.

ČOLAKOVIĆ, R. *Winning Freedom*, trans. A Brown. London, Lincolns Prager, 1962.

—— *Kazivanje o Jednom Pokoljenju*, vol. i (of which *Winning Freedom* is a translation), Zagreb 1964, and vol. ii, Sarajevo, 1968.

CONQUEST, R. *The Great Terror: Stalin's purge of the 'thirties*, London, Macmillan, 1968.

## SELECT BIBLIOGRAPHY

ČOROVIĆ, J. *Istorija Jugoslavije*, Zagreb, 1933.

CRNJA, Z. *Cultural History of Croatia*, Zagreb, 1962.

CRANKSHAW, E. *Russia without Stalin: The Emerging Pattern*, London M. Joseph, 1956.

—— *Khrushchev*, London, Collins, 1966.

—— *The Fall of the House of Habsburg*, London, Longmans, 1963.

DALMAS, L. *Le Communisme Yuogoslave Depuis la Rupture avec Moscou*, Paris, 1950.

DAMJANOVIĆ, P. *Tito na Čelu Partije*, Belgrade, 1968.

DAVIDSON, B. *Partisan Picture*, London, Bedford Books, 1946.

DEAKIN, F. W. 'Britanija i Jugoslavija 1941–1945', in *Jugoslovenski Istorijiski Časopis*, no. 2, 1963.

—— *The Brutal Friendship*, London, Weidenfeld & Nicolson, 1962.

DEDIJER, V. *Josip Broz Tito–Prilozi za Biografiju*, Belgrade, 1953.

—— *Tito Speaks* (translation of part of the above), London, Weidenfeld & Nicolson, 1953.

—— *Dnevnik*, 3 vols. Belgrade, 1945, 1946 and 1950.

—— *With Tito Through the War 1941–1944* (translation of parts of above diary), Alexander Hamilton, London, 1951.

—— *The Beloved Land*, London, Macgibbon & Kee, 1961.

—— *The Road to Sarajevo*, Macgibbon & Kee, 1967.

—— *Stalin's Last Battle*, London, 1969.

—— *Jugoslavensko-Albanski Odnosi 1938–49*, Belgrade, 1951.

DEUTSCHER, I. *Stalin*, Oxford U.P., 1949; Penguin, 1966.

DJILAS, M. *The New Class: An Analysis of the Communist System*, New York, Praeger; London, Thames & Hudson, 1957.

—— *Conversations with Stalin*, London, Hart-Davis, 1962.

—— *Land Without Justice*, London, Methuen, 1958.

DJONLAGIĆ, A., *et al*. *Yugoslavia in the Second World War*, Belgrade, 1967.

DJONOVIĆ, J. 'Contacts with Draža Mihailović from the Near East and North Africa', in *Glasnik SIKD 'Njegos'*, Chicago, July 1958.

DJORDJEVIĆ, J. 'Political Power in Yugoslavia', in *Government and Opposition*, ii, no. 2, January 1967.

DRACHKOVITCH, M. and LAZITCH, B., ed. *The Comintern: Historical Highlights*, New York, Praeger, 1966.

DRAGNICH, A. *Tito's Promised Land*, New Brunswick, Rutgers U.P., 1954.

ERLICH, V. ST. *Family in Transition: a study of 300 Yugoslav villages*, Princeton U.P., 1966.

FISCHER-GALATI, S., ed *Eastern Europe in the 'Sixties*, New York, Praeger, 1963.

FISHER, J. C. *Yugoslavia: A Multi-national State*, San Francisco, 1966.

## SELECT BIBLIOGRAPHY

FISK, W. M. and RUBINSTEIN, A. Z. 'Yugoslavia's Constitutional Court', in *East Europe*, New York, 1966.

FOTICH, C. *The War We Lost: Yugoslavia's Tragedy and the Failure of the West*, New York, Viking, 1948.

FRANKEL, J. 'Communism and the national question in Yugoslavia', in *Journal of Central European Affairs*, xv, April 1955.

GERŠKOVIĆ, L., ed. *Dokumenti o razvoju narodne vlasti*, Belgrade, 1948.

—— *Social and Economic System in Yugoslavia*, Belgrade, 1959.

HALPERIN, E. *The Triumphant Heretic; Tito's Struggle Against Stalin*, London, Heinemann, 1958.

HALPERN, J. M. *A Serbian Village*, Columbia U.P., 1958.

HODGKINSON, H. *West and East of Tito*, London, Gollancz, 1952.

HOFFMAN, G. and NEAL, W. F. *Tito's Yugoslavia*, Berkeley, Univ. of California Press, 1960.

HOPTNER, J. B. *Yugoslavia in Crisis 1934–1941*, Columbia U.P., 1962,

HORVAT, J. *Politička Povijest Hrvatske*, Zagreb, 1936.

HOWARD, M. *The Mediterranean Strategy in the Second World War*, London, Weidenfeld & Nicolson, 1968.

*Hronologija Oslobodilačke Borbe Naroda Jugoslavije 1941–45*, Belgrade, 1964. (Chronology of the Liberation War of the Yugoslav Peoples.)

HULL, C. *Memoirs*, 2 vols. New York, Macmillan; London, Hodder, 1948.

IONESCU, G. *The Politics of the European Communist States*, London, Weidenfeld & Nicolson, 1967.

JACKSON, G. D. *Comintern and Peasant in East Europe*, 1919–1930, New York, Columbia U.P., 1966.

JELAVICH, C. 'Serbian Nationalism and the Question of Union with Croatia in the Nineteenth Century', in *Balkan Studies*, v, 1962.

JOLL, J. *The Second International*, London, Weidenfeld & Nicolson, 1955.

JONES, W. *Twelve Months with Tito's Partisans*, Bedford, Bedford Books, 1946.

KARDELJ, E. *Collected Works*, 1953–1969, Belgrade, 1969.

KERNER, R., ed. *Yugoslavia*, Berkeley, California U.P., 1949.

KINGSCOTE, F. *Balkan Exit*, London, Bles, 1942.

KLJAKOVIĆ, V. 'Drugo Zasjedanje AVNO Ja i Politika Saveznika Prema Jugoslaviji', in *Značenje Drugog Zasjedanja AVNO Ja za Socijalističku revoluciju u Jugoslaviji, Zagreb, 1963*.

KNEZEVITCH, Z. L. *Why the Allies Abandoned the Yugoslav Army of General Mihailovich – With Official Memoranda and Documents*, Washington, 1945.

KOFOS, E. *Nationalism and Communism in Macedonia*, Salonika, 1959.

——'The Making of Yugoslavia's Peoples Republic of Macedonia', in *Balkan Studies*, iii, 1962.

KOLIŠEVSKI, L. *Macedonian National Question*, Belgrade, 1959.

KORBEL, J. *Tito's Communism*, Denver, Brown, 1951.

*Kriegstagebuch des Oberkommando der Wehrmacht*, vol. iii, Frankfurt, 1963.

KÜNREICH, H. *Partisanen Krieg in Europa 1939–45*. Berlin, Dietz, 1965.

LAWRENCE, C. *Irregular Adventure*, London, Faber, 1947.

LAZIĆ, B. *Tito et la Revolution Yougoslave*, Paris, 1957.

LEDERER, I. *Yugoslavia at the Paris Peace Conference*, Yale U.P., 1963.

LEVERKUEHN, P. *German Military Intelligence*, trans. R. H. Stevens and C. FitzGibbon, London, Weidenfeld & Nicolson, 1954.

MACARTNEY, C. A. *The Habsburg Empire 1790–1918*, London, Weidenfeld & Nicolson, 1969.

MAČEK, V. *In the Struggle for Freedom*, trans. E. and S. Gazi, New York, Speller, 1957.

MCKENZIE, K. E. *Comintern and World Revolution 1928–1943*, New York, Columbia U.P., 1963.

MACLEAN, F. *Eastern Approaches*, London, Cape, 1949.

—— *Disputed Barricade*, London, Cape, 1957.

—— 'Interview with President Tito', in *Borba*, 12 May 1964.

MCVICKER, C. P. *Titoism: Pattern for International Communism*, New York, St. Martins; London, Macmillan, 1957.

MARJANOVIĆ, J. *Potsetnik iz Istorije Konumističke Partije Jugoslavije 1919–1941*, Belgrade, 1953.

—— *Ustanak i Narodno-Oslobodilački Pokret u Srbiji 1941*, Belgrade, 1963.

—— 'Prilozi istoriji sukoba narodnooslobodilačkog pokreta i četnika Draže Mihailovića u Srbiji 1941 godine' in *Istorija XX Veka Zbornik Radova*, i, 1959.

MARKERT, W., ed. *Jugoslawien*, Cologne/Graz, 1954.

MARKHAM, R. H. *Tito's Imperial Communism*, Chapel Hill, Univ. of North Carolina Press, 1947.

MARKOVIĆ, S. *Der Komunismus in Jugoslavien*, Hamburg, 1922.

MARTIN, D. *Ally Betrayed: The Uncensored Story of Tito and Mihailović*, New York, Prentice-Hall; London, W. H. Allen, 1946.

MARLOFF, M. *Strategic Planning for Coalition Warfare 1943–1944*, Washington, D.C., 1959.

MOSELY, P. E. *The Kremlin and World Politics*, New York, 1960.

—— 'The Peasant Family: The *Zadruga* or Communal Joint-Family in the Balkans and its recent Evolution', in *The Cultural Approach to History*, ed. C. Ware, New York, Columbia U.P.; Oxford U.P., 1940.

MURPHY, R. D. *Diplomat Among Warriors*, New York, Doubleday, 1964.

*National Liberation Movement in Yugoslavia* (AFHQ Handbook, 1943).

NEAL, F. W. *Titoism in Action: The Reforms in Yugoslavia after 1948*, Univ. of California Press, 1958.

—— 'The Communist Party of Yugoslavia', in *American Political Science Review*, li, March 1957.

# SELECT BIBLIOGRAPHY

NEWMAN, B. *Tito's Yugoslavia*, London, Hale, 1952.

NOVAK, A. *I Served Tito*, Prague, 1951.

NOVAK, V. *Magnum Krimen*, Zagrab, 1948.

*Oslobodilački Rat Naroda Jugoslavije 1941–1945*, 2 vols. Belgrade, 1963 and 1965.

OSTOVIĆ, P. D. *The Truth about Yugoslavia*, New York, Roy Publishers, 1952.

PADEV, W. *Marshal Tito*, London, Muller, 1944.

PATTEE, R. *The Case of Cardinal Aloysius Stepinac*, Milwaukee, Bruce Publishers, 1953.

PARIS, E. *Genocide in Satellite Croatia, 1941–1945*, Chicago, n.d.

PAVLOWITCH, K. ST., 'The Formation of the Regency', in *Glasnik, SIKD 'Njegos'*, Chicago, June 1962.

PETER II, King of Yugoslavia, *A King's Heritage*, London, Cassell, 1955.

PIJADE, M. *Collected Works*, Zagreb, 1964.

——*About the Legend that the Yugoslav Uprising Owed its Existence to Soviet Assistance*, London, 1950.

PLENČA, D. *Medjunarodni Odnosi Jugoslavije u toku Drugog Svjetskog Rata*, Belgrade, 1962.

POPOVIĆ, M. *Jedinstvo Privrednog Sistema Samoupravljenje Planiranje*, Belgrade, 1962.

*Pregled Istorije Saveza Komunista Jugoslavije*, Belgrade, 1963.

PRIBICEVITCH, S. *La Dictature du Roi Alexandre*, Paris, 1929.

RADULOVIĆ, M. *Tito's Republic*, Wrotham, England, Coldharbour Press, 1951.

RANKOVIĆ, A. *Izabrani Govori i Članci, 1941–1945*, Belgrade, 1951.

RENDULIC, L. *Gekämpft, gesiegt, geschlagen*, Heidelberg, 1952.

*Revue d'Histoire de la Deuxieme Guerre Mondiale*, articles by A Kriegel on the Comintern No. 68, 1967, and by K. Meneghello-Dinčić on the Ustaši state in Croatia 1941–42 in no. 74, 1969.

RISTIĆ, D. N. *Yugoslavia's Revolution of 1941*, Hoover Institution Publications, 1966.

ROGERS, L. *Guerrilla Surgeon*, London, Collins, 1957.

ROOTHAM, J. *Miss Fire: The Chronicle of a British Mission to Mihailovitch, 1943–1944*, London, Chatto, 1946.

ROYAL INSTITUTE OF INTERNATIONAL AFFAIRS (RIIA). *Chronology of International Events and Documents*, London, 1932–61.

—— *The Soviet–Yugoslav Dispute*, London, RIIA, 1948.

SAUNDERS, H. ST G. *The Fight is Won*, vol. 3 of Richards, D., and Saunders, H. St G., *Royal Air Force 1939–1945*, London, H.M.S.O., 1954.

SETON-WATSON, H. *Eastern Europe Between the Wars, 1918–1941*, Cambridge U.P., 1945.

—— *The East European Revolution*, London, Methuen, 1951, 3rd edn., 1957.

—— *The Pattern of Communist Revolution*, London, Methuen, 1955; rev. edn, 1961.

SETON-WATSON, R. W. *The Rise of Nationality in the Balkans*, London, Constable, 1917.

SHOUP, P. S. *Communism and the Yugoslav National Question*, New York, Columbia U.P., 1968.

SKILLING, H. G. *The Government of Communist East Europe*, New York, Crowell, 1966.

SLESSOR, J. *The Central Blue*, London, Cassell, 1956.

*Soviet–Yugoslav Dispute*, London, Royal Institute of International Affairs, 1948.

STANOJEVIĆ, T. and MRAKOVIĆ, D. eds. *Tito Život i Rad*, Zagreb, 1962.

STETTINIUS, E. R. *Roosevelt and the Russians: The Yalta Conference*, New York, Doubleday, 1949.

SWEET-ESCOTT, B. *Baker Street Irregular*, London, Methuen, 1965.

SZABO, G. *Kroz Hrvatsko Zagorje*, Zagreb, n.d.

—— *Stari Zagreb*, Zagreb, n.d.

TAYLOR, A. J. P. *The Habsburg Monarchy*, rev. edn., London, Hamish Hamilton, 1948.

—— *The Origins of the Second World War*, London, Hamish Hamilton, 1963.

TENNYSON, H. *Tito Lifts the Curtain*, London, Rider, 1955.

TITO, J. B. *Political Report of the Central Committee of the Communist Party of Yugoslavia*, Belgrade, 1948.

—— *Workers Manage Factories*, Belgrade, 1950.

—— *Govori i Članci*, i–xvi, Zagreb, 1959–69.

—— *Selected Speeches and Articles*, Zagreb, 1963 (translation of selections from above).

—— *Selected Military Works*, Belgrade, 1966.

—— *Fifty Years of Revolutionary Struggle by the Communists of Yugoslavia*, Belgrade, 1969. Speech delivered at the Ninth Congress of the League of Communists of Yugoslavia, Belgrade, 1969.

*Tito Život i Rad*, see STANOJEVIĆ and MRAKOVIĆ, eds.

TOMAC, P. ed. *The Trial of Dragoljub–Draža Mihailović*, Belgrade, 1946.

TOMASEVITCH, J. *Peasants, Politics and Economic Change in Yugoslavia*, Stanford U.P., 1957.

TREVOR-ROPER, H. *The Last Days of Hitler*, rev. edn., Pan, 1960.

*Trial of Dragoljub–Draža Mihailović* (stenographic record and documents), Belgrade, 1946.

TROUTON, R. *Peasant Renaissance in Yugoslavia, 1900–1950*, London, Routledge & Kegan Paul, 1952.

ULAM, A. B. *Titoism and the Cominform*, Harvard U.P., 1952.

UNITED STATES, DEPARTMENT OF STATE. *Foreign Relations of the United States, Diplomatic Papers: The Conferences at Cairo and Teheran, 1943,* Washington, 1961.

VINTERHALTER, V. *Životnom Stazom Josipa Broza,* Belgrade, 1968 (cited in notes *Broz*).

*Vojna Enciklopedija,* vols. i–ix, Belgrade, 1958–67.

VUCINICH, W., ed. *Contemporary Yugoslavia,* Univ. of California Press, 1969.

WILSON, H. M., 1st Baron, *Eight Years Overseas,* London, Hutchinson, 1950.

WISKEMANN, E. *Age of the Dictators,* London, 1960.

ZILLIACUS, K. *Tito,* London, Michael Joseph, 1952.

# INDEX